Version 6.0

EXPLORING WORD FOR WINDOWS™

Robert T. Grauer

Maryann Barber

University of Miami

Prentice Hall, Englewood Cliffs, New Jersey 07632

Library of Congress Cataloging in Publication Data

Grauer, Robert T. [date]
Exploring Word for Windows, version 6.0 / Robert T. Grauer, Maryann Barber.
p. cm.
Includes index.
ISBN 0-13-079526-7
1. Microsoft Word for Windows. 2. Word processing. I. Barber. Maryann M. II. Title.
Z52.5.M523G74 1994
652.5' 536—dc20 94–11262
CIP

Acquisitions editor: P. J. Boardman
Editorial /production supervisor: Greg Hubit Bookworks
Interior and cover design: Suzanne Behnke
Production coordinator: Patrice Fraccio
Managing editor: Mary Cavaliere
Developmental editor: Harriet Serenkin
Editorial assistants: Renee Pelletier / Dolores Kenny

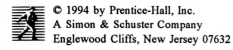

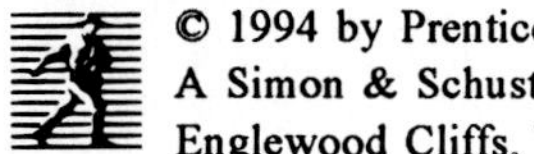

Printed in the United States of America
10 9 8 7 6 5

ISBN 0-13-079526-7

Prentice Hall International (UK) Limited, *London*
Prentice Hall of Australia Pty. Limited, *Sydney*
Prentice Hall of Canada Inc., *Toronto*
Prentice Hall Hispanoamericano, S.A., *Mexico*
Prentice Hall of India Private Limited, *New Delhi*
Prentice Hall of Japan, Inc., *Tokyo*
Simon & Schuster Asia Pte. Ltd., *Singapore*
Editora Prentice Hall do Brasil, Ltda., *Rio de Janeiro*

Contents

3

The Tools: Preparing a Résumé and Cover Letter 91

4

The Professional Document: Headers, Footers, Styles, and Tables 139

5

Desktop Publishing: Creating a Newsletter 177

Appendix A: Object Linking and Embedding 2.0: Sharing Data Among Programs 215

Preface

Exploring Word for Windows 6.0 is one of several books (modules) in the Prentice Hall *Exploring Windows* series. Other modules include *Microsoft Excel 5.0, WordPerfect for Windows 6.0, Lotus for Windows 4.0, Microsoft Access 2.0, PowerPoint 4.0*, and an introductory module, *Exploring Windows 3.1.* The books are independent of one another but possess a common design, pedagogy, and writing style intended to serve the application courses in both two- and four-year schools.

Each book in the series is suitable on a stand-alone basis for any course that teaches a specific application; alternatively, several modules can be bound together for a single course that teaches multiple applications. The initial component, *Exploring Windows 3.1,* assumes no previous knowledge and includes an introductory section for the individual who has never used a computer.

The *Exploring Windows* series will appeal to students in a variety of disciplines including business, liberal arts, and the sciences. Each module has a consistent presentation that stresses the benefits of the Windows environment, especially the common user interface that performs the same task in identical fashion across applications. Each module emphasizes the benefits of multitasking, demonstrates the ability to share data between applications, and stresses the extensive on-line help facility to facilitate learning. Students are taught concepts, not just keystrokes or mouse clicks, with hands-on exercises in every chapter providing the necessary practice to master the material.

The *Exploring Windows* series is different from other books, both in its scope as well as the way in which material is presented. Students learn by doing. Concepts are stressed and memorization is minimized. Shortcuts and other important Windows information are consistently highlighted in the many boxed tips that appear throughout the series. Every chapter contains an average of two directed exercises at the computer, but equally important are the less structured end-of-chapter problems that not only review the information but extend it as well. The end-of-chapter material is a distinguishing feature of the entire series, an integral part of the learning process, and a powerful motivational tool for students to learn and explore.

FEATURES AND BENEFITS

- *Exploring Word for Windows* presents concepts as well as keystrokes and mouse clicks, so that students learn the theory behind the applications. They are not just taught what to do but are provided with the rationale for why they are doing it, enabling them to extend the information to additional learning on their own.
- No previous knowledge is assumed on the part of the reader as a fast-paced introduction brings the reader or new user up to speed immediately.
- Practical information, beyond application-specific material, appears throughout the series. Students are cautioned about computer viruses and taught the importance of adequate backup. The *Exploring Windows* module, for example, teaches students to extend the warranty of a new computer and points out the advantages of a mail-order purchase.

- Problem solving and troubleshooting are stressed throughout the series. The authors are constantly anticipating mistakes that students may make and tell the reader how to recover from problems that invariably occur.
- Tips, tips, and more tips present application shortcuts in every chapter. Windows is designed for the mouse, but experienced users gravitate toward keyboard shortcuts once they have mastered basic skills. The series presents different ways to accomplish a given task, but in a logical and relaxed fashion.
- A unique Buying Guide in the introductory module presents a thorough introduction to PC hardware from the viewpoint of purchasing a computer. Students learn the subtleties in selecting a configuration—for example, how the resolution of a monitor affects its size, the advantages of a local bus, and the Intel CPU processor index.

ACKNOWLEDGMENTS

We want to thank the many individuals who helped bring this project to its successful conclusion. We are especially grateful to our editor at Prentice Hall, P. J. Boardman, without whom the series would not have been possible, and to Harriet Serenkin, the developmental editor, whose vision helped shape the project. Gretchen Marx of Saint Joseph College produced an outstanding set of Instructor Manuals. Greg Hubit was in charge of production. Deborah Emry, our marketing manager at Prentice Hall, developed the innovative campaign that helped make the series a success. Delores Kenny helped coordinate all phases of the project.

We also want to acknowledge our reviewers, who through their comments and constructive criticism made this a far better book.

Lynne Band, Middlesex Community College
Stuart P. Brian, Holy Family College
Jerry Chin, Southwest Missouri State University
Dean Combellick, Scottsdale Community College
Paul E. Daurelle, Western Piedmont Community College
David Douglas, University of Arkansas
Raymond Frost, Central Connecticut State University
James Gips, Boston College
Wanda D. Heller, Seminole Community College
Ernie Ivey, Polk Community College
Jane King, Everett Community College
John Lesson, University of Central Florida
Alan Moltz, Naugatuck Valley Technical Community College
Nancy Monthofen, Scottsdale Community College
Delores Pusins, Hillsborough Community College
Gale E. Rand, College Misericordia
David Rinehard, Lansing Community College
Marilyn Salas, Scottsdale Community College
Sally Visci, Lorain County Community College
David Weiner, University of San Francisco
Jack Zeller, Kirkwood Community College

A final word of thanks to the unnamed students at the University of Miami who make it all worthwhile. And, most of all, thanks to you, our readers, for choosing this book. Please feel free to contact us with any comments and suggestions. We can be reached most easily on the Internet.

Robert T. Grauer
RGRAUER@UMIAMI.MIAMI.EDU

Maryann Barber
MBARBER@UMIAMI.MIAMI.EDU

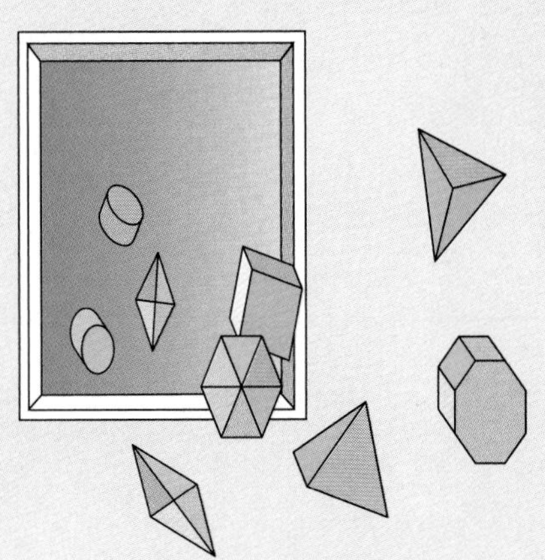

Word for Windows: What Will Word Processing Do for Me?

CHAPTER OBJECTIVES

After reading this chapter you will be able to:

1. Explain the concept of a common user interface and its advantage in learning a new application.
2. Describe the basic mouse operations; use a mouse and/or the equivalent keyboard shortcuts to select commands from a pull-down menu.
3. Discuss the function of a dialog box; describe the different types of dialog boxes and the various ways in which information is supplied.
4. Explain the functions of the minimize and maximize or restore buttons; describe the use of the scroll bar and its associated scroll box.
5. Access the on-line help facility and explain its various capabilities.
6. Define word wrap; differentiate between a hard and soft return.
7. Distinguish between the insertion and overtype modes; explain how to switch from one mode to the other.
8. Create, save, retrieve, edit, and print a simple document using Word for Windows.

OVERVIEW

Have you ever produced what you thought was the perfect term paper only to discover that you omitted a sentence or misspelled a word, or that the paper was three pages too short or one page too long? Wouldn't it be nice to make the necessary changes, and then be able to reprint the entire paper with the touch of a key? Welcome to the world of word processing, where you are no longer stuck with having to retype anything. Instead, you retrieve your work from disk, display it on the monitor and revise it as necessary, then print it at any time, in draft or final form.

This chapter provides a broad-based introduction to word processing and ***Word for Windows.*** It begins, however, with a discussion of basic Windows concepts, applicable to Windows applications in general, and to Word for Windows in particular. The emphasis is on the common user interface and consistent command structure that facilitates learning within the Windows environment. Indeed, you may already know much of this material, but that is precisely the point; that is, once you know one Windows application, it is that much easier to learn the next.

The second half of the chapter presents (or perhaps reviews) essential concepts of word processing. The hands-on exercises at the conclusion of the chapter allow you to apply all of the material at the computer, and are indispensable to the learn-by-doing philosophy we follow throughout the text.

THE WINDOWS DESKTOP

The ***desktop*** is the centerpiece of Microsoft Windows and is analogous to the desk on which you work. There are physical objects on your real desk and there are ***windows*** (framed rectangular areas) and ***icons*** (pictorial symbols) displayed on the Windows desktop. The components of a window are explained within the context of Figure 1.1, which contains the opening Windows screen on our computer.

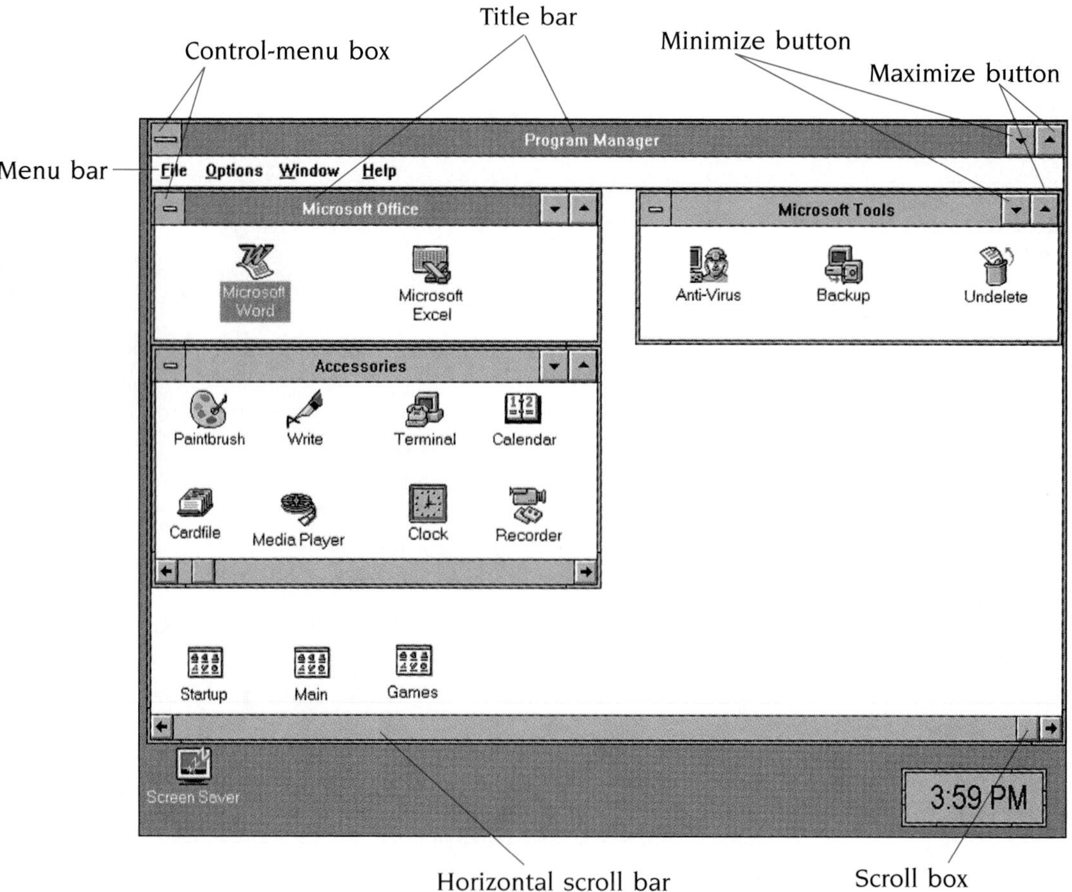

FIGURE 1.1 Program Manager

Your desktop may be different from ours, just as your real desk is arranged differently from that of your friend. You can expect, however, to see a window titled Program Manager. You may or may not see other windows within Program Manager such as the Accessories, Microsoft Tools, and Microsoft Office windows shown in Figure 1.1.

Program Manager is crucial to the operation of Windows. It starts automatically when Windows is loaded and it remains active the entire time you are working in Windows. Closing Program Manager closes Windows. Program Manager is in essence an organizational tool that places applications in groups (e.g., Microsoft Office), then displays those groups as windows or group icons.

Regardless of the windows that are open on your desktop, every window contains the same basic elements: a title bar, control-menu box, and buttons to minimize and to maximize or restore the window. The ***title bar*** displays the name of the window—for example, Microsoft Office in Figure 1.1. The ***control-menu box*** accesses a pull-down menu that lets you select operations relevant to the window. The ***maximize button*** enlarges the window so that it takes the entire desktop. The ***minimize button*** reduces a window to an icon (but keeps the program open in memory). A ***restore button*** (a double arrow not shown in Figure 1.1) appears after a window has been maximized and returns the window to its previous size (the size before it was maximized).

Other elements, which may or may not be present, include a horizontal and/or vertical scroll bar and a menu bar. A horizontal (vertical) ***scroll bar*** will appear at the bottom (right) border of a window when the contents of the window are not completely visible. The ***scroll box*** appears within the scroll bar to facilitate moving within the window. A ***menu bar*** is found in the window for Program Manager, but not in the other windows. This is because Program Manager is a different kind of window, an application window rather than a document window.

An ***application window*** contains a program (application). A ***document window*** holds data for a program and is contained within an application window. The distinction between application and document windows is made clearer when we realize that Program Manager is a program and requires access to commands contained in pull-down menus located on the menu bar.

MICROSOFT TOOLS

The Microsoft Tools group is created automatically when you install (or upgrade to) MS-DOS 6.0. The name of each icon (Antivirus, Backup, and Undelete) is indicative of its function, and each program is an important tool in safeguarding your data. The Antivirus program allows you to scan disks for known viruses (and remove them when found). The Backup utility copies files from the hard disk to one or more floppy disk(s) in case of hard disk failure. The Undelete program allows you to recover files that you accidentally erased from a disk.

Common User Interface

One of the most significant benefits of the Windows environment is the ***common user interface,*** which provides a sense of familiarity when you begin to learn a new application. All applications work basically the same way. Hence, once you know one Windows application, even one as simple as the Paintbrush accessory, it will be that much easier for you to learn Word for Windows. In similar fashion, it will take you less time to learn Excel once you know Word, because both applications share a common menu structure with consistent ways to select commands from those menus.

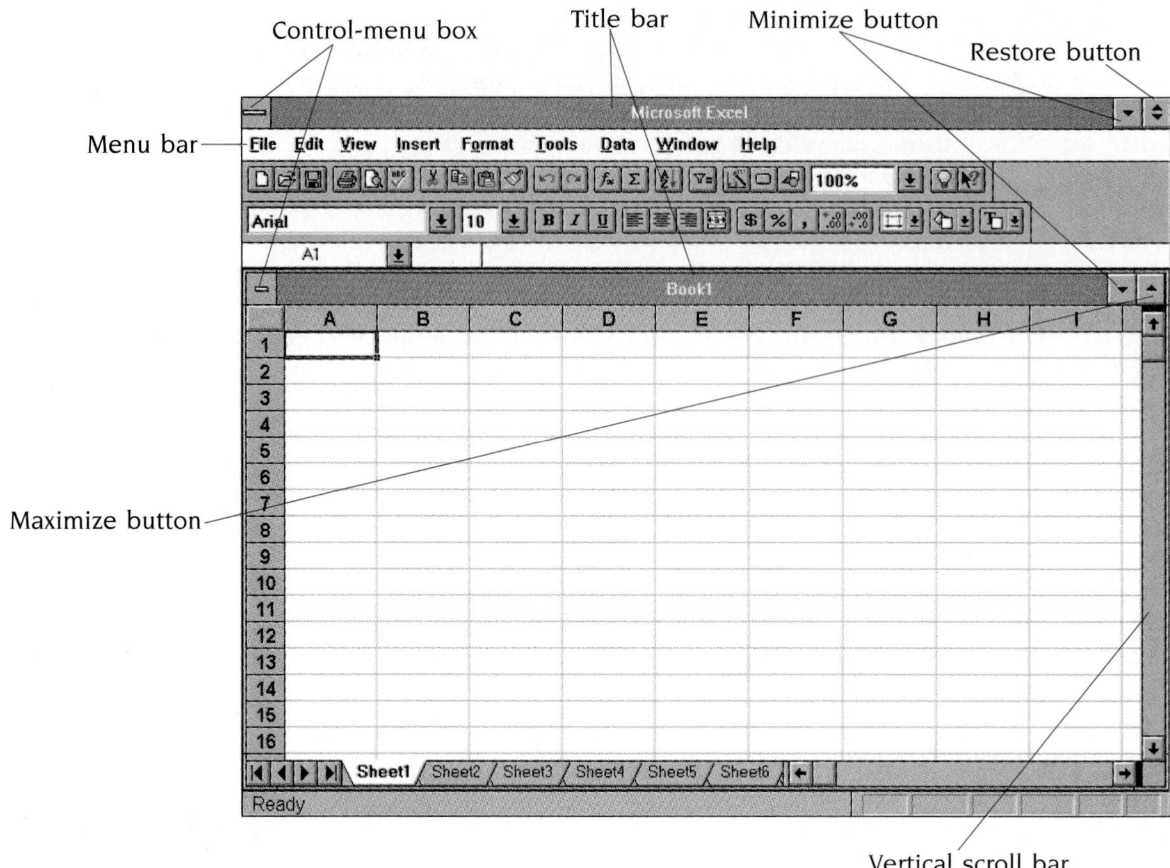

(a) Microsoft Excel Version 5.0

FIGURE 1.2 Common User Interface

Consider, for example, Figures 1.2a and 1.2b, containing windows for Excel and Word, respectively. The applications are very different, yet the windows have many characteristics in common. You might even say that they have more similarities than differences, a remarkable statement considering the programs accomplish very different tasks. A document window (Book1) is contained within the application window for Excel. In similar fashion, a document window (Document1) is present within the application window for Word.

The application windows for Excel and Word contain the same elements as any other application window: a title bar, menu bar, and control-menu box; and minimize and maximize or restore buttons. The menu bars are almost identical; that is, the File, Edit, View, Insert, Format, Tools, Window, and Help menus are present in both applications. (The only difference between the menu bars is that Excel has a Data menu whereas Word has a Table menu.)

The commands within the menus are also consistent in both applications. The File menu contains the commands to open and close a file, the Edit menu has commands to cut, copy, and paste text, and so on. The means for accessing the pull-down menus are also consistent; that is, click the menu name (see mouse basics later in the chapter) or press the Alt key plus the underlined letter of the menu name—for example, Alt+F to pull down the File menu.

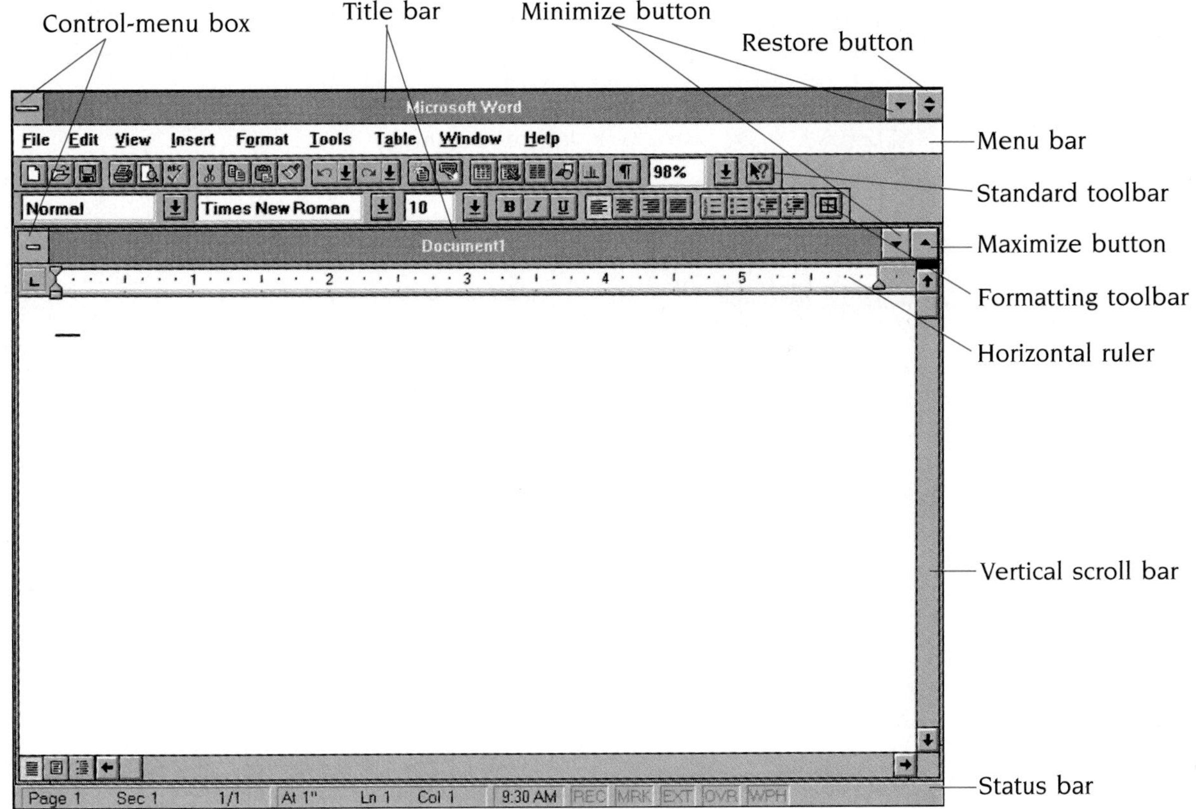

(b) Word for Windows Version 6.0

FIGURE 1.2 Common User Interface (continued)

WORD FOR WINDOWS

We concentrate on the ***Word for Windows*** screen in Figure 1.2b. Do not be concerned if your screen is different from ours because you can change it to suit your personal preferences. What is important is that you recognize the basic elements in the Word Window, which include toolbars, the ruler, and the status bar.

Toolbars provide immediate access to common commands. Seven built-in toolbars are available, two of which are shown in the figure. The toolbars can be displayed or hidden by using the View menu as described in the hands-on exercises later in the chapter.

The ***Standard toolbar*** appears immediately below the menu bar and contains buttons for the most basic commands in Word, such as opening and closing a file, printing a document, and so on. The ***Formatting toolbar,*** under the Standard toolbar, provides access to various formatting operations such as boldface, italics, or underlining. (Toolbars are also present in the Excel window. Many of the buttons are the same in both applications.)

The toolbars may at first appear overwhelming, but there is absolutely no need to memorize what the individual buttons do. That will come with time. We suggest, however, that you will have a better appreciation for the various buttons if you consider them in groups according to their general function as shown in Figure 1.3.

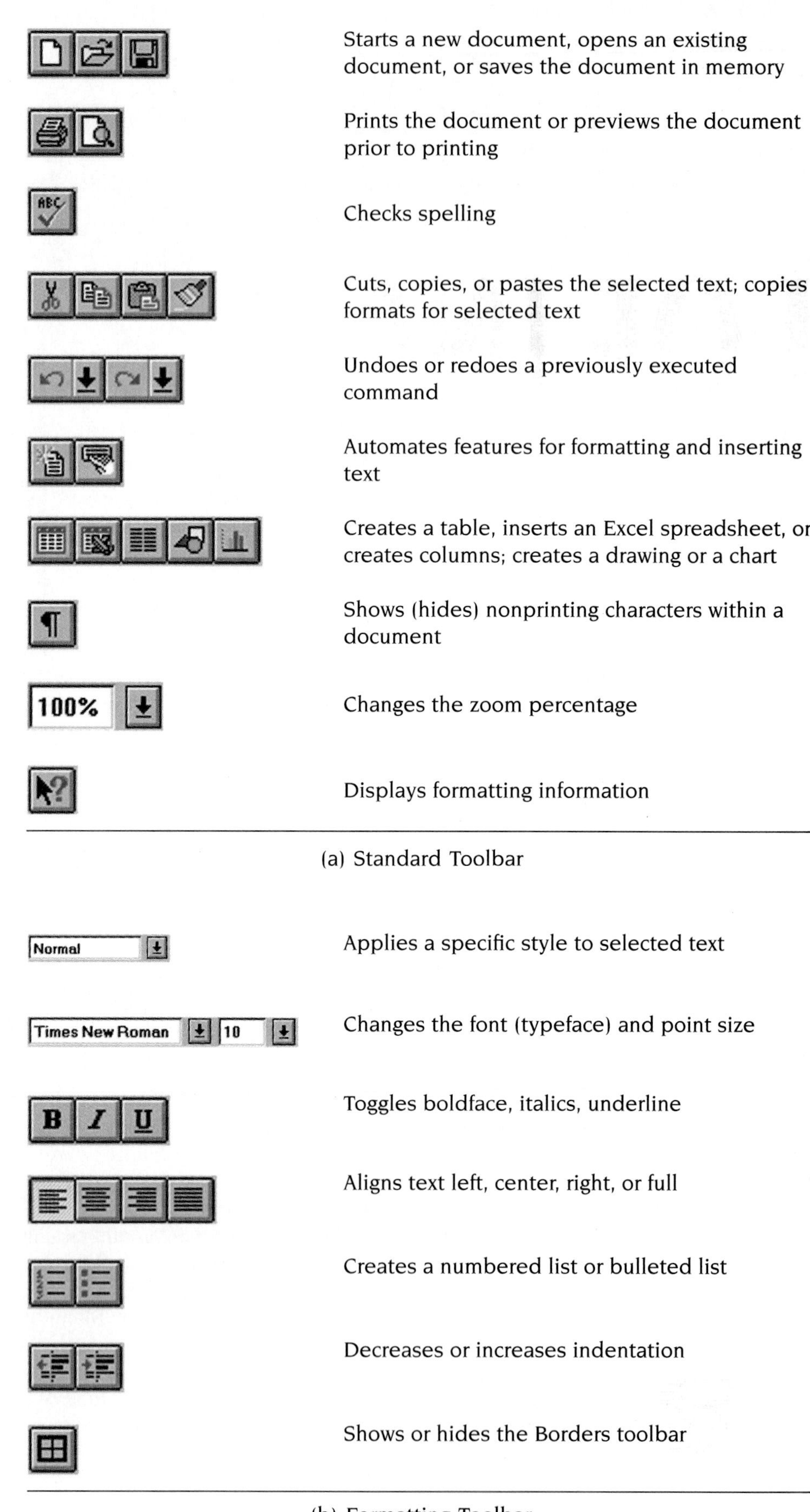

Starts a new document, opens an existing document, or saves the document in memory
Prints the document or previews the document prior to printing
Checks spelling
Cuts, copies, or pastes the selected text; copies formats for selected text
Undoes or redoes a previously executed command
Automates features for formatting and inserting text
Creates a table, inserts an Excel spreadsheet, or creates columns; creates a drawing or a chart
Shows (hides) nonprinting characters within a document
100%
Changes the zoom percentage
Displays formatting information
(a) Standard Toolbar
Normal
Applies a specific style to selected text
Times New Roman
10
Changes the font (typeface) and point size
B
I
U
Toggles boldface, italics, underline
Aligns text left, center, right, or full
Creates a numbered list or bulleted list
Decreases or increases indentation
Shows or hides the Borders toolbar
(b) Formatting Toolbar

FIGURE 1.3 Toolbars

The ***horizontal ruler*** is displayed underneath the toolbars and enables you to change margins, tabs, and indents for all or part of a document. A ***vertical ruler*** (not shown in the figure) shows the vertical position of text on the page.

The ***status bar*** at the bottom of the figure displays information about the document. It also shows the status (settings) of various indicators, such as OVR to show that the Word is in the overtype (as opposed to the insertion) mode as explained later in the chapter.

WORKING IN WINDOWS

The next several pages take you through the basic operations common to Windows applications in general, and to Word for Windows in particular. You may already be familiar with much of this material, in which case you are already benefitting from the common user interface. We begin with the mouse and describe how it is used to access pull-down menus and to supply information in dialog boxes. We also emphasize the ***on-line help*** facility that is present in every Windows application.

The Mouse

The mouse (or track ball) is essential to Word as it is to all Windows applications, and you will need to be comfortable with its four basic actions:

- To ***point*** to an item, move the mouse pointer to the item.
- To ***click*** an item, point to it, then press and release the left mouse button. You can also click the right mouse button to display a shortcut menu with commands applicable to the item you are pointing to.
- To ***double click*** an item, point to it, then click the left mouse button twice in succession.
- To ***drag*** an item, move the pointer to the item, then press and hold the left button while you move the item to a new position.

The mouse is a pointing device—move the mouse on your desk and the ***mouse pointer,*** typically a small arrowhead, moves on the monitor. The mouse pointer assumes different shapes according to the nature of the current action. You will see a double arrow when you change the size of a window, an I-beam to insert text, a hand to jump from one help topic to the next, or a circle with a line through it to indicate that an attempted action is invalid.

The mouse pointer will also change to an hourglass to indicate Windows is processing your most recent command, and that no further commands may be issued until the action is completed. The more powerful your computer, the less frequently the hourglass will appear. Conversely, the less powerful your system, the more you will see the hourglass.

A right-handed person will hold the mouse in his or her right hand and click the left button. A left-handed person may want to hold the mouse in the left hand and click the right button. If this sounds complicated, it's not, and you can master the mouse with the on-line tutorial provided in Windows (see step 2 in the hands-on exercise on page 17).

MOUSE TIP FOR LEFTIES

Customize the mouse to reverse the actions of the left and right buttons. Double click the Main group icon in Program Manager to open the group, then double click the Control Panel icon. Double click the Mouse icon, click the Swap Left/Right Buttons check box, then click OK.

Word is designed for a mouse, but it provides keyboard equivalents for almost every command, with toolbars and the ruler offering still other ways to accomplish the most frequent operations. You may at first wonder why there are so many different ways to do the same thing, but you will come to recognize the many options as part of Word's charm. The most appropriate technique depends on personal preference, as well as the specific situation.

If, for example, your hands are already on the keyboard, it is faster to use the keyboard equivalent. Other times, your hand will be on the mouse and that will be the fastest way. It is not necessary to memorize anything, nor should you even try; just be flexible and willing to experiment. The more you do, the easier it will be!

MOUSE TIP: PICK UP THE MOUSE

It seems that you always run out of room on your real desk, just when you need to move the mouse a little further. The solution is to pick up the mouse and move it closer to you—the pointer will stay in its present position on the screen, but when you put the mouse down, you will have more room on your desk in which to work.

Pull-down Menus

Pull-down menus, such as those in Figure 1.4, are essential to all Windows applications. A pull-down menu is accessed by clicking the menu name (within the menu bar) or by pressing the Alt key plus the underlined letter in the menu name—for example, Alt+H to pull down the Help menu.

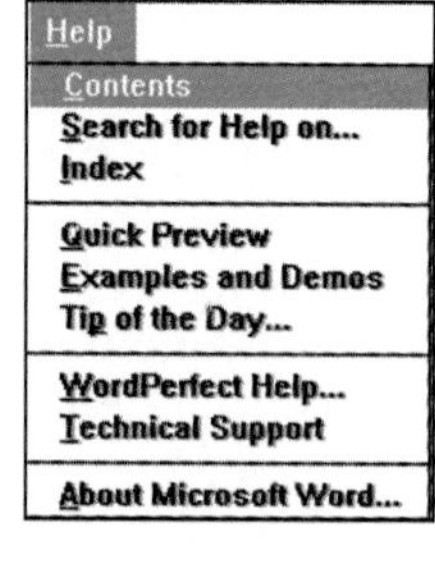

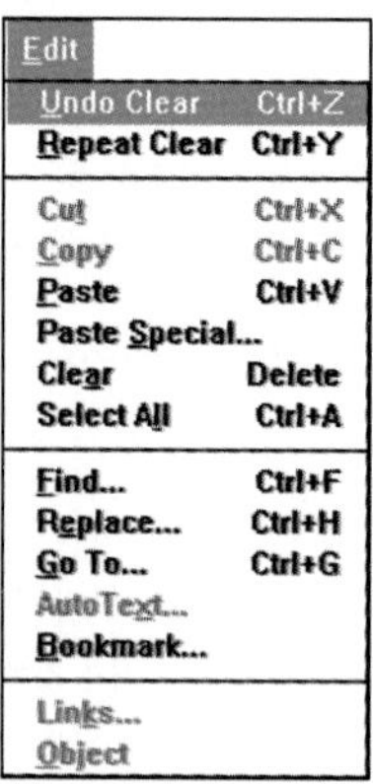

FIGURE 1.4 Pull-down menus

Menu options (commands) are executed by clicking the command once the menu has been pulled down or by pressing the underlined letter (e.g., press C to execute the Close command in the File menu). You can also bypass the menu entirely if you know the equivalent keystrokes shown to the right of the command in the menu (e.g., Ctrl+X, Ctrl+C, or Ctrl+V in the Edit menu to cut, copy, and paste text, respectively). A ***dimmed command*** (e.g., the Copy command within the Edit menu) indicates that the command is not currently executable; that is, some additional action has to be taken for the command to become available.

Many commands are followed by an ***ellipsis*** (. . .) to indicate that additional information is required to execute the command. For example, selection of the Find command in the Edit menu requires the user to specify the text to be found. The additional information is entered into a dialog box, which appears immediately after the command has been selected.

Dialog Boxes

A ***dialog box*** appears whenever additional information is needed to execute a command—that is, whenever a menu option is followed by an ellipsis. The information can be supplied in different ways, which in turn leads to different types of dialog boxes as shown in Figure 1.5.

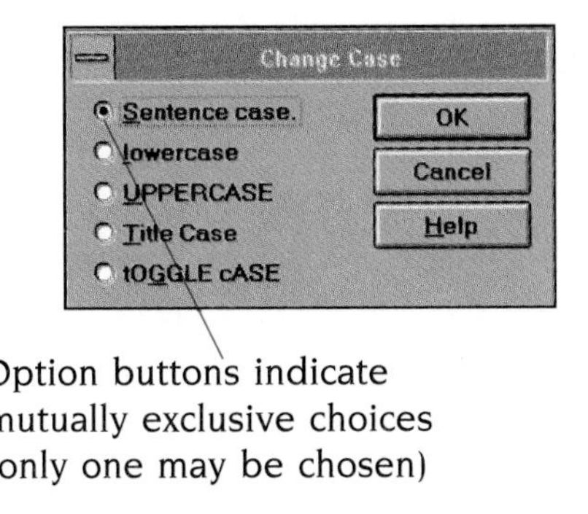

(a) Option (radio) Buttons

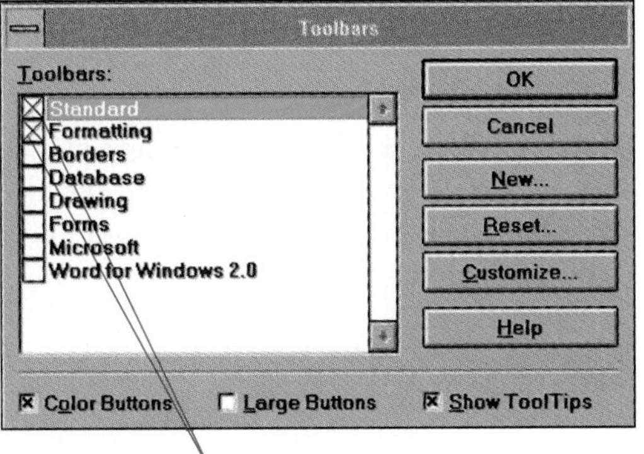

Options are not mutually exclusive (more than one may be chosen)

(b) Check Boxes

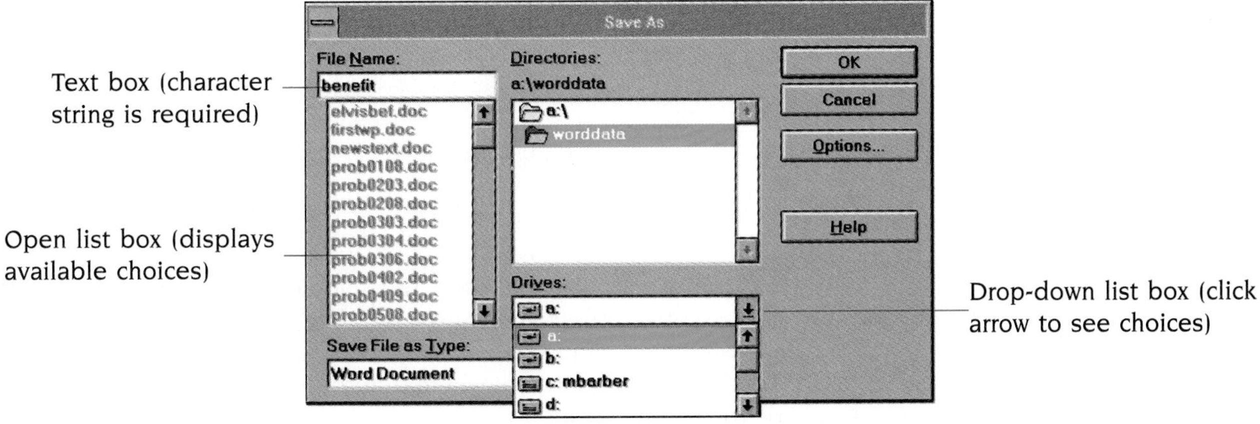

(c) Text Boxes and List Boxes

FIGURE 1.5 Dialog Boxes

The ***option (radio) buttons*** in Figure 1.5a indicate mutually exclusive choices, one of which must be chosen; that is, you must choose Sentence case, lowercase, UPPERCASE, Title Case, or tOGGLE cASE. ***Check boxes*** are used instead of option buttons if the options are not mutually exclusive, that is, if several options can be selected at the same time such as the Standard and Formatting toolbars in Figure 1.5b. The individual options are selected (cleared) by clicking on the appropriate check box.

A ***text box*** indicates that a character string is required—for example, a file name in the text box of Figure 1.5c. Some text boxes are initially empty and display a flashing vertical bar to indicate the position of the insertion point for the text you will enter. Other text boxes already contain an entry, in which case you can click anywhere in the box to establish the insertion point and edit the entry.

An ***open list box,*** such as the list of file names or directories in Figure 1.5c, displays the available choices, any one of which is selected by clicking on the desired item. A ***drop-down list box,*** such as the list of available drives or file types, conserves space by showing only the current selection; click the arrow of a drop-down list box to produce a list of available options.

All three dialog boxes in Figure 1.5 contain one or more ***command buttons*** to initiate an action. The function of a command button should be apparent from its name. For example, Cancel returns to the previous screen with no action taken, OK accepts the information and closes the dialog box, and Help provides additional explanation.

On-line Help

Word for Windows provides extensive on-line help, which is accessed by pulling down the ***Help menu*** or by pressing the F1 function key. The Word for Windows Help menu was shown earlier in Figure 1.4 and contains the following choices:

Contents	Displays a list of help topics
Search for Help on . . .	Searches for help on a specific subject
Index	An alphabetical index of all Help topics
Quick Preview	Highlights new features in Word for Windows 6.0 and suggests tips for WordPerfect users coverting to Word
Examples and Demos	Demonstrates major features in Word
Tip of the day . . .	Accesses the Tip of the Day dialog box
WordPerfect Help . . .	Detailed help in converting from WordPerfect to Word
Technical Support	Describes the different types of technical support available
About Microsoft Word . . .	Indicates the specific release of Word you are using

The Contents command displays the window of Figure 1.6a and provides access to all elements within the Help facility. A Help window contains all of the elements found in any other application window: a title bar, minimize and maximize or restore buttons, a control-menu box, and optionally, a vertical and/or horizontal scroll bar. There is also a menu bar with additional commands made available through the indicated pull-down menus.

The ***help buttons*** near the top of the help window enable you to move around more easily; that is, you can click a button to perform the indicated function. The *Contents button* returns to the screen in Figure 1.6a from elsewhere within Help. The *Search button* produces the screen of Figure 1.6b and allows you to look for information on a specific topic. Type a key word in the text box, and the corresponding term will be selected within the upper list box. Double click the highlighted item to produce a list of available topics on that subject, then double

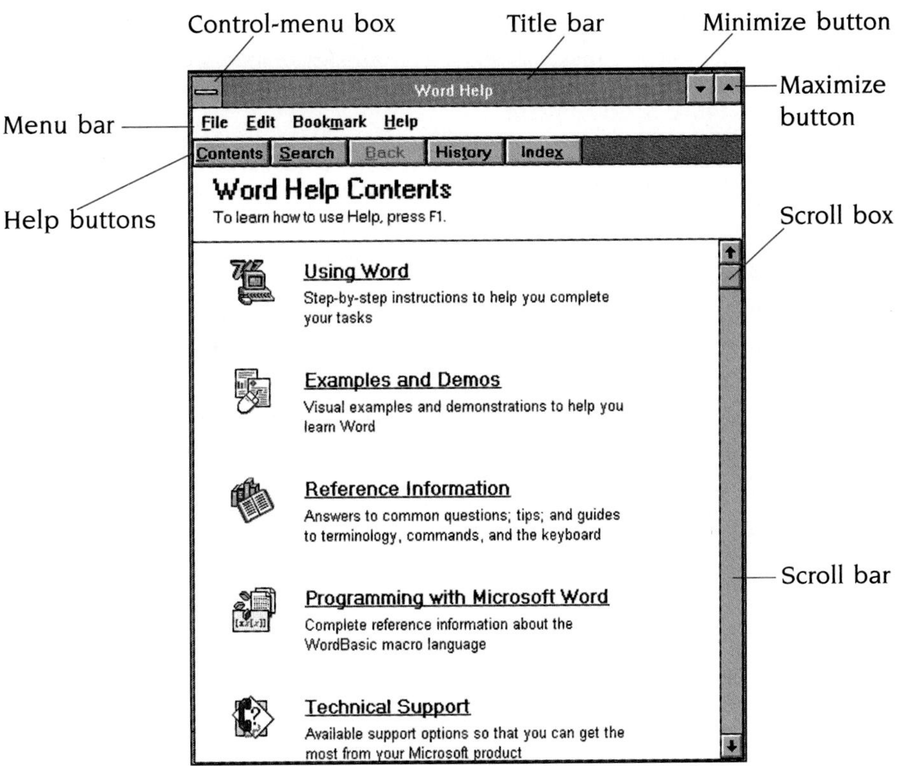

(a) Opening Screen

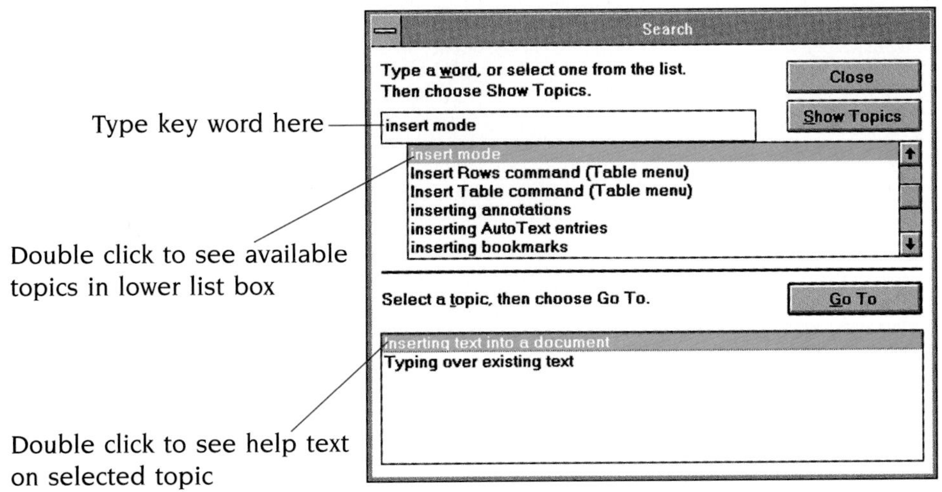

(b) Search Command

FIGURE 1.6 Getting Help

click the topic you want in the lower list box to see the actual help text, such as the screen shown in Figure 1.6c.

The *Back button* returns directly to the previous help topic. The *History button* is more general as it displays a list of all topics selected within the current session and makes it easy to return to any of the previous topics. The *Index button* produces a window containing an alphabetical index of the Help topics.

The ***Tip of the Day*** in Figure 1.6d appears automatically whenever you start Word. The tip can also be accessed on demand by pulling down the Help menu and clicking Tip of the Day. You can see additional tips by clicking the appropriate command button.

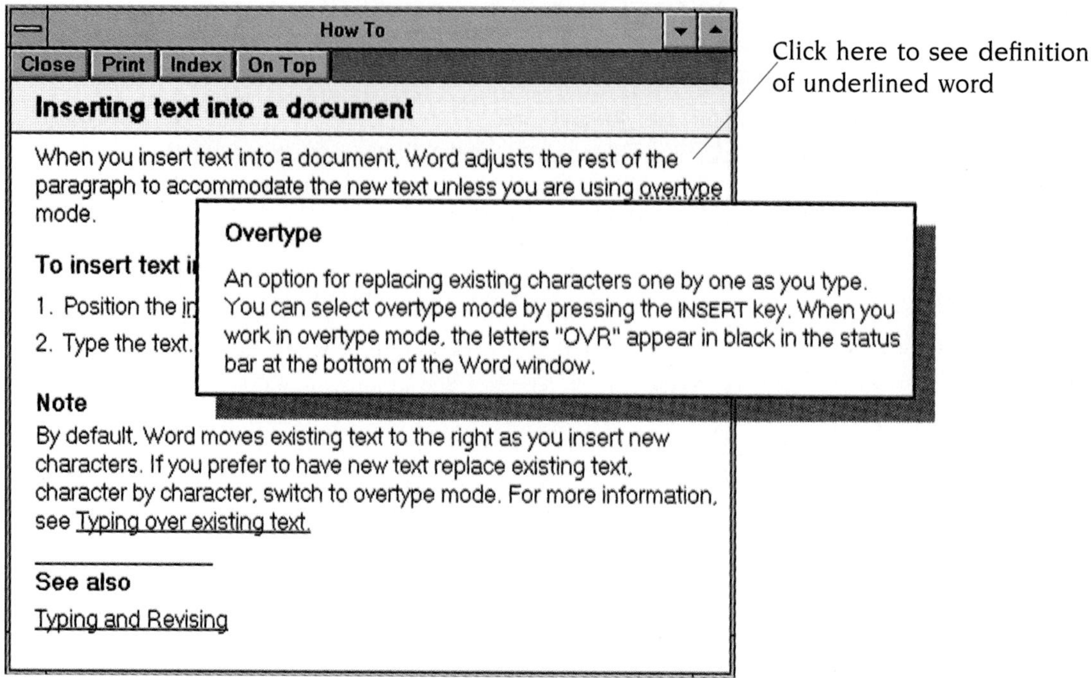

(c) Help text

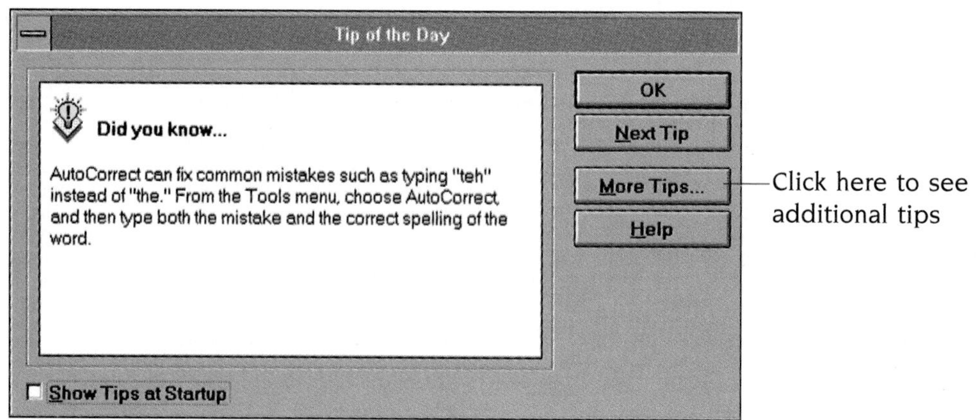

(d) Tip of the Day

FIGURE 1.6 Getting Help (continued)

ABOUT MICROSOFT WORD

About Microsoft Word on the Help menu displays information about the specific release of Word for Windows including the product serial number. Execution of the command produces a dialog box with a System Information command button; click the button to learn about the hardware installed on your system including the amount of memory and available space on the hard drive.

THE BASICS OF WORD PROCESSING

All word processors, be they DOS- or Windows-based, adhere to certain basic concepts that must be understood if you are to use the program effectively. The next several pages introduce ideas that are applicable to any word processor (and which you may already know). We follow the conceptual material with a hands-on exercise that gives you the opportunity to practice all that you have learned.

Insertion Point

The ***insertion point*** is a flashing vertical line that marks the place where text will be entered. The insertion point is always at the beginning of a new document, but it can be moved anywhere within an existing document. If, for example, you wanted to add text to the end of a document, you would move the insertion point to the end of the document, then begin typing. The ***end-of-file marker*** is the horizontal line that indicates the end of the document and beyond which the insertion point cannot be moved.

Toggle Switches

Suppose you sat down at the keyboard and typed an entire sentence without pressing the Shift key. The sentence would be in all lowercase letters. Then you pressed the Caps Lock key and retyped the sentence, again without pressing the Shift key. This time the sentence would be in all uppercase letters. You could repeat the process as often as you like. Each time you pressed the Caps Lock key, the sentence would switch from lowercase to uppercase and vice versa.

The point of this example is to introduce the concept of a ***toggle switch,*** a device that causes the computer to alternate between two states. The Caps Lock key is an example of a toggle switch; each time you press it, newly typed text will change from uppercase to lowercase and back again. We will see several other examples of toggle switches as we proceed in our discussion of word processing.

Insertion versus Overtype

Word for Windows is always in one of two modes, ***insertion*** or ***overtype,*** and uses a toggle switch (the Ins key) to alternate between the two. The status bar displays OVR when the overtype mode is in effect. The indicator is dim when the insertion mode is active, as was shown earlier in Figure 1.2.

Press the Ins key once and you switch from insertion to overtype; press the Ins key a second time and you go from overtype back to insertion. Text that is entered into a document during the insertion mode moves existing text to the right to accommodate the characters being added. Text entered from the overtype mode replaces (overtypes) existing text. Text is always entered or replaced immediately to the right of the insertion point.

The insertion mode is best when you enter text for the first time, but either mode can be used to make corrections. The insertion mode is the better choice when the correction requires you to add new text. The overtype mode is easier when you are substituting one character(s) for another. The difference is illustrated in Figure 1.7.

Figure 1.7a displays the text as it was originally entered, with two misspellings. The letters *se* have been omitted from the word *insertion,* whereas an *x* has been erroneously typed instead of an *r* in the word *overtype.* The insertion mode is used in Figure 1.7b to add the missing letters, which in turn moves the rest of the line to the right. The overtype mode is used in Figure 1.6c to replace the *x* with an *r.*

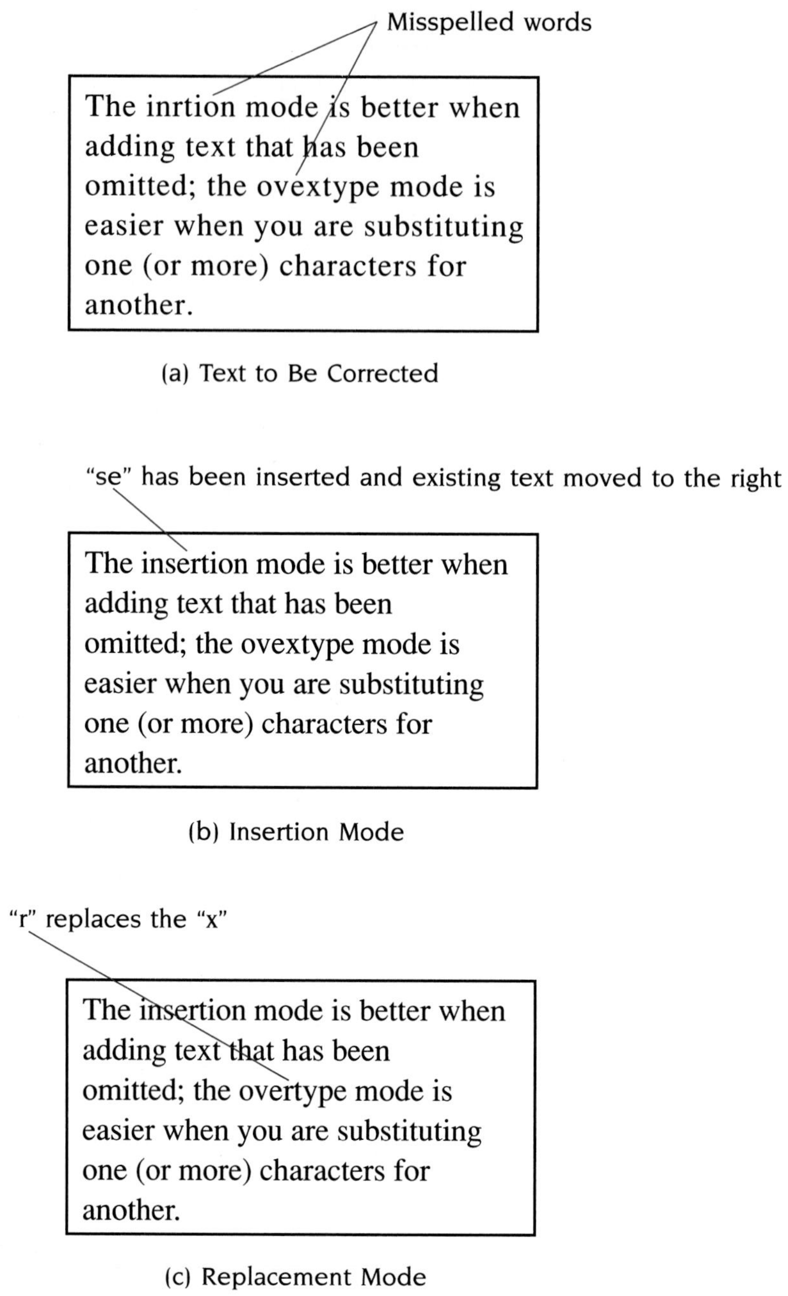

Misspelled words

The inrtion mode is better when adding text that has been omitted; the ovextype mode is easier when you are substituting one (or more) characters for another.

(a) Text to Be Corrected

"se" has been inserted and existing text moved to the right

The insertion mode is better when adding text that has been omitted; the ovextype mode is easier when you are substituting one (or more) characters for another.

(b) Insertion Mode

"r" replaces the "x"

The insertion mode is better when adding text that has been omitted; the overtype mode is easier when you are substituting one (or more) characters for another.

(c) Replacement Mode

FIGURE 1.7 Insertion and Replacement Modes

Deleting Text

The backspace and Del keys delete one character immediately to the left or right of the insertion point, respectively. The choice between them depends on when you need to erase a character(s). The backspace key is easier if you want to delete a character immediately after typing it. The Del key is preferable during subsequent editing.

You can delete a block of text by selecting it (i.e., dragging the mouse over the text), then pressing the Del key. And finally, you can delete and replace text in one operation by selecting the text to be replaced and then typing the new text in its place.

THE UNDO COMMAND

The **_Undo command_** reverses the effect of the most recent operation and is invaluable at any time, but especially when text is accidentally deleted. Pull down the Edit menu and click Undo (or click the Undo button on the Standard toolbar).

Word Wrap

Newcomers to word processing have one major transition to make from a typewriter, and it is an absolutely critical adjustment. Whereas a typist returns the carriage at the end of every line, just the opposite is true of a word processor; that is, you type continually *without* pressing the enter key because the word processor automatically wraps text from one line to the next. This concept is known as ***word wrap*** and is illustrated in Figure 1.8.

The word *primitive* does not fit on the current line in Figure 1.8a, and is automatically shifted to the next line, *without* the user having to press the enter key. The user continues to enter the document with additional words being wrapped to subsequent lines as necessary. The only time you use the enter key is at the end of a paragraph, or when you want the cursor to move to the next line, and the end of the current line doesn't reach the right margin.

Word wrap is closely associated with another concept, that of hard and soft carriage returns. A ***hard return*** is created by the user when he or she presses the enter key at the end of a paragraph. A ***soft return*** is created by the word processor as it wraps text from one line to the next. The location of the soft returns changes automatically as a document is edited (e.g., as text is inserted or deleted, or as margins or fonts are changed). The location of the hard returns can be changed only by the user, who must intentionally insert or delete each hard return.

There are two hard returns in Figure 1.8b, one at the end of each paragraph. There are also seven soft returns in the first paragraph (one at the end of every line except the last) and four soft returns in the second paragraph. Now suppose the margins in the document are made smaller (that is, the line is made longer) as shown in Figure 1.8c. The number of soft returns drops to four and two (in the first and second paragraphs, respectively) as more text fits on a line and fewer lines are needed. The revised document still contains the two original hard returns, one at the end of each paragraph.

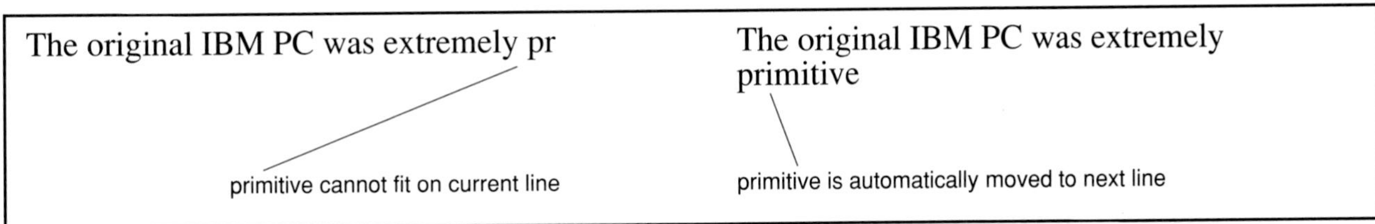

(a) Entering the Document

FIGURE 1.8 Word Wrap

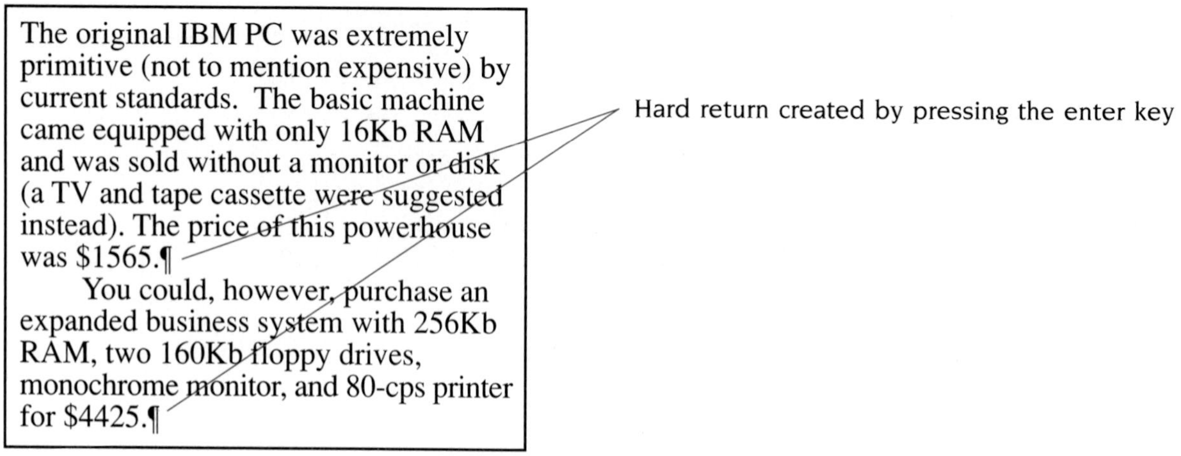

The original IBM PC was extremely primitive (not to mention expensive) by current standards. The basic machine came equipped with only 16Kb RAM and was sold without a monitor or disk (a TV and tape cassette were suggested instead). The price of this powerhouse was $1565.¶

You could, however, purchase an expanded business system with 256Kb RAM, two 160Kb floppy drives, monochrome monitor, and 80-cps printer for $4425.¶

Hard return created by pressing the enter key

(b) Completed Document

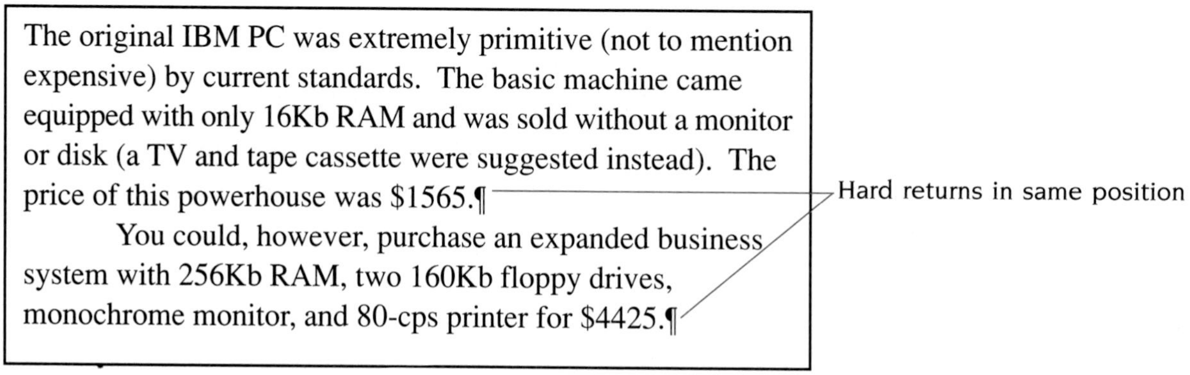

The original IBM PC was extremely primitive (not to mention expensive) by current standards. The basic machine came equipped with only 16Kb RAM and was sold without a monitor or disk (a TV and tape cassette were suggested instead). The price of this powerhouse was $1565.¶

You could, however, purchase an expanded business system with 256Kb RAM, two 160Kb floppy drives, monochrome monitor, and 80-cps printer for $4425.¶

Hard returns in same position

(c) Completed Document

FIGURE 1.8 Word Wrap (continued)

LEARNING BY DOING

We believe strongly in learning by doing, and thus there comes a point where you must sit down at the computer if the discussion is to have real meaning. The exercises in this chapter are linked to one another in that you create a simple document in Exercise 1, then retrieve and edit that document in Exercise 2. The ability to save and retrieve a document is critical, and you do not want to spend an inordinate amount of time entering text, unless you are confident in your ability to retrieve it later.

The first exercise also introduces you to the data disk provided by your instructor and that can be used to store the documents you create. (Alternatively, you can store the documents on a hard disk if you have access to your own computer.) The data disk also contains a variety of documents that are used in the hands-on exercises throughout the text.

HANDS-ON EXERCISE 1:

Creating a Document

Objective To load Word for Windows, then create, save, and print a simple document. The exercise introduces you to the data disk provided by your instructor and reviews basic Windows operations: pull-down menus, dialog boxes, on-line help, and the use of a mouse. Use Figure 1.9 as a guide in doing the exercise.

Step 1: Load Windows

- Type **WIN** and press **enter** to load Windows if it is not already loaded.
- The appearance of your desktop will be different from ours, but it should resemble Figure 1.1 at the beginning of the chapter. You will most likely see a window containing Program Manager, but if not, you should see an icon titled Program Manager near the bottom of the screen; double click this icon to open the Program Manager window.

Step 2: Master the mouse

- A mouse is essential to the operation of Word as it is to all other Windows applications, and it is important that you master its operation. The easiest way to practice is with the mouse tutorial found in the Help menu of Windows itself.
- Click the **Help menu.** Click **Windows Tutorial.**
- Type **M** to begin, then follow the on-screen instructions.
- Exit the tutorial when you are finished.

Step 3: Install the data disk

- Do this step *only* if you have your own computer and want to copy the files from the data disk to the hard drive.
- Place the data disk in drive A (or whatever drive is appropriate).
- Pull down the **File menu.** Click **Run.**
- Type **A:INSTALL C** in the text box. Click **OK.** (The drive letters in the command, A and C, are both variable. If, for example, the data disk were in drive B and you wanted to copy its files to drive D, you would type the command **B:INSTALL D**)
- Follow the on-screen instructions.

Step 4: Load Word for Windows

- Double click the icon for the group containing Word for Windows—for example, Microsoft Office, if that group is not already open. Double click the Program icon for **Word** (or Microsoft Word).
- Click the **maximize button** (if necessary) so that the application window containing Word takes the entire screen as shown in Figure 1.9a.
- Do not be concerned if your screen is different from ours as we include a troubleshooting section immediately following this exercise.

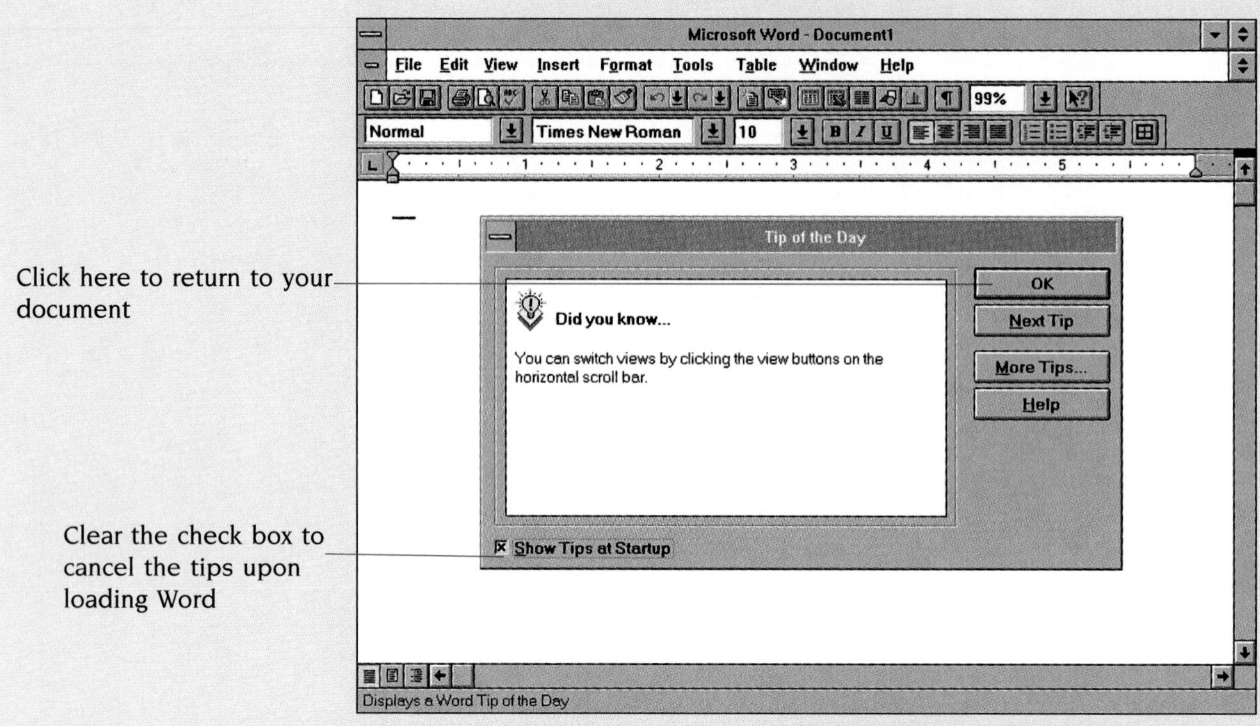

(a) Opening Word Screen with the Tip of the Day (steps 4 and 5)

FIGURE 1.9 Hands-on Exercise 1

DOUBLE CLICKING FOR BEGINNERS

If you are having trouble double clicking, it is because you are not clicking quickly enough, or more likely, because you are moving the mouse (however slightly) between clicks. Relax, hold the mouse firmly in place, and try again.

Step 5: Tip of the Day

- Word displays a tip of the day every time it is loaded. If you do not see a tip, pull down the **Help menu** and click **Tip of the Day.**
  - — To cancel the tips when you start Word, **clear** the box to **Show Tips at Startup.**
  - — To see a tip when you start Word, **click** the box to **Show Tips at Startup.**
- Click **OK** to begin working on your document.

Step 6: Create the document

- Create the document in Figure 1.9b by typing just as you would on a typewriter with one exception—do *not* press the enter key at the end of a line because Word will automatically wrap text from one line to the next.
- Press the **enter key** at the end of the paragraph.
- Proofread the document and correct any errors. Use the **Ins key** to toggle between the insertion and overtype mode as appropriate.

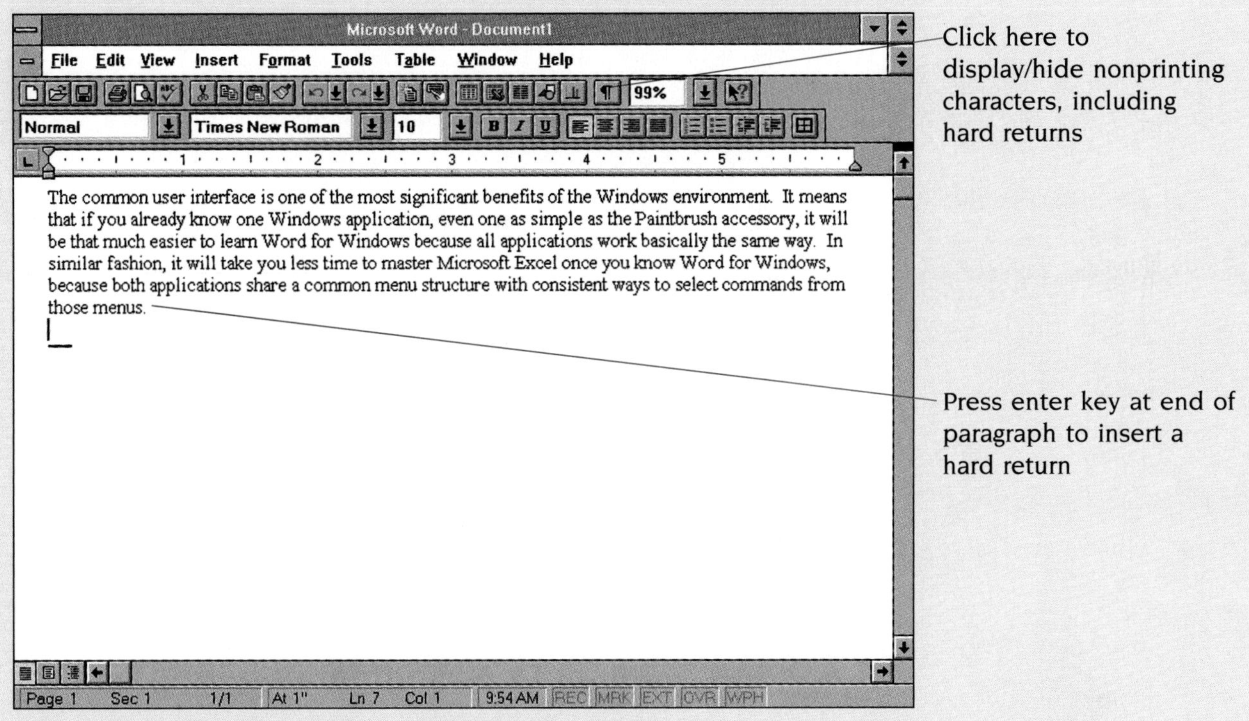

(b) Create the Document (step 6)

FIGURE 1.9 Hands-on Exercise 1 (continued)

DISPLAY THE HARD RETURNS

Click the Show/Hide button on the Standard Toolbar to display the hard returns (paragraph marks) and other nonprinting characters (such as tab characters or blank spaces) contained within a document. The Show/Hide button (denoted by the ¶ symbol indicating a hard return) functions as a toggle switch: the first time you click it, the hard returns are displayed, the second time you press it, the returns are hidden; and so on.

Step 7: Save the document

- Pull down the **File menu.** Click **Save.**
- Alternatively you can press **Alt+F** to pull down the File menu, then type the letter **S,** or you can click the **save button** on the Standard toolbar. Regardless of the technique you choose you should see the Save As dialog box in Figure 1.9c.
- Click the **drop-down list box** in the middle of the screen to specify the appropriate drive, drive C or drive A, depending on whether or not you installed the data disk in step 3.
- Scroll through the directory list box until you come to the **WORDDATA** directory. Double click this directory to make it the active directory.
- Click in the text box for File Name. Click and drag over DOC1.DOC, then type **BENEFIT** as the name of your document (the DOC extension is added automatically).
- Click **OK** or press the **enter key.**

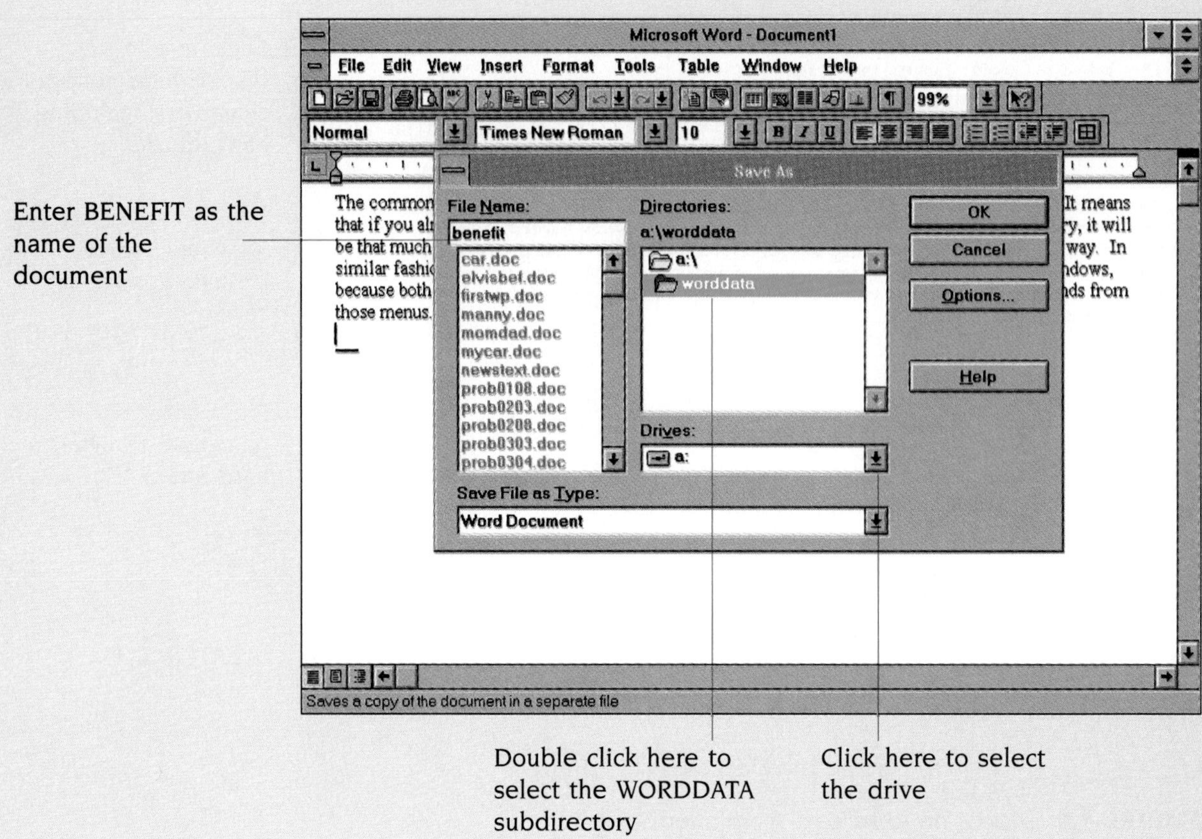

(c) The Save Command (step 7)

FIGURE 1.9 Hands-on Exercise 1 (continued)

> **LEARN TO TYPE**
>
> The ultimate limitation of any word processor is the speed at which you enter data; hence the ability to type quickly is invaluable. Learning how to type is far from an insurmountable problem, especially with the availability of computer-based typing programs. As little as a half hour a day for a couple of weeks will have you up to speed, and if you do any significant amount of writing at all, the investment will pay off many times.

Step 8: Print the document

- Pull down the **File menu.**
- Click **Print** to produce the dialog box of Figure 1.9d.
- Click the **OK** command button to print the document.
- You can also click the **Print icon** on the Standard toolbar to print the document without seeing the dialog box.

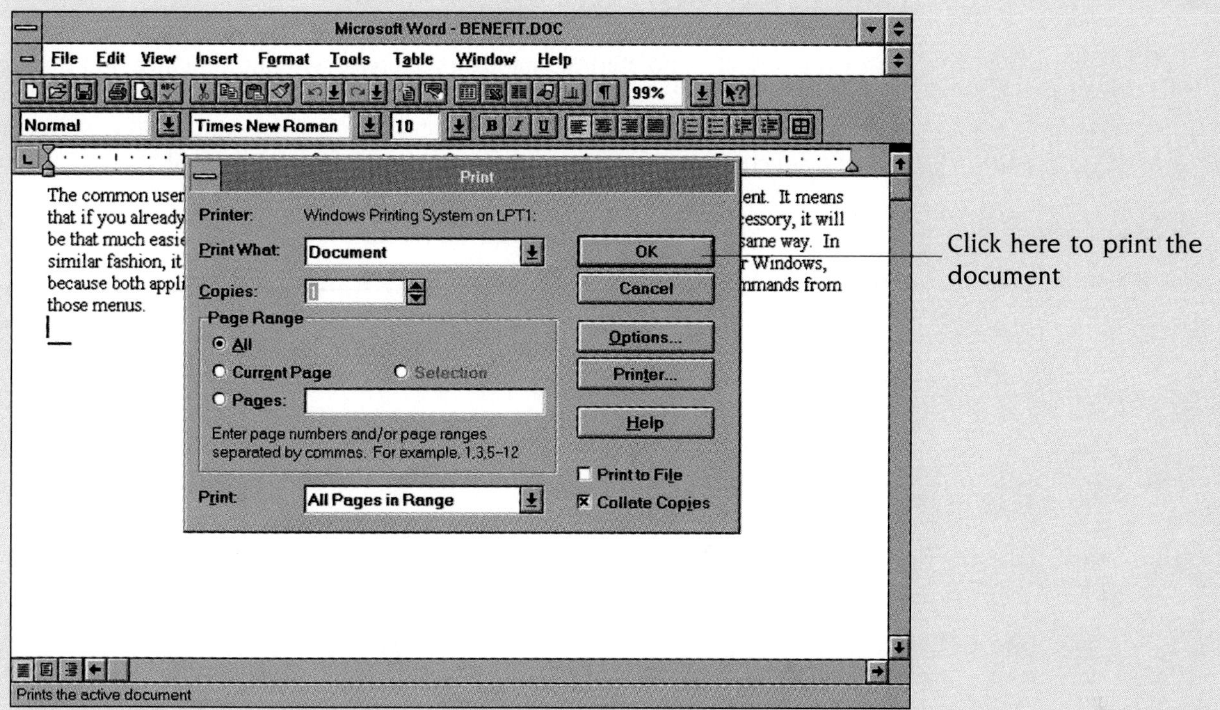

(d) The Print Command (step 8)

FIGURE 1.9 Hands-on Exercise 1 (continued)

EXECUTE COMMANDS QUICKLY

The fastest way to select a command from a pull-down menu is to point to the menu name, then drag the pointer (i.e., press and hold the left mouse button) to the desired command and release the mouse. The command is executed when you release the button.

Step 9: Exit Word

- The easiest way to exit (close) Word is to double click the **control-menu box** at the left of the title bar. Alternatively, you can pull down the **File menu** and click **Exit,** or you can press **Alt+F4** prior to pulling down the File menu.
- Exit Word and return to Program Manager.

Step 10: Exit Windows

- The consistent command structure within Windows means that the same operation is accomplished the same way in different applications; that is, you can exit from Program Manager using any of the techniques described in the previous step.
- Pull down the **File menu** in Program Manager.
- Select the **Exit Windows** command. You will see an informational message indicating that you are leaving Windows, and requiring that you click the **OK** command button to confirm the operation.

TROUBLESHOOTING

We trust that you completed the hands-on exercise without difficulty, and that you were able to create, save, and print the document in Figure 1.9. There is, however, one area of potential confusion in that Word offers different views of the same document depending on the preferences of the individual user. It is very likely that your screen will not match ours and, indeed, there is no requirement that it should. The *contents* of your document, however, should be identical to ours.

Figure 1.9 displayed the document in the ***Normal view.*** Figure 1.10 displays an entirely different view called the ***Page Layout view.*** Each view has its advantages. The Normal view is faster, but the Page Layout view more closely resembles the printed page as it displays the top and bottom margins, a vertical ruler, and other elements not seen in the Normal view. The Normal view is better for entering text and editing. The Page Layout view is used to apply the finishing touches and check a document prior to printing.

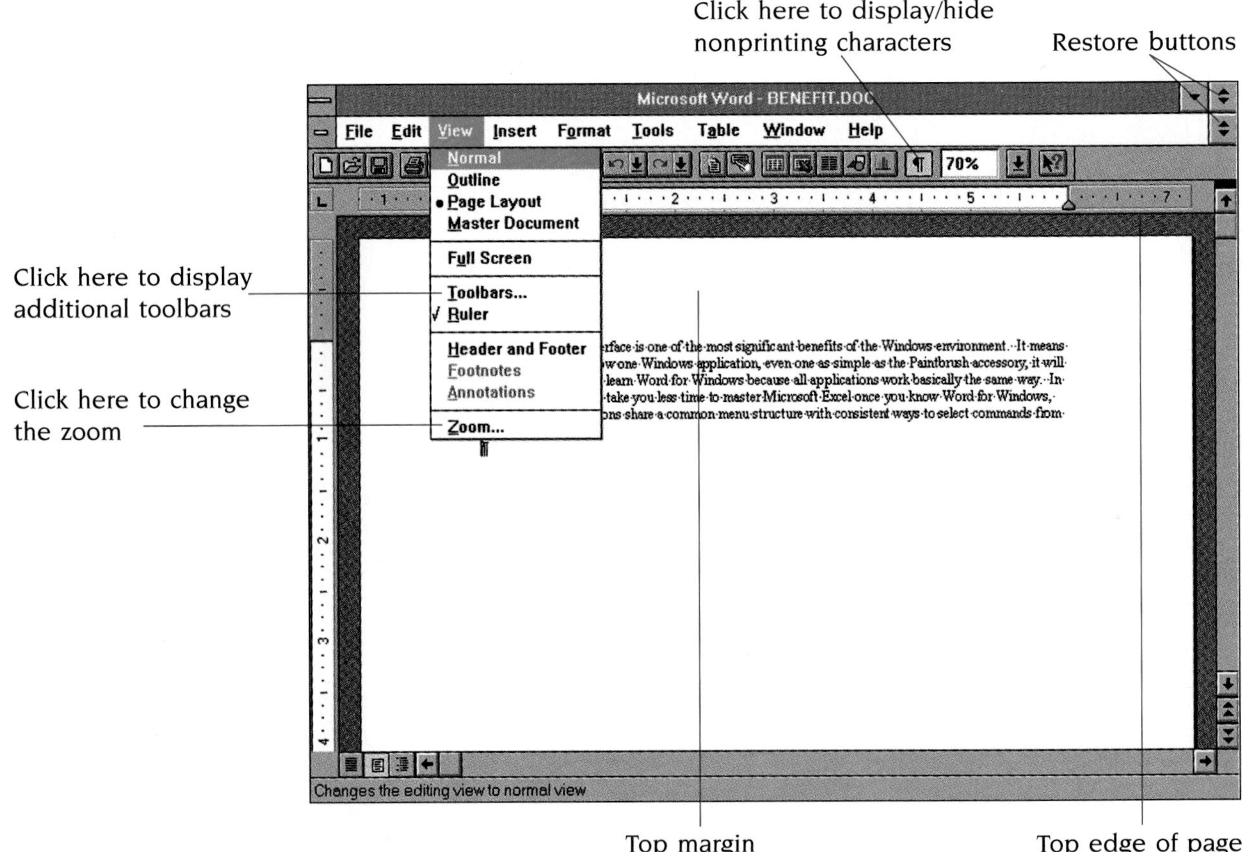

FIGURE 1.10 Troubleshooting

Your screen may or may not match either figure, and you will undoubtedly develop preferences of your own. The following suggestions will help you match the screens of Figure 1.9:

- If the application window for Word does not take the entire screen, and/or the document does not take the entire window within Word, click the maximize button in the application and/or the document window. There are two restore buttons in Figure 1.9b to indicate that the application window and its associated document window have been maximized.

- If the text does not come up to the top of the screen—that is, you see the top edge of the page (as in Figure 1.10)—it means that you are in the Page Layout view instead of the Normal view. Pull down the View menu and click Normal to match the document in Figure 1.9b.
- If the text seems unusually large or small, it means that you or a previous user elected to zoom in or out to get a different perspective on the document. Pull down the View menu, click ***Zoom,*** then click Page Width so that the text takes the entire line as in Figure 1.9b.
- If you see the ¶ and other nonprinting symbols it means that you or a previous user elected to display these characters. Click the Show/Hide button on the Standard Toolbar to make the symbols disappear.
- If the Standard or Formatting toolbar is missing and/or a different toolbar is displayed, pull down the View menu, click Toolbars, then click the appropriate toolbars on or off. If the ruler is missing, pull down the View menu and click Ruler.

THE WRONG KEYBOARD

Word for Windows facilitates conversion from WordPerfect by providing an alternative (software-controlled) keyboard that implements WordPerfect conventions. If you are sharing your machine with others, and if various keyboard shortcuts do not work as expected, it could be because someone else has implemented the WordPerfect keyboard. Pull down the Tools menu, click Options, then click the General tab in the dialog box. Clear the check box next to Navigation keys for WordPerfect users to return to the normal Word for Windows keyboard.

HANDS-ON EXERCISE 2:

Retrieving a Document

Objective To retrieve an existing document, revise it, and save the revision; to demonstrate the Undo command and on-line help. Use Figure 1.11 as a guide in the exercise.

Step 1: Retrieve a document

- Repeat the necessary steps from the first exercise to load Word.
- Pull down the **File menu.** Click **Open.**
- Alternatively you can press **Alt+F** to pull down the File menu and type the letter **O,** or you can click the **open button** on the Standard toolbar. Regardless of the technique you choose, you should see a dialog box similar to the one in Figure 1.11a.
- Click the appropriate drive, drive C or drive A, as in the first exercise.
- Double click the **WORDDATA** directory to make it the active directory.
- Double click **BENEFIT.DOC** to retrieve the document from the first exercise.

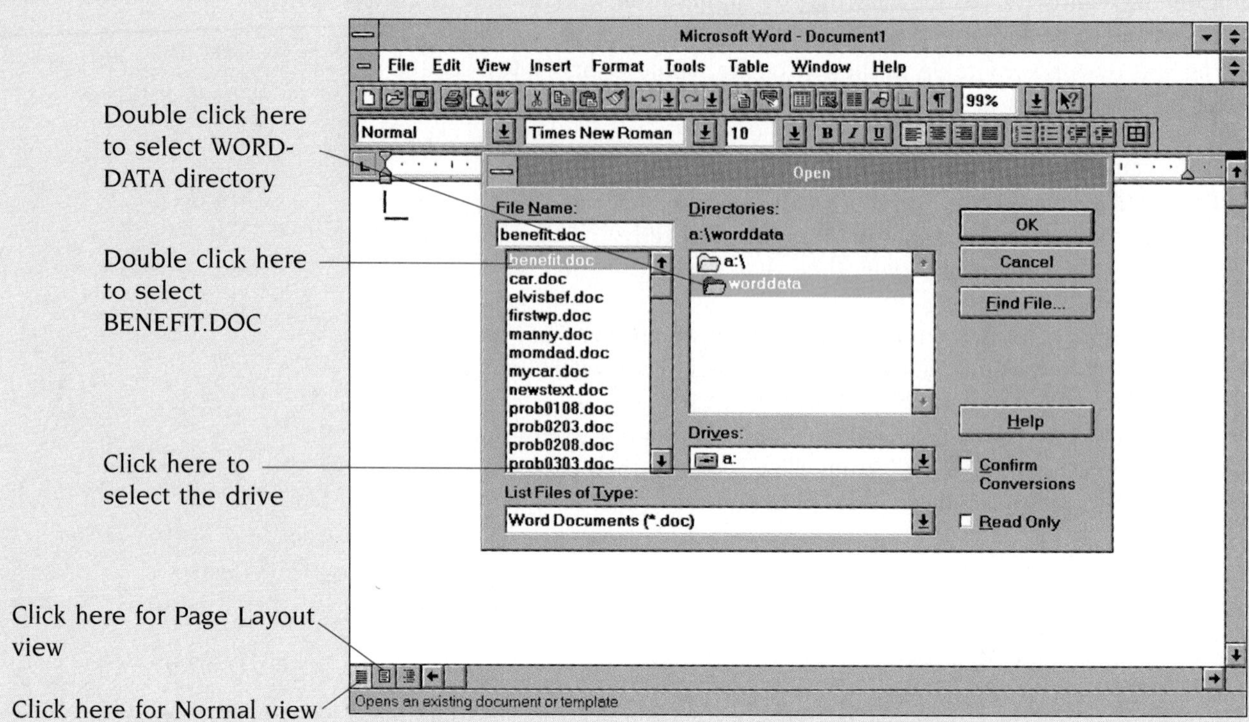

(a) The Open Command (step 1)

FIGURE 1.11 Hands-on Exercise 2

Step 2: The view menu (troubleshooting)

- To change views in the document, pull down the **View menu** and click **Normal** or **Page Layout.** You can also click the appropriate icon at the bottom of the application window.
- To hide or display toolbars, pull down the **View menu,** click **Toolbars,** then click to check or clear the boxes for the individual toolbars.
- To change the size and amount of text displayed in the window, pull down the **View menu,** click **Zoom,** then click the desired percentage. (We suggest 100% or Page Width.)
- There may still be subtle differences between your screen and ours, depending on the resolution of your monitor. These variations, if any, need not concern you at all as long as you are able to complete the exercise.

CHANGE TOOLBARS WITH THE RIGHT MOUSE BUTTON

You can display (hide) toolbars with the right mouse button provided at least one toolbar is visible. Point to any toolbar, then click the right mouse button to display a shortcut menu listing the available toolbars. Click the individual toolbars on or off as appropriate.

Step 3: Display the hard returns

- The **Show/Hide icon** on the Standard toolbar functions as a toggle switch to display (hide) the hard returns (and other nonprinting characters) in a document.
- Click the **Show/Hide icon** to display the hard returns as in Figure 1.11b.
- Click the **Show/Hide icon** a second time to hide the nonprinting characters.
- Display or hide the paragraph markers as you see fit.

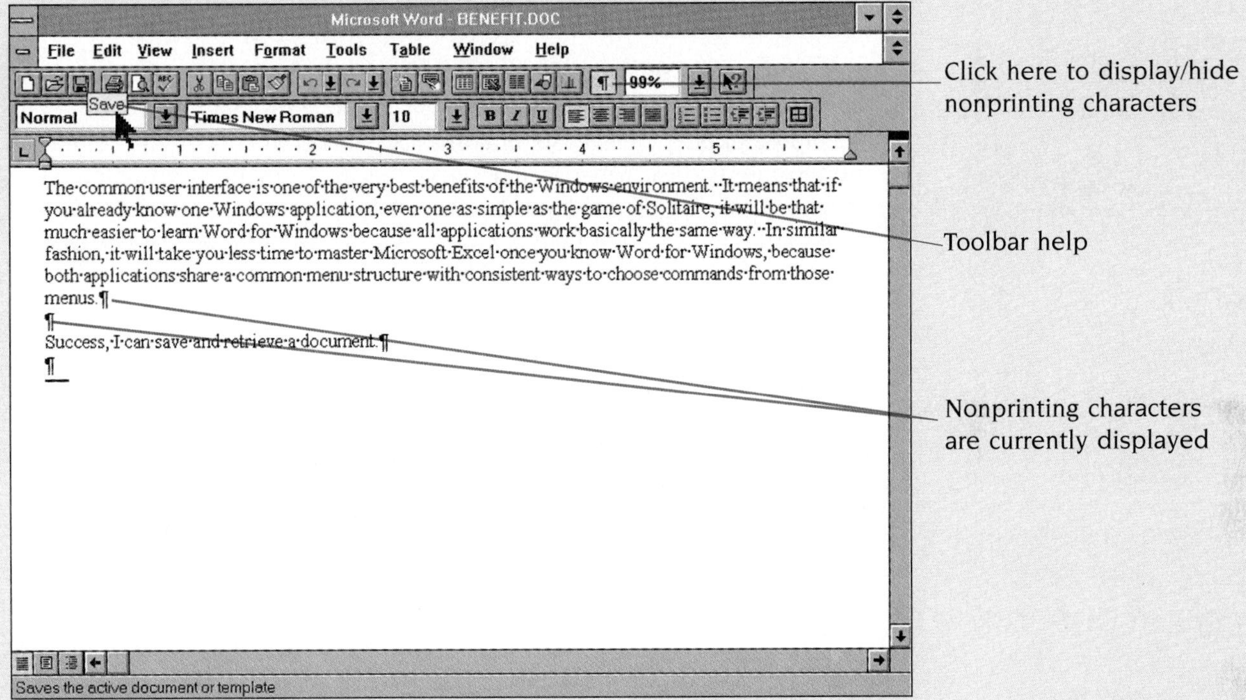

(b) Corrected Document with Paragraph Markers (steps 2, 3, and 4)

FIGURE 1.11 Hands-on Exercise 2 (continued)

TOOLBAR HELP

Point to any button on any toolbar and Word displays the name of the toolbar button, which is indicative of its function. If pointing to a button has no effect, pull down the View menu, click Toolbars, and check the box to Show Tool Tips.

Step 4: Modify the document

- Press **Ctrl+End** to move to the end of the document.
- Press the **enter key** once or twice to add a blank line(s).
- Add the sentence, **Success, I can save and retrieve a document!**
- Make the following additional modifications to practice editing:
  - Change the phrase, *most significant* to **very best.**
  - Change *Paintbrush accessory* to **game of Solitaire.**
  - Change the word *select* to **choose.**

- Switch between the insertion and overtype modes as necessary. Press the **Ins key** or double click the **OVR** indicator on the status bar to toggle between the insertion and overtype modes.

Step 5: Save the changes

- It is very, very important to save your work repeatedly during a session.
- Pull down the **File menu** and click **Save,** or click the **save button** on the Standard toolbar. This time you will not see a dialog box, because the document is saved automatically under the existing name (BENEFIT.DOC).

> **THE INSERTION POINT VERSUS THE I-BEAM**
>
> The mouse pointer changes to an ***I-beam*** whenever you move the pointer into the editing area. The I-beam is very different from the insertion point; you must click the mouse to position the insertion point if you scroll using the mouse. The insertion point changes automatically if you use the keyboard to move through the document.

Step 6: Deleting text

- Point to the first character in the document. **Press and hold the left mouse button** as you drag the mouse over the first sentence. Release the mouse.
- The sentence should remain highlighted (selected) as in Figure 1.11c. The selected text is the text that will be affected by the next command.
- Click anywhere else in the document to deselect the text.
- Repeat the process to reselect the first sentence.
- Press the **Del** key to delete the highlighted text (the first sentence) from the document.

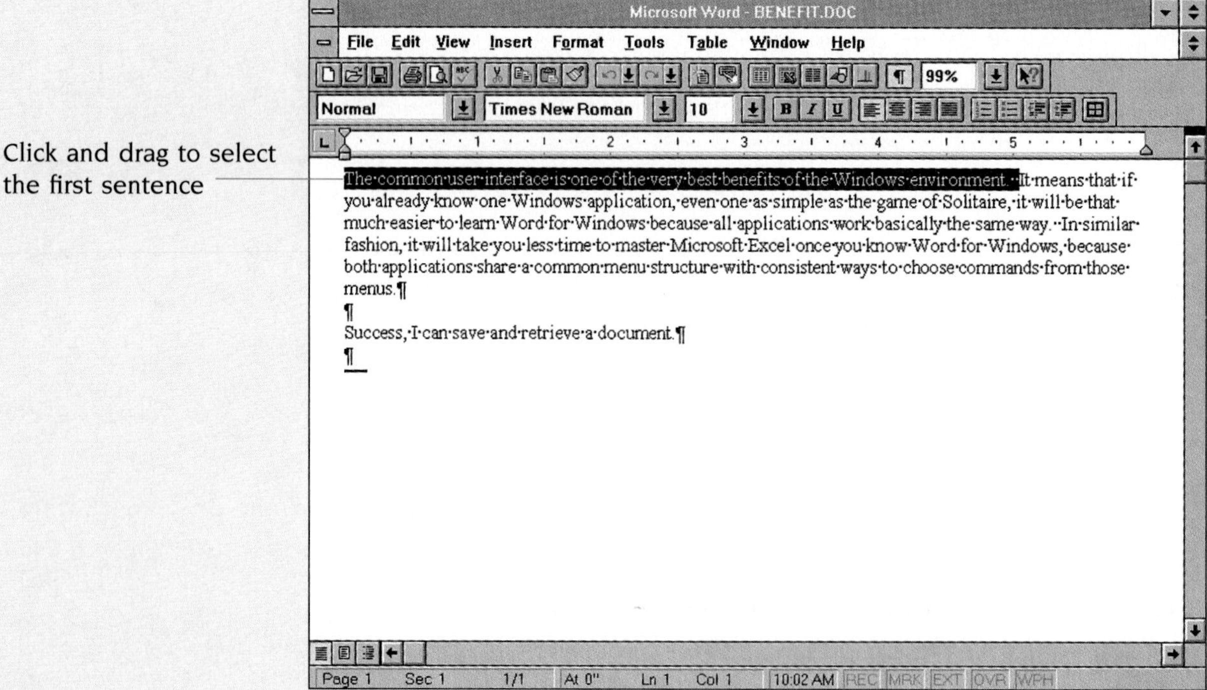

(c) Selecting Text (step 6)

FIGURE 1.11 Hands-on Exercise 2 (continued)

Step 7: The Undo command

- Pull down the **Edit menu** as in Figure 1.11d.
- Click **Undo** to reverse (undo) the previous command.
- The deleted text should be returned to your document. The Undo command is a tremendous safety net and can be used at almost any time.
- Click anywhere outside the highlighted text to deselect the sentence.

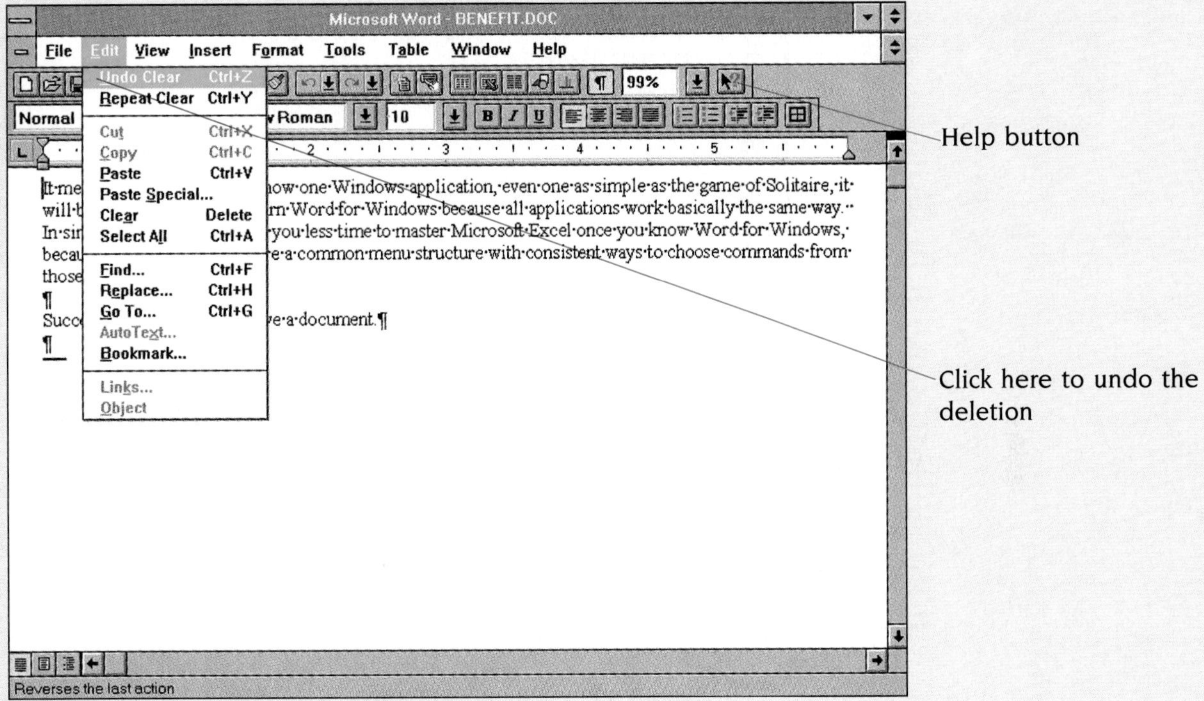

(d) The Undo Command (step 7)

FIGURE 1.11 Hands-on Exercise 2 (continued)

Step 8: On-line help

- Pull down the **Help menu.** Click **Search for Help on.** Type **undo** in the text box.
- Double click **Undo command (Edit menu)** when you see it appear in the upper list box.
- Double click **Undo command (Edit menu)** when it appears in the lower list box to produce a screen similar to Figure 1.11e. Read the help screen.
- Double click the **control-menu box** in the help screen to exit Help and return to the document.

HELP TIPS

Click the Help button on the Standard toolbar (the mouse pointer changes to include a large question mark), then click any other toolbar icon to display a help screen with information about that button. Double click the Help button to produce the Search dialog box that is normally accessed through the Help menu.

Double click here to return to the document

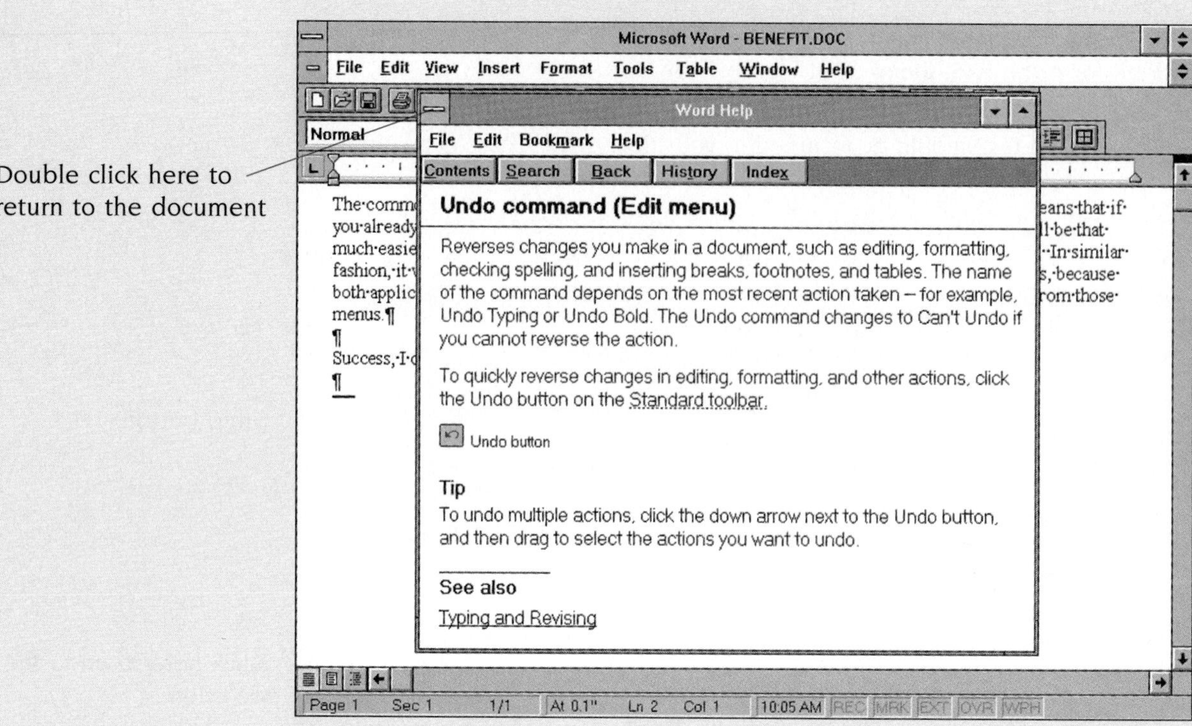

(e) On-line Help (step 8)

FIGURE 1.11 Hands-on Exercise 2 (continued)

Step 9: Print the revised document

- Save the document a final time.
- Print the revised document.
- Exit Word (and Windows) as you did at the end of the previous exercise.

SUMMARY STATISTICS

Pull down the File menu, click Summary Info, then click the Statistics command button. The resulting dialog box displays information about the current document including its approximate size, the date it was created, the date it was last saved, and the total editing time. You can print this information together with the document by setting the appropriate option. Pull down the Tools menu, click Options, click the Print tab, then check the box to print summary information. The summary statistics will appear the next time you print a document.

SUMMARY

The common user interface ensures that all Windows applications are similar in appearance and work basically the same way, with common conventions and a consistent menu structure. It provides you with an intuitive understanding of any application, even before you begin to use it, and means that once you learn one application, it is that much easier to learn the next.

The mouse is essential to Word as it is to all other Windows applications, but keyboard equivalents are provided for virtually all operations. The Standard and Formatting toolbars offer yet another way to execute common commands. On-line help provides detailed information about all aspects of Word.

A word processor is always in one of two modes, insertion or overtype, and uses a toggle switch (the Ins key) to alternate between the two. The insertion point marks the place within a document where text is added or replaced.

The enter key is pressed at the end of a paragraph, not the end of a line, because Word automatically wraps text from one line to the next. A hard return is created by the user when he or she presses the enter key; a soft return is created by Word as it wraps text and begins a new line.

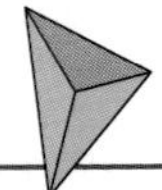

Key Words and Concepts

Application window
Check box
Click
Command button
Common user interface
Control-menu box
Desktop
Dialog box
Dimmed command
Document window
Double click
Drag
Drop-down list box
Ellipsis
End-of-file marker
Formatting toolbar
Hard return
Help button
Help menu
Horizontal ruler
I-beam
Icon
Index button
Insertion mode
Insertion point
Maximize button
Menu bar
Minimize button
Mouse pointer
Normal view
On-line help
Open list box
Option button
Overtype mode
Page Layout view
Point
Program Manager
Pull-down menu
Restore button
Scroll bar
Scroll box
Soft return
Standard toolbar
Status bar
Text box
Tip of the Day
Title bar
Toggle switch
Toolbar
Undo command
Vertical ruler
View menu
Windows
Word for Windows
Word wrap
Zoom

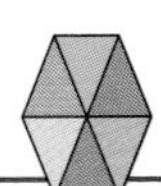

Multiple Choice

1. When entering text within a document, the enter key is normally pressed at the end of every:
(a) Line
(b) Sentence
(c) Paragraph
(d) All of the above

2. Which of the following is true regarding scrolling?
(a) You can scroll a document in a vertical direction
(b) You can scroll a document in a horizontal direction
(c) Both (a) and (b)
(d) Neither (a) nor (b)

3. Which of the following will execute a command from a pull-down menu?
   (a) Clicking on the command once the menu has been pulled down
   (b) Typing the underlined letter in the command
   (c) Both (a) and (b)
   (d) Neither (a) nor (b)
4. The File Open command:
   (a) Brings a document from disk into memory
   (b) Brings a document from disk into memory, then erases the document on disk
   (c) Stores the document in memory on disk
   (d) Stores the document in memory on disk, then erases it from memory
5. The File Save command:
   (a) Brings a document from disk into memory
   (b) Brings a document from disk into memory, then erases the document on disk
   (c) Stores the document in memory on disk
   (d) Stores the document in memory on disk, then erases the document from memory
6. What is the easiest way to change the phrase, *revenues, profits, gross margin,* to read *revenues, profits, and gross margin*?
   (a) Use the insertion mode, position the insertion point before the *g* in gross, then type the word *and* followed by a space
   (b) Use the insertion mode, position the insertion point after the *g* in gross, then type the word *and* followed by a space
   (c) Use the overtype mode, position the insertion point before the *g* in gross, then type the word *and* followed by a space
   (d) Use the overtype mode, position the insertion point after the *g* in gross, then type the word *and* followed by a space
7. What happens if you press the Ins key *twice in a row* from within Word?
   (a) You will be in the insertion mode
   (b) You will be in the overtype mode
   (c) You will be in the same mode you were in before pressing the key at all
   (d) You will be in the opposite mode you were before pressing the key at all
8. What is the significance of three dots next to a menu option?
   (a) The option is not accessible
   (b) A dialog box will appear if the option is selected
   (c) A help window will appear if the option is selected
   (d) There are no equivalent keystrokes for the particular option
9. What is the significance of a menu option that appears faded (dimmed)?
   (a) The option is not currently accessible
   (b) A dialog box will appear if the option is selected
   (c) A help window will appear if the option is selected
   (d) There are no equivalent keystrokes for the particular option
10. Which of the following elements may be found within a help window?
   (a) Title bar, menu bar, and control-menu box
   (b) Minimize, maximize, and/or a restore button
   (c) Vertical and/or horizontal scroll bars
   (d) All of the above

11. A document has been entered into Word with a given set of margins which are subsequently changed. What can you say about the number of hard and soft returns before and after the change in margins?
    (a) The number of hard returns is the same, but the number and/or position of the soft returns is different
    (b) The number of soft returns is the same, but the number and/or position of the hard returns is different
    (c) The number and position of both hard and soft returns is unchanged
    (d) The number and position of both hard and soft returns is different

12. Which of the following is an example of a toggle switch within Word?
    (a) The Ins key
    (b) The Caps Lock key
    (c) The Show/Hide button on the Standard toolbar
    (d) All of the above

13. Which of the following is true regarding a dialog box?
    (a) Option buttons indicated mutually exclusive choices
    (b) Check boxes imply that multiple options may be selected
    (c) Both (a) and (b)
    (d) Neither (a) nor (b)

14. Which of the following will exit Word and return to Windows?
    (a) Double clicking the control-menu box in the title bar for Word
    (b) Pressing Alt+F4 from anywhere within Word
    (c) Pulling down the File menu and clicking on Exit
    (d) All of the above

15. Which of the following actions will end a Windows session?
    (a) Double clicking on the control-menu box of the Program Manager
    (b) Double clicking on the control-menu box of Word
    (c) Both (a) and (b)
    (d) Neither (a) nor (b)

ANSWERS

1. c
2. c
3. c
4. a
5. c
6. a
7. c
8. b
9. a
10. d
11. a
12. d
13. c
14. d
15. a

EXPLORING WORD

1. Use Figure 1.12 to identify the elements of a Word screen by matching each element with the appropriate letter:

____ Restore button	____ Minimize button
____ Control-menu box	____ Vertical scroll bar
____ Standard toolbar	____ Scroll box
____ Formatting toolbar	____ Menu bar
____ Horizontal ruler	____ Status bar

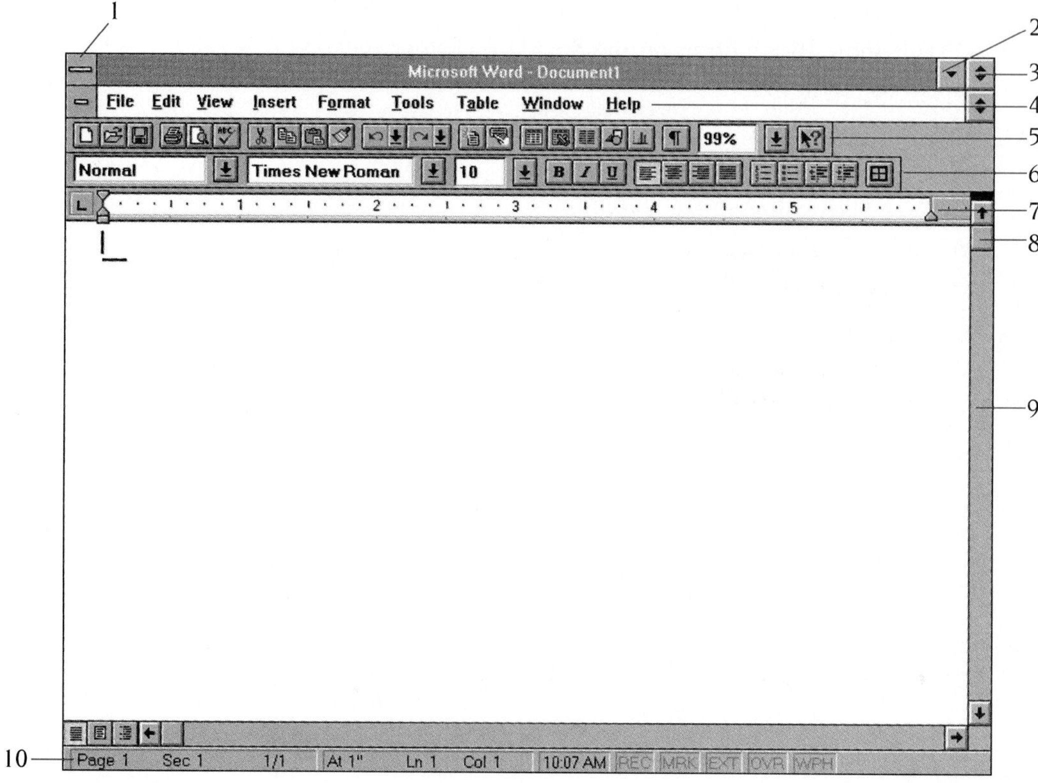

FIGURE 1.12 Screen for Problem 1

2. The common user interface: Answer the following with respect to Figures 1.2a and 1.2b that appeared earlier in the chapter.
   a. Which pull-down menus are common to both Excel and Word?
   b. How do you access the Edit menu in Excel? in Word?
   c. How do you open a file in Word? Do you think the same command will work in Excel as well?
   d. Which icons correspond to the Open and Save commands in the Excel toolbar? Which icons correspond to the Open and Save commands in the Word toolbar?
   e. Which icons will boldface, italicize, and underline selected type? Are the icons descriptive of the tasks they perform?
   f. What do your answers to parts a through e tell you about the advantages of a common user interface?
3. What is the difference between:
   a. The insertion and overtype modes?

b. Deleting a character using the backspace and Del keys?
c. Typing when text is selected versus typing when no text has been selected?
d. The I-beam and the insertion point?
e. The insertion point and the end-of-file marker?
f. The Standard and Formatting toolbars?
g. The normal and page layout views?
h. A hard and soft carriage return?

4. Troubleshooting: The informational messages in Figure 1.13 appeared (or could have appeared) in response to various commands issued during the chapter.
   a. Which command produced the message in Figure 1.13a? What action is necessary to correct the indicated problem?
   b. Which command produced the message in Figure 1.13b? When would No be an appropriate response to this message?
   c. The message in Figure 1.13c appeared in response to a File Open command in conjunction with the file shown earlier in Figure 1.11a. What is the most likely corrective action?

(a) Informational Message 1

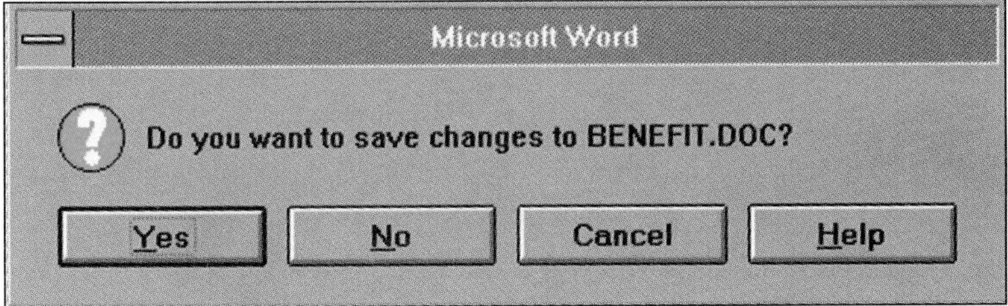

(b) Informational Message 2

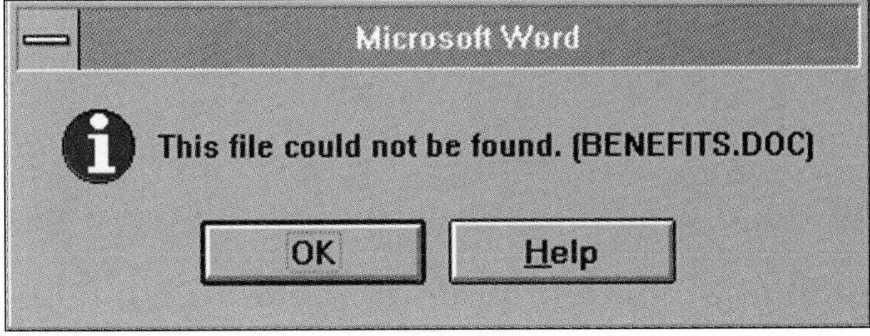

(c) Informational Message 3

FIGURE 1.13 Informational Messages for Problem 4

5. Answer the following with respect to the dialog box in Figure 1.14.
   a. Which command produced the dialog box?
   b. Can the Print to File and Collate Copies boxes be checked at the same time?
   c. What happens if you click the Collate Copies box, given that it is already checked?
   d. Which options (if any) are mutually exclusive?
   e. What do the three dots following the Options command button indicate?
   f. What happens when you click the Cancel command button? Which key has the same effect?
   g. What happens when you click the OK command button? Which key has the same effect as clicking on the OK button when it is highlighted?

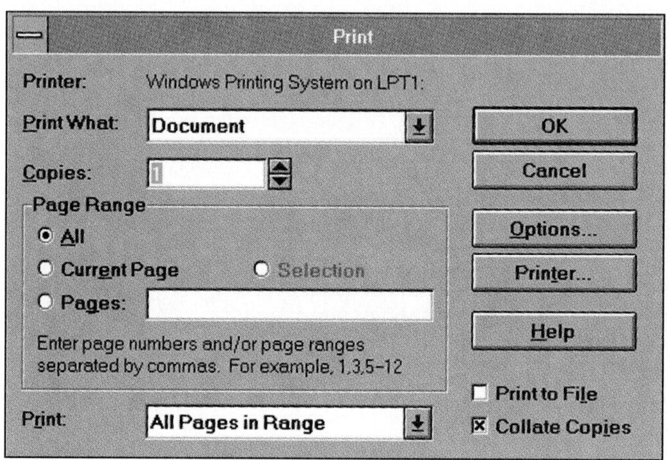

FIGURE 1.14 Dialog Box for Problem 5

6. Exploring help: Answer the following with respect to Figure 1.15:
   a. What is the significance of the scroll box that appears within the scroll bar?
   b. What happens if you click the down (up) arrow within the scroll bar?
   c. What happens if you press the maximize button? Might this action eliminate the need to scroll within the help window?
   d. How do you print the help topic shown in the window?
   e. What keystroke will move you to the beginning of a line? to the end of a line?
7. Answer the following with respect to Figure 1.16:
   a. What is the name of the document currently being edited?
   b. Which view is selected, Page Layout view or Normal?
   c. Is the ruler present? the Formatting toolbar? the Standard toolbar? How do you cause the missing elements to reappear?
   d. Which mode is active, insertion or overtype? How do you switch from one mode to the other?
   e. How do you display (hide) the hard carriage returns? Are the hard returns displayed in the figure?
   f. Has the application window for Word been maximized? Has the document window within Word been maximized?
   g. Add your name at the top of the document, then create and print the entire document. Submit the completed document to your instructor.

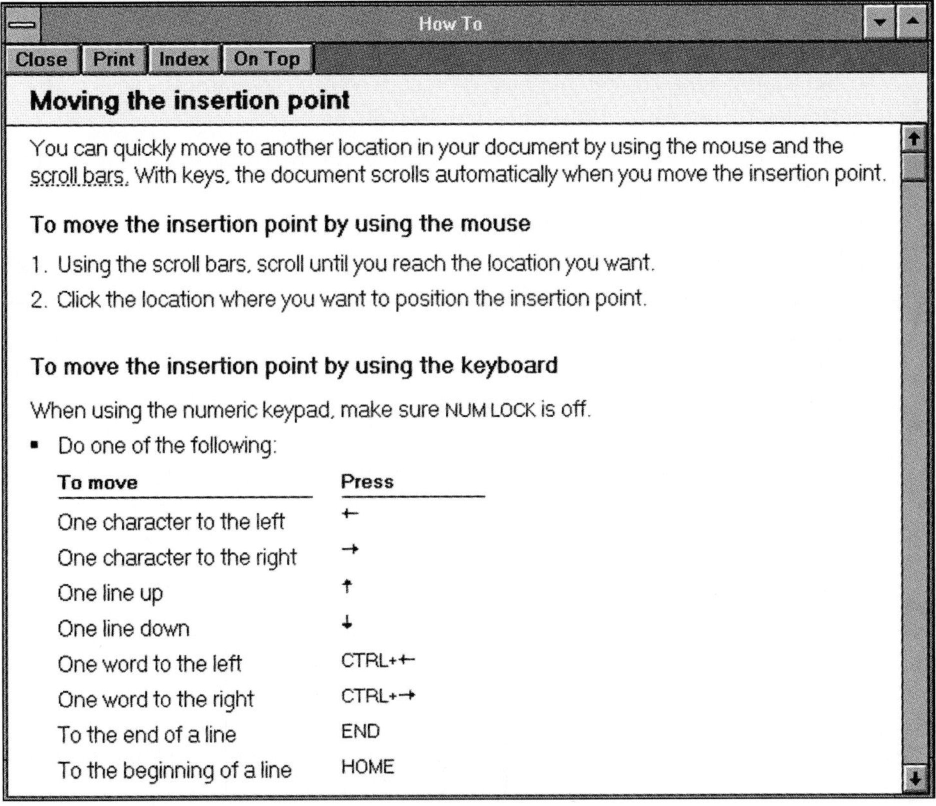

How To
Close
Print
Index
On Top
Moving the insertion point
You can quickly move to another location in your document by using the mouse and the scroll bars. With keys, the document scrolls automatically when you move the insertion point.
To move the insertion point by using the mouse
1. Using the scroll bars, scroll until you reach the location you want.
2. Click the location where you want to position the insertion point.
To move the insertion point by using the keyboard
When using the numeric keypad, make sure NUM LOCK is off.
Do one of the following:
To move
Press
One character to the left ←
One character to the right →
One line up ↑
One line down ↓
One word to the left CTRL+←
One word to the right CTRL+→
To the end of a line END
To the beginning of a line HOME

FIGURE 1.15 Screen for Problem 6

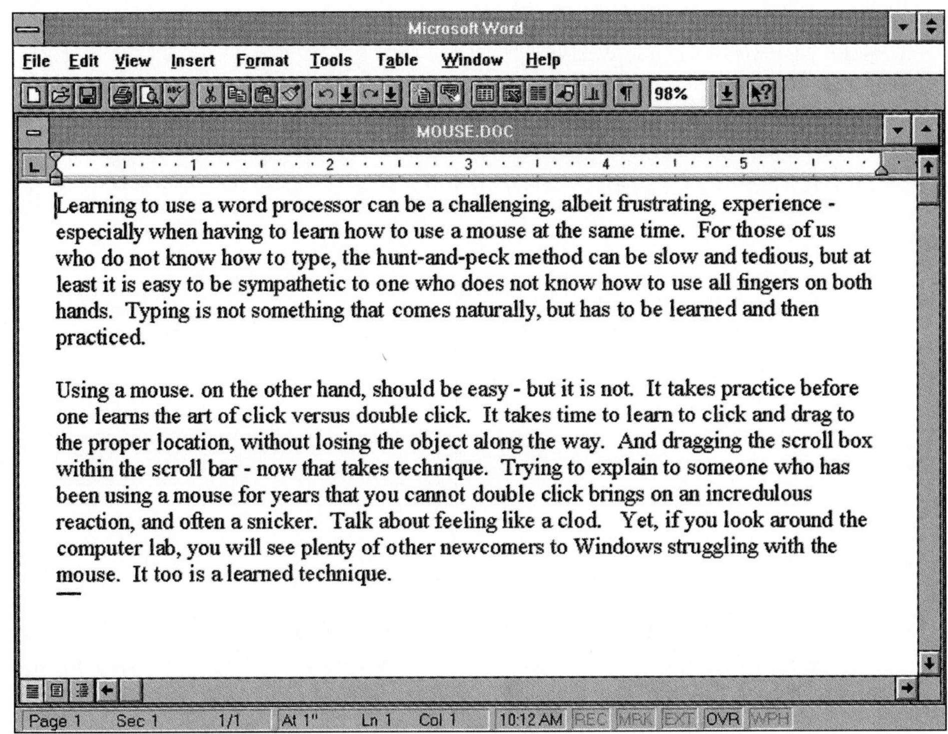

Microsoft Word
File Edit View Insert Format Tools Table Window Help
98%
MOUSE.DOC
Learning to use a word processor can be a challenging, albeit frustrating, experience - especially when having to learn how to use a mouse at the same time. For those of us who do not know how to type, the hunt-and-peck method can be slow and tedious, but at least it is easy to be sympathetic to one who does not know how to use all fingers on both hands. Typing is not something that comes naturally, but has to be learned and then practiced.
Using a mouse. on the other hand, should be easy - but it is not. It takes practice before one learns the art of click versus double click. It takes time to learn to click and drag to the proper location, without losing the object along the way. And dragging the scroll box within the scroll bar - now that takes technique. Trying to explain to someone who has been using a mouse for years that you cannot double click brings on an incredulous reaction, and often a snicker. Talk about feeling like a clod. Yet, if you look around the computer lab, you will see plenty of other newcomers to Windows struggling with the mouse. It too is a learned technique.
Page 1 Sec 1 1/1 At 1" Ln 1 Col 1 10:12 AM REC MRK EXT OVR WPH

FIGURE 1.16 Screen for Problem 7

8. Retrieve the PROB0108.DOC document in Figure 1.17 from the WORDDATA subdirectory, then make the following changes:
   a. Select the text *Your name* and replace it with your name.
   b. Replace *January 1, 1994* with the current date.
   c. Insert the phrase *one or* in line 2 so that the text reads . . . *one or more characters than currently exist.*
   d. Delete the word *And* from sentence 4 in line 5, then change the *w* in *when* to a capital letter to begin the sentence.
   e. Change the phrase *most efficient* to *best.*
   f. Place the insertion point at the end of sentence 2, make sure you are in the insertion mode, then add the following sentence: *The insertion mode adds characters at the insertion point while moving existing text to the right in order to make room for the new text.*
   g. Place the insertion point at the end of the last sentence, press the enter key twice in a row, then enter the following text: *There are several keys that function as toggle switches of which you should be aware. The Ins key switches between the insertion and overtype modes, the Caps Lock key toggles between upper- and lowercase letters, and the Num Lock key alternates between typing numbers and using the cursor control keys.*
   h. Save the revised document, then print it and submit it to your instructor.

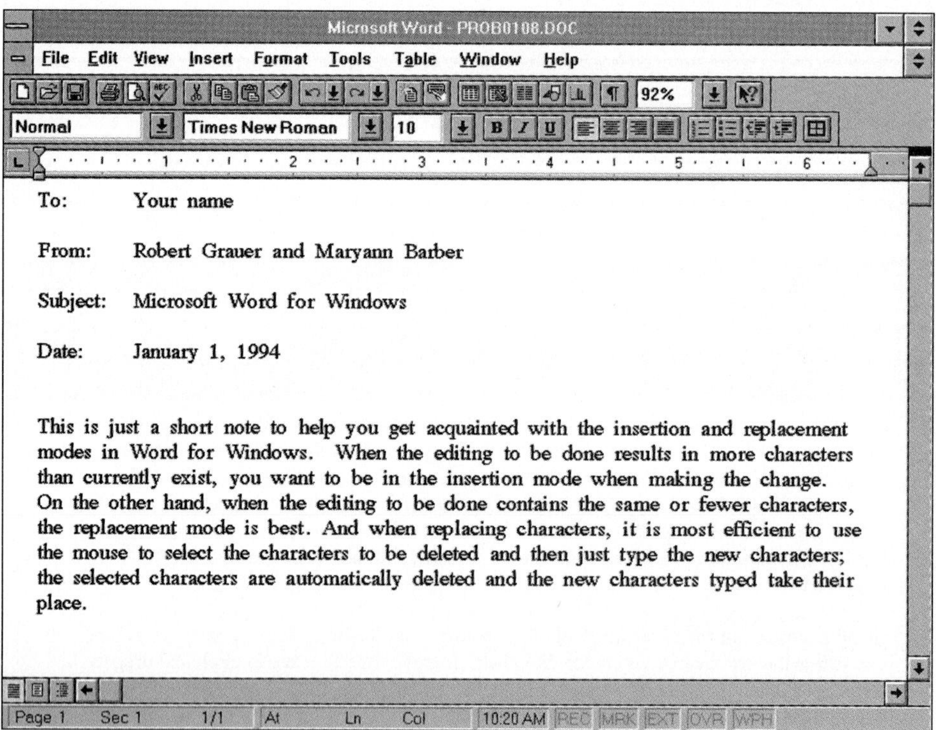

To: Your name

From: Robert Grauer and Maryann Barber

Subject: Microsoft Word for Windows

Date: January 1, 1994

This is just a short note to help you get acquainted with the insertion and replacement modes in Word for Windows. When the editing to be done results in more characters than currently exist, you want to be in the insertion mode when making the change. On the other hand, when the editing to be done contains the same or fewer characters, the replacement mode is best. And when replacing characters, it is most efficient to use the mouse to select the characters to be deleted and then just type the new characters; the selected characters are automatically deleted and the new characters typed take their place.

FIGURE 1.17 Screen for Problem 8

9. Prepare a one-page memo (approximately 250 words) from student to instructor detailing your background. Include any previous knowledge of computers you may have, prior computer courses you have taken, your objectives for the course, and so on. Also, indicate whether you own a PC,

whether you have access to one at work, and/or whether you are considering purchase. Include any other information about yourself and/or your computer-related background. Your one page of text should consist of at least two paragraphs. After you have created your memo, print it and submit it to your instructor.

10. Write a short essay (three to four paragraphs) describing your favorite fictional character—whether it be a character from a cherished novel or short story, a classic or recently released movie, or even a mythological tale. Give a brief physical and/or psychological description of the character, an explanation of the role he/she plays in the fictional world in which he/she exists, and the reasons why this character has inspired you to feel as you do. When you have completed the essay, proofread it for errors, make any corrections necessary, then print it and submit it to your instructor for a grade.

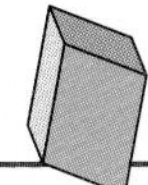

Case Studies

It's a Mess

Newcomers to word processing quickly learn the concept of word wrap and the distinction between hard and soft returns. This lesson was lost, however, on your friend who created the document HELPME.DOC on the data disk. The first several sentences were entered without any hard returns at all, whereas the opposite problem exists toward the end of the document. This is a good friend and her paper is due in one hour. Please help.

Planning for Disaster

Do you have a backup strategy? Do you even know what a backup strategy is? You had better learn, because sooner or later you will wish you had one. You will erase a file, be unable to read from a floppy disk, or worse yet suffer a hardware failure in which you are unable to access the hard drive. The problem always seems to occur the night before an assignment is due. The ultimate disaster is the disappearance of your computer, by theft or natural disaster (e.g., Hurricane Andrew or the Los Angeles earthquake). Describe in 250 words or less the backup strategy you plan to implement in conjunction with your work in this class.

A Letter Home

You really like this course and want very much to have your own computer, but you're strapped for cash and have decided to ask your parents for help. Write a one-page letter describing the advantages of having your own system and how it will help you in school. Tell your parents what the system will cost, and that you can save money by buying through the mail. Describe the configuration you intend to buy (don't forget to include the price of software), and then provide prices from at least three different companies. Cut out the advertisements and include them in your letter. Bring your material to class and compare your research with that of your classmates.

Computer Magazines

A subscription to a computer magazine should be given serious consideration if you intend to stay abreast in a rapidly changing field. The reviews on new products are especially helpful and you will appreciate the advertisements should you need to buy. Go to the library or a newsstand and obtain a magazine that appeals to you, then write a brief review of the magazine for class. Describe the features you like and don't like. Devote at least one paragraph to an article or other item you found useful.

2

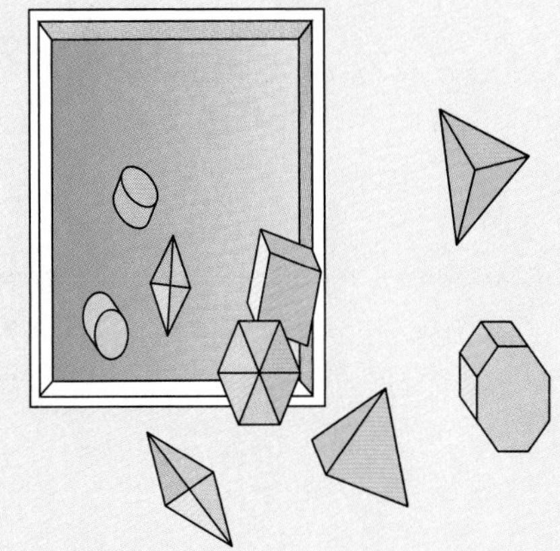

Gaining Proficiency: Editing and Formatting

CHAPTER OBJECTIVES

After reading this chapter you will be able to:

1. Define the select-then-do methodology; describe several shortcuts with the mouse and/or the keyboard to select text.
2. Use the clipboard and/or the drag-and-drop capability to move and copy text within a document.
3. Use the Find and Replace commands to substitute one character string for another.
4. Differentiate between the Save and Save As commands; describe various backup options that can be selected.
5. Define scrolling; scroll to the beginning and end of a document.
6. Distinguish between the Normal and Page Layout views; state how to change the view and/or magnification of a document.
7. Explain TrueType; distinguish between a serif and a sans serif typeface; use the Format Font command to change the font and/or type size.
8. Use the Format Paragraph command to change line spacing, alignment, tabs and indents, and to control pagination; use the Borders and Shading command to box and shade text.
9. Describe the Undo and Redo commands and how they are related to one another.
10. Use the Page Setup command to change the margins and/or orientation; differentiate between a soft and hard page break.

OVERVIEW

The previous chapter taught you the basics of Word for Windows and enabled you to create and print a simple document. The present chapter significantly extends your capabilities by offering a variety of commands that let you change the contents and appearance of a document. These operations are known as editing and formatting, respectively.

You will learn how to move and copy text within a document, how to find and replace one character string with another, and how to implement various backup options. You will also learn the basics of typography and be able to switch between the different fonts included within Windows. You will be able to change the justification, indentation, and line spacing. You will learn how to change margins and page orientation, and how to create a page break. All of these commands are used in three hands-on exercises that are the very essence of the chapter.

As you read the chapter, realize that there are many different ways to accomplish the same task and that it would be impossible to cover them all. Our approach is to present the overall concepts and suggest the ways we think are most appropriate at the time we introduce the material. We also offer numerous shortcuts in the form of boxed tips that appear throughout the chapter and urge you to explore further on your own. It is not necessary for you to memorize anything as on-line help is always available. Be flexible and willing to experiment.

WRITE NOW, EDIT LATER

You write a sentence, then change it, and change it again, and one hour later you've produced a single paragraph. It happens to every writer—you stare at a blank screen and flashing cursor and are unable to write. The best solution is to brainstorm and write down anything that pops into your head, and to keep on writing. Don't worry about typos or spelling errors because you can fix them later. Above all, resist the temptation to continually edit the few words you've written because overediting will drain the life out of what you are writing. The important thing is to get your ideas on paper.

SELECT THEN DO

Virtually every operation in Word takes place within the context of a ***select-then-do*** methodology; that is, you select a block of text, then you execute the command to operate on that text. The most basic way to select text is by dragging the mouse. Click at the beginning of the selection, press and hold the left mouse button as you move to the end of the selection, then release the mouse.

There are, however, a variety of shortcuts to facilitate the process. You can double click anywhere within a word to select the word. You can press the Ctrl key and click the mouse anywhere within a sentence to select the sentence. Additional shortcuts are presented in each of the hands-on exercises, at which point you will have an opportunity to practice.

Selected text is affected by any subsequent operation; for example, clicking the boldface or italics icon changes the selected text to boldface or italics, respectively. You can also drag the selected text to a new location, press the Del key to erase the selected text, or execute any other editing or formatting command. The selected text remains highlighted until you click elsewhere in the document.

SHORTCUT MENUS

Point anywhere within a document, then click the right mouse button to display a ***shortcut menu.*** Shortcut menus contain commands appropriate to the item you have selected. Click in the menu to execute a command, or click outside the menu to close the menu without executing a command.

MOVING AND COPYING TEXT

The ability to move and/or copy text is essential in order to develop any degree of proficiency in editing. A move operation removes the text from its current location and places it elsewhere in the same (or even a different) document; a copy operation retains the text in its present location and places a duplicate elsewhere. Either operation can be accomplished using the Windows clipboard and a combination of the ***Cut, Copy,*** and ***Paste commands.*** (A shortcut, using the mouse to ***drag and drop*** text from one location to another, is described on page 55.)

The ***clipboard*** is a temporary storage area available to any Windows application. Selected text is cut or copied from a document and placed into the clipboard from where it can be pasted to a new location(s). A move requires that you select the text and execute a Cut command to remove the text from the document and place it in the clipboard. You then move the insertion point to the new location, and finally you paste the text from the clipboard into the new location. A copy operation necessitates the same steps except that the selected text is copied rather than cut.

The Cut, Copy, and Paste commands are found in the Edit menu, or alternatively, can be executed by clicking the appropriate icons on the toolbar. The contents of the clipboard are replaced by each subsequent Cut or Copy command. They are unaffected by the Paste command; that is, the contents of the clipboard can be pasted into multiple locations in a document.

DELETE WITH CAUTION

You work too hard developing your thoughts to see them disappear in a flash. Hence, instead of deleting large blocks of text, try moving them to the end of your document where they can be recalled later if you change your mind. A related practice is to remain in the insert mode (as opposed to overtype) to prevent the inadvertent deletion of existing text as new ideas are added.

UNDO, REPEAT, AND REDO COMMANDS

The ***Undo command*** was used in Chapter 1 but is repeated here because it is invaluable at any time, especially when text is accidentally deleted. Pull down the Edit menu and click Undo (or click the Undo button on the Standard toolbar) to reverse the effect of the most recent operation. Use the command whenever something happens to your document that is confusing or different from what you had intended.

The ***Repeat command*** (also in the Edit menu) repeats the most recent editing or formatting change. Use the command whenever you want to make the same revision several times in a document; for example, when you want to add the same

100 LEVELS OF UNDO

Incredible, perhaps, but Word enables you to undo the last 100 changes to a document. Click the arrow next to the Undo button on the Standard toolbar to produce a list of your previous actions, then click the action you want to undo.

phrase in multiple places in a long document.

The ***Redo command*** works in conjunction with the Undo command; that is, every time a command is undone it can be redone at a later time.

FIND AND REPLACE COMMANDS

The ***Find command*** enables you to locate a specific occurrence of a character string in order to perform a subsequent editing or formatting operation. The ***Replace command*** incorporates the Find command and allows you to locate and optionally replace (one or more occurrences of) a character string with a different character string.

The two strings are known as the find and replacement strings, respectively. Each may consist of a single letter, a word, a sentence, or any combination of text. The two strings do *not* have to be the same length; for example, you could replace *16* with *sixteen.* The commands are illustrated in Figure 2.1.

The search may or may not be ***case sensitive.*** A case-sensitive search (where Match Case is selected as in Figure 2.1a) matches not only the characters, but the use of upper- and lowercase letters; that is, *There* is different from *there,* and a search on one will not identify the other. A ***case-insensitive*** search (where Match Case is *not* selected) is just the opposite and finds both *There* and *there.* The search may also specify a match on the ***whole word only,*** which will identify *there,* but not *therefore* or *thereby.*

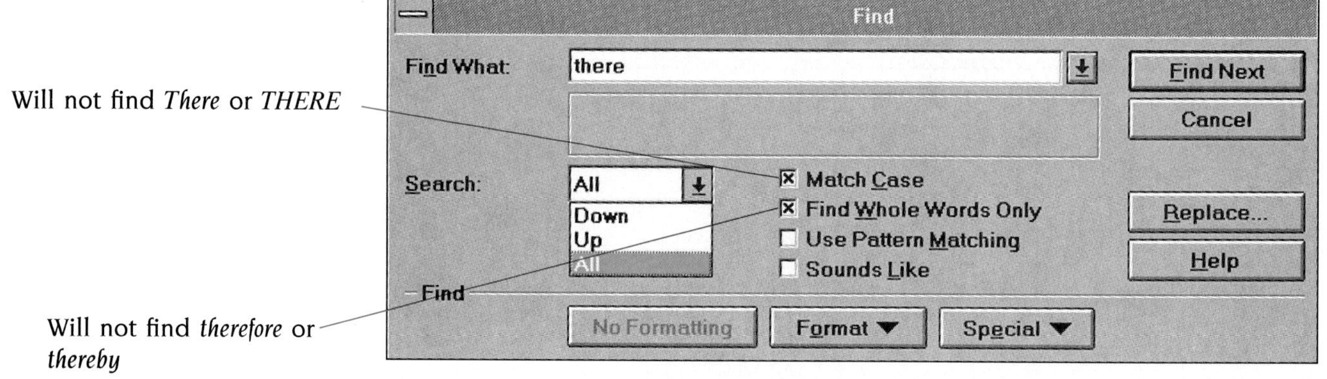

(a) Find Command

FIGURE 2.1 Find and Replace Commands

The Replace command in Figure 2.1b implements either ***selective replacement,*** which lets you examine the character string in context and decide whether to replace it, or ***automatic replacement,*** where the substitution is made automatically. The latter often produces unintended consequences and is generally not recommended; for example, if you substitute the word *text* for *book,* the phrase *text book* would become *text text,* which is not what you had in mind.

Selective replacement is implemented in Figure 2.1b by clicking the Find Next command button, then clicking (or not clicking) the Replace button to make the substitution. Automatic or ***global replacement*** (through the entire document) is implemented by clicking the Replace All button.

The Find and Replace commands can include formatting and/or special characters. You can, for example, change all italicized text to boldface, or you can change five consecutive spaces to a tab character. You can also introduce a wild card into the search string; for example, find all four-letter words that begin with "f" and end with "l" such as "fall", "fill", or "fail." You can even search for a word based on how it sounds; for example, search for Marion, check the Sounds Like check box, and find both Marion and Marian.

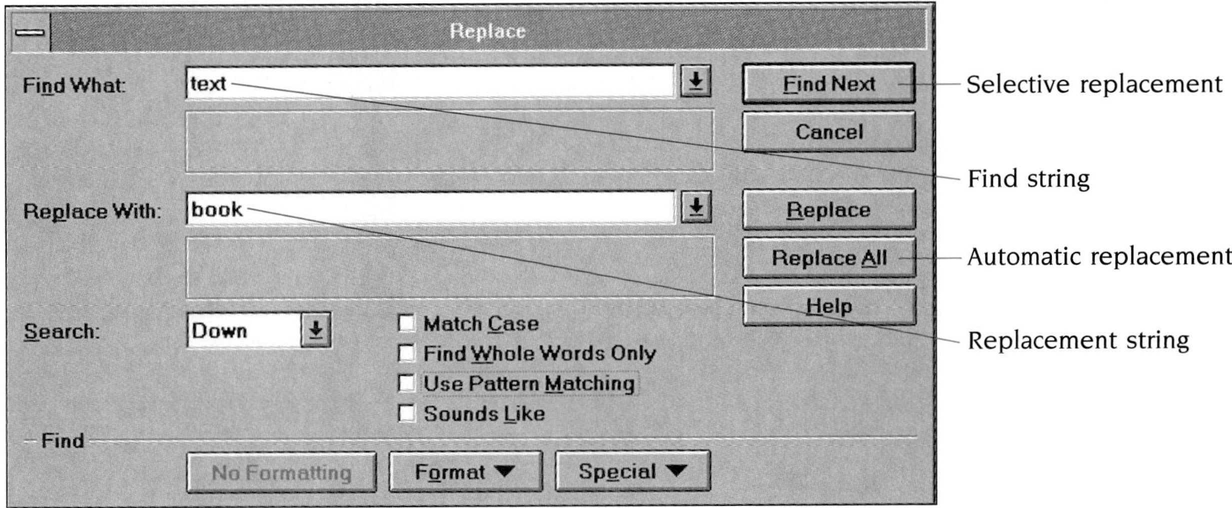

(b) Replace Command

FIGURE 2.1 Find and Replace Commands (continued)

SAVE COMMAND

The ***Save command*** copies the document currently being edited (the document in memory) to a permanent storage medium, that is, to disk. The initial execution of the command requires you to assign a filename (from one to eight characters) and automatically assigns the extension DOC to the document. All subsequent executions of the Save command will save the document under the name you entered, replacing the previously saved version with the new one. The ***Save As command*** saves the document under a different name. It is useful when you want to retain a copy of the original document as well as the document on which you are making changes.

We cannot overemphasize the importance of periodically saving a document, so that if something does go wrong, you won't lose all of your work. Nothing is more frustrating than to lose two hours of effort, due to an unexpected problem in Windows or to a temporary loss of power. Save your work frequently, at least once every 15 minutes. Pull down the File menu and click Save, or click the save icon on the Standard toolbar. Do it!

QUIT WITHOUT SAVING

There will be times when you do not want to save the changes to a document—for example, when you have edited it beyond recognition and wish you had never started. Pull down the File menu and click the Close command, then click No in response to the message asking whether you want to save the changes to the document. Pull down the File menu, click Open to reopen the file, then start over from the beginning.

Backup Options

Word offers several different ***backup*** options. We believe the most important is the option that creates a backup copy in conjunction with every Save command as illustrated in Figure 2.2. (See step 3 in the hands-on exercise for instructions on how to establish this option.)

Step 1 – Create FOX.DOC

The fox jumped over the fence

Saved to disk

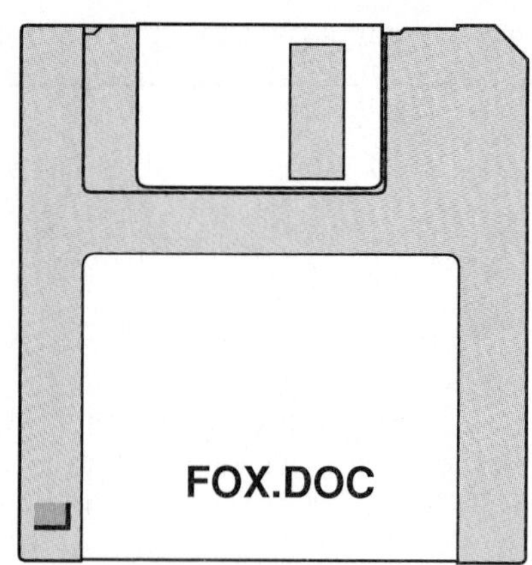

Step 2 – Retrieve FOX.DOC

The fox jumped over the fence

Retrieve FOX.DOC

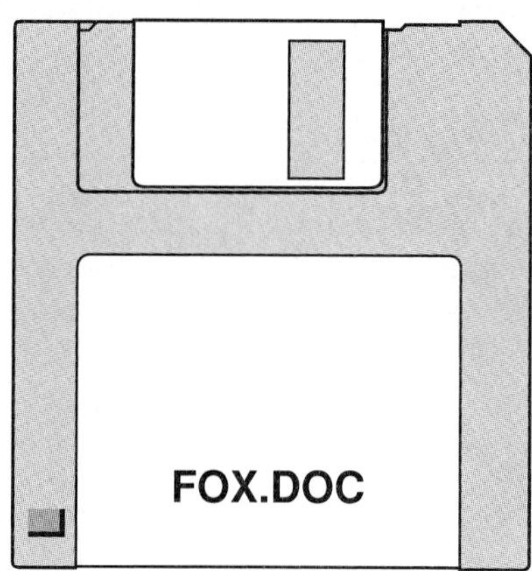

Step 3 – Edit and save FOX.DOC

The quick brown fox jumped over the fence

Saved to disk

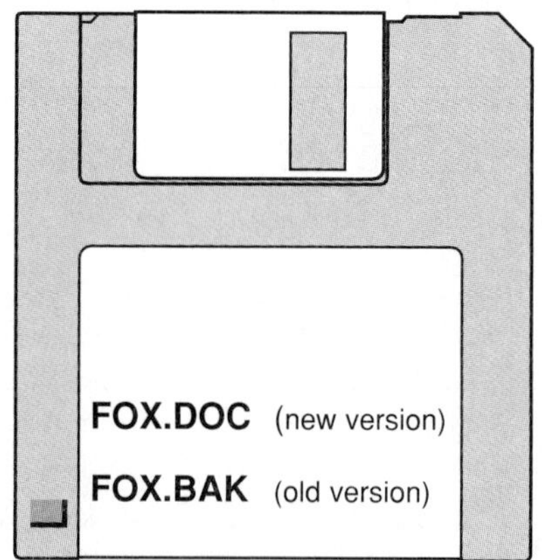

FIGURE 2.2 Backup Procedures

Assume, for example, that you have created the simple document, *The fox jumped over the fence,* and saved it under the name FOX.DOC. Assume further that you edit the document to read, *The quick brown fox jumped over the fence,* and that you saved it a second time. The second Save command changes the name of the original document from FOX.DOC to FOX.BAK, then saves the current contents of memory as FOX.DOC. In other words, the disk now contains two versions of the document: the current version (FOX.DOC) and the most recent previous version (FOX.BAK), to which the ***BAK extension*** was automatically assigned.

The cycle goes on indefinitely, with FOX.DOC always containing the current version, and FOX.BAK the most recent previous version. Thus if you revise and save the document a third time, FOX.DOC will contain the latest revision while FOX.BAK would contain the previous version alluding to the quick brown fox. The original (first) version of the document disappears entirely since only two versions are kept.

The contents of FOX.DOC and FOX.BAK are different. The latter enables you to retrieve the previous version if you inadvertently edit beyond repair or accidentally erase the current version of FOX.DOC. Should this occur (and it will), you can always retrieve its predecessor and at least salvage your work prior to the last save operation.

KEEP DUPLICATE COPIES OF IMPORTANT FILES

It is absolutely critical to maintain duplicate copies of important files on a separate disk stored away from the computer. In addition, you should print each new document at the end of every session, saving it before printing (power failures happen when least expected, for example, during the print operation). Hard copy is not as good as a duplicate disk, but it is better than nothing.

SCROLLING

Scrolling is necessary when a document is too large to be viewed in its entirety. Figure 2.3a, for example, displays the top portion of a document as it would appear on the monitor. Figure 2.3b shows the entire (printed) document. To see the complete document in the monitor, you need to scroll, whereby new lines will be brought into view as the old lines disappear.

Scrolling comes about automatically as you reach the bottom of the screen. Entering a new line of text, clicking on the down arrow within the scroll bar, or

SCROLLING TIP

Scroll quickly through a document by clicking above or below the scroll box to scroll up or down an entire screen. Move to the top, bottom, or an approximate position within a document by dragging the scroll box to the corresponding position in the scroll bar; for example, dragging the scroll box to the middle of the bar moves the mouse pointer to the middle of the document. Realize, however, that both techniques move the mouse pointer, but *not* the insertion point; that is, you must click the mouse after scrolling to change the position of the insertion point.

Insertion point

Drag the scroll box to scroll quickly through the document (to the beginning, end, or approximate position)

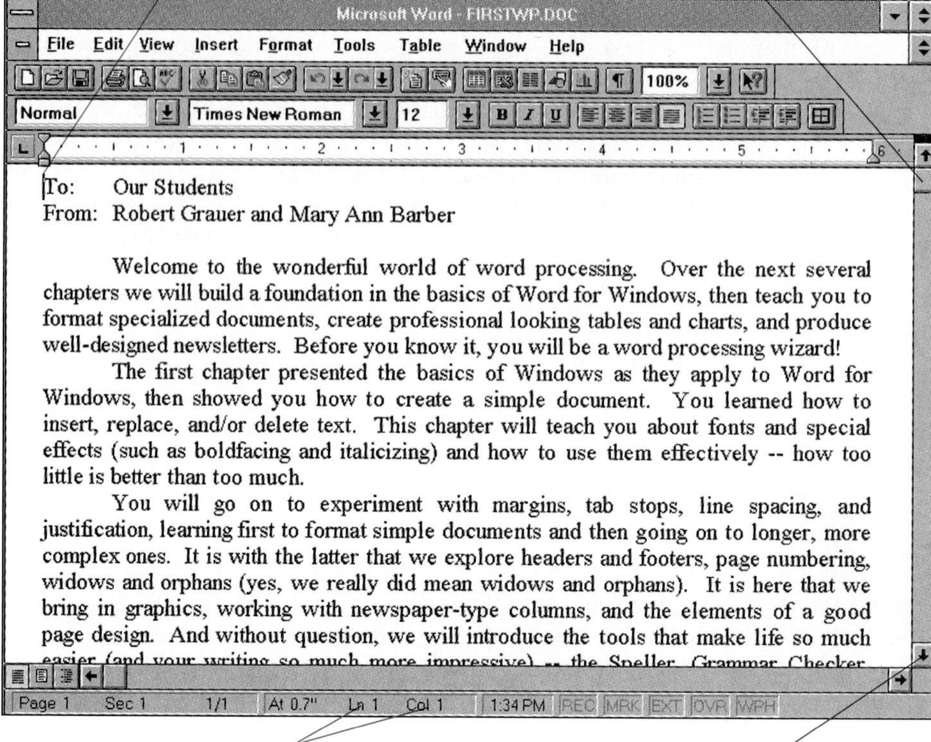

Indicates position of insertion point

Click here to bring a new line into view

(a) Screen Display

FIGURE 2.3 Scrolling

pressing the down arrow key brings a new line into view at the bottom of the screen and simultaneously removes a line at the top. (The process is reversed at the top of the screen.)

Scrolling occurs most often in a vertical direction as shown in Figure 2.3. It can also occur horizontally, when the length of a line in a document exceeds the number of characters that can be displayed horizontally on the screen. Note, too, the position of the insertion point in Figure 2.3a and how this information is communicated on the status bar.

VIEW MENU

The ***View menu*** provides different views of a document. Each view can be displayed at different magnifications, which in turn determine the amount of scrolling necessary to see remote parts of a document.

The ***Normal view*** is the default and the one you use most of the time. The ***Page Layout*** view more closely resembles the printed document and displays the top and bottom margins, headers and footers, and other features that do not appear in the Normal view. The Normal view is faster, however, because Word spends less time formatting the display.

To: Our Students
From: Robert Grauer and Mary Ann Barber

Welcome to the wonderful world of word processing. Over the next several chapters we will build a foundation in the basics of Word for Windows, then teach you to format specialized documents, create professional looking tables and charts, and produce well-designed newsletters. Before you know it, you will be a word processing wizard!

The first chapter presented the basics of Windows as they apply to Word for Windows, then showed you how to create a simple document. You learned how to insert, replace, and/or delete text. This chapter will teach you about fonts and special effects (such as boldfacing and italicizing) and how to use them effectively -- how too little is better than too much.

You will go on to experiment with margins, tab stops, line spacing, and justification, learning first to format simple documents and then advancing to longer, more complex ones. It is with the latter that we explore headers and footers, page numbering, widows and orphans (yes, we really did mean widows and orphans). It is here that we bring in graphics, working with newspaper-type columns, and the elements of a good page design. And without question, we will introduce the tools that make life so much easier (and your writing so much more impressive) -- the Speller, Grammar Checker, Thesaurus, Glossaries, and Styles.

If you are wondering what all these things are, read on in the text and proceed with the hands-on exercises. Create a simple newsletter, then really knock their socks off by adding graphics, fonts, and Word Art. Create a simple calendar and then create more intricate forms that no one will believe were done by little old you. Create a résumé with your beginner's skills and then make it look like so much more with your intermediate (even advanced) skills. Last, but not least, run a mail merge to produce the cover letters that will accompany your résumé as it is mailed to companies across the United States (and even the world).

It is up to you to practice, for it is only through working at the computer that you will learn what you need to know. Experiment and don't be afraid to make mistakes. Practice and practice some more.

Our goal is for you to learn and to enjoy what you are learning. We have great confidence in you, and in our ability to help you discover what you can do. And to prove us right, we'd love to have you mail us copies of documents that you have created.
Write to us at the following address:

Dr. Robert Grauer/Ms. Mary Ann Barber
University of Miami
421 Jenkins Building
Coral Gables, Florida 33124

We look forward to hearing from you and hope that you will like our text book. You are about to embark on a wonderful journey toward computer literacy. Be patient, be inquisitive, and enjoy.

(b) Printed Document

FIGURE 2.3 Scrolling (continued)

The ***Zoom command*** displays the document on the screen at different magnifications such as 75%, 100%, or 200%. (The Zoom command does not affect the size of the text on the printed page.) A Zoom percentage (magnification) of 100% displays the document in the approximate size of the text on the printed page. You can increase the percentage to 200% to make the characters appear larger. You can also decrease the magnification to 75% to see more of the document at one time.

You can also let Word determine the magnification for you, by selecting one of three additional Zoom options—Page Width, Whole Page, or Many Pages. Figure 2.4a, for example, displays a two-page document in Page Layout view. Figure 2.4b shows the corresponding settings in the Zoom command. (The 29% magnification is determined automatically once you specify the number of pages as shown in the figure.)

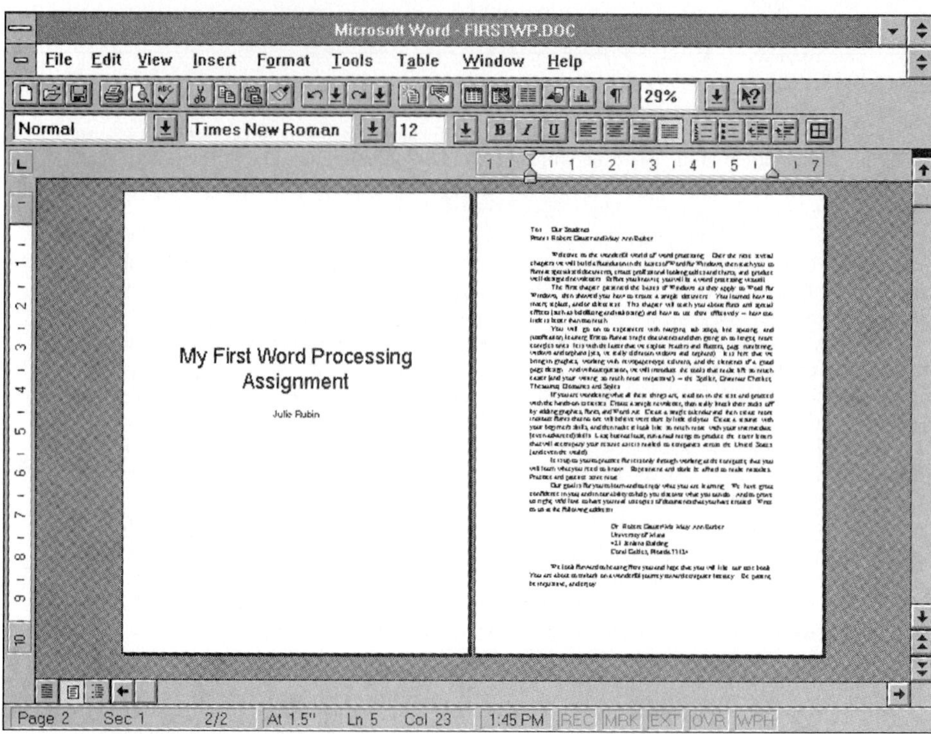

(a) Page Layout View (Zoom to Many Pages)

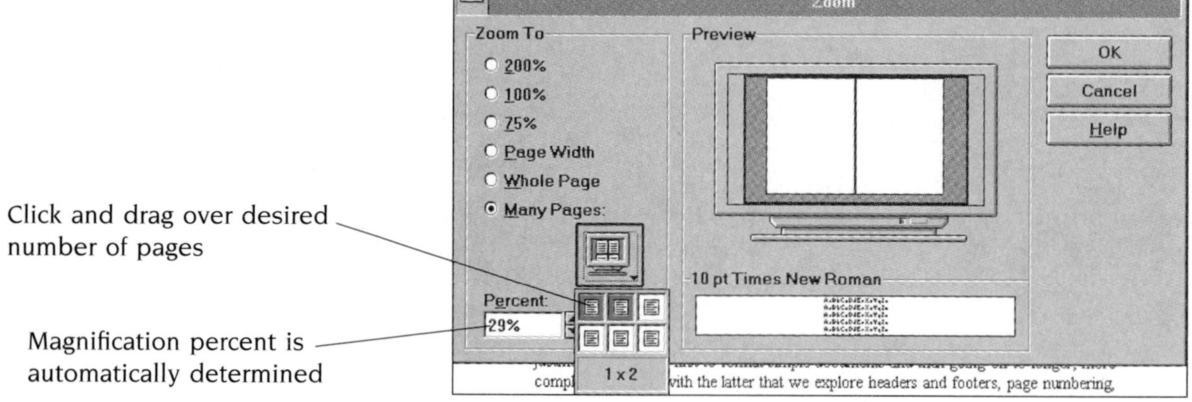

(b) Zoom Command

FIGURE 2.4 View Menu and Zoom Command

HANDS-ON EXERCISE 1:

Editing

Objective To edit an existing document; to change the view and magnification of a document; to scroll through a document. To use the Find, Replace, and Save As commands; to move and copy text using the clipboard and the drag-and-drop facility. Use Figure 2.5 as a guide in the exercise.

Step 1: Load the practice document

- Load Word as described in the hands-on exercises from Chapter 1.
- Pull down the **File menu** and click **Open** (or click the Open icon on the Standard toolbar).
- Click drive C or drive A, depending on whether or not you copied the data disk to your hard drive.
- Scroll through the directory list box until you come to the **WORDDATA** directory. Double click this directory.
- Scroll through the file list box until you come to the **FIRSTWP.DOC.** Double click the file name to open the document as shown in Figure 2.5a.

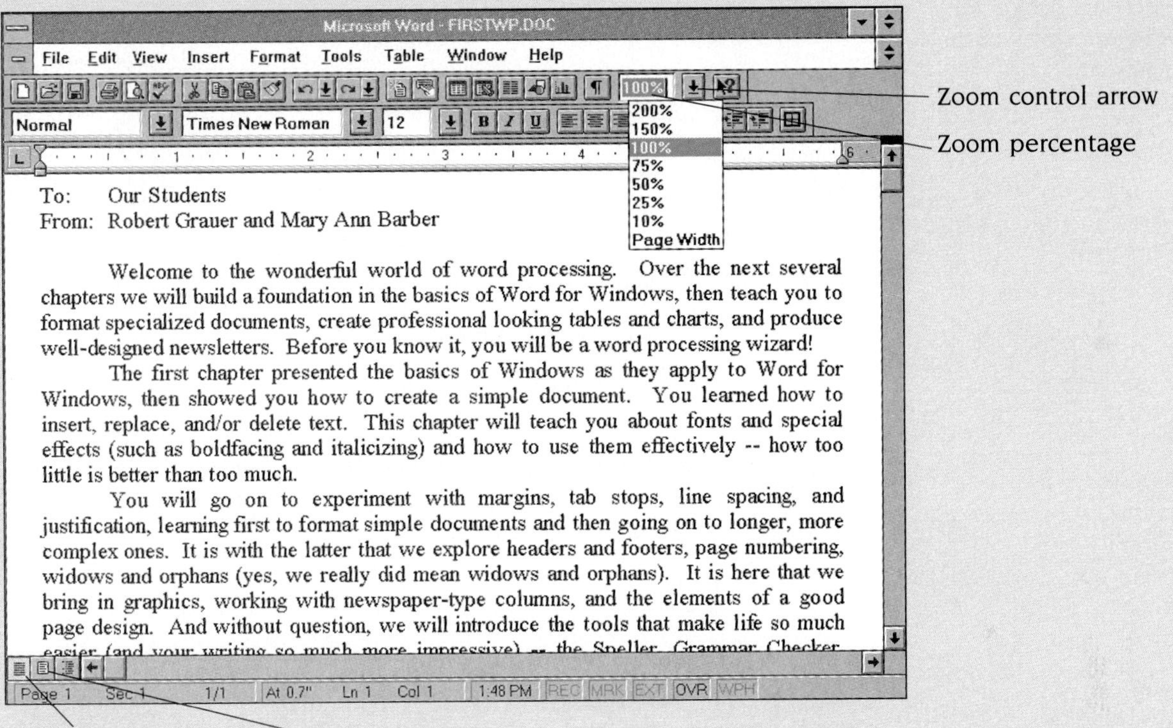

(a) The View Menu and Zoom Control (steps 1 and 2)

FIGURE 2.5 Hands-on Exercise 1

Step 2: The View menu

- Change the view:

  — Pull down the **View menu.** Click **Normal.**
  or Click the **Normal view icon** on the status bar.
- Change the zoom percentage:

  — Pull down the **View menu.** Click **Zoom.** Click **100%.** Click **OK.**
  or Click the **Zoom control arrow** on the Standard toolbar, drag to 100%, and release the mouse.

Step 3: Establish Automatic Backup (The BAK file)

- Pull down the **Tools menu.** Click **Options.**
- Click the **Save tab** to produce the dialog box of Figure 2.5b.

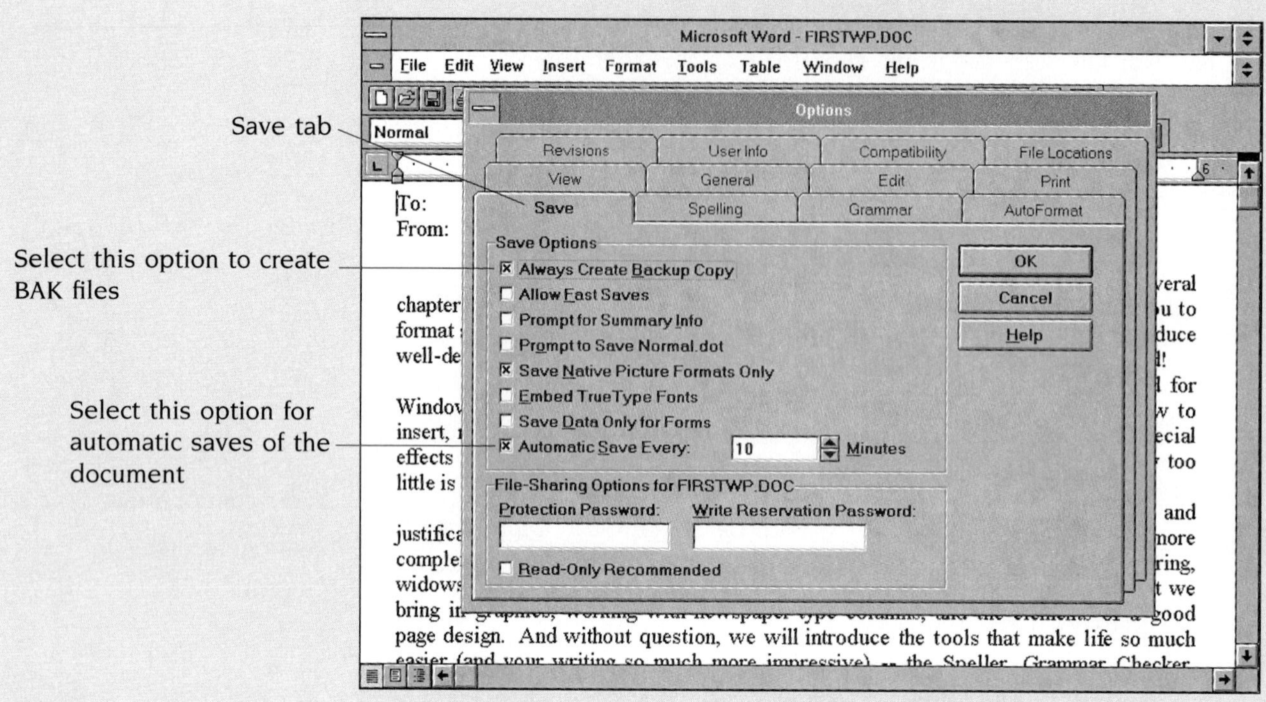

(b) The Options Command

FIGURE 2.5 Hands-on Exercise 1 (continued)

- Click the first check box to choose **Always Create Backup Copy** (creation of a BAK file). Adjust the other options as you see fit; for example, you can specify that the document be saved every 10 minutes.
- Click **OK.**

> **CHANGE THE DEFAULT DIRECTORY**
>
> The ***default directory*** is the directory where Word retrieves (saves) documents unless it is otherwise instructed. To change the default directory, pull down the Tools menu, click Options, click the File Locations tab, click Documents, and click the Modify command button. Enter the name of the new directory (for example, C:\WORDDATA), click OK, then click the Close button. The next time you access the File menu the default directory will reflect these changes.

Step 4: The Save As command

- Pull down the **File menu.** Click the **Save As** command to produce the dialog box in Figure 2.5c.
- Enter a filename from one to eight characters, for example, **PRACTICE** (the DOC extension is added automatically), and press **enter.**
- There are now two identical copies of the file on disk—FIRSTWP.DOC, which we supplied, and PRACTICE.DOC, which you just created. The title bar of the document window shows the latter name.

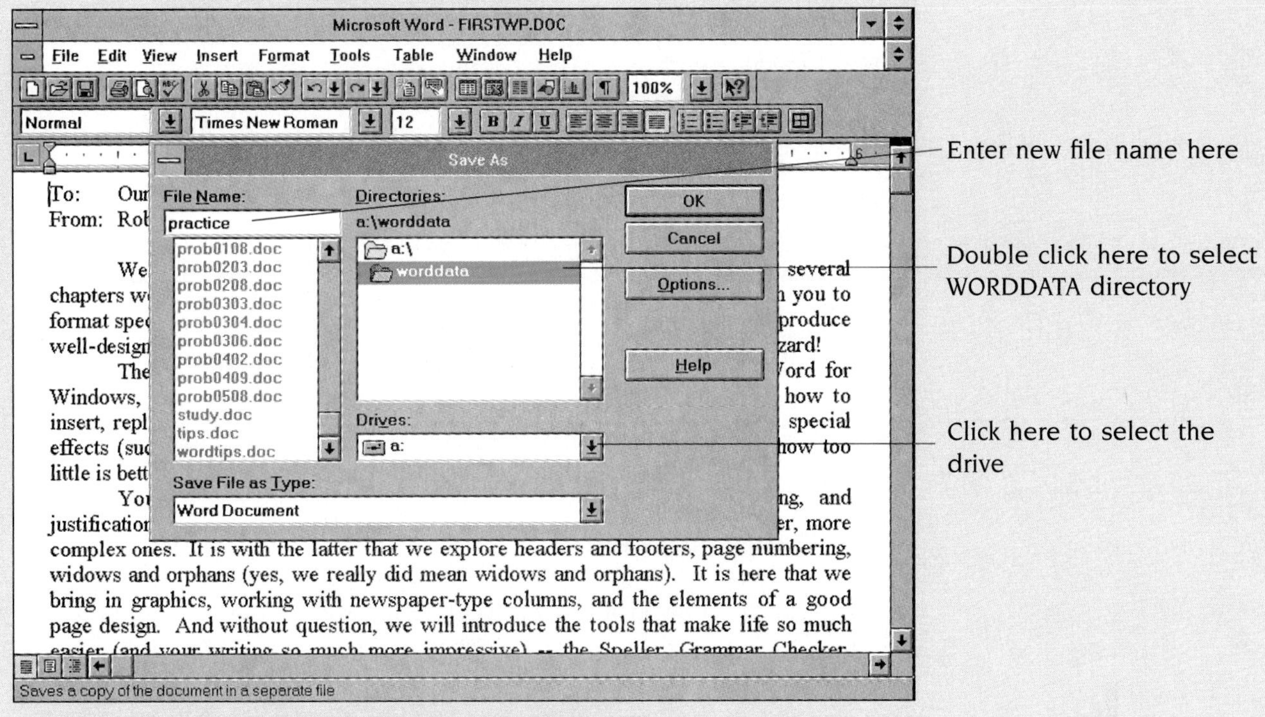

(c) Save As Command (step 4)

FIGURE 2.5 Hands-on Exercise 1 (continued)

Step 5: Scrolling

- Click the **down arrow** at the bottom of the vertical scroll bar to move down in the document, causing the top line to disappear and be replaced with a new line at the bottom.
- Click the **down arrow** several times to move through the document, then click the **up arrow** key to scroll in the other direction.
- Drag the **scroll box** to the bottom of the scroll bar, to the top of the scroll bar, then to the middle of the scroll bar, noting that in every instance the insertion point does *not* follow the scrolling; that is, you must **click the mouse** to move the insertion point to the new location after scrolling with the mouse.

KEYBOARD SHORTCUTS: MOVING WITHIN A DOCUMENT

Press **Ctrl+Home** and **Ctrl+End** to move to the beginning and end of a document. Press **Home** and **End** to move to the beginning and end of a line. Press **PgUp** or **PgDn** to scroll one screen in the indicated direction. The advantage to scrolling via the keyboard (instead of the mouse) is that the insertion point moves as you scroll.

Step 6: Insertion versus Overtype

- Press the **Ins** key once or twice until you clearly see OVR in one of the status boxes at the bottom of the screen.

- Press the **Ins** key once more so that OVR becomes dim. You are now in the insert mode.
- Press **Ctrl+Home** to move to the beginning of the document, click immediately before the period ending the first sentence, press the **space bar,** then add the phrase **and desktop publishing.**
- Drag the **scroll box** to scroll to the bottom of the document, and click immediately before the M in Ms. Mary Ann Barber.
- Press the **Ins** key (OVR should appear in the status bar) to toggle to the replacement mode, then type **Dr.** to replace Ms.
- Press **Ctrl+Home** to move to the beginning of the document. Click and drag the mouse to select the phrase **Our Students.** Type your name to replace the highlighted text.
- Pull down the **File menu** and click **Save** (or click the **Save icon**) to save the changes.

Step 7: Find and Replace

- Press **Ctrl+Home** to move to the beginning of the document.
- Pull down the **Edit menu.** Click **Replace** to produce the dialog box of Figure 2.5d.
- Type **text** in the Find What text box.
- Press the **Tab key.** Type **book** in the Replace With text box.
- Click the **Find Next button** to find the first occurrence of the word "text." The dialog box remains on the screen and the first occurrence of "text" is highlighted. This is *not* an appropriate substitution; that is, you should not substitute "book" for "text" at this point.
- Click the **Find Next button** to move to the next occurrence. This time the substitution is appropriate.
- Click **Replace** to make the change and automatically move to the next occurrence where the substitution is again inappropriate.
- Click **Find Next** a final time. Word will indicate that it has finished searching the document. Click **OK.**
- Change the Find and Replace strings to **Mary Ann** and **Maryann,** respectively.
- Click the **Replace All button** to make the substitution globally without confirmation. Word will indicate that it has finished searching and that two replacements were made. Click **OK.**
- Click the **Close command button** to close the dialog box. Save the document.

Step 8: The clipboard

- Press **PgDn** to scroll toward the end of the document until you come to the paragraph beginning *It is up to you.*
- Select the sentence *Practice and practice some more* by dragging the mouse over the sentence. (Be sure to include the period.) The sentence will be highlighted as shown in Figure 2.5e.
- Pull down the **Edit menu.** Click **Copy** to copy the selected text to the clipboard.
- Scroll to the end of the document. **Click the mouse** (to move the insertion point). Press the **enter key** twice.
- Pull down the **Edit menu.** Click **Paste** to copy the selected sentence.

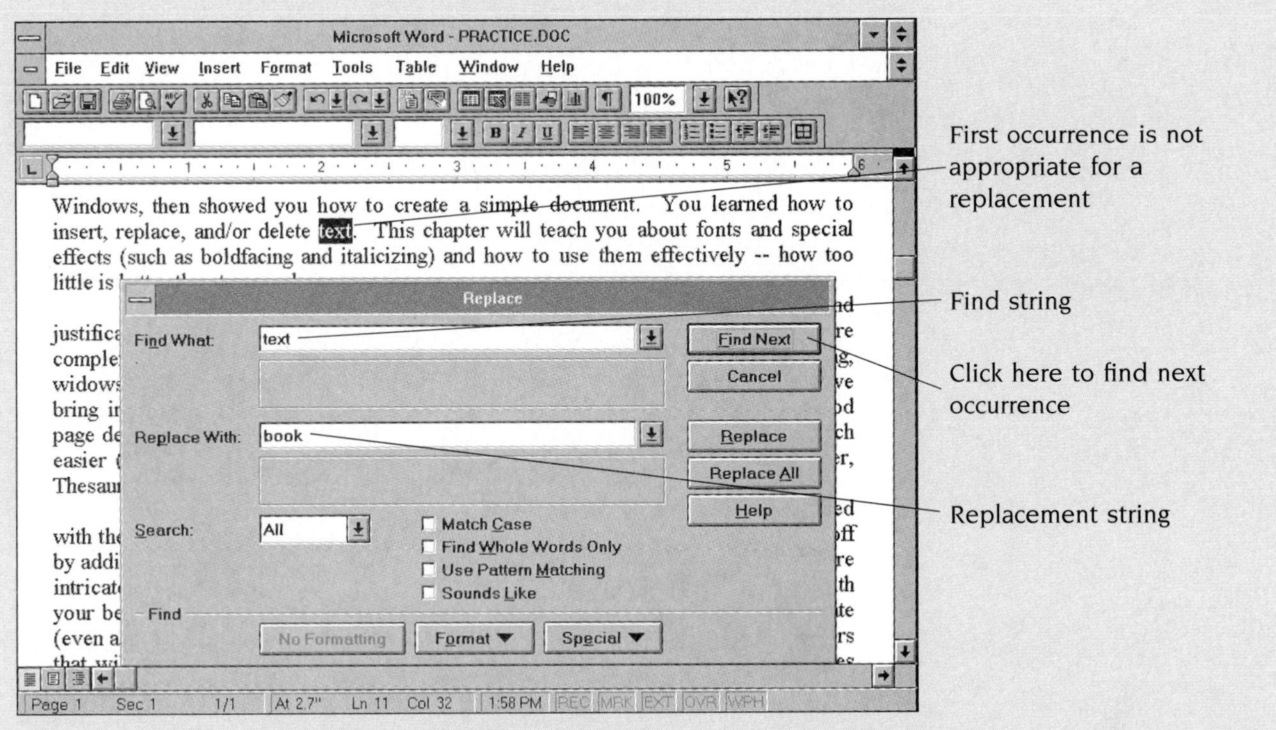

(d) Replace Command (step 7)

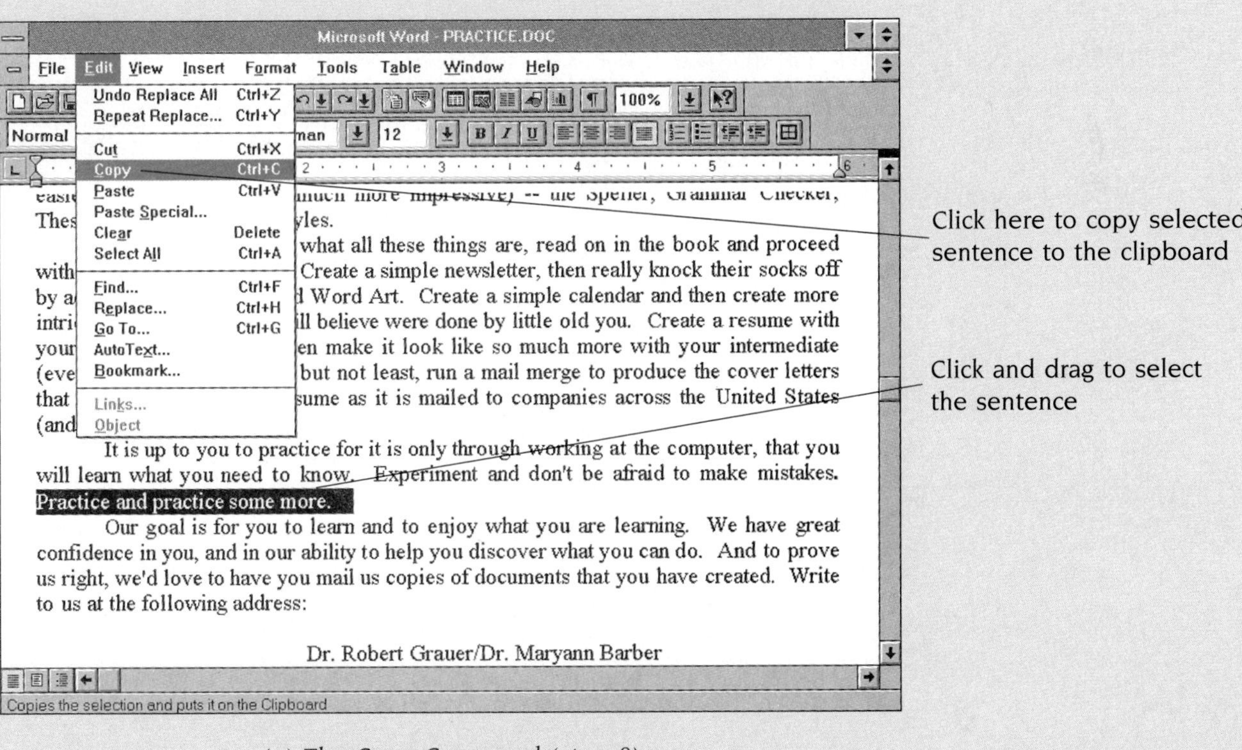

(e) The Copy Command (step 8)

FIGURE 2.5 Hands-on Exercise 1 (continued)

- Move the insertion point to the end of the first paragraph (ending with the word "wizard"). Press the **space bar** twice.
- Pull down the **Edit menu.** Click **Paste** to copy the sentence a second time.
- Save the document.

CUT, COPY, AND PASTE

Ctrl+X, **Ctrl+C**, and **Ctrl+V** are shortcuts to cut, copy, and paste, respectively, and apply to Word for Windows, Excel, and Windows applications in general. (The shortcuts are easier to remember when you realize that the operative letters, X, C, and V are next to each other at the bottom left side of the keyboard.) You can also use the Cut, Copy, and Paste icons on the Standard toolbar, which are also found on the Standard toolbar in Excel.

Step 9: Undo and Redo

- Click the **down arrow** next to the Undo tool to display the previously executed actions as in Figure 2.5f.
- The list of actions corresponds to the editing commands you have issued since the start of the exercise. (Your list will be different from ours if you deviated from any instructions in the hands-on exercise.)
- Click the **down arrow** for the Redo command. You will hear a beep indicating that there are no actions to be redone; that is, the Undo command has not yet been issued and so there is nothing to redo.

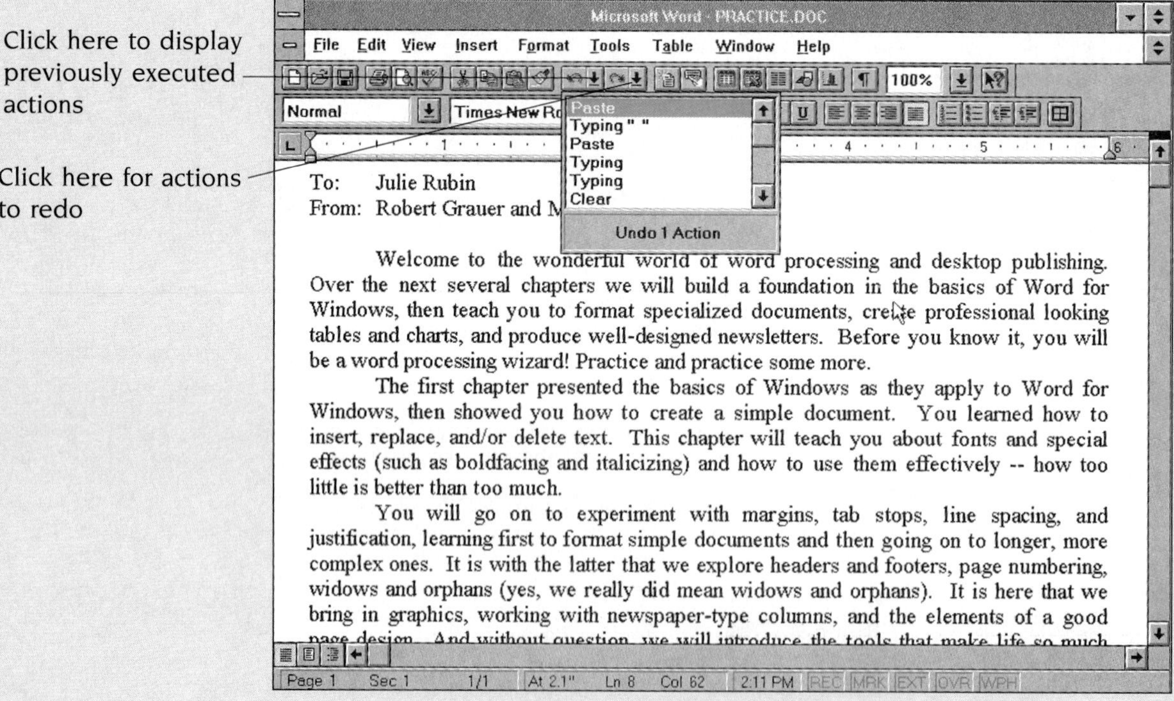

(f) The Undo Command (step 9)

FIGURE 2.5 Hands-on Exercise 1 (continued)

- Click the **down arrow** for the Undo command. Click **Paste** (the first command on the list) to undo the most recent editing command; the sentence, *Practice and practice some more,* disappears from the end of the first paragraph.
- Click the remaining steps on the undo list to retrace your steps through the exercise. When the list is empty you will have the document as it existed at the start of the exercise.
- Click the **down arrow** for the Redo command. This time you will see the list of commands you have undone; click each command in sequence and you will restore the document.

Step 10: Drag and drop

- This step takes a little practice, but it is well worth it.
- Use the Find command to locate and select the phrase **format specialized documents,** as shown in Figure 2.5g. (Be sure to include the comma and the space after the comma.)
- Drag the phrase to its new location immediately before the word "and," then release the mouse button to complete the move. (A dotted vertical bar appears as you drag the text to indicate its new location.)
- Click the **drop-down list box** for the **Undo** command; click **Move** to undo the move.
- To copy the selected text, press and hold the **Ctrl key** as you drag the text to its new location.
- Practice the drag-and-drop procedure several times until you are confident you can move and copy with precision.
- Save the document.

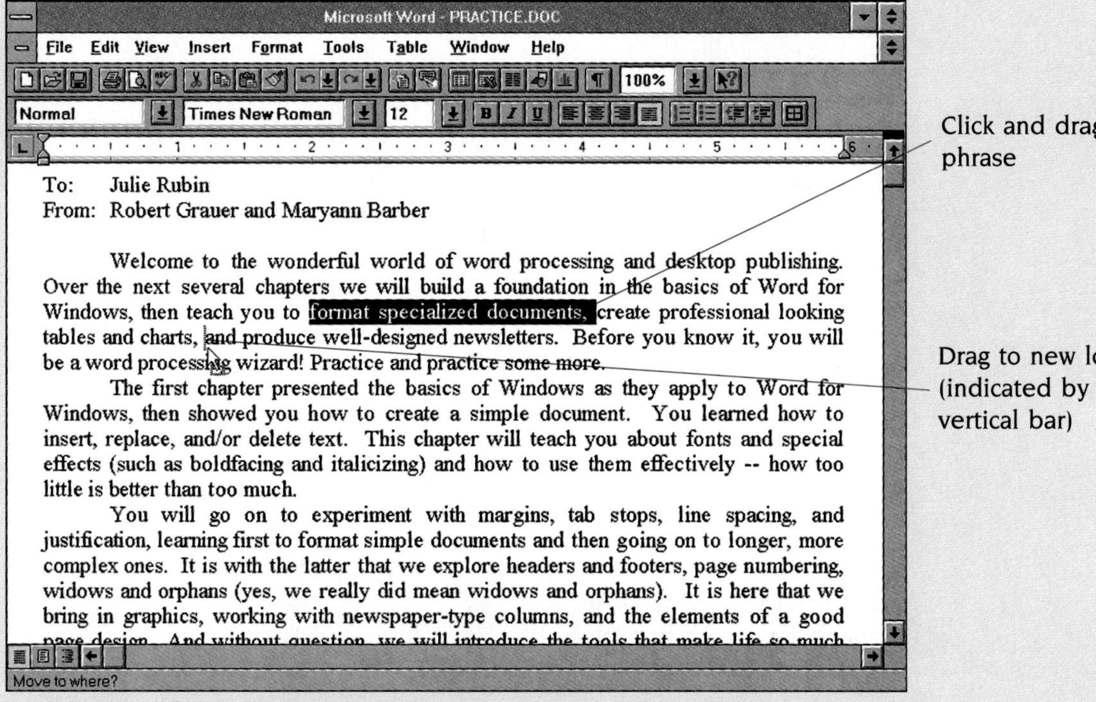

(g) Drag and Drop (step 10)

FIGURE 2.5 Hands-on Exercise 1 (continued)

Step 11: Print the completed document

- ➤ Pull down the **View menu** and select **Page Layout** (or click the **Page Layout button** on the status bar).
- ➤ Pull down the **View menu,** click **Zoom,** and select **Whole Page** (or use the Zoom control box on the Standard toolbar.)
- ➤ Your screen should match Figure 2.5h, which shows the completed document.
- ➤ Pull down the **File menu,** click **Print,** and click **OK** (or click the **Print button** on the Standard toolbar) to print the completed document.
- ➤ Pull down the **File menu** and click **Exit** (or double click the **control-menu box**) to quit **Word.**

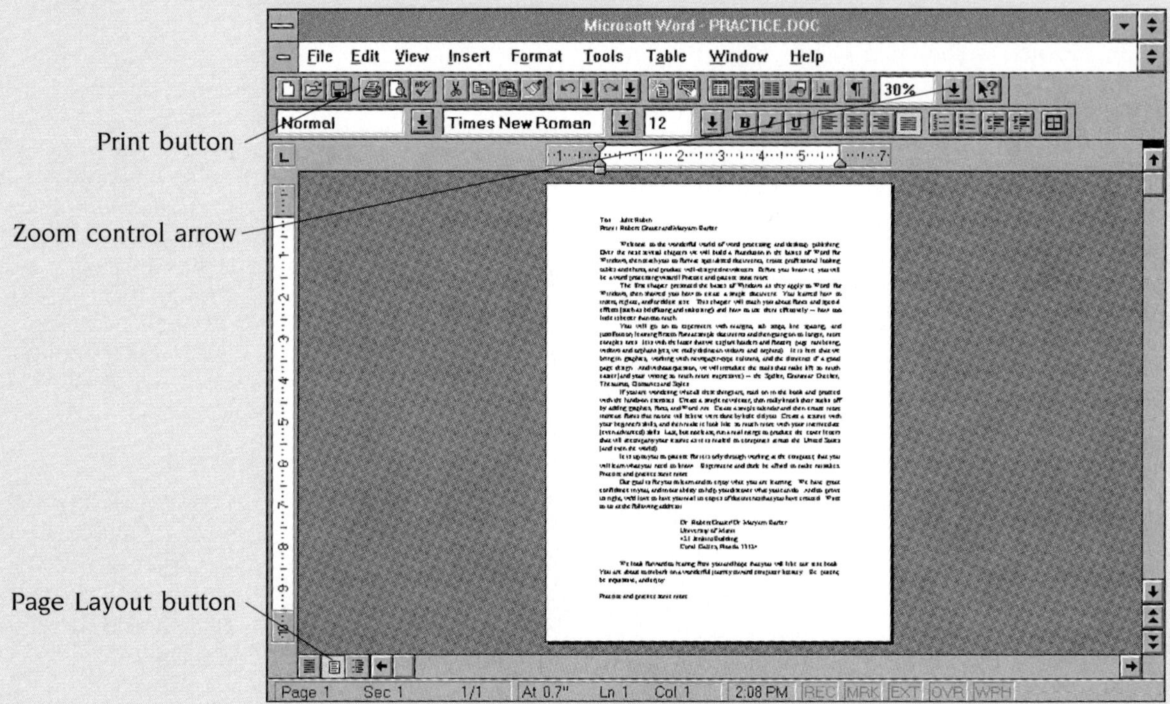

(h) The Completed Document (step 11)

FIGURE 2.5 Hands-on Exercise 1 (continued)

TYPOGRAPHY

Typography is the process of selecting typefaces, type styles, and type sizes. The importance of these decisions is obvious, for the ultimate success of any document depends greatly on its appearance. Type should reinforce the message without calling attention to itself and should be consistent with the information you want to convey.

Typeface

A ***typeface*** is a complete set of characters (upper- and lowercase letters, numbers, punctuation marks, and special symbols). Figure 2.6 illustrates two typefaces, ***Times New Roman*** and ***Arial,*** that are supplied with Windows, and which in turn are accessible from Word.

The type you choose should be consistent with the message you want to convey, neither too large nor too small, neither too bold nor too reserved. A serif typeface has tiny cross strokes that end the main strokes of each letter; a sans serif typeface does not.

(a) Times New Roman

The type you choose should be consistent with the message you want to convey, neither too large nor too small, neither too bold nor too reserved. A serif typeface has tiny cross strokes that end the main strokes of each letter; a sans serif typeface does not.

(b) Arial

FIGURE 2.6 Typefaces

One definitive characteristic of any typeface is the presence or absence of tiny cross lines that end the main stroke of each letter. A ***serif typeface*** has these lines; a ***sans serif*** (sans from the French for *without*) does not. Times New Roman is an example of a serif typeface. Arial is a sans serif typeface.

Serifs help the eye to connect one letter with the next and are generally used with large amounts of text. This book, for example, is set in a serif typeface. A sans serif typeface is more effective with smaller amounts of text and appears in headlines, corporate logos, airport signs, and so on. Serif typefaces convey a sense of authority; sans serif typefaces produce a more informal result.

Any typeface can be set in different styles (e.g., regular, boldface, or italics). A ***font*** (as the term is used in Windows) is a specific typeface in a specific style; for example, **Arial bold** or *Times New Roman italic.*

TYPOGRAPHY TIP: USE RESTRAINT

More is not better especially in the case of too many typefaces and styles, which produce cluttered documents that impress no one. Try to limit yourself to a maximum of two typefaces per document, but choose multiple sizes and/or styles within those typefaces. Use boldface or italics for emphasis, but do so in moderation, because if you emphasize too many elements the effect is lost.

Type Size

Type size is a vertical measurement and is specified in points. One ***point*** is equal to 1/72 of an inch; that is, there are 72 points to the inch. The measurement is made from the top of the tallest letter in a character set (for example, an uppercase T) to the bottom of the lowest letter (for example, a lowercase y). Most documents are set in 10 or 12 point type; newspaper columns may be set as small as 8 point type. Type sizes of 14 points or higher are ineffective for large amounts of text. Figure 2.7 shows the same phrase set in varying type sizes.

Some typefaces appear larger (smaller) than others even though they may be set in the same point size. The type in Figure 2.6a, for example, looks smaller than the corresponding type in Figure 2.6b even though both are set in the same point size. This is because the Arial typeface users longer ascenders (strokes that climb upward from the baseline) and longer descenders (strokes that reach downward) than the Times New Roman design.

This is Arial 8 point type

This is Arial 10 point type

This is Arial 12 point type

This is Arial 18 point type

This is Arial 24 point type

(a) Sans Serif Typeface

This is Times New Roman 8 point type

This is Times New Roman 10 point type

This is Times New Roman 12 point type

This is Times New Roman 18 point type

This is Times New Roman 24 point type

(b) Serif Typeface

FIGURE 2.7 Type Size

TrueType

Windows 3.1 supports a new type of font technology known as ***TrueType,*** which uses the same fonts for the monitor and the printer. This means that your document is truly WYSIWYG, and that the fonts you see on the monitor will be identical to those in the printed document. Equally important, TrueType fonts are scalable, so that you can select any font in any size, from 4 to 127 points. And finally, TrueType fonts are accessible from any Windows application; that is, you can use the same fonts in Excel as in Word.

Windows itself includes 14 TrueType fonts: *Times New Roman* (in regular, bold, italic, and bold italic styles), *Arial* (in regular, bold, italic, and bold italic styles) *Courier New* (in regular, bold, italic, and bold italic styles), and two special fonts: *Symbol* and *Wingdings.* Word for Windows provides several additional fonts, giving you a great deal of flexibility in the documents you create.

All fonts are classified as either monospaced or proportional. A ***monospaced font*** such as Courier New has a fixed pitch (uniform character width). Monospaced fonts are used in tables and financial projections where items must be precisely lined up, one beneath the other. A ***proportional font***—for example, Times New Roman or Arial—allocates a different amount of space for each character according to the width of the character. Proportional fonts create a more professional appearance and are appropriate for most documents.

FORMAT FONT COMMAND

The ***Format Font command*** gives you complete control over the size and style of the text in a document. Execution of the command produces the dialog box in Figure 2.8, in which you specify the font (typeface), style, and point size. You can choose any of the special effects and/or change the underline options (whether or not spaces are to be underlined). You can even change the color of the text on the monitor, but you need a color printer for the printed document. The Character Spacing tab produces a different set of options in which you control the spacing of the characters.

The Preview box shows the text as it will appear in the document. The message at the bottom of the dialog box indicates that Times New Roman is a TrueType font and that the same font will be used on both the screen and the printer.

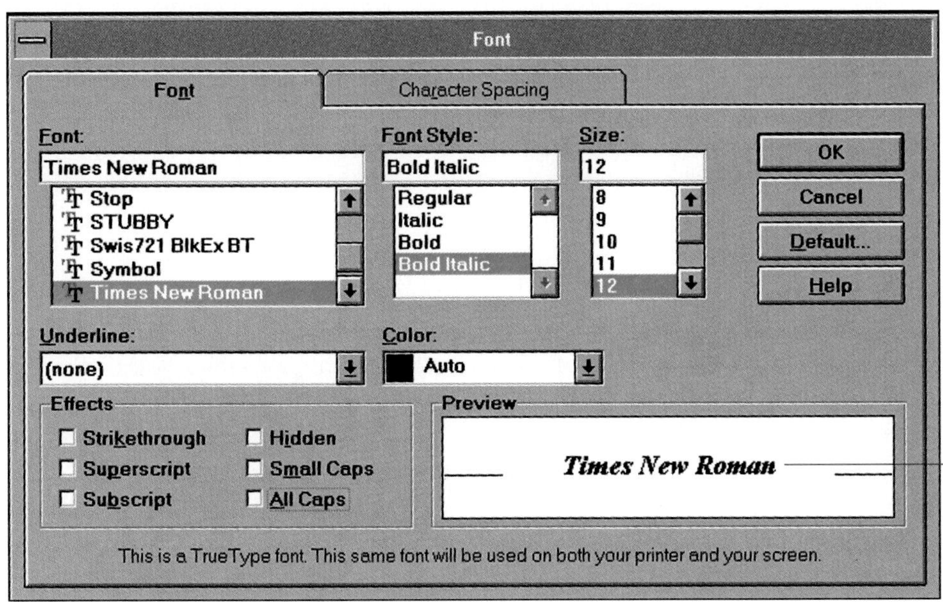

FIGURE 2.8 The Format Font Command

FORMAT PAINTER

The **Format Painter** copies the formatting of the selected text to other places in a document. Select the text with the formatting you want to copy, then double click the Format Painter button on the Standard Toolbar. The mouse pointer changes to a paintbrush to indicate that you can paint other areas in the document with the current formatting; just drag the paintbrush over the additional text, which will assume the identical formatting characteristics as the original selection. Repeat the painting process as often as necessary, then click the Format Painter button a second time to return to normal editing.

PAGE SETUP COMMAND

The ***Page Setup command*** in the File menu lets you change margins, paper size (and orientation), paper source, and/or layout. All parameters are accessed from the dialog box in Figure 2.9 by clicking the appropriate tab within the dialog box.

The default margins are indicated in Figure 2.9a and are one inch on the top and bottom of the page, and one-and-a-quarter inches on the left and right. You can change any (or all) of these settings by entering a new value in the appropriate text box, either by typing it explicitly or clicking the up/down arrow. The margins in the figure apply to the whole document regardless of the position of the insertion point. (Different margins can be in effect for different parts of a document by creating sections, a concept discussed in Chapter 5.)

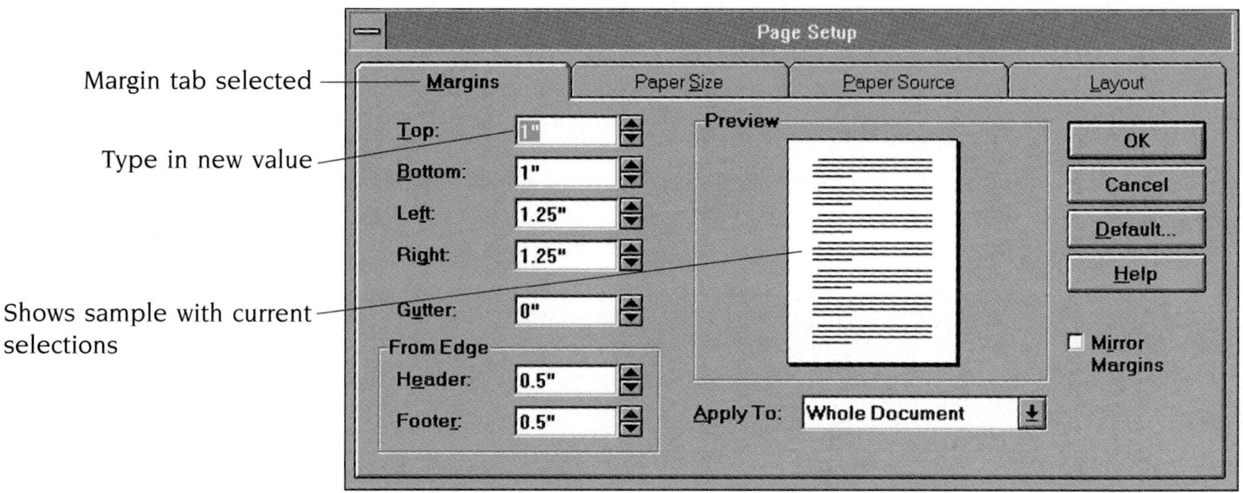

(a) Margins

FIGURE 2.9 Page Setup Command

The Paper Size tab within the Page Setup command enables you to change the orientation of a page as shown in Figure 2.9b. ***Portrait orientation*** is the default. ***Landscape orientation*** flips the page 90 degrees so that its dimensions are 11 × 8½ rather than the other way around. Note, too, the Preview box in the figure, which shows how the document will appear with the selected parameters.

The Paper Source tab is used to specify which tray should be used on printers with multiple trays, and is helpful when you want to load different types of paper simultaneously. The Layout tab is used to create headers and footers and is discussed in Chapter 4.

Page Breaks

One of the first concepts you learned was that of word wrap, whereby Word inserts a soft return at the end of a line in order to begin a new line. The number and location of the soft returns change automatically as you add or delete text within a document. Soft returns are very different from the hard returns inserted by the user, whose number and location remain constant.

In much the same way, Word creates a ***soft page break*** to go to the top of a new page when text no longer fits on the current page. And just as you can insert a hard return to start a new paragraph, you can insert a ***hard page break*** to force any part of a document to begin on a new page. (Press **Ctrl+Enter** to create a hard page break.)

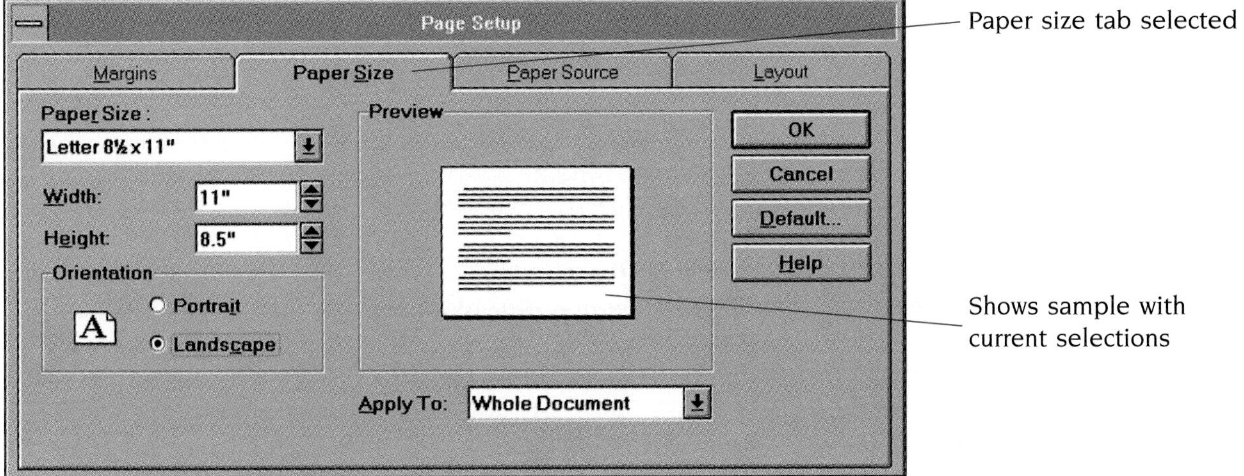

(b) Size and Orientation

FIGURE 2.9 Page Setup Command (continued)

AN EXERCISE IN DESIGN

The following exercise has you retrieve an existing document from the data disk, then experiment with various typefaces, type styles, and point sizes. The original document uses a monospaced (typewriter style) font, without boldface or italics, and you are asked to improve its appearance. The first step directs you to save the document under a new name so that you can always return to the original if necessary.

There is no right and wrong with respect to design and you are free to choose any combination of fonts that appeal to you. The exercise takes you through various formatting options but lets you make the final decision. It does, however, ask you to print the final document and submit it to your instructor.

IMPOSE A TIME LIMIT

A word processor is supposed to save time and make you more productive. It will do exactly that provided you use the word processor for its primary purpose—writing and editing. It is all too easy, however, to lose sight of that objective and spend too much time formatting the document. Concentrate on the content of your document rather than its appearance. Impose a time limit on the amount of time you will spend on formatting. End the session when the limit is reached.

HANDS-ON EXERCISE 2:

Character Formatting

Objective Experiment with character formatting; to change fonts and to use boldface and italics; to copy formatting with the Format Painter; to insert a page break and see different views of a document. Use Figure 2.10 as a guide in the exercise.

Step 1: Load the practice document.

- Pull down the **File menu.** Click **Open** (or click the Open icon on the Standard toolbar).
- If you have not yet changed the default directory:
  - — Click the appropriate drive.
  - — Scroll through the directory list box until you come to the **WORDDATA** directory.
  - — Double click the **WORDATA** directory.
- Double click **TIPS.DOC** to open the document.
- Pull down the **File menu.** Click the **Save As** command to save the file as **MYTIPS.DOC.** The title bar reflects MYTIPS.DOC, but you can always return to the original TIPS.DOC document if you edit the duplicated file beyond repair.
- Pull down the **View menu** and click **Normal** (or click the **Normal View button** on the Status Bar).
- Set the magnification (zoom) to **Page Width.**

TIP: SELECTING TEXT

The ***selection bar,*** a blank column at the far left of the document window, makes it easy to select a line, paragraph, or the entire document.

- To select a line, move the mouse pointer to the selection bar, point to the line, and click the left mouse button.
- To select a paragraph, move the mouse pointer to the selection bar, point to any line in the paragraph, and double click the mouse.
- To select the entire document, move the mouse pointer to the selection bar and press the **Ctrl** key while you click the mouse.

Step 2: Shortcut menu

- Select the first tip as shown in Figure 2.10a.
- Click the **right mouse button** to produce the Shortcut menu shown in the figure. The Shortcut menu contains commands from both the Edit and Format menus.
- Click outside the menu to close the menu without executing a command.
- Press the **Ctrl key** as you click the selection bar to select the entire document, then click the **right mouse button** to display the Shortcut menu.
- Click **Font** to execute the Format Font command.

Step 3: Changing fonts

- Click the **down arrow** on the Font list box of Figure 2.10b to scroll through the available fonts. Select a different font—for example, Times New Roman.
- Click the **down arrow** in the Font Size list box to choose a point size.
- Click **OK** to change the font and point size for the selected text.
- Pull down the **Edit menu** and click **Undo** (or click the **Undo button** on the Standard toolbar) to return to the original font.
- Experiment with different fonts and/or different point sizes until you are satisfied with the selection; we chose 12 point Times New Roman.
- Save the document.

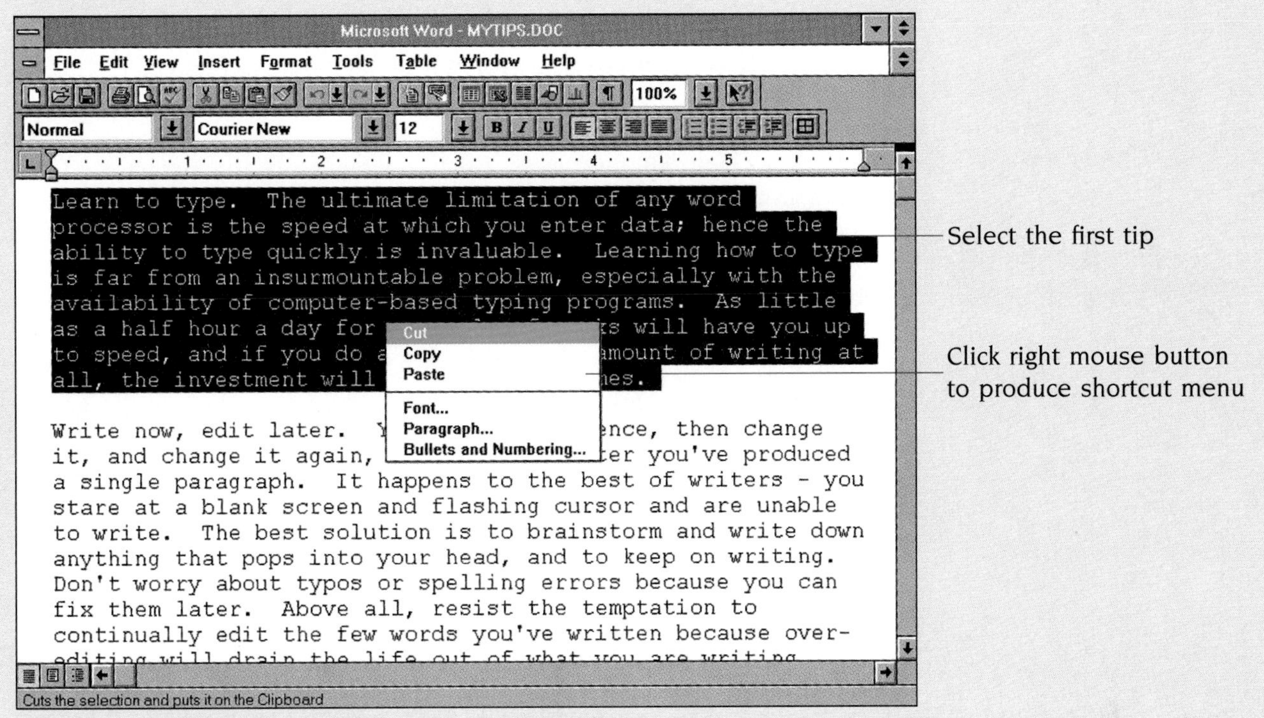

(a) Shortcut Menu (step 2)

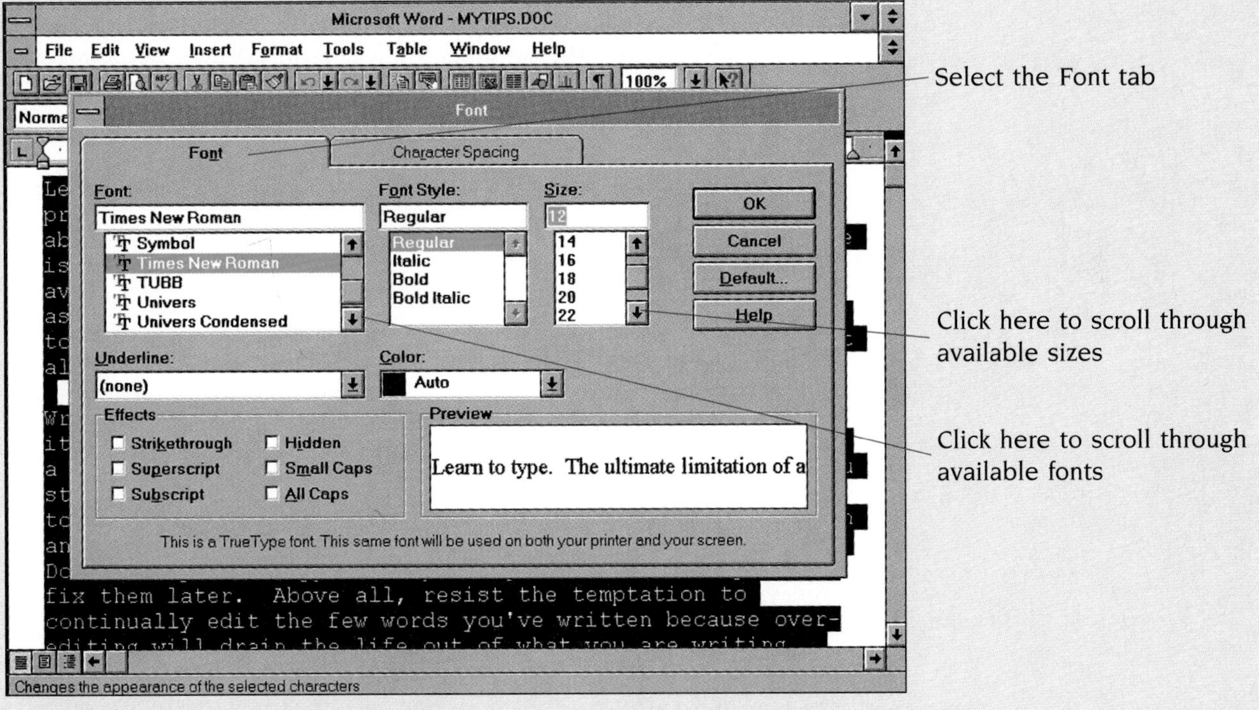

(b) The Format Font Command (step 3)

FIGURE 2.10 Hands-on Exercise 2

Step 4: Boldface and italics

➤ Drag the mouse over the sentence **Learn to Type** at the beginning of the document.

- Click the **Italics button** on the Formatting toolbar to italicize the selected phrase. The phrase should remain highlighted.
- Click the **Boldface button** to boldface the selected text; the text is now in boldface and italics.
- Experiment with different styles (boldface, italics, underlining, or boldface-italics) until you are satisfied. The italics, boldface, and underline buttons function as toggle switches; that is, clicking the italics button when text is already italicized returns the text to normal.
- Save the document.

DESELECTING TEXT

The effects of a formatting change are often difficult to see when text is highlighted. Thus, it is often necessary to deselect the text in order to see the results of a formatting command.

Step 5: The Format Painter

- Click anywhere within the sentence **Learn to Type.**
- **Double click** the **Format Painter button** on the Standard toolbar. The mouse pointer changes to a paintbrush as shown in Figure 2.10c.
- Drag the mouse pointer over the next title, **Write now, edit later,** and release the mouse. The formatting from the original sentence (boldface italics in Figure 2.10c) has been applied to this sentence as well.
- Drag the mouse pointer (in the shape of a paintbrush) over the remaining titles in the document to copy the formatting.
- Click the **Format Painter button** after you have painted the last tip.
- Save the document.

DIALOG BOX SHORTCUTS

You can use the mouse to click an option button, to mark a check box on or off, or to pull down a drop-down list box and select an option. You can also use a keyboard shortcut for each of these actions.

- Press Tab (Shift+Tab) to move forward (backward) from one field or command button to the next
- Press Alt plus the underlined letter to move directly to a field or command button
- Press Enter to activate the highlighted command button
- Press Esc to exit the dialog box without taking action
- Press the Space Bar to toggle check boxes on or off
- Press the down arrow to open a list box once the list has been accessed; press the up or down arrow to move between options in a list box

Step 6: Change margins

- Press **Ctrl+End** to move to the end of the document as shown in Figure 2.10d.
- You will see a dotted line indicating a soft page break. (If you do not see

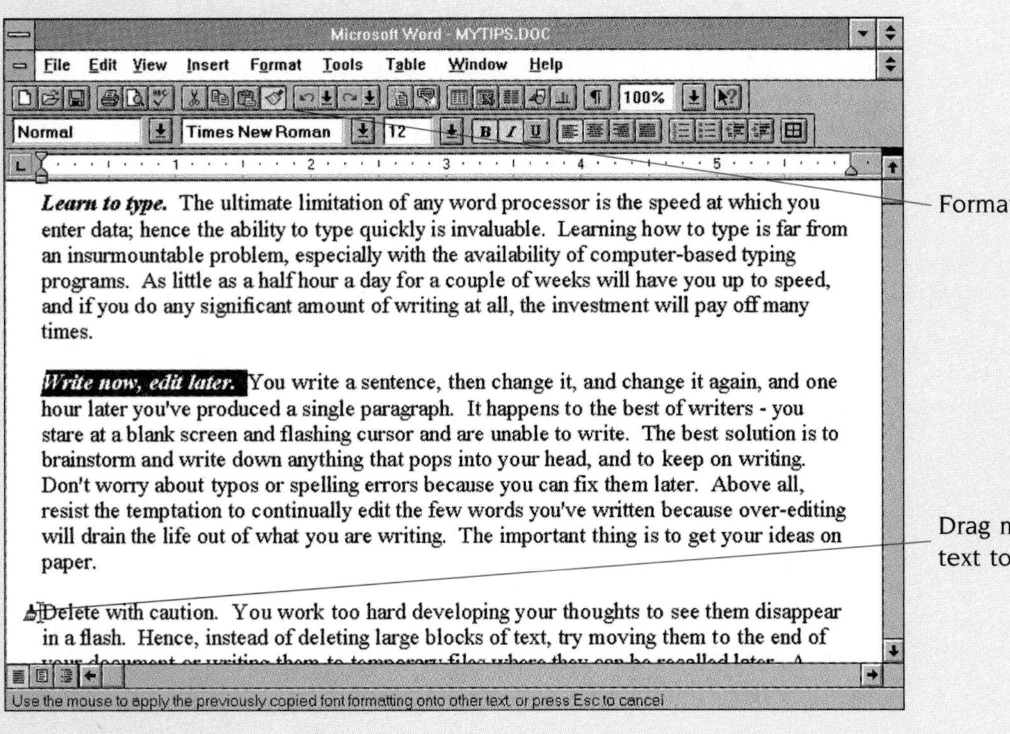

(c) The Format Painter (step 5)

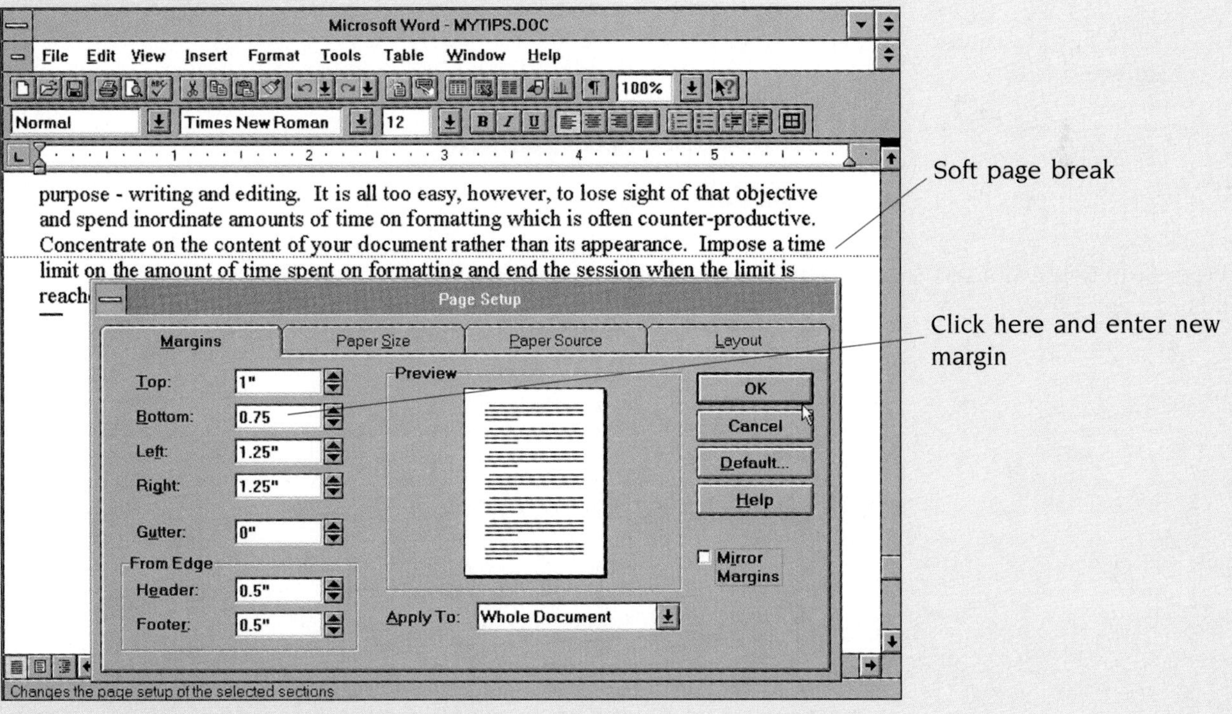

(d) Change Margins (step 6)

FIGURE 2.10 Hands-on Exercise 2 (continued)

the page break, it means that your document fits on one page because you used a different font and/or a smaller point size; we used 12 point Times New Roman.)

- Pull down the **File menu.** Click **Page Setup.**
- Change the bottom margin to **.75** inch. Click **OK.** The page break disappears because we can fit more text on the page.
- Save the document.

Step 7: Create a title page

- Press **Ctrl+Home** to move to the beginning of the document.
- Press **enter** three or four times to add a few blank lines.
- Press **Ctrl+Enter** to insert a hard page break. You will see the words "Page Break" in the middle of a dotted line as shown in Figure 2.10e.
- Press the **up arrow key** two times.
- Enter the title **Word Processing Tips.** Select the title and format it in a larger point size, such as 24 points.
- Enter your name on the next line in a different point size, such as 14 points.
- Select both the title and your name as shown in the figure. Click the **Center justification button** on the Standard toolbar.
- Save the document.

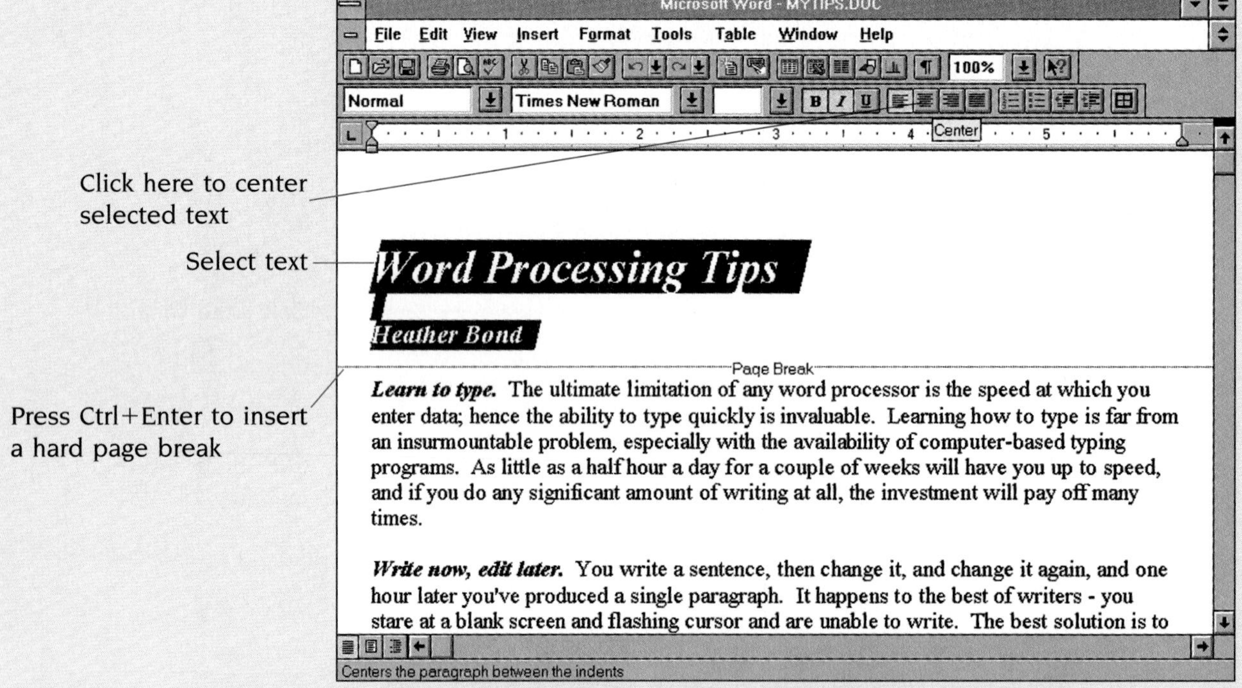

(e) Create the Title Page (step 7)

FIGURE 2.10 Hands-on Exercise 2 (continued)

Step 8: The completed document

- Pull down the **View menu** and click **Page Layout** (or click the **Page Layout button** on the status bar).

- Click the **Zoom control arrow** on the Standard toolbar and drag to select **Two Pages.** Release the mouse to view the completed document in Figure 2.10f.
- Exit Word.

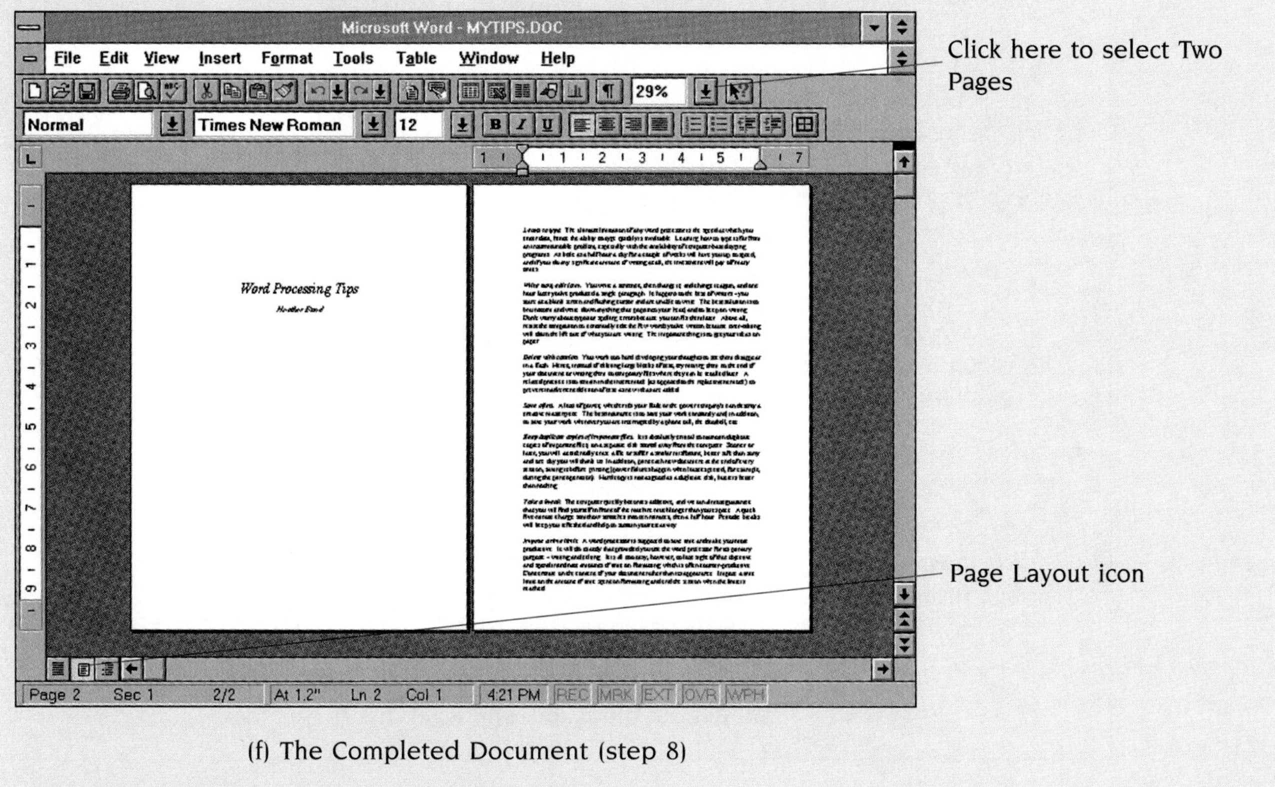

(f) The Completed Document (step 8)

FIGURE 2.10 Hands-on Exercise 2 (continued)

PARAGRAPH FORMATTING

A change in typography is only one way to alter the appearance of a document. You can also change its indentation, ***alignment,*** or line spacing, or you can include borders or shading for added emphasis. All of these features are implemented at the paragraph level and affect the entire paragraph, regardless of the position of the insertion point when the command is executed.

Alignment

Text can be aligned in four different ways as shown in Figure 2.11. It may be fully justified (flush left/flush right), left aligned (flush left with a ragged-right margin), right aligned (flush right with a ragged-left margin), or centered within the margins (ragged left and right).

Left-aligned text is perhaps the easiest to read. The first letters of each line align with each other, helping the eye to find the beginning of each line. The lines themselves are of irregular length. There is uniform spacing between words. The ragged margin on the right adds white space to the text, giving it a lighter and more informal look.

Fully justified text produces lines of equal length, with the spacing between words adjusted to align at the margins. It may be more difficult to read than text

We, the people of the United States, in order to form a more perfect Union, establish justice, insure domestic tranquility, provide for the common defense, promote the general welfare, and secure the blessings of liberty to ourselves and our posterity, do ordain and establish this Constitution for the United States of America.

(a) Fully Justified (flush left/flush right)

We, the people of the United States, in order to form a more perfect Union, establish justice, insure domestic tranquility, provide for the common defense, promote the general welfare, and secure the blessings of liberty to ourselves and our posterity, do ordain and establish this Constitution for the United States of America.

(b) Left Aligned (flush left/ragged right)

We, the people of the United States, in order to form a more perfect Union, establish justice, insure domestic tranquility, provide for the common defense, promote the general welfare, and secure the blessings of liberty to ourselves and our posterity, do ordain and establish this Constitution for the United States of America.

(c) Right Aligned (flush right/ragged left)

We, the people of the United States, in order to form a more perfect Union, establish justice, insure domestic tranquility, provide for the common defense, promote the general welfare, and secure the blessings of liberty to ourselves and our posterity, do ordain and establish this Constitution for the United States of America.

(d) Centered (ragged left/ragged right)

FIGURE 2.11 Alignment

that is left aligned because of the uneven (sometimes excessive) word spacing and/or the greater number of hyphenated words needed to justify the lines.

Type that is centered or right justified is restricted to limited amounts of text where the effect is more important than the ease of reading. Centered text, for example, appears frequently on wedding invitations or formal announcements. Right-justified text is used with figure captions and short headlines.

Tabs

Anyone who has used a typewriter is familiar with the function of the Tab key; that is, press Tab and the insertion point moves to the next ***tab stop*** (a measured position to align text at a specific place.) The Tab key functions identically within Word except it is more powerful because you can choose from four different types of tab stops (left, center, right, and decimal). You can also specify a ***leader character,*** typically dots or hyphens, to draw the reader's eye across the page. Tabs are often used to create tables within a document.

The default tab stops are set every 1/2 inch and are left aligned. You can change the alignment and/or position with the Format Tabs command in Figure 2.12. Four types of alignment are possible:

- Left alignment, where the text *begins* at the tab stop and corresponds exactly to the Tab key on a typewriter

- Right alignment, where the text *ends* at the tab stop; right alignment is commonly used to align page numbers in a table of contents
- Center alignment, where text centers over the tab stop
- Decimal alignment, which lines up numeric values in a column on the decimal point

Figure 2.12 illustrates a dot leader in combination with a right tab to produce a Table of Contents. The default tab stops have been cleared in Figure 2.12a, in favor of a single right tab at 5.5 inches. The option button for a dot leader has also been checked. The resulting document is shown in Figure 2.12b.

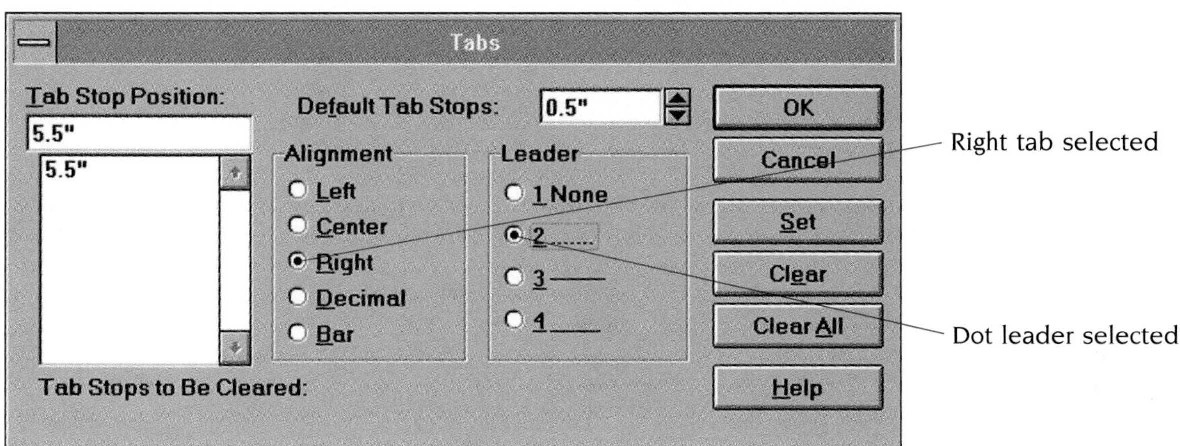

(a) Tab Stops

Right tab with a dot leader

Chapter 1: Introduction 3
Chapter 2: Gaining Proficiency 32
Chapter 3: The Tools 61
Chapter 4: The Professional Document 99
Chapter 5: Desktop Publishing 124

(b) Table of Contents

FIGURE 2.12 Tabs

Indents

Individual paragraphs can be indented so that they appear to have different margins from the rest of a document. Indentation is established at the paragraph level; thus different indentation can be in effect for different paragraphs. One paragraph may be indented from the left margin only, another from the right margin only, and a third from both the left and right margins. The first line of any paragraph may be indented differently from the rest of the paragraph. And finally, a paragraph may be set with no indentation at all, so that it aligns on the left and right margins.

The indentation of a paragraph is determined by three settings: the ***first-line indent,*** the ***left indent,*** and the ***right indent.*** The default values for all three parameters are zero, and produce a paragraph with no indentation as shown in Figure 2.13a. Positive values for the left and right indents offset the paragraph from both margins as shown in Figure 2.13b.

The left and right indents are defined as the distance between the text and the left and right margins, respectively. Both parameters are set to zero in this paragraph, and so it aligns on both margins.

(a) No Indents

Positive values for the left and right indents offset a paragraph from the rest of a document and are often used for long quotations. This paragraph has left and right indents of one-half inch each.

(b) Left and Right Indents

In addition to setting left and right indents, you can indent the first line of a paragraph. This paragraph uses a first-line indent, which is equivalent to pressing the Tab key at the beginning of a paragraph.

(c) First Line Indent

A hanging indent sets the first line of a paragraph to left of the remaining lines. Hanging indents are used for added emphasis and often appears with numbered or bulleted lists.

(d) Hanging Indent

FIGURE 2.13 Indents

The first-line indent affects only the first line in the paragraph as shown in Figure 2.13c (and is an alternative to pressing the Tab key). A ***hanging indent,*** as shown in Figure 2.13d, is often used with bulleted or numbered lists.

Indents affect an entire paragraph and can be set when the insertion point is anywhere within the paragraph. To change the indentation of multiple paragraphs, first select the paragraphs, then set the indentation.

INDENTS VERSUS MARGINS

Indents measure the distance between the text and the margins. Margins mark the distance from the text to the edge of the page. Indents are determined at the paragraph level, whereas margins are established at the section (document) level. The left and right margins are set (by default) to 1.25 inches each; the left and right indents default to zero. The first-line indent is measured from the setting of the left indent and can be either positive or negative.

FORMAT PARAGRAPH COMMAND

The ***Format Paragraph command*** sets the indentation, tab stops, line spacing, and alignment for the selected paragraph(s). The command also provides a preview that lets you see the options in effect—for example, a hanging indent, line spacing of 1.5 lines, and full justification as shown in Figure 2.14a.

Figure 2.14b illustrates an entirely different set of options in which you control the text flow (pagination) of a document. You are already familiar with the concept of ***page breaks,*** and the distinction between soft page breaks (inserted by Word) versus hard page breaks (inserted by the user). The check boxes in Figure 2.14b enable you to prevent awkward page breaks that detract from the appearance of a document.

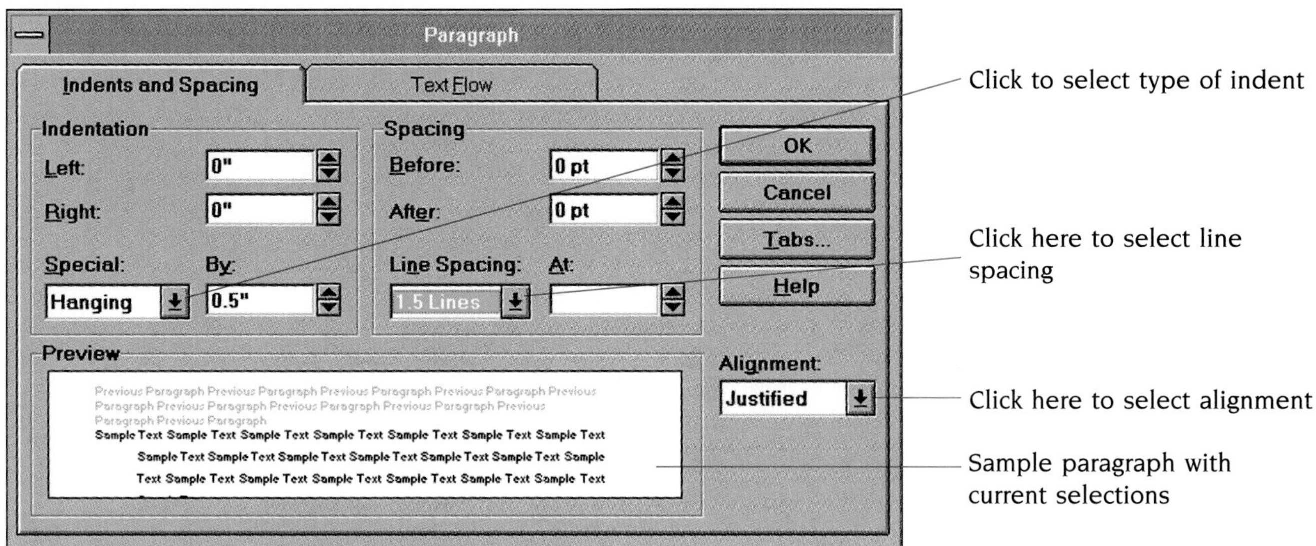

(a) Indents and Spacing

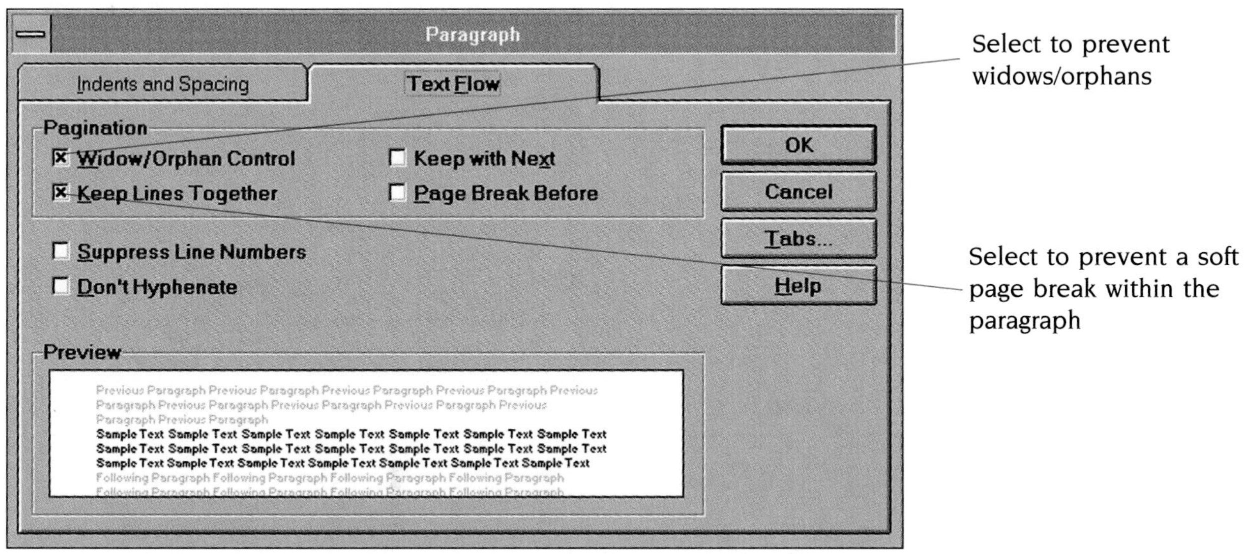

(b) Text Flow

FIGURE 2.14 The Format Paragraph Command

You might, for example, want to prevent ***widows and orphans,*** terms used to describe isolated lines that seem lost and out of place. A widow refers to the last line of a paragraph appearing by itself at the top of a page; an orphan is the first line of a paragraph appearing by itself at the bottom of a page.

You can also impose additional controls by clicking one or more check boxes. Use the Keep Lines Together option to prevent a break within a paragraph—that is, to ensure that the entire paragraph appears on the same page. Use the Keep with Next option to prevent a page break between the selected paragraph and the following paragraph.

FORMATTING AND THE PARAGRAPH MARK

The ***paragraph mark*** ¶ at the end of a paragraph does more than just indicate the presence of a hard return. It also stores all of the formatting in effect for the paragraph. Hence in order to preserve the formatting when you move or copy a paragraph, you must include the paragraph mark in the selected text. Click the Show/Hide button on the toolbar to display the paragraph mark and make sure it has been selected.

Borders and Shading

The ***Borders and Shading command*** in Figure 2.15 puts the finishing touches on a document. It lets you create boxed and/or shaded text as well as place horizontal or vertical lines around a paragraph. You can choose from several different line styles in any color (assuming you have a color printer). You can place a uniform border around a paragraph (choose Box), or you can create a ***drop shadow effect*** with thicker lines at the right and bottom. You can also apply lines to selected sides of a paragraph(s) by clicking the desired sides within the Border sample box and then selecting a line style.

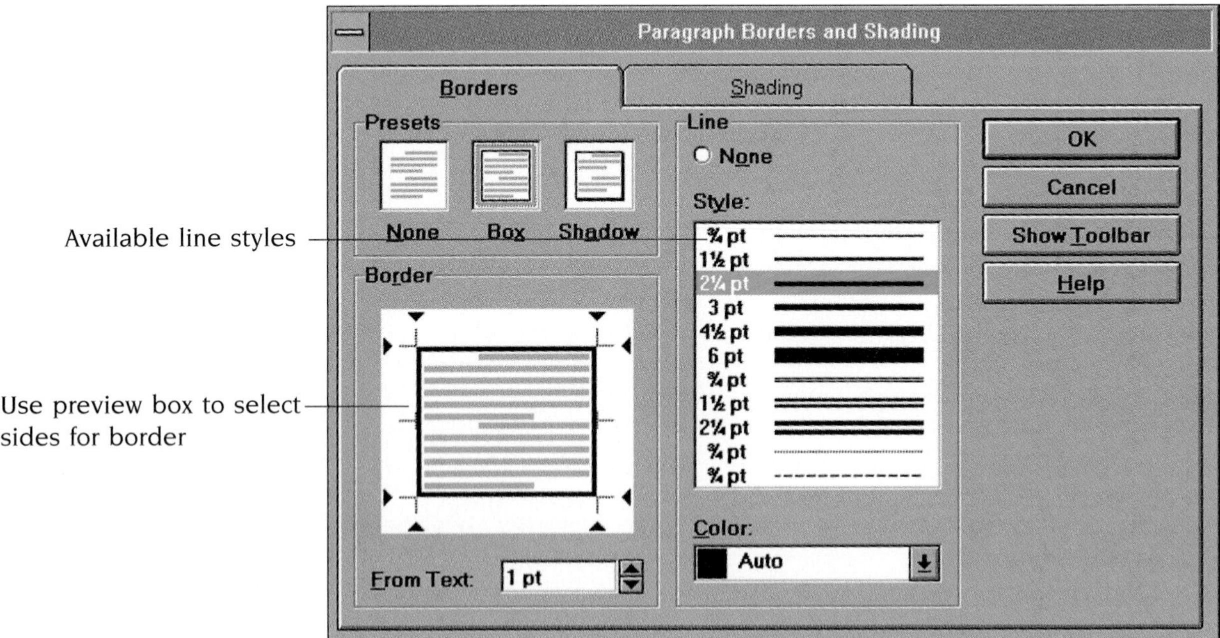

(a) Borders

FIGURE 2.15 Paragraph Borders and Shading

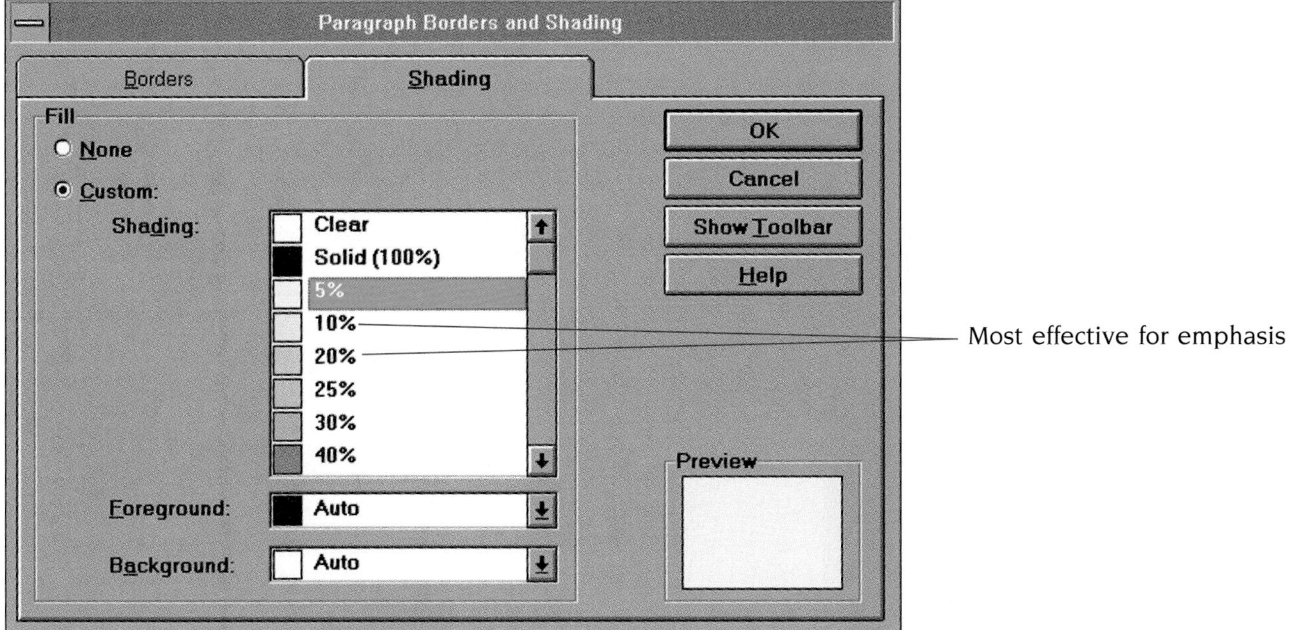

(b) Shading

FIGURE 2.15 Paragraph Borders and Shading (continued)

Shading is implemented independently of the border. Clear (no shading) is the default. Solid (100%) shading creates a solid box where the text is unreadable. Shading of 10 or 20 percent is generally most effective to add emphasis to the selected paragraph.

HELP WITH FORMATTING

It's all too easy to lose sight of the formatting in effect, so Word provides a Help button on the Standard toolbar. Click the button, and the mouse pointer assumes the shape of a large question mark. Click anywhere in a document to display the formatting in effect at that point. Click the Help button a second time to exit Help.

HANDS-ON EXERCISE 3:

Paragraph Formatting

Objective To practice line spacing, alignment, justification, tabs and indents; to implement widow and orphan protection; to box and shade a selected paragraph. Use Figure 2.16 as a guide in the exercise.

Step 1: Load the practice document.

- Open the **MYTIPS** document from the previous exercise.
- Pull down the **File menu.** Save the document as **MYTIPS2.DOC.**
- If necessary change to the Page Layout view. Pull down the **Zoom control**

button and click **Two Pages** to match the view in Figure 2.16a.

➤ Select the entire second page as shown in the figure.

➤ Press the **right mouse button** to produce the shortcut menu.

➤ Click **Paragraph** to produce the dialog box in Figure 2.16b.

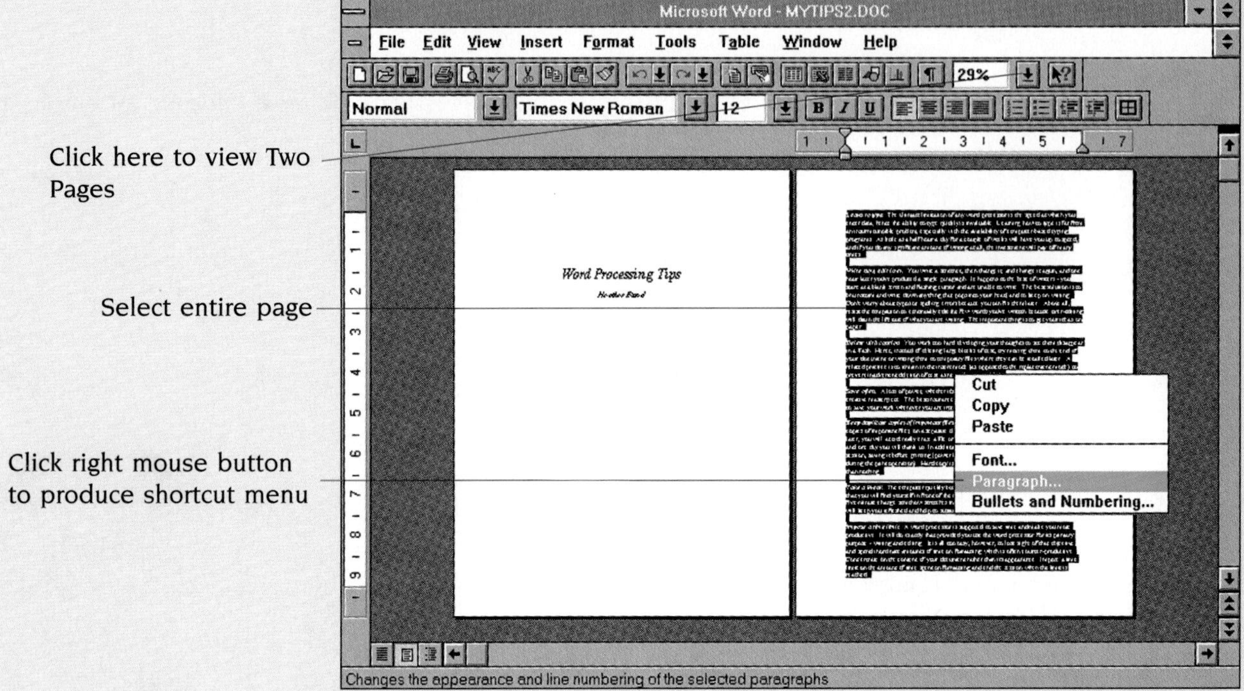

(a) Select Then Do (step 1)

FIGURE 2.16 Hands-on Exercise 3

SELECT TEXT WITH THE F8 EXTEND KEY

Position the insertion point at the beginning of the text you want to select, then press the F8 (extend) key The letters EXT will appear in the status bar. Use the arrow keys to extend the selection in the indicated direction; for example, press the down arrow key to select the line. You can also press any character—for example, a letter, space, or period—to extend the selection to the first occurrence of that character. Press Esc to cancel the selection mode.

Step 2: Line spacing, justification, and text flow

➤ If necessary, click the **Indents and Spacing tab** to view the options in Figure 2.16b.

➤ Click the **down arrow** on the list box for Line Spacing and select **1.5 Lines.**

➤ Click the **down arrow** on the Alignment list box and select **Justified** as shown in Figure 2.16b.

➤ Click the tab for **Text Flow.** Check the box for **Keep Lines Together.** If necessary, check the box for **Widow/Orphan Control.**

➤ Click **OK** to accept all of the settings in the dialog box; that is, you need to

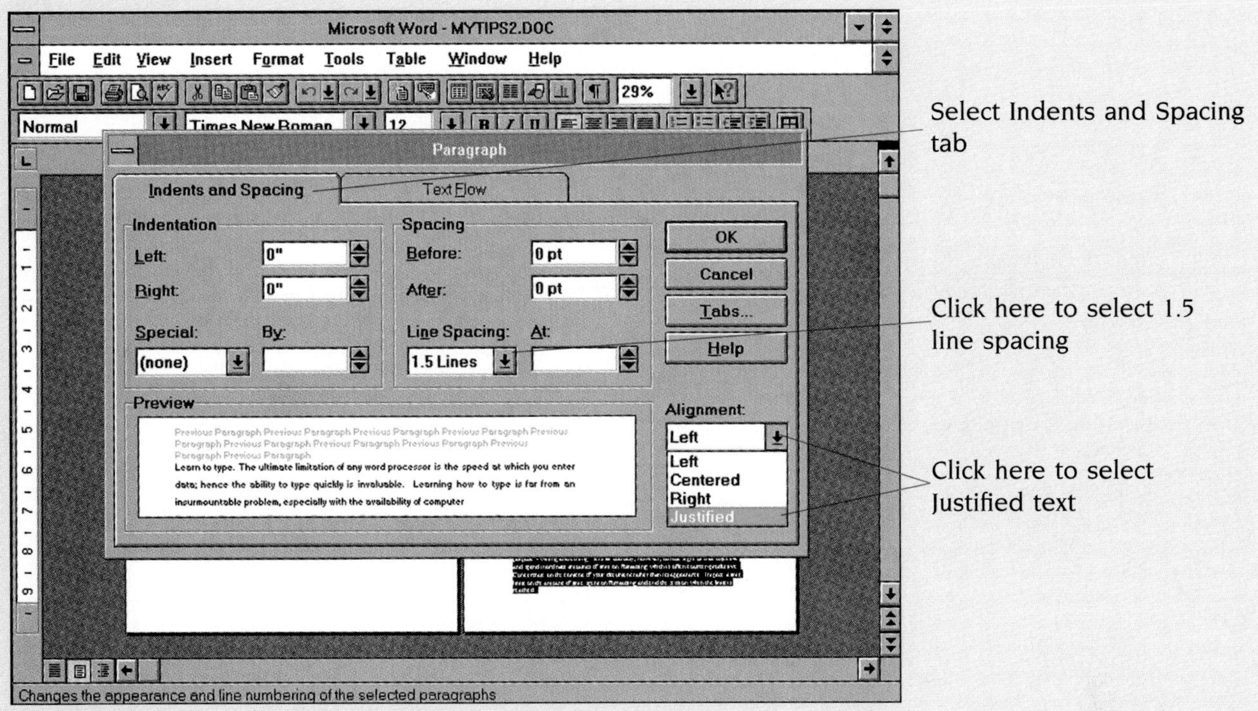

(b) Format Paragraph Command (step 2)

FIGURE 2.16 Hands-on Exercise 3 (continued)

click OK only once to accept the settings for Indents and Spacing and Text Flow.

- Click anywhere in the document to deselect the text and see the effects of the formatting changes. The document is fully justified and the line spacing has increased.
- Save the document.

PARAGRAPH FORMATTING AND THE INSERTION POINT

Indents, tabs, line spacing, justification, and text flow are set at the paragraph level and affect the entire paragraph. The position of the insertion point within the paragraph does not matter; that is, the insertion point can be anywhere within the paragraph when the Format Paragraph command is executed.

Step 3: Tabs

- Pull down the **View menu,** click **Zoom,** then select **Page Width** (or use the **Zoom control box** on the Standard toolbar to achieve the same result).
- Scroll through the document until you see the first paragraph. Click at the beginning of the first paragraph.
- Press the **Tab key** to indent the paragraph as shown in Figure 2.16c. The first line is indented .5 inch corresponding to the first tab stop.
- Pull down the **Format menu.** Click **Tabs** to produce the dialog box in Figure 2.16c.

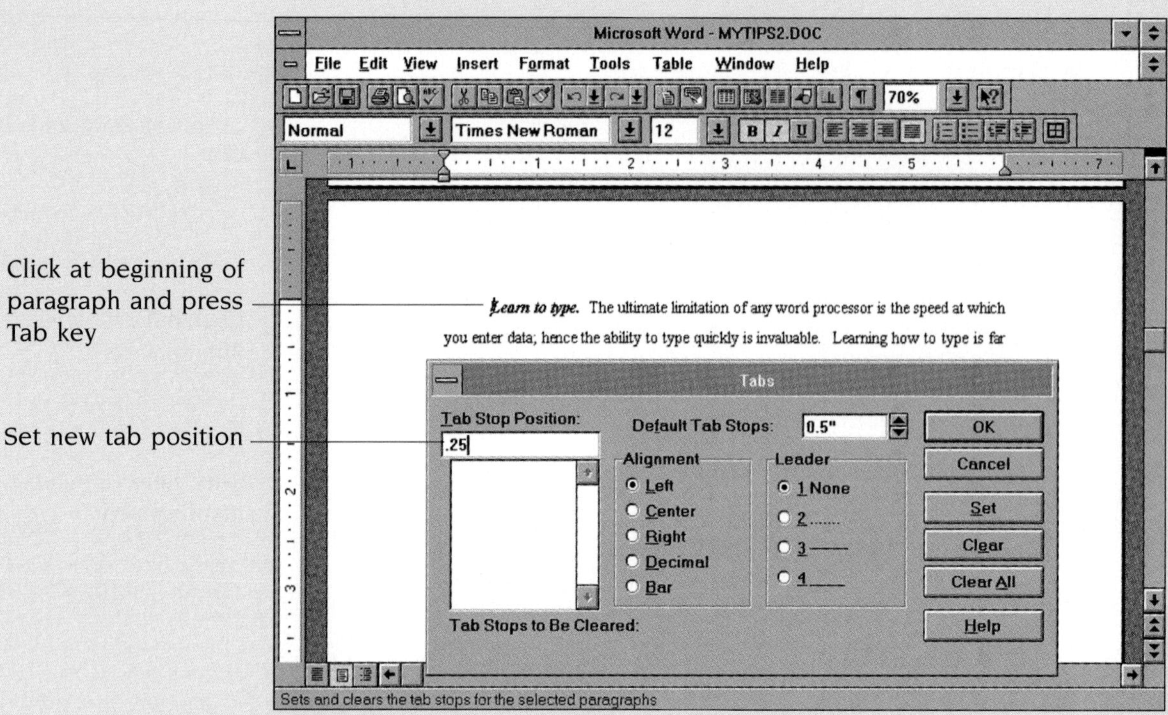

(c) Format Tabs Command (step 3)

FIGURE 2.16 Hands-on Exercise 3 (continued)

- Click the **Tab Stop Position** text box. Type **.25.** Click **OK.** The indentation in the paragraph changes to .25 inch corresponding to the new tab stop.
- Decide whether or not to indent the remaining paragraphs. (We opted to remove the Tab by clicking at the beginning of the paragraph and pressing the **backspace key.**)

TABS AND THE RULER

Use the ruler to insert or delete a tab stop and/or change the type of tab. Select the paragraph (or paragraphs) in which you want to change the tab settings. To insert a tab stop, click the Tab Alignment button on the left of the ruler until you see the symbol for the tab stop you want:

└ ***Left tab***
⊥ ***Centered tab***
┘ ***Right tab***
⊥̇ ***Decimal tab***

then click the position on the ruler where you want the tab stop to be. To delete an existing tab stop, just drag it off the ruler. Use the Format Tabs command for more precise settings.

Step 4: Indents

- Select the second paragraph as shown in Figure 2.16d. (The second paragraph will not be indented.)

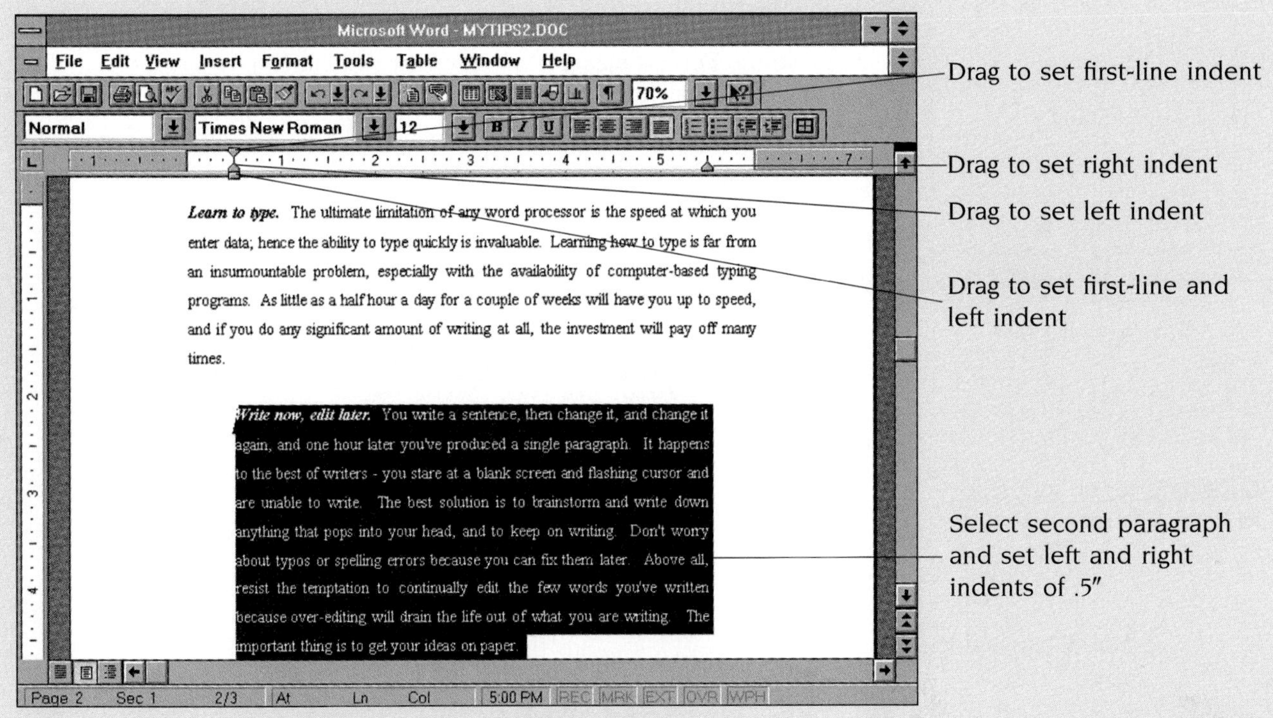

(d) Indents and the Ruler (step 4)

FIGURE 2.16 Hands-on Exercise 3 (continued)

- Pull down the **Format menu** and click **Paragraph** (or press the **right mouse button** to produce the shortcut menu and click **Paragraph**).
- If necessary, press the **Indents and Spacing tab** in the Paragraph dialog box.
- Click the **up arrow** on the Left Indentation text box to set the **Left Indent** to **.5** inch. Set the **Right indent** to **.5** inch. Click **OK.** Your document should match Figure 2.16d.
- Save the document.

INDENTS AND THE RULER

Use the ruler to change the first-line, left, and/or right indents. Select the paragraph (or paragraphs) in which you want to change indents, then drag the appropriate indent markers to the new location.

First-line indent only	drag the top triangle at the left margin
Left indent only	drag the bottom triangle at the left margin (the box will also move)
First-line *and* left indent	drag the box on the bottom at the left margin
Right indent	drag the triangle at the right margin

If the first line indent changes when you wanted to change only the left indent, it means you dragged the box instead of the triangle. Click the Undo button and try again. (You can always use the Format Paragraph command rather than the ruler if you continue to have difficulty.)

Step 5: Borders and Shading

- Pull down the **Format menu.** Click **Borders and Shading** to produce the dialog box in Figure 2.16e.
- If necessary, click the **Borders tab.** Click the rectangle labeled **Box** under Presets. Click a style for the line around the box.
- Click the **Shading Tab.** Click **10%** within the open list box.
- Click **OK** to accept the settings for both Borders and Shading.
- Save the document.

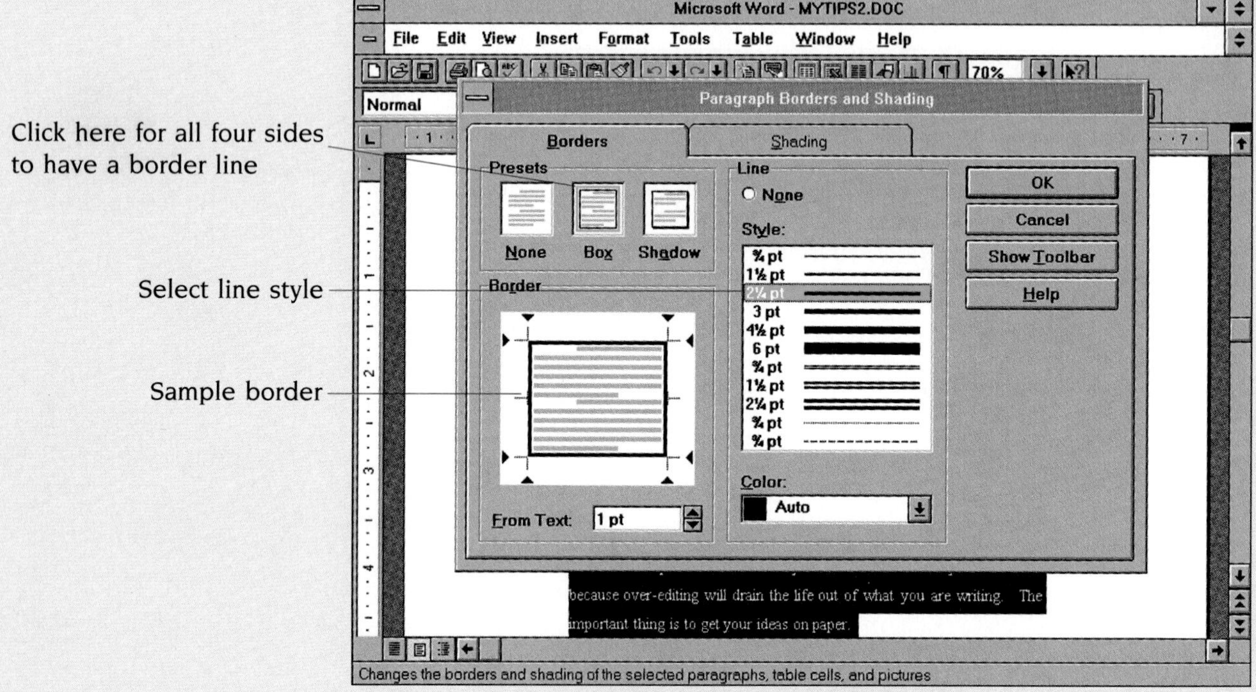

(e) Borders and Shading (step 5)

FIGURE 2.16 Hands-on Exercise 3 (continued)

THE BORDERS BUTTON

Click the Borders button on the Formatting toolbar to display (hide) the Borders toolbar, which contains icons for all capabilities within the Borders and Shading command. The Borders toolbar contains a list box for the line width, icons for the border styles, and a second list box for shadings.

Step 6: Help with Formatting

- Click outside the selected text to see the effects of the Borders and Shading command.
- Click the **Help button** on the Standard toolbar. The mouse pointer changes to include a large question mark.
- Click inside the boxed paragraph to see the formatting in effect for this paragraph as shown in Figure 2.16f.

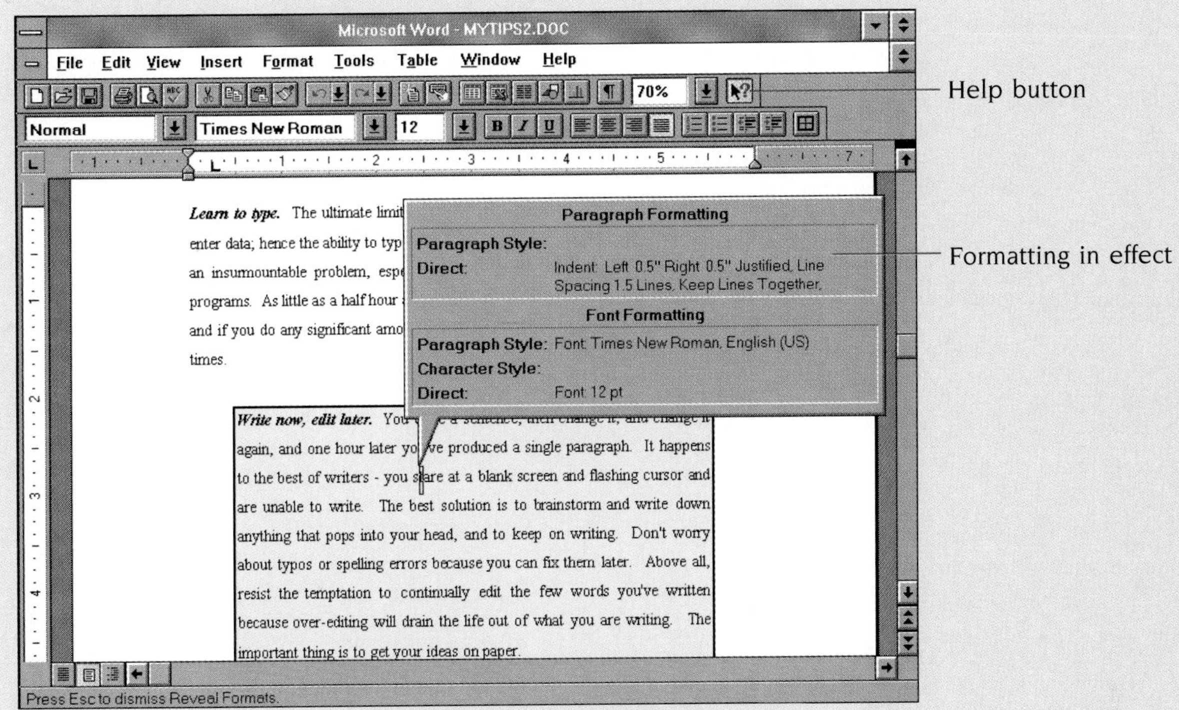

(f) Help Command (step 6)

FIGURE 2.16 Hands-on Exercise 3 (continued)

- Click the **Help button** a second time to exit help. The mouse pointer returns to normal.

> **THE INCREASE INDENT AND DECREASE INDENT BUTTONS**
>
> The Formatting toolbar provides yet another way to indent (unindent) a paragraph(s). The Increase Indent button moves the entire paragraph to the right; that is, it indents the paragraph to the next tab stop and wraps the text to fit the new indentation. The Decrease Indent button moves the paragraph one tab stop back (to the left).

Step 7: The Zoom Command

- Pull down the **View menu.** Click **Zoom** to produce the dialog box in Figure 2.16g.
- Click the **Many Pages** option button. Click the icon within the monitor and drag to display three pages across as shown in the figure. Release the mouse. Click **OK.**

Step 8: The Completed Document

- Your screen should match the one in Figure 2.16h, which displays all three pages of the document.
- The Page Layout view displays both a vertical and a horizontal ruler.
- The boxed and indented paragraph is clearly shown in the second page.

- The soft page break between pages two and three occurs between tips rather than within a tip; that is, the text of each tip is kept together on the same page.
- Save the document. Exit Word.

Click and drag over three pages

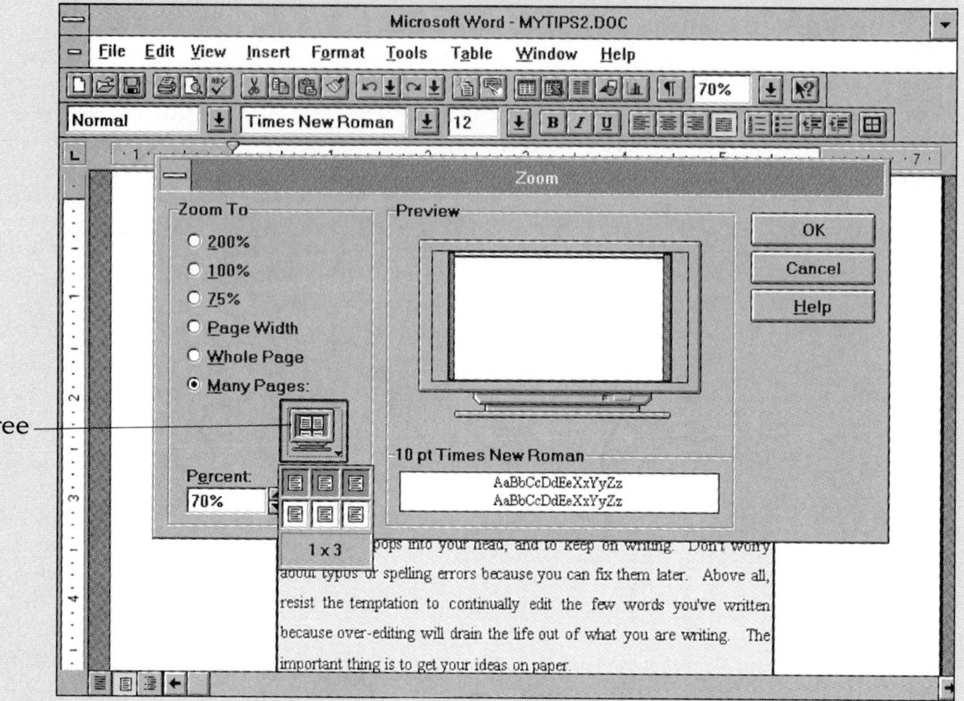

(g) The View Zoom Command (step 7)

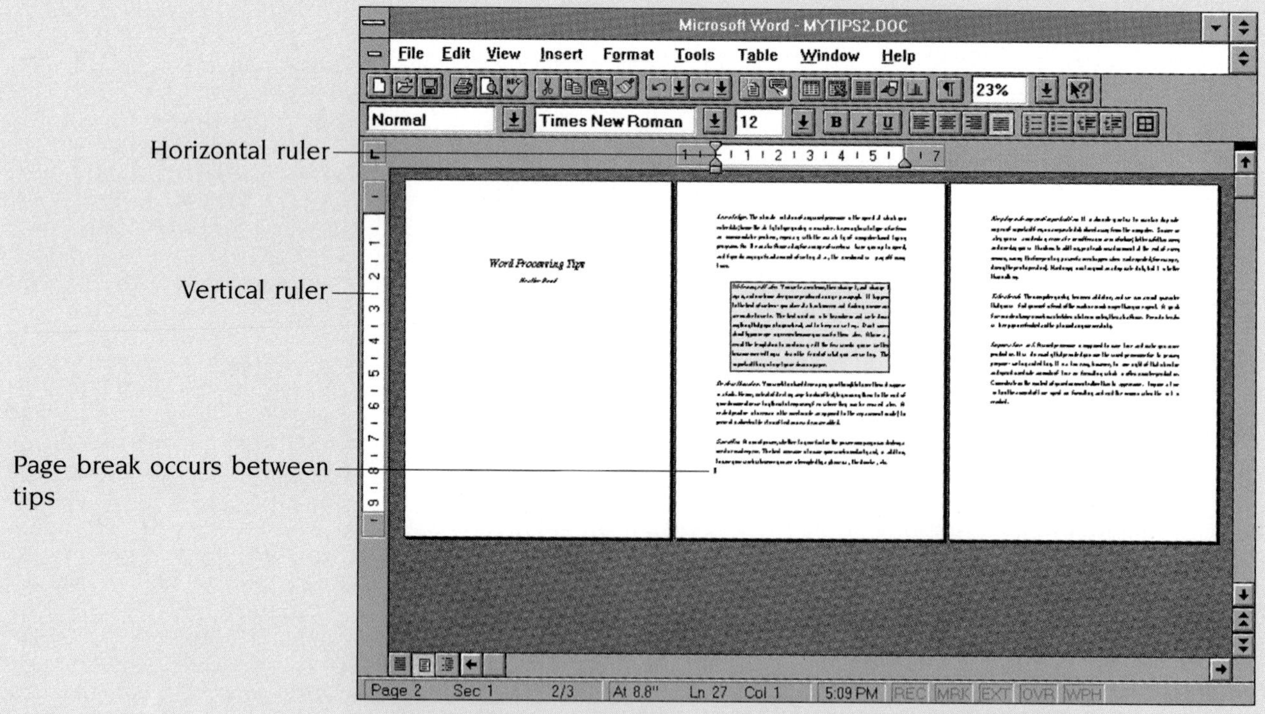

(h) The Completed Document (step 8)

FIGURE 2.16 Hands-on Exercise 3 (continued)

SUMMARY

Virtually every operation in Word is done within the context of select-then-do; that is, select the text, then execute the necessary command. Text may be selected by dragging the mouse, by using the selection bar to the left of the document, or by using the keyboard. Text is deselected by clicking anywhere within the document.

The Find and Replace commands locate a designated character string, then optionally replace one or more occurrences of that string with a different character string. The search may be case sensitive and/or restricted to whole words as necessary.

Text is moved or copied through a combination of the Cut, Copy, and Paste commands and/or the drag-and-drop facility. The contents of the clipboard are replaced by any subsequent Cut or Copy command, but are unaffected by the Paste command; that is, the same text can be pasted into multiple locations.

The Undo command reverses the effect of previous commands. The Undo and Redo commands work in conjunction with one another; that is, every command that is undone can be redone at a later time.

Scrolling occurs when a document is too large to be seen in its entirety. Scrolling with the mouse changes what is displayed on the screen, but does not move the insertion point; that is, you must click the mouse to move the insertion point. Scrolling via the keyboard (for example, PgUp and PgDn) changes what is seen on the screen as well as the location of the insertion point.

The Page Layout view displays top and bottom margins, headers and footers, and other elements not seen in the Normal view. The Normal view is faster because Word spends less time formatting the display. Both views can be seen at different magnifications.

The Save command copies the document in memory to disk under its existing name. The Save As command saves the document under a different name. It is useful when you want to retain a copy of the current document prior to all changes as well as a copy of the revised document.

TrueType fonts are scalable and accessible from any Windows application. The Format Font command enables you to choose the typeface (e.g., Times New Roman or Arial), style (e.g., boldface or italics), and point size.

The Format Paragraph command determines line spacing, justification, tabs and indents, text flow, borders, and shading. All are set at the paragraph level and affect the entire paragraph. Margins are set in the Page Setup command and affect the entire document (or section).

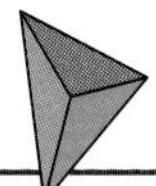

Key Words and Concepts

Alignment
Arial
Automatic replacement
Backup
BAK extension
Borders and Shading command
Case-insensitive replacement
Case-sensitive replacement
Centered tab
Clipboard
Copy command
Cut command
Decimal tab
Default directory
Drag and drop
Drop shadow effect
Find command
First-line indent
Font
Format Font command
Format Painter
Format Paragraph command
Global replacement
Hanging indent
Hard page break
Landscape orientation
Leader character

Left indent
Left tab
Monospaced font
Normal view
Page break
Page Layout view
Page Setup command
Paragraph mark
Paste command
Point size
Portrait orientation
Proportional font
Redo command
Replace command
Right indent
Right tab
Ruler
Sans serif typeface
Save As command
Save command
Scrolling
Select-then-do
Selection bar
Selective replacement
Serif typeface
Shortcut menu
Soft page break
Tab stop
Times New Roman
TrueType
Typeface
Type size
Typography
Undo Command
View menu
Whole word replacement
Widows and orphans
Zoom command

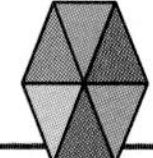

Multiple Choice

1. Which of the following commands does *not* place data onto the clipboard?
   (a) Cut
   (b) Copy
   (c) Paste
   (d) All of the above

2. What happens if you select a block of text, copy it, move to the beginning of the document, paste it, move to the end of the document, and paste the text again?
   (a) The selected text will appear in three places: at the original location, and at the beginning and end of the document
   (b) The selected text will appear in two places: at the beginning and end of the document
   (c) The selected text will appear in just the original location
   (d) The situation is not possible; that is, you cannot paste twice in a row without an intervening cut or copy operation

3. What happens if you select a block of text, cut it, move to the beginning of the document, paste it, move to the end of the document, and paste the text again?
   (a) The selected text will appear in three places: at the original location and at the beginning and end of the document
   (b) The selected text will appear in two places: at the beginning and end of the document
   (c) The selected text will appear in just the original location
   (d) The situation is not possible; that is, you cannot paste twice in a row without an intervening cut or copy operation

4. Which of the following are set at the paragraph level?
   (a) Borders and shading
   (b) Tabs and indents
   (c) Line spacing and justification
   (d) All of the above

5. How do you change the font for *existing* text within a document?
   (a) Select the text, then choose the new font
   (b) Choose the new font, then select the text
   (c) Either (a) or (b)
   (d) Neither (a) nor (b)
6. The Page Setup command can be used to change:
   (a) The margins in a document
   (b) The orientation of a document
   (c) Both (a) and (b)
   (d) Neither (a) nor (b)
7. Which of the following is a true statement regarding indents?
   (a) Indents are measured from the edge of the page rather than from the margin
   (b) The left, right, and first-line indents must be set to the same value
   (c) The insertion point can be anywhere in the paragraph when indents are set
   (d) Indents must be set with the Format Paragraph command
8. The spacing in an existing multipage document is changed from single spacing to double spacing. What can you say about the number of hard and soft page breaks before and after the formatting change?
   (a) The number of soft page breaks is the same, but the number and/or position of the hard page breaks is different
   (b) The number of hard page breaks is the same, but the number and/or position of the soft page breaks is different
   (c) The number and position of both hard and soft page breaks are the same
   (d) The number and position of both hard and soft page breaks are different
9. The default tab stops are set to:
   (a) Left indents every ½ inch
   (b) Left indents every ¼ inch
   (c) Right indents every ½ inch
   (d) Right indents every ¼ inch
10. Which of the following describes the Arial and Times New Roman fonts?
    (a) Arial is a sans serif font, Times New Roman is a serif font
    (b) Arial is a serif font, Times New Roman is a sans serif font
    (c) Both are serif fonts
    (d) Both are sans serif fonts
11. The find and replacement strings must be
    (a) The same length
    (b) The same case, either upper or lower
    (c) The same length and the same case
    (d) None of the above
12. Assume that you are in the middle of a multipage document. How do you scroll to the beginning of the document and simultaneously change the insertion point?
    (a) Press Ctrl+Home
    (b) Drag the scroll bar to the top of the scroll box
    (c) Both (a) and (b)
    (d) Neither (a) nor (b)

13. A right-handed person will normally:
    (a) Click the right and left mouse button to access a pull-down menu and shortcut menu, respectively
    (b) Click the left and right mouse button to access a pull-down menu and shortcut menu, respectively
    (c) Click the left mouse button to access either type of menu
    (d) Click the right mouse button to access either type of menu

14. Which of the following deselects a selected block of text?
    (a) Clicking anywhere outside the selected text
    (b) Clicking any alignment icon on the toolbar
    (c) Clicking the boldface, italics, or underline buttons
    (d) All of the above

15. Which command saves the document in memory and creates a backup copy with the BAK extension?
    (a) The Save command, provided the proper backup option has been set
    (b) The Save As command, provided the proper backup option has been set
    (c) The Save command irrespective of the backup options in effect
    (d) The Save As command irrespective of the backup options in effect

ANSWERS

1. c	**6.** c	**11.** d
2. a	**7.** c	**12.** a
3. b	**8.** b	**13.** b
4. d	**9.** a	**14.** a
5. a	**10.** a	**15.** a

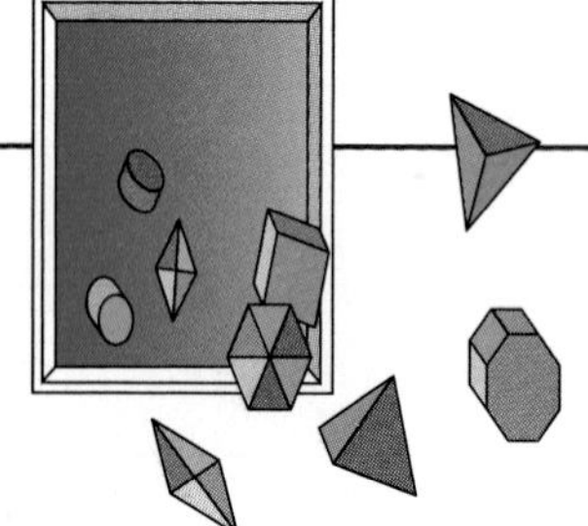

EXPLORING WORD

1. Use Figure 2.17 to match each action with its result; a given action may be used more than once.

Action		Result
a. Click at 1	___	Undo the previous two commands
b. Click at 2	___	Cut the selected text from the document
c. Click at 3	___	Change the alignment of the current paragraph to fully justified
d. Click at 4	___	Change the font of the selected text to Arial
e. Click at 5	___	Change the left and right margins to 1.5″
f. Click at 6	___	Change the size of the selected text to 16 point
g. Click at 7	___	Boldface the selected text
h. Click at 8	___	Change to the Page Layout view
i. Click at 9	___	Paint another word with the same format as the currently selected word
j. Click at 10	___	Change the magnification to Whole Page

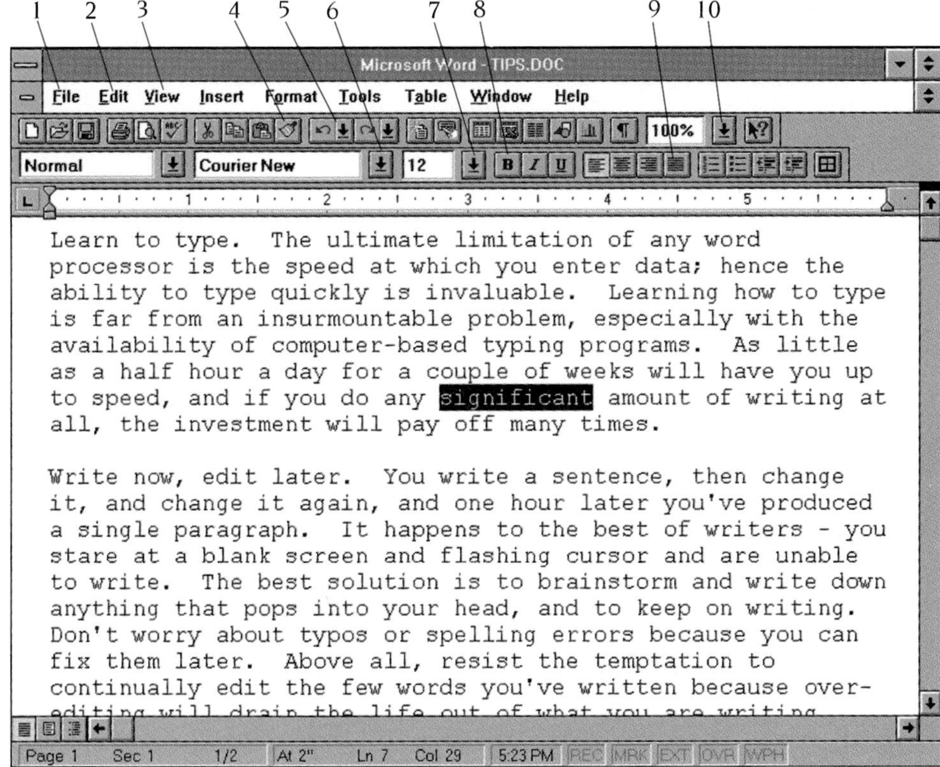

FIGURE 2.17 Screen for Problem 1

2. Use the Preamble to the Constitution as the basis for the following exercise, which you are to complete and submit to your instructor. Enter the text as shown below:

We, the people of the United States, in order to form a more perfect Union, establish justice, insure domestic tranquility, provide for the common defense, promote the general welfare, and secure the blessings of liberty to ourselves and our posterity, do ordain and establish this Constitution for the United States of America.

   a. Choose any typeface you like, but specify italic as the style, and 10 points as the size. Use single spacing and left justification.
   b. Copy the preamble to a new page, then change the specifications for the copied text to double spacing and full justification. Use the same typeface as before, but choose regular rather than italic for the style.
   c. Create a title page for your assignment, containing your name, course name, and appropriate title. Use a different typeface for the title page than for the rest of the document. Set the title in at least 24 points. Submit all three pages to the instructor.

3. Figure 2.18 displays an additional practice document on the data disk.
   a. Open the document PROB0203.DOC on the data disk.
   b. Copy the sentence, *Discretion is the better part of valor,* to the beginning of the first paragraph.
   c. Move the second paragraph to the end of the document.
   d. Change the typeface of the entire document to 12 point Arial.
   e. Change all whole word occurrences of *feel* to *think.*
   f. Change the spacing of the entire document from single spacing to 1.5. Change the justification of the entire document to fully justified.

g. Set the phrases *Format Font Command* and *Format Paragraph Command* in italics.

h. Indent the second paragraph .25 inch on both the left and right.

i. Box and shade the last paragraph.

j. Create a title page that precedes the document. Set the title, *Discretion in Design,* in 24 point Arial bold and center it approximately two inches from the top of the page. Right justify your name toward the bottom of the document in 12 point Arial regular.

k. Save the modified document as SOLUTION.DOC.

l. Print the revised document and submit it to your instructor.

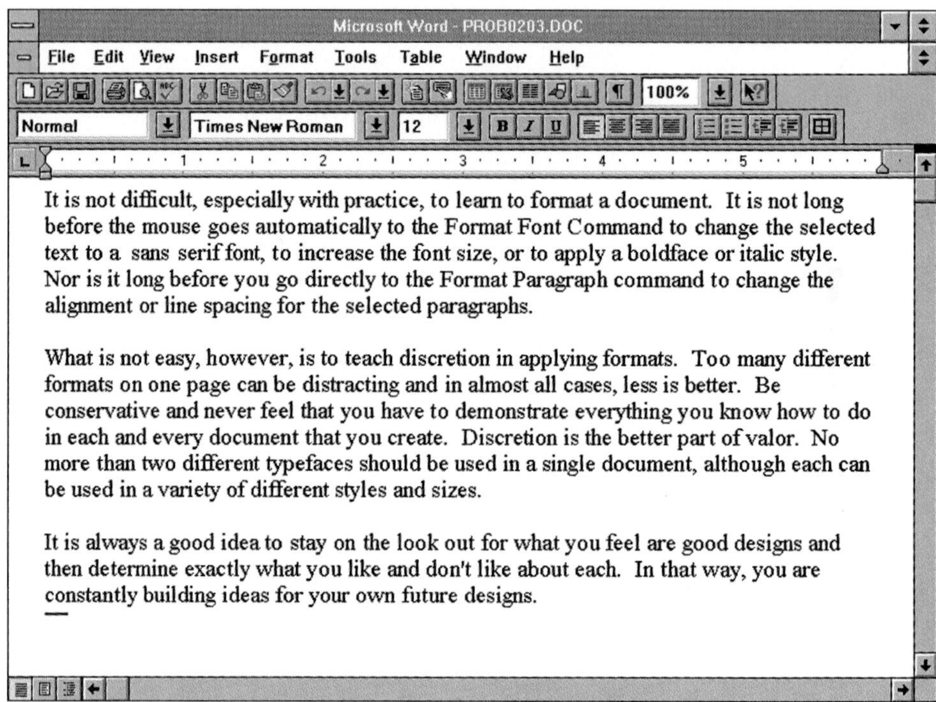

FIGURE 2.18 Screen for Problem 3

4. Prepare a personal ad for placement in a newspaper that could be distributed to the class at large. Any writing style is acceptable, but try to make it creative. A poem or limerick would be fine. The only requirement is to demonstrate proficiency in the use of a word processor, with adherence to the following specifications:

a. Fully justified text

b. A line length of 4 inches

c. Boldface the information for a reply (centered on the last line), which should consist of the last four digits of your social security number and the first two characters of your last name.

d. A sample appears below:

Dynamic professor seeks motivated students for exciting course in Windows applications. Presentation of Windows concepts, Word, Microsoft Excel, and Presentation graphics. Approximately 10 homework assignments, two tests, and a final. No previous knowledge of computers is required.

Respond to 1234GR

5. Describe at least one way, using the mouse or keyboard, to do each of the following. (The answers are found in the boxed tips throughout the chapter. Alternatively, you can access the on-line help facility to find the information.) How do you:

   a. Scroll to the beginning or end of a document? Does the action you describe also change the insertion point?
   b. Select a sentence? a paragraph? the entire document?
   c. Set the left and right indents?
   d. Insert an additional tab stop?
   e. Copy the formatting in a block of text to multiple places in the same document?
   f. Change highlighted text to boldface, italics, or underlining?
   g. Change the line spacing and justification for a selected paragraph?
   h. Save the document under a different name?
   i. Box and shade a selected paragraph?

6. Word for Windows can be used to prepare any kind of document, not only one that is limited to traditional text—for example, the set of dots below. Recreate the figure below consisting of multiple rows of dots. (To make life really interesting, you might try doing this with the fewest number of commands possible. Compare your solution to that of your neighbor.)

   The figure represents the children's game of *dots,* in which the players take turns connecting two adjacent dots. Each player is allowed one line per turn, except in the event that the last line drawn completes a box. In that case, the player puts his or her initial in the box and goes again. The player with the most boxes at the end of the game wins. Most of the action takes place at the end of the game, at which time runs of 10, 20, or 30 boxes are possible.

```
. . . . . . . . . . . . . . .

. . . . . . . . . . . . . . .

. . . . . . . . . . . . . . .

. . . . . . . . . . . . . . .

. . . . . . . . . . . . . . .

. . . . . . . . . . . . . . .

. . . . . . . . . . . . . . .

. . . . . . . . . . . . . . .

. . . . . . . . . . . . . . .

. . . . . . . . . . . . . . .

. . . . . . . . . . . . . . .
```

7. The boxed tips that have appeared throughout the chapter have been collected into a single file, PROB0207.DOC, and placed on the data disk. Open the file and format the tips in the most attractive way possible. Add a title page with your name, but indicate that the tips were taken from *Exploring Word for Windows* by Grauer and Barber. Print the formatted document and submit it to your instructor.

8. The document in Figure 2.19 exists on the data disk but with no formatting. Open the file PROB0208.DOC, then implement the changes below so that your file matches the document in the figure.
   a. Set top and bottom margins of 2 inches each.
   b. Set left and right margins of 1 inch each.
   c. Establish 1.5 line spacing for the document. Leave an extra line between the paragraphs.
   d. Change the typeface for the body of the document to 12 point Times New Roman.
   e. Find the word Arial within the document, then change its typeface to 12 point Arial.
   f. Use italics and boldface italics on the highlighted terms as shown in the figure.
   g. Set the title of the document in 18 point Arial bold. Center the title.
   h. Fully justify the document (flush left/flush right).
   i. Place a border around the entire document.

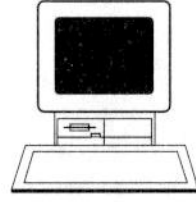

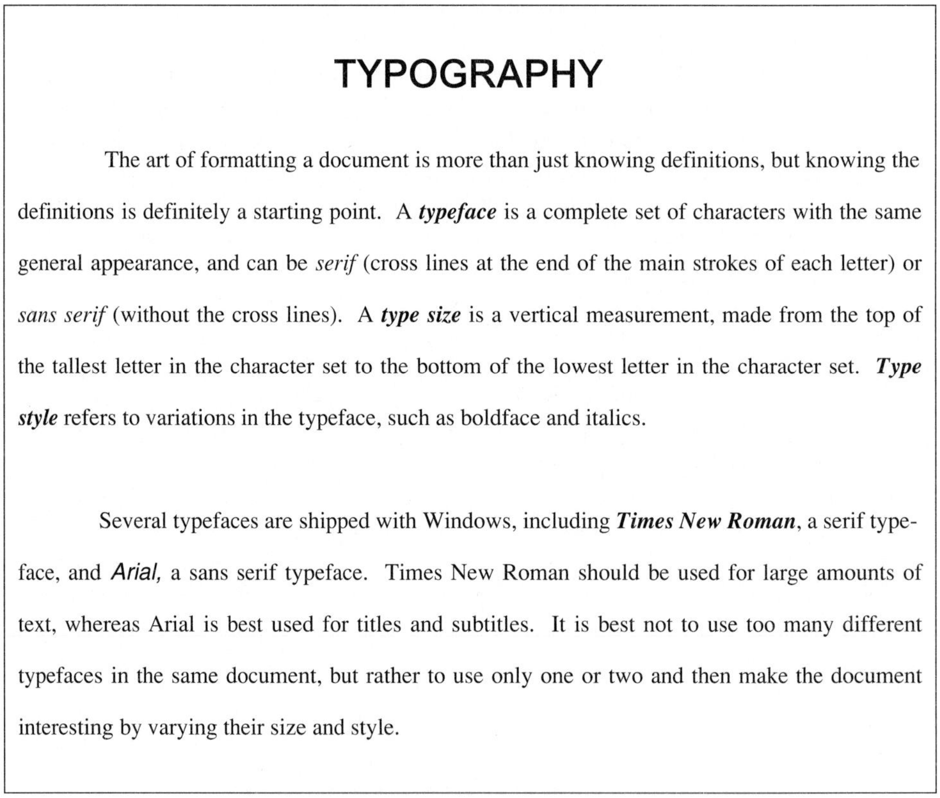

TYPOGRAPHY

The art of formatting a document is more than just knowing definitions, but knowing the definitions is definitely a starting point. A ***typeface*** is a complete set of characters with the same general appearance, and can be *serif* (cross lines at the end of the main strokes of each letter) or *sans serif* (without the cross lines). A ***type size*** is a vertical measurement, made from the top of the tallest letter in the character set to the bottom of the lowest letter in the character set. ***Type style*** refers to variations in the typeface, such as boldface and italics.

Several typefaces are shipped with Windows, including ***Times New Roman***, a serif typeface, and *Arial,* a sans serif typeface. Times New Roman should be used for large amounts of text, whereas Arial is best used for titles and subtitles. It is best not to use too many different typefaces in the same document, but rather to use only one or two and then make the document interesting by varying their size and style.

FIGURE 2.19 Document for Problem 8

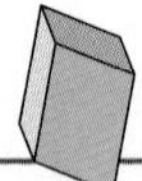

Case Studies

Computers Past and Present

The ENIAC was the scientific marvel of its day and the world's first operational electronic computer. It could perform 5,000 additions per second, weighed 30 tons, and took 1,500 square feet of floor space. The price was a modest $486,000 in 1946 dollars. The story of the ENIAC and other influential computers of the authors' choosing is found in the file HISTORY.DOC, which we forgot to format, so we are asking you to do it for us. Be sure to use appropriate emphasis to highlight the names of the various computers.

Your Own Reference Manual

The clipboard is a temporary storage area available to all Windows applications. Selected text is cut or copied from one document into the clipboard, from where it can be pasted into another document altogether. Use on-line help to obtain detailed information on several topics within Word for Windows, then use the Edit Copy command to copy the information to the clipboard, and paste it into a new document, which will become your personal reference manual. To really do an outstanding job, you will have to format the reference manual after the information has been copied from the clipboard. Be sure to include a title page.

Fonts, Fonts, and More Fonts

In the beginning fonts were expensive and Courier was good enough. Then came TrueType and all of a sudden font packages that used to cost hundreds of dollars were sold for almost nothing. The problem is that fonts have gotten out of hand and most of us have many more than we use. Do you really need all of the fonts on your system? Do you have any idea how much disk space the fonts require? Which fonts are your favorites and where did you get them? In what type of documents are they used? Can you suggest some type of strategy for font management and selection? Answer these questions in a nicely formatted report of one to two pages.

Your First Consultant's Job

Go to a real installation—for example, a doctor's or an attorney's office, the company where you work, or the computer lab at school. Determine the backup procedures that are in effect, then write a one-page report indicating whether the policy is adequate and, if necessary, offering suggestions for improvement. Your report should be addressed to the individual in charge of the business and it should cover all aspects of the backup strategy—that is, which files are backed up and how often, and what software is used for the backup operation. Use appropriate emphasis (for example, bold italics) to identify any potential problems. This is a professional document (it is your first consultant's job), and its appearance must be perfect in every way.

3

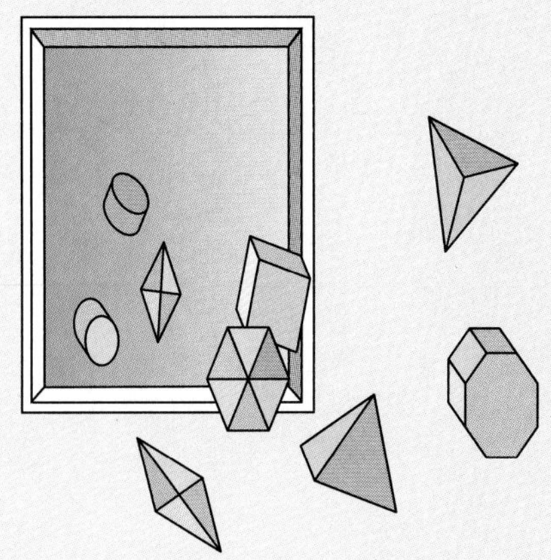

The Tools: Preparing a Résumé and Cover Letter

CHAPTER OBJECTIVES

After reading this chapter you will be able to:

1. Describe the AutoCorrect feature.
2. Implement a spell check; describe the function of the custom dictionary.
3. Use the thesaurus to look up synonyms and antonyms.
4. Explain the objectives and limitations of the grammar checker.
5. Insert symbols and a date field into a document.
6. Create an envelope.
7. Use wizards and templates to create a document.
8. Distinguish between the main document and data source used in a mail merge; create and print a set of form letters.

OVERVIEW

Is summer vacation or graduation coming close and the pressure for a job getting to you? Would you like to prepare a professional résumé and associated cover letter, and be able to mail it to multiple potential employers? In this chapter, we tell you how as we present the tools to add the finishing touches to a document and make it as error free as possible. We show you how to use a spelling checker and introduce the thesaurus as a means of adding precision to your writing. We present the grammar checker as a convenient way of finding a variety of errors but remind you that there is no substitute for carefully proofreading the final document.

The chapter is built around a résumé and the associated cover letter to a potential employer. We show you how to add the date to a letter, how to insert special symbols, and how to create and print an envelope. We present the concept of a mail merge, which takes the tedium out of sending form letters, as it creates the same letter many times, changing the addressee's name and address from letter to letter. The chapter also introduces the wizards and templates built into Word to help you create professionally formatted documents quickly and easily.

We believe this to be a very enjoyable chapter that will add significantly to your capability in Word for Windows. As always, learning is best accomplished by doing, and the hands-on exercises are essential to master the material.

THE SPELLING CHECKER

The ***spelling checker*** is an integral part of any full-featured word processor. You are well advised to use it because spelling errors make your work look sloppy and discourage the reader before he or she has read what you had to say. They can cost you a job, a grade, a lucrative contract, or an award you deserve.

The spelling checker can be used at any time; for example, to check an individual word, a block of selected text, or the document as a whole. Each word is checked against a built-in dictionary, with any mismatch (a word found in the document but not the built-in dictionary) flagged as an error.

The dictionary included with Word is limited to standard English and does not include many proper names, acronyms, abbreviations, or specialized terms, and hence, the use of any such item is considered a misspelling. You can, however, add such words to a ***custom dictionary*** so that they will not be flagged in the future. You can also purchase specialized dictionaries containing medical or legal terminology, or even a foreign language dictionary. The spelling checker will inform you of repeated words and irregular capitalization. It cannot, however, flag properly spelled words that are used improperly, and thus cannot tell you that *Two bee or knot too be* is not the answer.

The spelling checker is called from the Tools menu or by clicking the Spell Check icon on the Standard toolbar. Its capabilities are illustrated in conjunction with the text in Figure 3.1a. The spelling checker goes through the document and returns the errors one at a time, offering several options for each mistake. You can change the misspelled word to one of the alternatives suggested by Word, leave the word as is, or you can add the word to a custom dictionary.

The first error is *embarassing* with Word's suggestion(s) for correction displayed in the list box in Figure 3.1b. To accept the highlighted suggestion, click the ***Change command button*** and the substitution will be made automatically in the document. To accept an alternate suggestion, click the desired word, then click the Change command button. You can also click the AutoCorrect button so that in the future, the mistake will be corrected as it is typed, as described in the next section.

The spelling checker detects both irregular capitalization and duplicated words as shown in Figures 3.1c and 3.1d, respectively. The error in Figure 3.1e, *Grauer,* is not a misspelling per se, but a proper noun not found in the standard dictionary. No correction is required, and the appropriate action is to skip the word (taking no further action)—or better yet, add it to the custom dictionary so that it will not be flagged in future sessions. And finally, we could not resist including the example in Figure 3.1f, which shows another use of the spelling checker.

A spelling checker will catch embarassing mistakes, iRregular capitalization, and duplicate words words. It will also flag proper nouns, for example Robert Grauer, but you can add these terms to an auxiliary dictionary so that they will not be flagged in the future. It will not, however, notice properly spelled words that are used incorrectly; for example, Two bee or knot to be is not the answer.

(a) The Text

FIGURE 3.1 The Spelling Checker

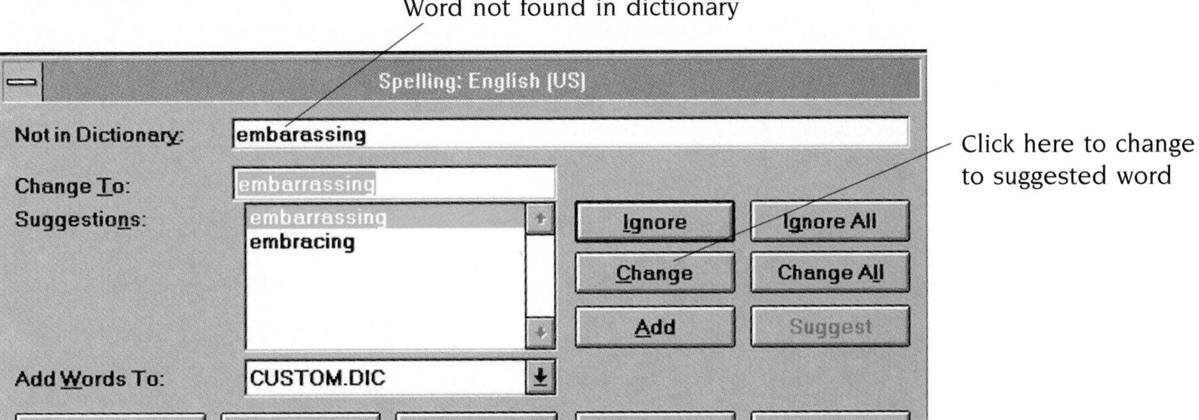

(b) Ordinary Misspelling

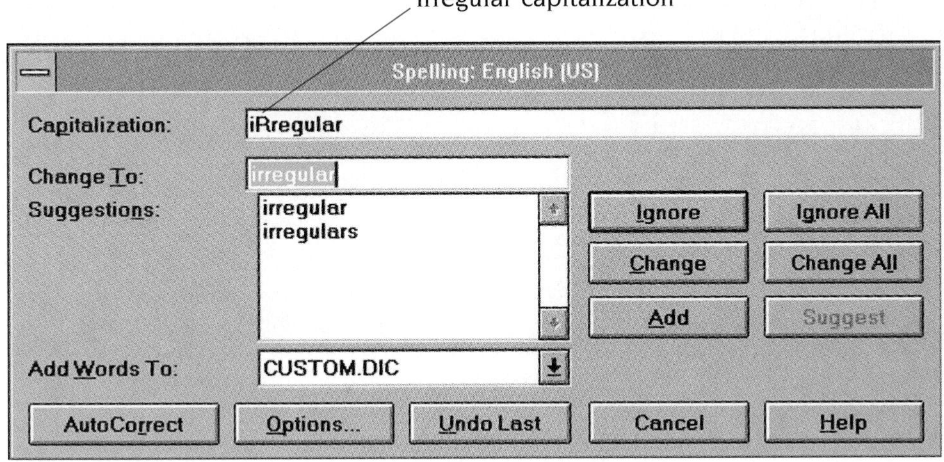

(c) Irregular Capitalization

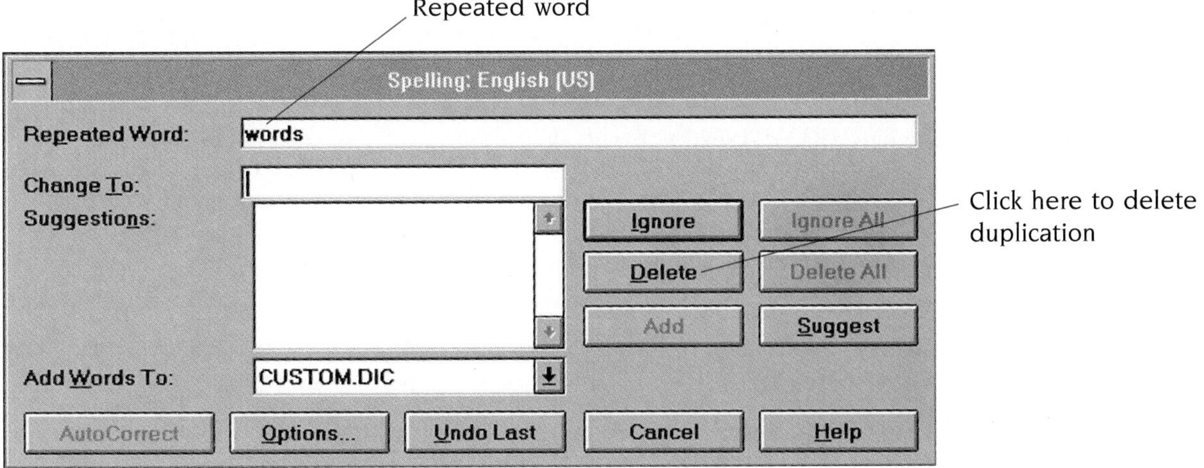

(d) Duplicated Word

FIGURE 3.1 The Spelling Checker (continued)

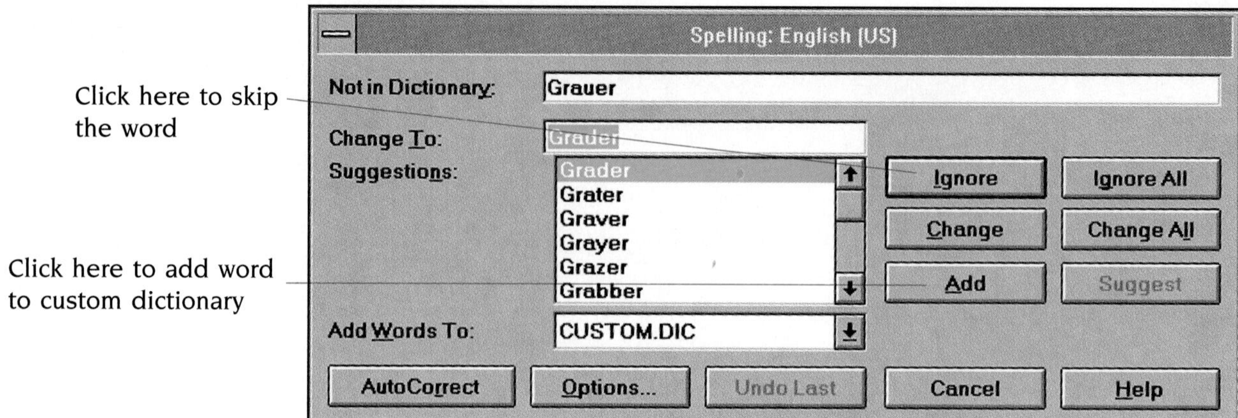

(e) Proper Noun

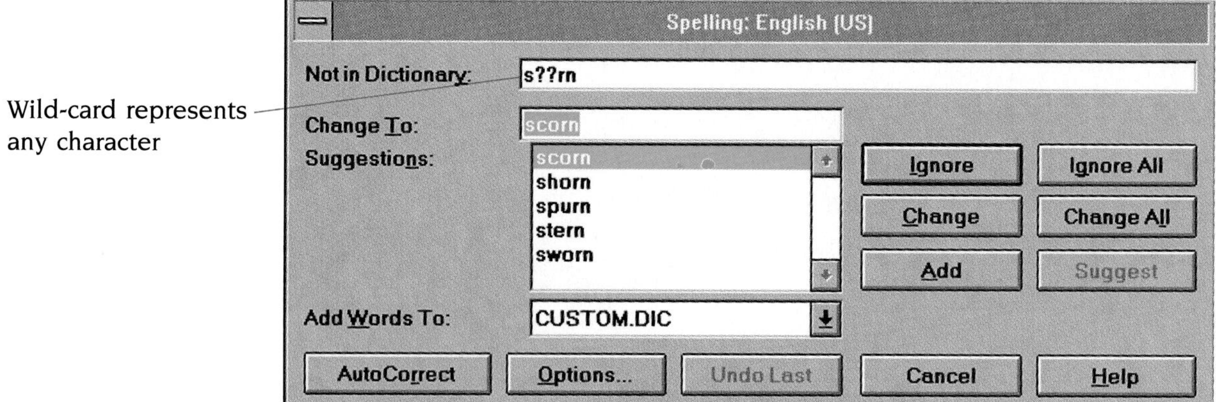

(f) Help with Crosswords

FIGURE 3.1 The Spelling Checker (continued)

HELP IN CROSSWORDS

Quick, what is a five-letter word, meaning severe or firm, with the pattern S _ _ R N? If you answered stern, you don't need our help. But if not, you might want to use the spelling checker to come up with the answer. Type the pattern using a question mark for each unknown character—for example, S??RN—then click the spelling checker icon on the toolbar. Word will return all of the matching words in the dictionary (scorn, shorn, spurn, stern, and sworn). It's then a simple matter to pick out the word that fits.

AutoCorrect

The ***AutoCorrect feature*** corrects mistakes as they are made without any effort on your part. It makes you a better typist. If, for example, you typed *teh* instead of *the,* Word would change the spelling without even telling you. Word will also change *adn* to *and, i* to *I,* and occu*r*ence to occu*rr*ence.

Word includes a predefined table of common mistakes and uses that table to make substitutions whenever it encounters an error it recognizes. You can add additional items to the table to include the frequent errors you make. You can also use the feature to define your own shorthand; for example, *cis* for Computer Information Systems as shown in Figure 3.2.

The AutoCorrect feature will change ordinary quotes (" ") to smart quotes (“ ”). It will also correct mistakes in capitalization; for example, it will capitalize the first letter in a sentence, recognize that MIami should be Miami, and capitalize the days of the week.

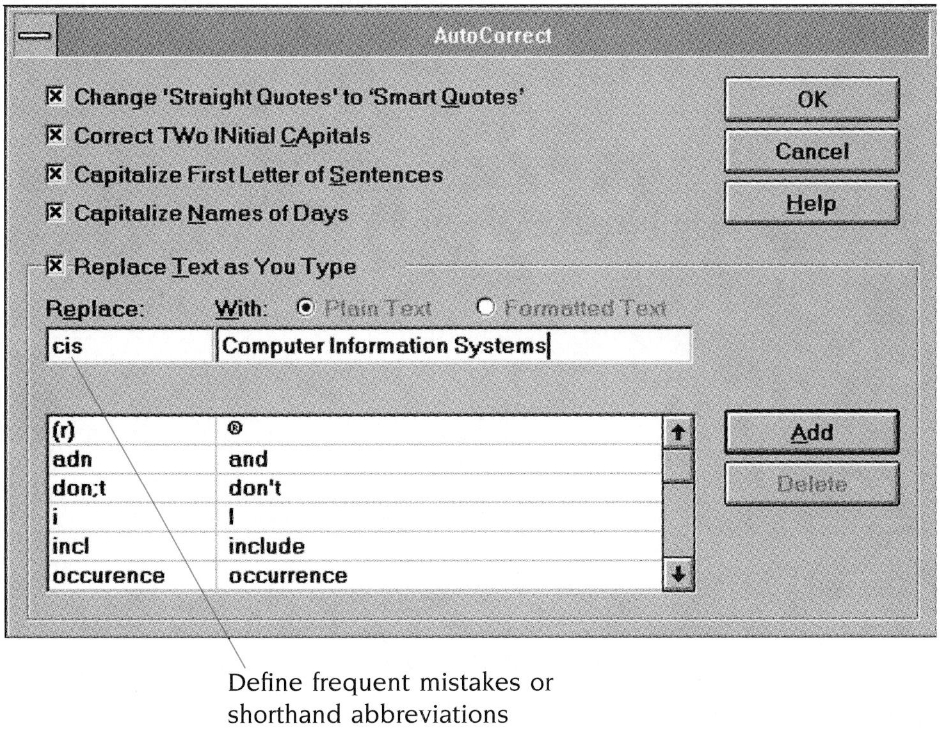

Define frequent mistakes or shorthand abbreviations

FIGURE 3.2 AutoCorrect

THESAURUS

Mark Twain said the difference between the right word and almost the right word is the difference between a lightning bug and lightning. The ***thesaurus*** is the second major tool in a word processor, and to our way of thinking, is as essential as a spelling checker. The thesaurus is both fun and educational; it helps you to avoid repetition, and it polishes your writing.

The thesaurus is called from the Tools menu (or with the **Shift+F7** keyboard equivalent). You position the cursor at the appropriate word within the document, then invoke the thesaurus and follow your instincts. The thesaurus recognizes multiple meanings and forms of a word (for example, adjective, noun, and verb) as in Figure 3.3a, and (by double clicking) allows you to look up any listed meaning to produce additional choices as in Figure 3.3b.

Substitutions in the document are made automatically by selecting the desired ***synonym*** and clicking the ***Replace button.*** You can explore further alternatives by selecting a synonym and clicking on the ***Look Up button.*** The thesaurus also provides a list of ***antonyms*** for most entries as in Figure 3.3c.

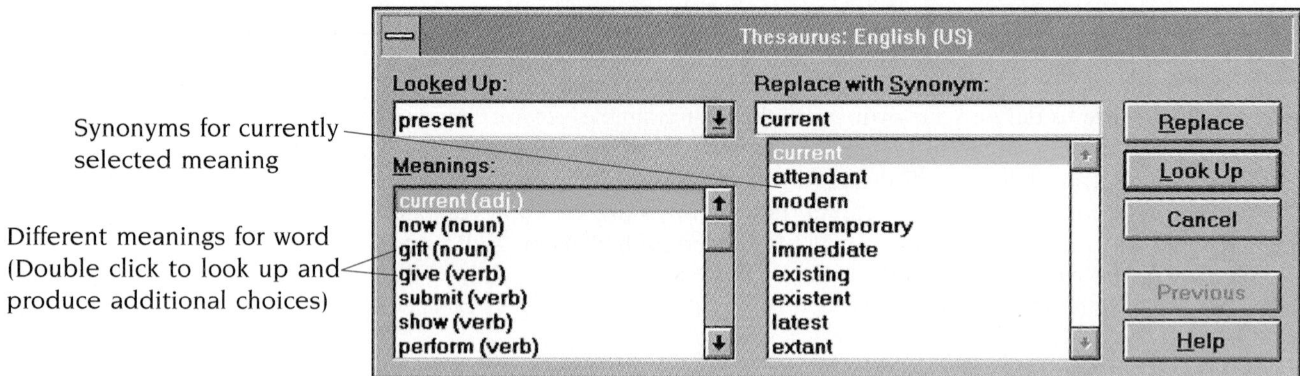

(a) Initial Word

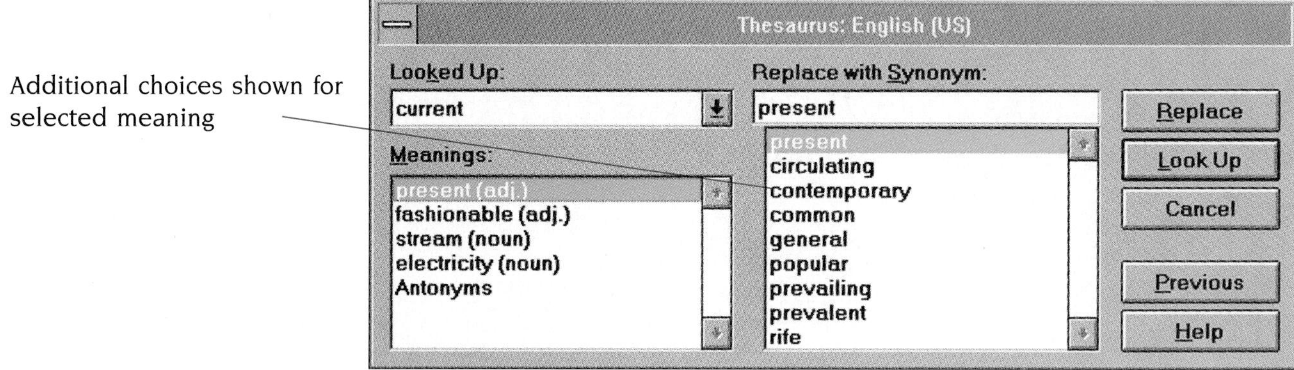

(b) Alternate Forms

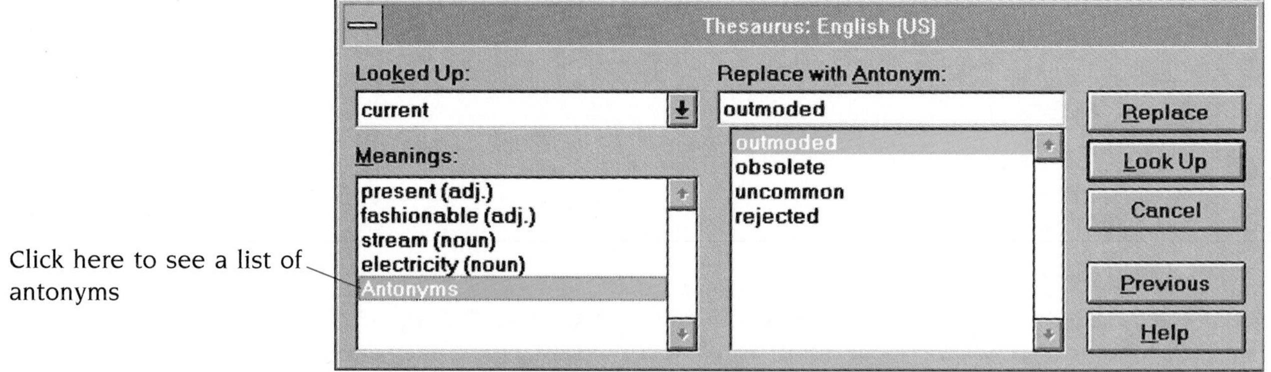

(c) Antonyms

FIGURE 3.3 The Thesaurus

GRAMMAR CHECKER

The ***grammar checker*** attempts to catch mistakes in punctuation, writing style, and word usage by comparing strings of text within a document to a series of predefined rules. As with the spelling checker, errors are brought to the screen where you can accept the suggested correction and make the replacement automatically, or more often, edit the highlighted text and make your own changes.

You can also ask the grammar checker to explain the rule it is attempting to enforce. Unlike a spelling checker the grammar checker is subjective, and what seems appropriate to you may be objectionable to someone else. The English language is also too complex for the grammar checker to detect every error, although it will find many errors.

The grammar checker caught the inconsistent phrase in Figure 3.4a and suggested the appropriate correction (*catch* instead of *catches*). In Figure 3.4b, it suggested the elimination of the superfluous comma. These examples show the grammar checker at its best, but much of the time it is more subjective and less capable. It objects, for example, to the phrase *all men are created equal* in Figure 3.4c, citing excessive use of the passive voice; whether or not you accept the suggestion is entirely up to you. Note, too, that the entire paragraph in Figure 3.4d went through without error, showing that there is simply no substitute for carefully proofreading every document.

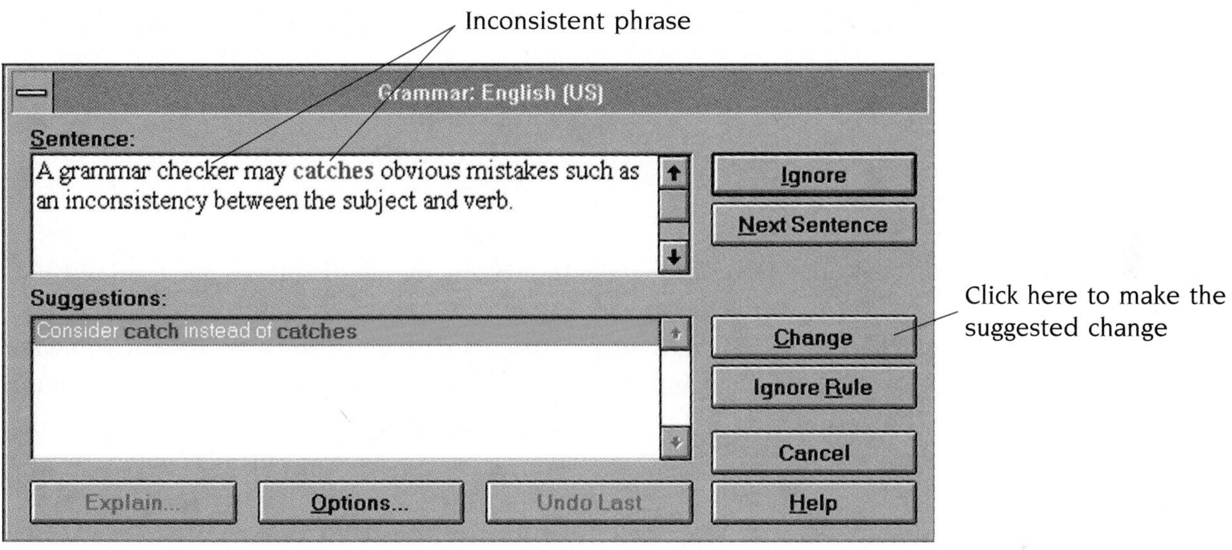

(a) Inconsistent Verb

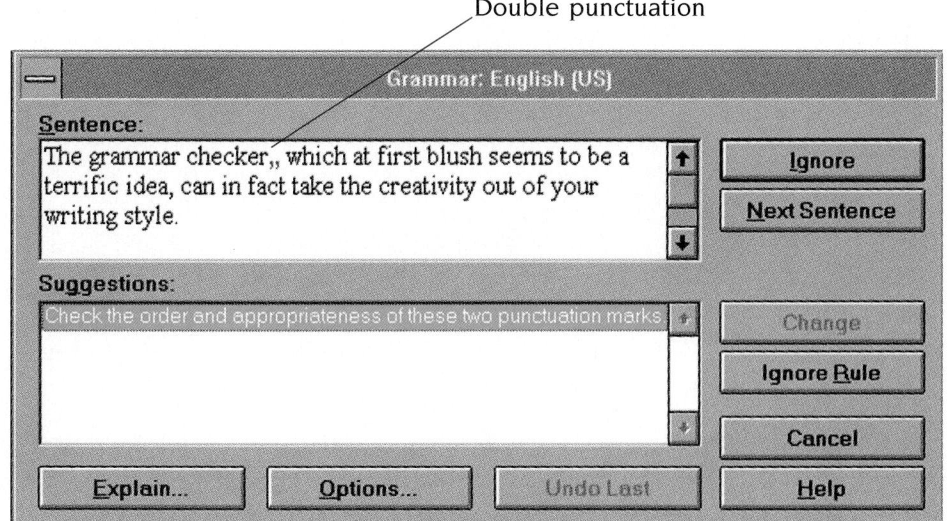

(b) Doubled Punctuation

FIGURE 3.4 The Grammar Checker

Click here to ignore suggestion

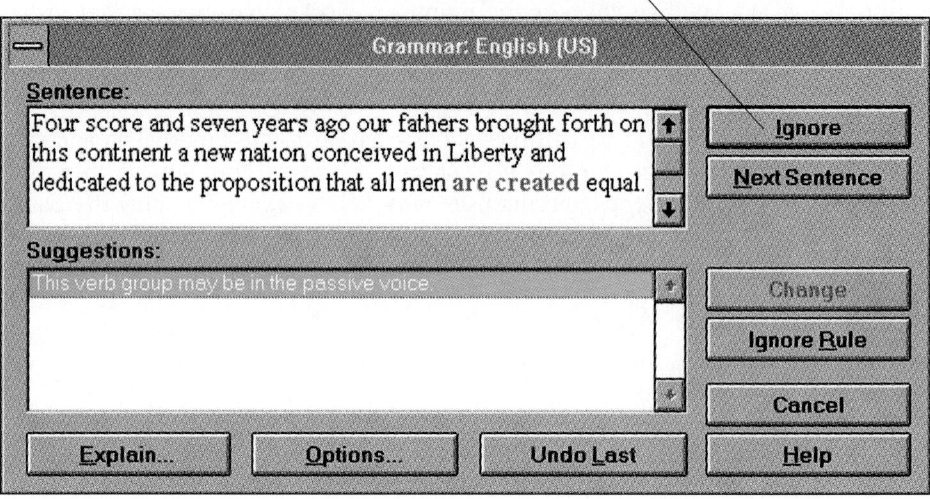

(c) Subjective Rules

Most items are not notice because English is just to complicated and the grammar program will accept this entire paragraph even though it contains many errors and this sentence is very long and the paragraph does not make any cents. It did not find any mistakes in the next sentence that used notice rather than noticed, to instead of too, and cents instead of sense. It does not object to misplaced tenses such as yesterday I will go to the store or tomorrow I went to the store.

(d) Limitations

FIGURE 3.4 The Grammar Checker (continued)

CASUAL OR BUSINESS WRITING

Word enables you to change almost every aspect of its environment to suit your personal preference. One option you may want to change is the rules in effect within the grammar checker—for example, whether Word should check for business or casual writing. Pull down the Tools menu, click Options, then click the Grammar tab. Choose the option(s) you want, then click OK.

LEARNING BY DOING

The hands-on exercise that follows shortly is based on the cover letter and accompanying résumé shown in Figure 3.5. The cover letter includes the date and requires an envelope in which it can be mailed. Both requirements are used to introduce additional capabilities within Word for Windows.

ELVIS AARON PRESLEY
1 Graceland Mansion
Memphis, Tennessee

Professional Objective

To emerge from hiding and perform once more before live audiences at major Las Vegas night clubs

Academic Background

1953 - Graduated from Humes High School, Memphis, Tennessee

Work Experience

1954 - 1977, Featured Singer - Concert Circuit
Traveled extensively on the concert circuit, including 22 club appearances in Las Vegas and Lake Tahoe

1956 - 1977, Recording Artist
Recorded 72 albums, including *Loving You, Elvis' Christmas Album, Elvis Is Back, G.I. Blues, Blue Hawaii, Elvis for Everyone, How Great Thou Art, Worldwide 50 Gold Award Hits, Moody Blues*

1956 - 1972, Recording Artist
Recorded 38 Top Ten hits, 18 of which climbed to #1 on the chart, including *Heartbreak Hotel, Hound Dog, Don't Be Cruel, Love Me Tender, All Shook Up, Teddy Bear, Jailhouse Rock, Hard Headed Woman, Stuck on You, It's Now or Never, Are You Lonesome Tonight, Good Luck Charm,* and *Suspicious Minds.*

1956 - 1972, Movie and Television Star
Performed in 38 feature length movies, including *Love Me Tender, Jailhouse Rock, Blue Hawaii, Viva Las Vegas, The Trouble with Girls,* and *Elvis on Tour.*

Featured on 15 television shows, including *The Milton Berle Show, The Steve Allen Show, Ed Sullivan's Toast of the Town,* and the *Today Show.*

1958 - 1960, Soldier, United States Army
Served in the United States Army as a tank crewman with the Third Armored Division. Stationed in Germany.

Honors

Picture placed on United States Postage Stamp
3 Grammy Awards
Male Entertainer of the Year

References

Colonel Thomas Andrew Parker, Manager
John Q. Public, Elvis Impersonator's Association
Priscilla Presley, Actress

(a) Résumé

FIGURE 3.5 The Presley Comeback

ELVIS PRESLEY

Graceland Mansion
Memphis, TN 38116
(901) 332-3322

November 28, 1993

Mr. David Letterman
1697 Broadway
New York, NY 10019

Dear Mr. Letterman,

I am seeking an engagement as the lead act at a Las Vegas night club. I have extensive experience both in private clubs and road tours throughout the United States, and have enclosed my résumé for your review.

It has been some time since I have been in the public eye, but I have never stopped singing or living my music. I am well aware of current trends and have many new songs that will, without question, catch the public's imagination. Everyone needs a gimmick in today's market and I have several extraordinary ideas in mind.

I would welcome the opportunity to meet you to discuss my ideas and audition my new act. Please contact me at the above address or call me at 1-800-HOUND-DOG. I look forward to hearing from you.

Sincerely,

Elvis

(b) Cover Letter

FIGURE 3.5 The Presley Comeback (continued)

THIRTY SECONDS IS ALL YOU HAVE . . .

Thirty seconds is the average amount of time a personnel manager spends skimming your résumé and deciding whether or not to call you for an interview. It doesn't matter how much training you've had or how good you are if your résumé and cover letter fail to project a professional image. Know your audience and use the vocabulary of your targeted field. Be positive and describe your experience from an accomplishment point of view. Maintain a separate list of references and have it available on request. Be sure all information is accurate. Be conscientious about the design of your résumé, and proofread the final documents very carefully.

The Insert Date Command

The ***Insert Date command*** puts the date (and/or time) into a document. The date is not inserted as a specific value, but as a ***field*** (or code) that is updated automatically when the document is printed. (The date may also be updated manually by the appropriate command from a pull-down or shortcut menu.) Word recognizes the entry in the document as a ***date field*** and retrieves the date from the computer's internal clock, saving you the work of manually updating the document.

The date may be printed in a variety of formats as shown in Figure 3.6. Note that the Insert as Field box is checked, so that the date is inserted as a field. If the box were not checked, the date would be inserted as ***date text*** and would remain the same, regardless of when the document is retrieved.

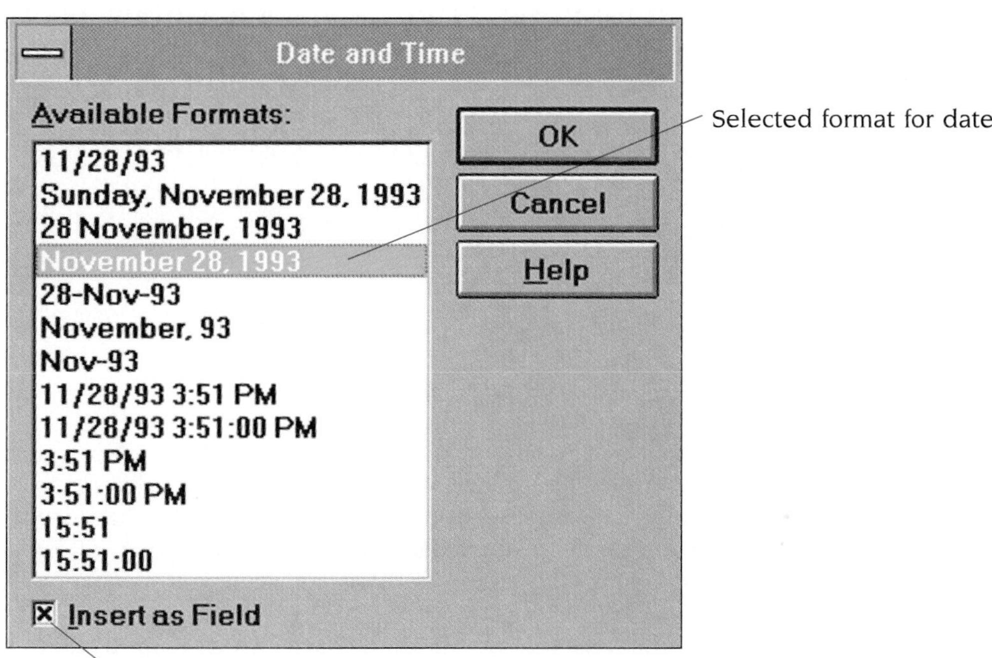

FIGURE 3.6 Insert Date and Time Command

> **DAYLIGHT SAVINGS TIME**
>
> The date field uses the computer's internal clock and calendar to obtain the current time and date. But what if your computer has the wrong information? Open the Main group in Program Manager, double click the Control Panel icon, then double click the Date/Time icon to open a dialog box. Enter the correct time and date, click OK to accept the new settings, then close the Control Panel application.

The Insert Symbol Command

One quality that distinguishes the professional document is the use of typographic characters or foreign language symbols; for example, ™ rather than TM, © rather than (C), or ½ and ¼, rather than 1/2 and 1/4. Many of these symbols are contained within the Wingdings or Symbols fonts that are supplied with Windows.

The ***Insert Symbol command*** provides easy access to all of the fonts installed on your system. Choose the font—for example, Wingdings in Figure 3.7—select the desired symbol, then click the Insert command button to place the character into the document. Remember, too, that TrueType fonts are scalable, from 4 to 127 points, enabling you to create some truly unusual documents.

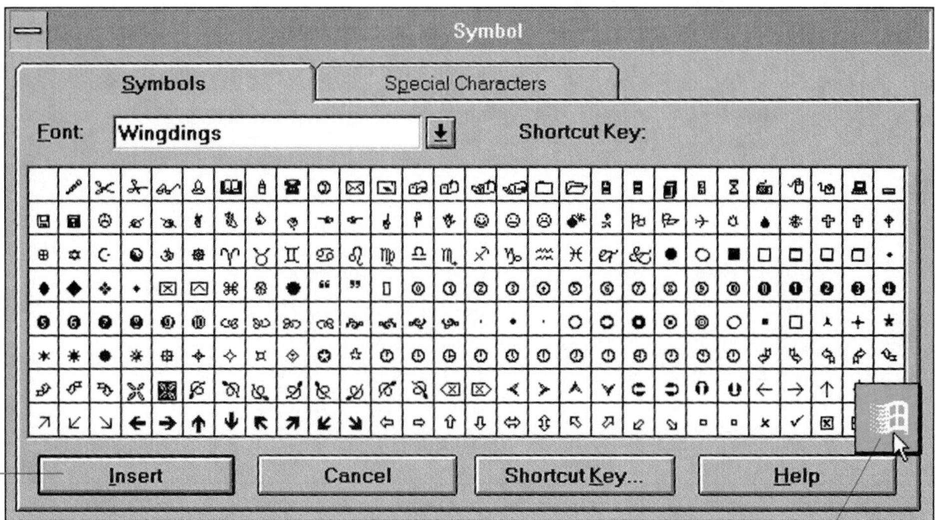

FIGURE 3.7 Insert Symbol Command

Creating an Envelope

Anyone who has used a word processor knows that printing an envelope poses potential problems in that the physical document (the envelope) is a different size than the letter it will contain. Word saves you the trouble of having to change margins and orientation by providing the ***Envelopes and Labels command*** in the Tools menu. Execution of the command produces a dialog box where you supply or edit the necessary addresses. Word takes care of the rest.

The addressee's information can be taken directly from the cover letter as described in step 8 of the following exercise. The return address can be entered directly in the dialog box, or it can be selected from a set of previously stored return addresses. Word also lets you choose from different size envelopes; it will even supply the postal bar code if you request that option.

HANDS-ON EXERCISE 1:

Proofing a Document

Objective To use the auto correction, spelling checker, thesaurus, and grammar checker; to insert the date and special symbols into a document; to create (and print) an envelope. Use Figure 3.8 as a guide.

Step 1: Load the practice document

- Pull down the **File menu** and click **Open** (or click the **File Open button** on the Standard toolbar).
- If you have not yet changed the default directory:
  - — Click the appropriate drive.
  - — Scroll through the directory list box until you come to the **WORDDATA** directory.
  - — Double click the **WORDDATA** directory.
- Double click **ELVISBEF.DOC** to open the document.
- Pull down the **File menu.** Click the **Save As** command to save the document as **ELVISAFT.DOC.** Click **OK.**
- The title bar reflects **ELVISAFT.DOC,** but you can always return to the original document if you edit the duplicated file beyond redemption.
- If necessary, change to the **Normal view** at **Page Width.**

Step 2: The date field

- Point to the date, click the **right mouse button** to produce the shortcut menu shown in Figure 3.8a, then click **Update Field.** The document displays today's date rather than the date in our letter because the date was inserted into the document as a field rather than text.
- Click anywhere in the date; the date is displayed in gray to indicate it is a field and not text.
- Press **Shift+F9** and the date is displayed as a date field.
- Press **Shift+F9** a second time and the field is replaced by the formatted date.

FIELD CODES VERSUS FIELD RESULTS

All fields are displayed in a document in one of two formats, as a ***field code*** or as a ***field result.*** A field code appears in braces and indicates instructions to insert variable data when the document is printed; a field result displays the information as it will appear in the printed document. You can toggle the display between the field code and field result by pressing **Shift+F9** during editing.

Step 3: AutoCorrect

- The phrase, *as the lead act,* has been omitted in the first sentence of the letter.
- Be sure you are in the insertion mode. Click immediately before the word *at* in the first line of the letter.
- Type the *misspelled* phrase **as teh lead act.** Try to look at the monitor as you type the word *teh* to see the AutoCorrect feature in action; Word will correct the misspelling and change *teh* to *the.*

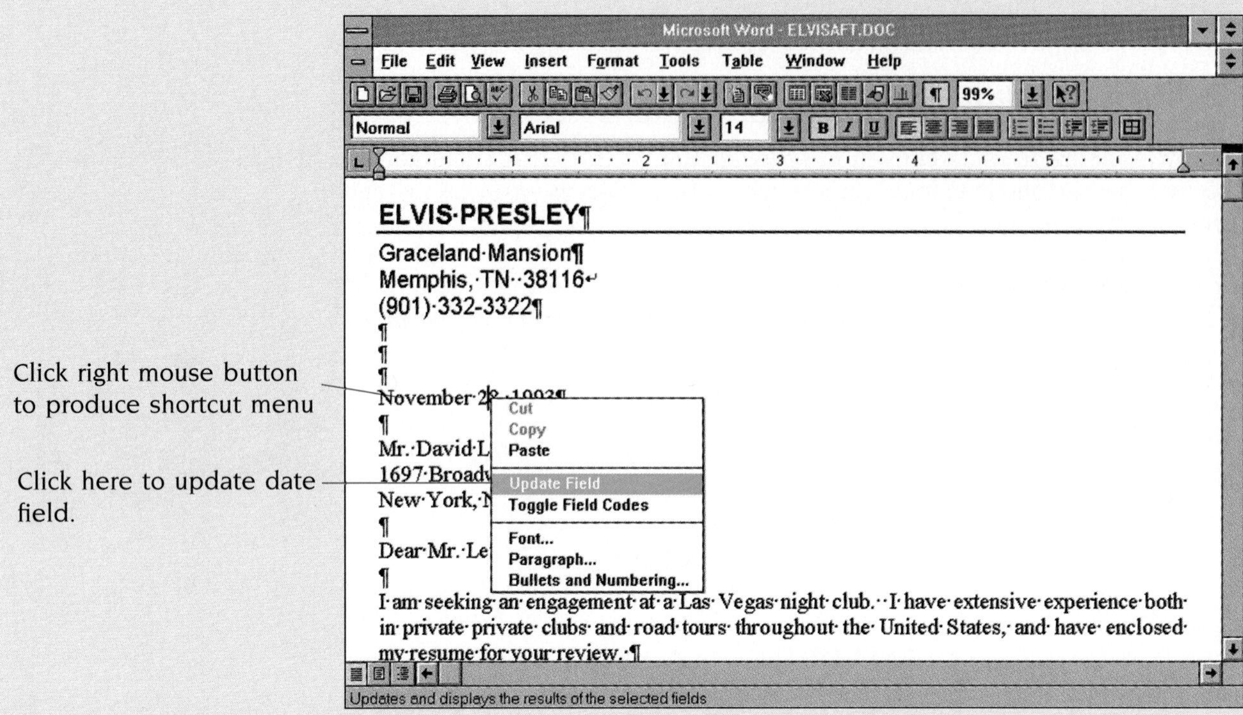

(a) The Date Field (step 2)

FIGURE 3.8 Hands-on Exercise 1

- If you did not see the correction being made, click the arrow next to the Undo command on the Standard toolbar and undo the last several actions. Click the arrow next to the Redo command and redo the corrections in order to see the typing and auto correction.
- Save the file.

> **CREATE YOUR OWN SHORTHAND**
>
> Use AutoCorrect to expand abbreviations such as "usa" for United States of America. Pull down the Tools menu, click AutoCorrect, type the abbreviation and the expanded entry, then click the Add command button. Click OK to exit the dialog box and return to the document. The next time you type usa in a document, it will automatically be expanded to the United States of America.

Step 4: The spelling checker

- Press **Ctrl+Home** to move to the beginning of the document.
- Pull down the **Tools menu.** Click **Spelling** (or click the **Spelling icon** on the toolbar) to initiate the spelling check. Presley is flagged as the first misspelling as shown in Figure 3.8b.
- Click the **Ignore command button** to accept Presley as written (or click the Add command button to add Presley to the custom dictionary). Ignore Graceland as well (or add it to the custom dictionary).

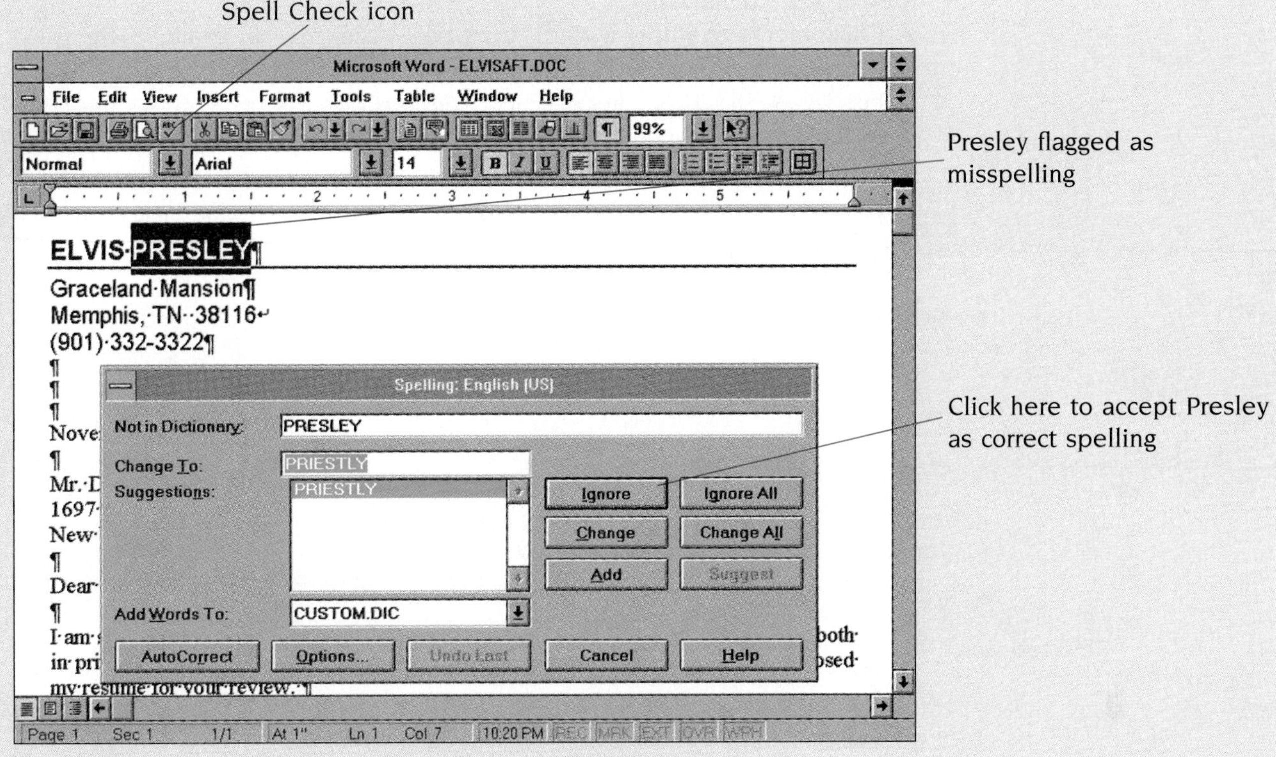

(b) The Spell Check (step 4)

FIGURE 3.8 Hands-on Exercise 1 (continued)

- Continue checking the document, which returns misspellings and other irregularities one at a time. Click the appropriate command button as each mistake is found:
  - — Click **Delete** to delete the second occurrence of the repeated word (private).
  - — Click **Change** to correct the irregular capitalization in everyone.
  - — Click **Change** to accept the correct spelling for gimmick.
  - — Click **Change** to accept the correct spelling for Sincerely.
- Click **OK** when the spelling check is complete.
- Save the document.

THE CUSTOM DICTIONARY

It's easy to add a word to the custom dictionary, but how do you delete a word if you've added it incorrectly? Word anticipates the problem and allows you to edit the custom dictionary as an ordinary Word document. Pull down the Tools menu, click Options, and select the Spelling tab. Click the custom dictionary you want (if there is more than one), click Edit, click Yes, then click OK. Make the necessary changes, save the file as text, then be sure to close the custom dictionary so that it is available the next time you run a spell check.

Step 5: The thesaurus

- Click anywhere within a word you wish to change—for example, the word **magnificent** in Figure 3.8c.
- Pull down the **Tools menu.** Click **Thesaurus** to display synonyms for the selected word (magnificent) as shown in the figure.
- Double click **grand** (in either list box) to display synonyms for this word.
- Click the **Previous command button** to return to the original synonyms for magnificent.
- Click **extraordinary** in the list of synonyms. Click **Replace.**
- Change other words as you see fit; for example, we changed **chance** to **opportunity.**
- Save the document.

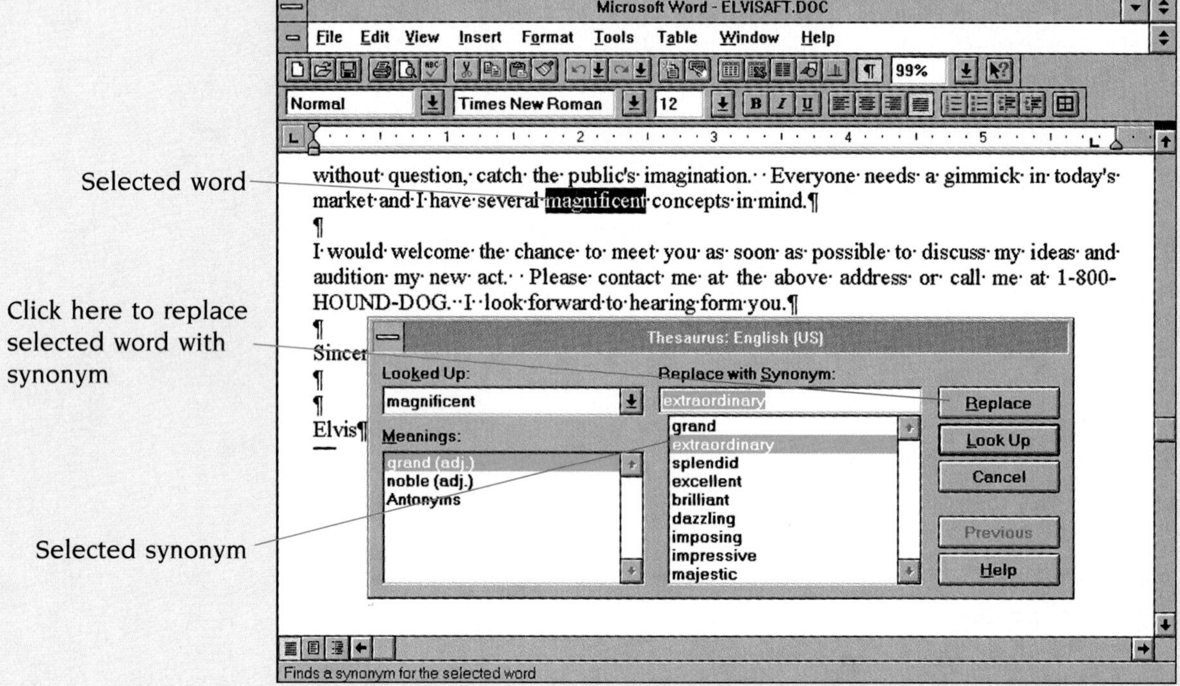

(c) The Thesaurus (step 5)

FIGURE 3.8 Hands-on Exercise 1 (continued)

TO CLICK OR DOUBLE CLICK

The thesaurus displays the different meanings and forms of the selected word. Click any meaning, and its synonyms appear in the synonym list box in the right of the window. Double click any meaning or synonym, and Word will look up the selected word and provide additional meanings and synonyms.

Step 6: The grammar checker

- Pull down the **Tools menu.** Click **Options.** Click the **Grammar tab** to customize the grammar checker.

- Click **Strictly (all rules).** Clear the box to **Check Spelling.** If necessary, click the box to **Show Readability statistics.**
- Click **OK.** Your options match ours and your results should match the steps in this exercise.
- Press **Ctrl+Home** to move to the beginning of the document.
- Pull down the **Tools menu** a second time. Click **Grammar** to begin checking the document. Suggestions for correction will be returned one at a time; you can accept or reject the suggestions as you see fit.
- Click the **Explain button** at any time to display an explanation of the rule as shown in Figure 3.8d. (Double click the **control-menu box** to close the explanation window.) We elected to keep the phrase *in the public eye* by clicking the **Ignore button,** but we accepted the next suggestion to change *concepts* to ideas.
- We deleted the phrase *as soon as possible,* by clicking in the document, selecting the phrase *as soon as possible,* and pressing the **Del key.**
- The grammar checker is not perfect, but it does detect one very significant error: the incorrect use of *form* rather than *from* in the last sentence.
- Click **OK** after viewing the readability statistics to return to the document.
- Save the document.

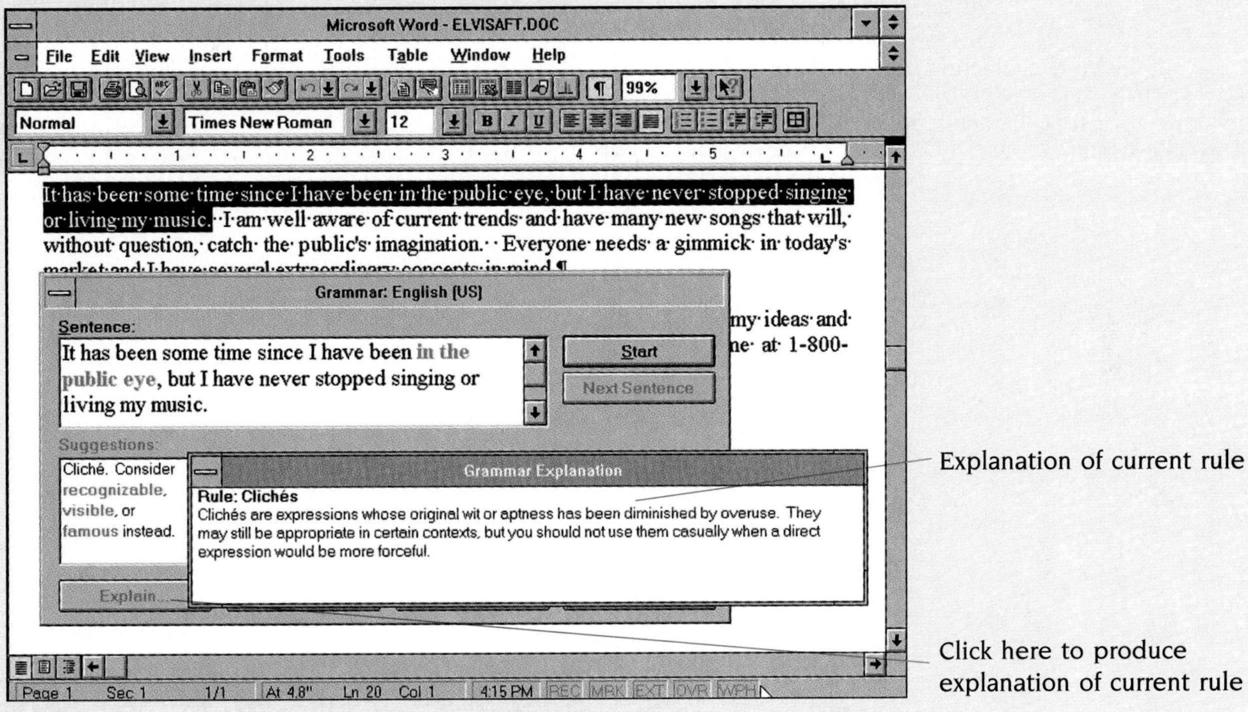

(d) The Grammar Checker (step 6)

FIGURE 3.8 Hands-on Exercise 1 (continued)

Step 7: Special characters

- The proper spelling of résumé places accents over both e's. Click before the first e in resume (in the first paragraph of the letter).
- Pull down the **Insert menu,** click **Symbol,** and choose **normal text** from the Font list box.

➤ Click the **é** as shown in Figure 3.8e. Click the **Insert button** to insert the character into the document.

➤ Click in the document window and delete the unaccented e. Click before the second e. Click **Insert.** Click **Close.** Delete the second unaccented e.

➤ Save the document.

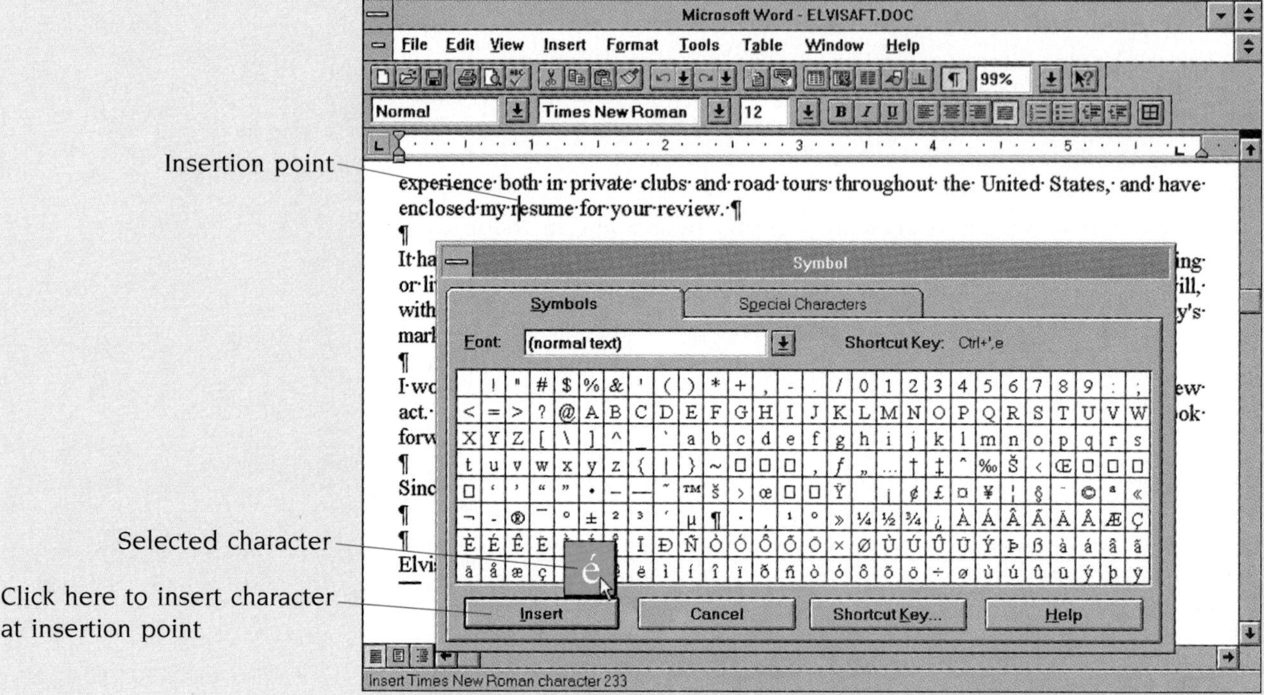

(e) Special Characters (step 7)

FIGURE 3.8 Hands-on Exercise 1 (continued)

Step 8: Create an envelope

➤ Pull down the **Tools menu.** Click **Envelopes and Labels** to produce the dialog box in Figure 3.8f.

➤ David Letterman's address should already be on the envelope because Word inserts the first address it finds; if this is not the case, just type the address yourself. Enter the return address as well.

➤ Click the **Add to document** command button. Click **Yes** or **No** depending on whether you want to change the default return address.

CUSTOMIZE THE TOOLBAR

The envelope button is a perfect addition to the Standard toolbar if you print envelopes frequently. Pull down the Tools menu, click Customize, then click the Toolbars tab in the dialog box. If necessary, click the arrow in the Categories list box, select Tools, then drag the envelope button to the Standard toolbar. Click Close. Click the envelope button the next time you need to create an envelope or label.

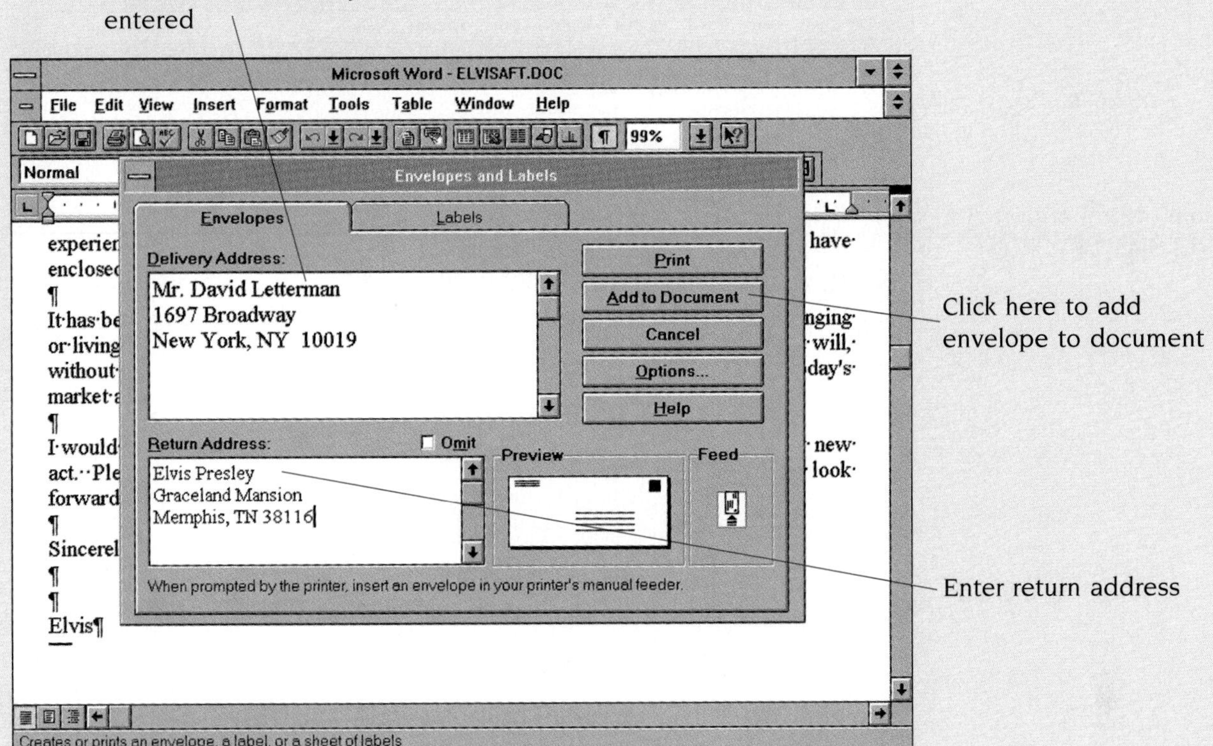

(f) Creating an Envelope (step 8)

FIGURE 3.8 Hands-on Exercise 1 (continued)

Step 9: The Completed Document

- Click the **Page Layout icon** on the status bar. Click the **Zoom control arrow** on the Standard toolbar and select **Two Pages.** You should see the completed letter and envelope as shown in Figure 3.8g.
- Do *not* print the envelope unless you can manually feed an envelope to the printer.
- Click the page containing the letter (page two in our document)
- Pull down the **File menu.** Click **Print.** Click the **Current Page command button.** Click **OK** to print only the letter.
- Pull down the **File menu.** Click **Close** to close the document, saving it if prompted.
- You are still in Word and ready to begin the next exercise.

PRINT SELECTED PAGES

Why print an entire document if you want only a few pages? Pull down the File menu and click Print as you usually do to initiate the printing process. Click the Pages option button, then enter the page numbers and/or page ranges you want; for example, 3, 6-8 will print page three and pages six through eight.

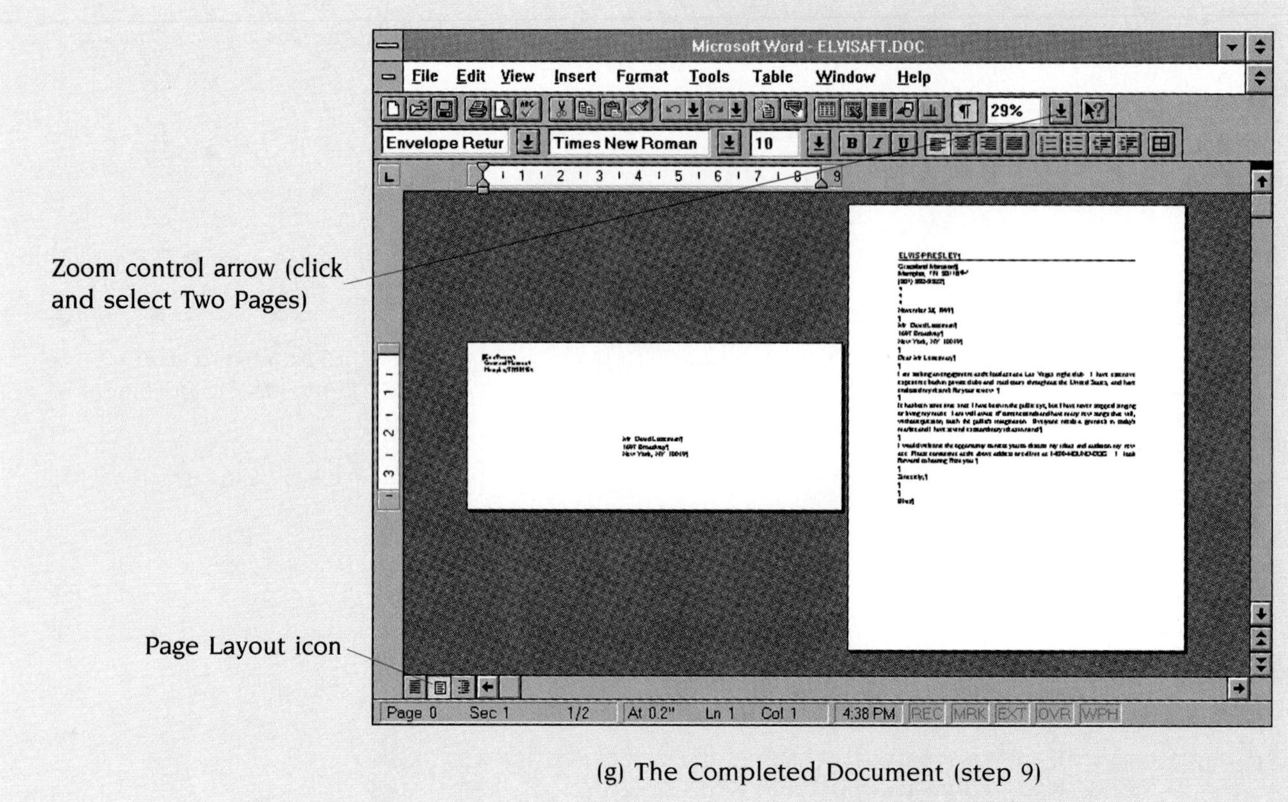

(g) The Completed Document (step 9)

FIGURE 3.8 Hands-on Exercise 1 (continued)

WIZARDS AND TEMPLATES

The letter to David Letterman and the accompanying résumé were based on designs (templates) provided by Word. Elvis supplied the content but Word took care of the formatting. That left Elvis free to concentrate on the message he wanted to deliver.

A ***template*** is a partially completed document that contains formatting, text, and/or graphics. It may be as simple as a memo or as complex as a résumé or newsletter. Word provides a variety of templates for common documents including a letter, memo, report, or fax cover sheet. You can design your own templates or you can use the ones built into Word. (Every document is in fact based on a general-purpose template known as the Normal Document Template; that is, unless you choose a different template, Word will base each new document on the Normal template.)

A ***wizard*** attempts to make the process even easier, by asking questions, then creating the template for you. Word supplies eight different wizards: Agenda, Award, Calendar, Fax Cover Sheet, Letter, Memo, Newsletter, and Résumé, four of which are illustrated in Figure 3.9.

Wizards and templates help you to create professionally designed documents, but they are only a beginning. The content is still up to you. Some wizards are easier to use than others. The calendar wizard, for example, asks you for the month, year, and type of calendar, then completes the document for you. The Fax Cover Sheet, Agenda, and Award wizards create a template, but require you to enter additional information. The ***Résumé wizard*** is more complex and requires a knowledge of styles in order to be used effectively. (Styles are covered in Chapter 4.)

	Sun	Mon	Tue	Wed	Thu	Fri	Sat
November		1	2	3	4	5	6
	7	8	9	10	11	12	13
	14	15	16	17	18	19	20
	21	22	23	24	25	26	27
	28	29	30				
1993							

(a) Calendar

The King of Rock and Roll   Graceland Mansion,   Memphis, TN 38116

FAX

Date: **11/28/93**
Number of pages including cover sheet: 2

To: David Letterman
Phone: (212) 975-4321
Fax phone: (212) 975-4351
CC:

From: Elvis Presley
Phone: (901) 332-3322
Fax phone: (901) 111-2222

REMARKS: ☐ Urgent ☐ For your review ☐ Reply ASAP ☐ Please comment

Dave,

This will confirm our meeting next Tuesday and my appearance on your show on Wednesday. Attached is a preliminary agenda for the meeting.

(b) Fax Cover Sheet

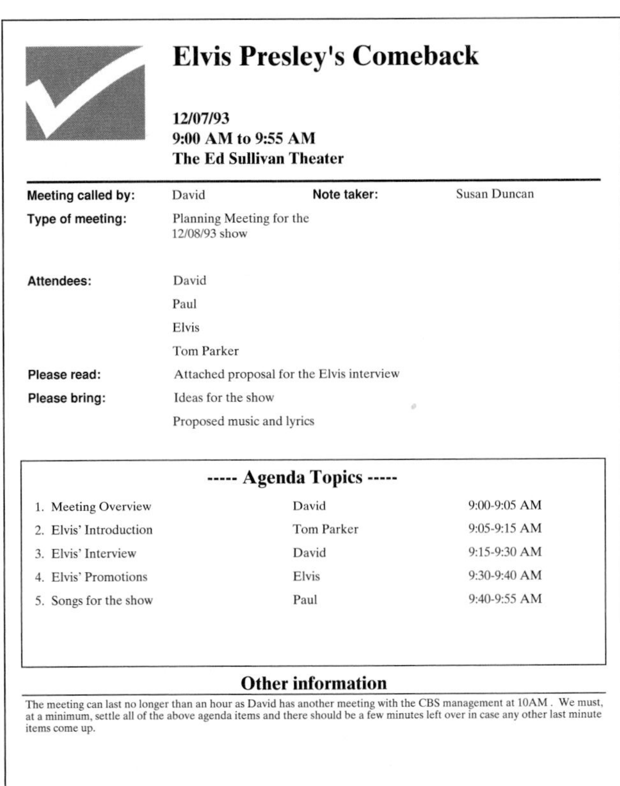

Elvis Presley's Comeback

12/07/93
9:00 AM to 9:55 AM
The Ed Sullivan Theater

Meeting called by: David   **Note taker:** Susan Duncan
Type of meeting: Planning Meeting for the 12/08/93 show

Attendees: David
Paul
Elvis
Tom Parker

Please read: Attached proposal for the Elvis interview
Please bring: Ideas for the show
Proposed music and lyrics

----- Agenda Topics -----

1. Meeting Overview	David	9:00-9:05 AM
2. Elvis' Introduction	Tom Parker	9:05-9:15 AM
3. Elvis' Interview	David	9:15-9:30 AM
4. Elvis' Promotions	Elvis	9:30-9:40 AM
5. Songs for the show	Paul	9:40-9:55 AM

Other information

The meeting can last no longer than an hour as David has another meeting with the CBS management at 10AM. We must, at a minimum, settle all of the above agenda items and there should be a few minutes left over in case any other last minute items come up.

(c) Agenda

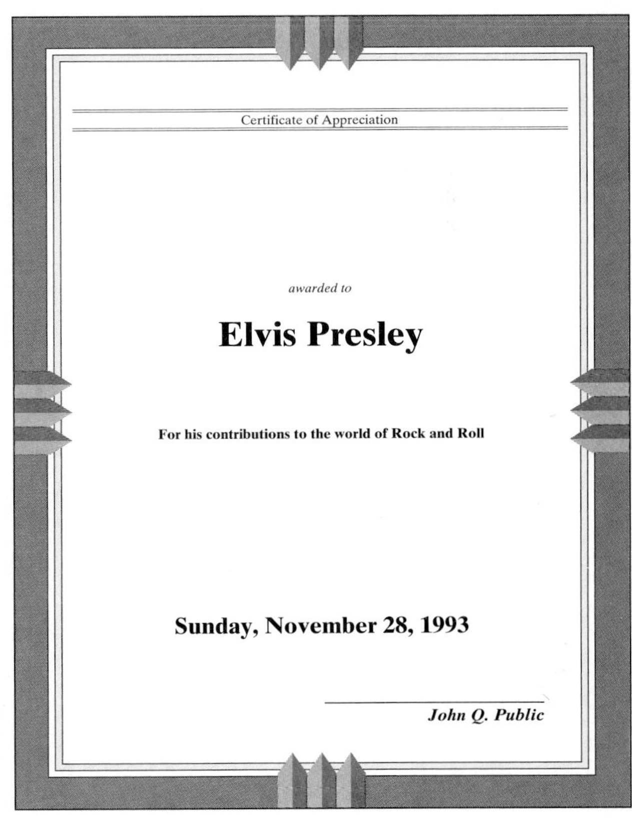

Certificate of Appreciation

awarded to

Elvis Presley

For his contributions to the world of Rock and Roll

Sunday, November 28, 1993

John Q. Public

(d) Award

FIGURE 3.9 What You Can Do with Wizards

Any document that is created with a wizard or template can be saved under its own name, then edited like any other document. Wizards and templates are illustrated in the following exercise, which also shows you how to work with multiple documents at the same time.

HANDS-ON EXERCISE 2:

Wizards and Templates

Objective To use wizards and templates to create two documents based on existing templates. To view multiple documents at the same time. Use Figure 3.10 as a guide.

Step 1: The File New command

- If necessary, change to the **Page Layout** view at **Page Width.**
- Pull down the **File menu.** Click **New** to produce the dialog box in Figure 3.10a.
- Double click **Fax Wizard** in the open list box to start the Fax Wizard.

Double click here to select the Fax Wizard

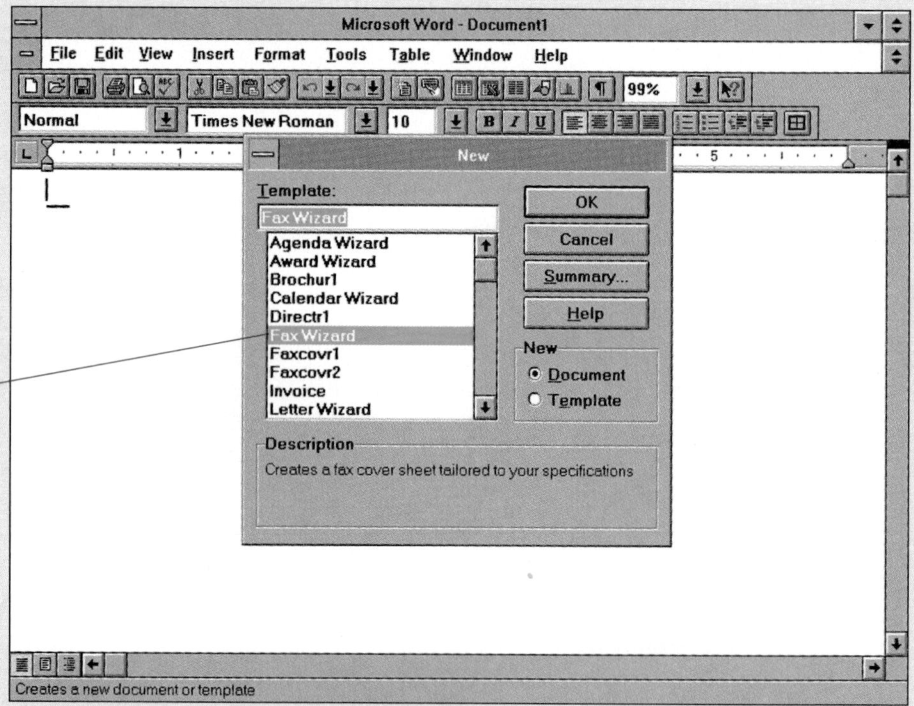

(a) The File New Command (step 1)

FIGURE 3.10 Hands-on Exercise 2

Step 2: The Fax Wizard

- The ***Fax Wizard*** asks a series of questions in order to build a template. Each question is displayed in its own screen.
- Click **Portrait** orientation as shown in Figure 3.10b. Click the **Next command button.**

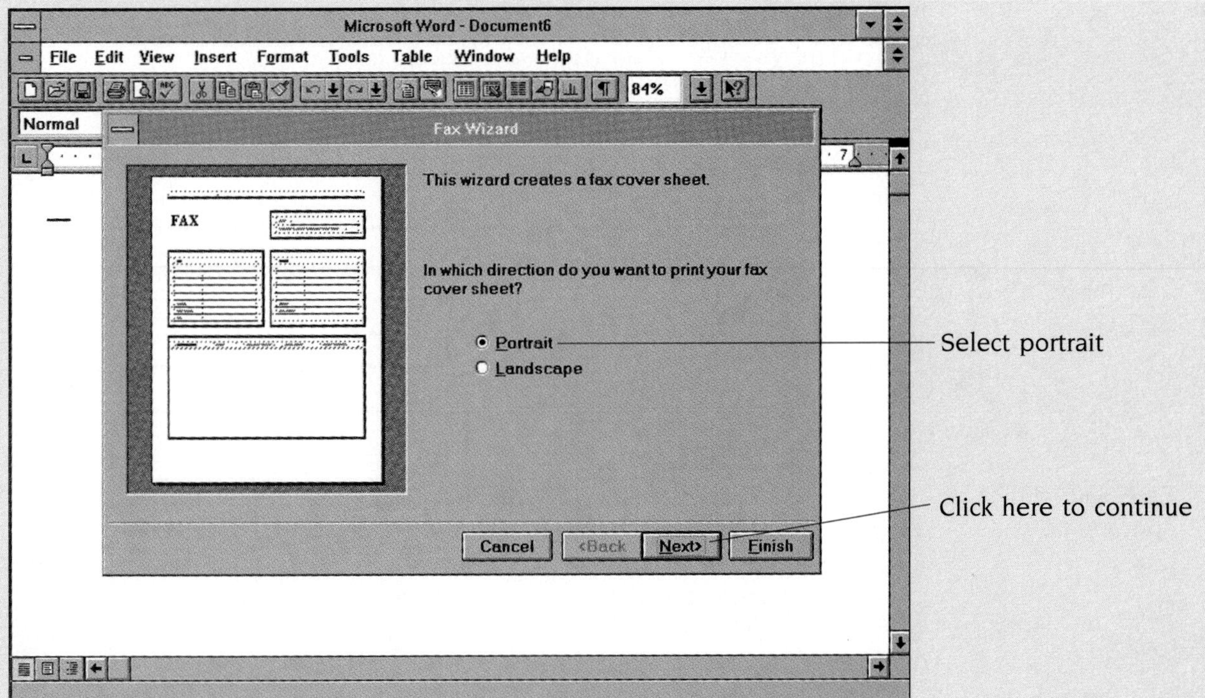

(b) The Fax Wizard (step 2)

FIGURE 3.10 Hands-on Exercise 2 (continued)

- Choose a style for the cover sheet. (We chose Jazzy.) Click **Next.**
- Enter your name, your company's name, and your mailing address (or enter the corresponding information for Elvis). Click **Next.**
- Click in the text boxes to enter your telephone number and your fax number. Click **Next.**
- You will see a message indicating that the Fax Wizard has all the information it needs. Click Yes or No depending on whether or not you want help as you complete the fax.
- Click the **Finish command button.**
- Save the document as **ELVISFAX.DOC.**

Step 3: Complete the Fax

- Figure 3.10c displays the Fax cover sheet created by the Fax Wizard based on the answers you supplied.
- Type David Letterman's name and phone number as shown in the figure.
- Click in the **Remarks** area. Type the text of the fax as shown in Figure 3.10d.
- Click the **Spell check icon** on the Standard toolbar to begin a spell check. Correct any misspellings.
- Save the file.

Step 4: The Agenda Wizard

- Pull down the **File menu.** Click **New** to produce the dialog box that displays the available wizards.
- Double click the **Agenda Wizard** in the open list box to start the Agenda Wizard.

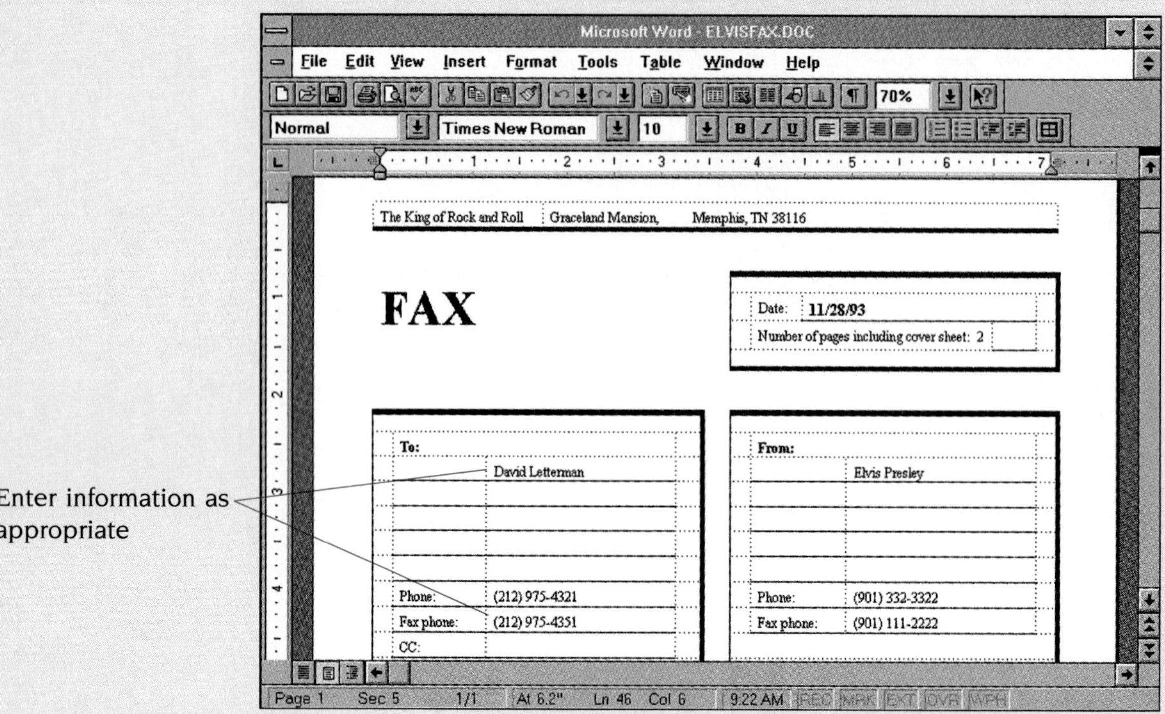

(c) Complete the Fax (step 3)

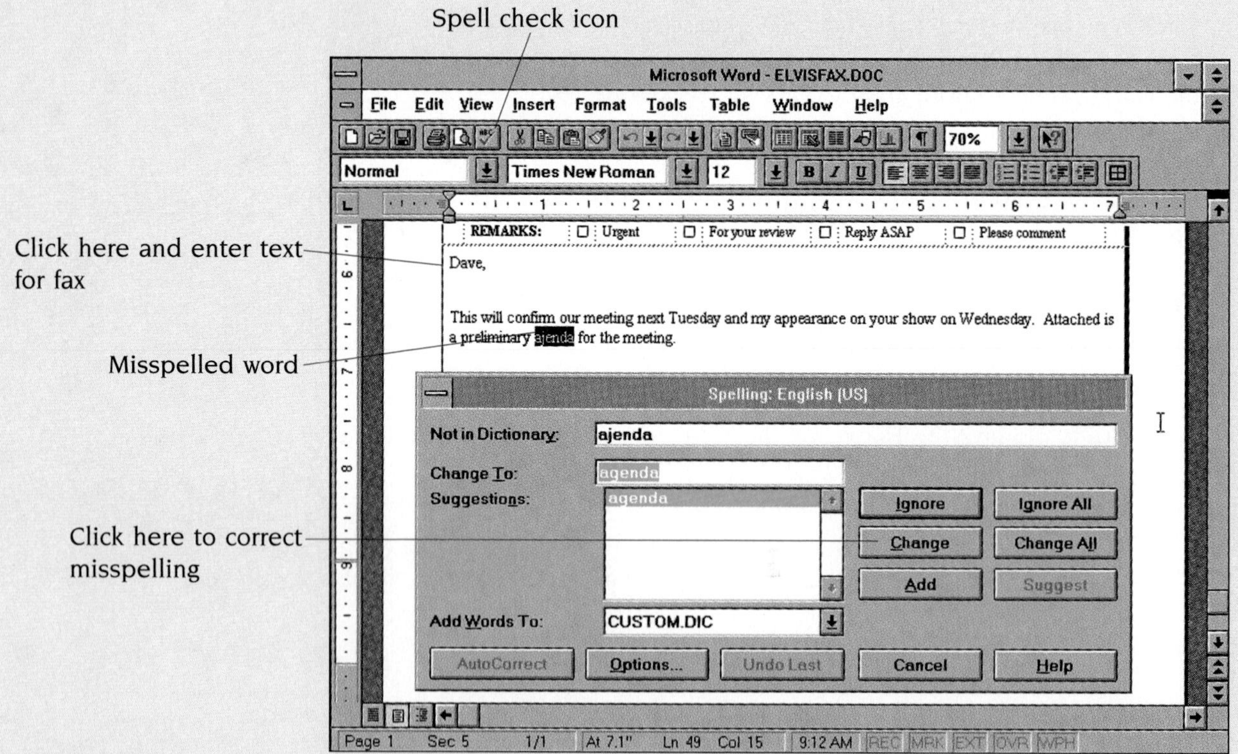

(d) The Spell Check (step 3)

FIGURE 3.10 Hands-on Exercise 2 (continued)

- The ***Agenda Wizard*** asks a series of questions in order to build a template. Each question is displayed in its own screen.
- Click the option button for the style you want—for example, **Boxes** in Figure 3.10e. Click **Next.**
- Enter the Date and Starting Time of the meeting. Click **Next.**
- Enter the main topic to be discussed and the location of the meeting. Click **Next.**
- Check (clear) the boxes corresponding to the items you want (don't want) placed on the agenda; for example, check the boxes for **Please Read** and **Please Bring.** Click **Next.**
- Check the boxes for the persons you want mentioned on the agenda; for example, check the boxes for attendees and the note taker. Click **Next.**

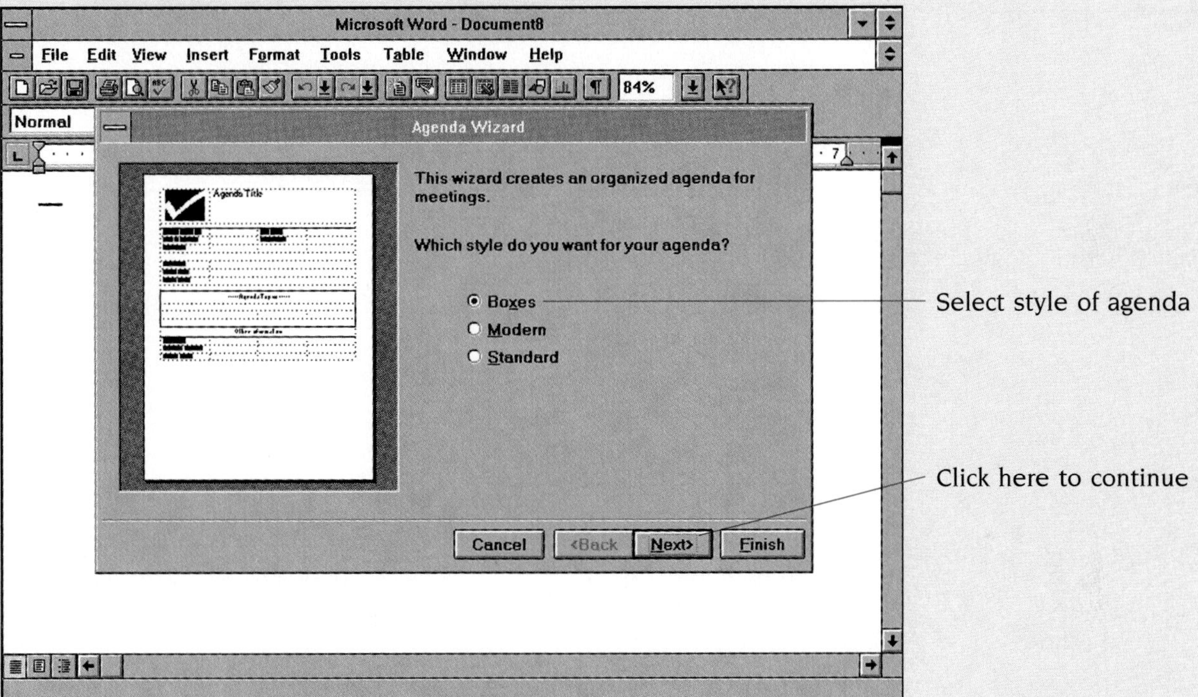

(e) The Agenda Wizard (step 4)

FIGURE 3.10 Hands-on Exercise 2 (continued)

RETRACE YOUR STEPS

Wizards guide you every step of the way but what if you make a mistake? Click the Back command button to return to a previous step and enter a different answer, then continue working with the wizard.

Step 5: The Agenda Wizard (continued)

- Continue to answer the questions posed by the Agenda Wizard.
- Enter the Agenda topics as shown in Figure 3.10f; press the **Tab key** to move

Enter agenda topics (press Tab to move from text box to text box)

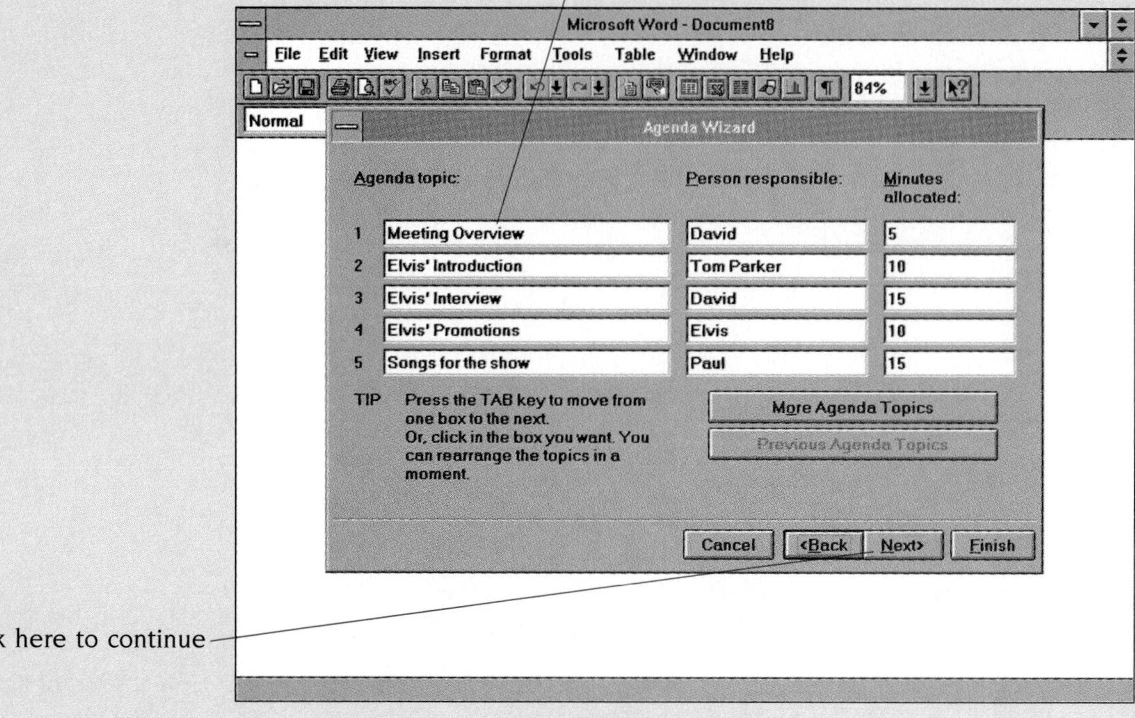

Click here to continue

(f) The Agenda Wizard (step 5)

FIGURE 3.10 Hands-on Exercise 2 (continued)

from one text box to the next. Click the **Next command button** when you have completed the topics.

- If necessary, reorder the topics by clicking the desired topic, then clicking the **Move Up** or **Move Down** command button. Click **Next** when you are satisfied with the agenda.
- Click the **Yes** or **No** button depending on whether you want a form to record the minutes of the meeting. Click **Next.**
- You will see a message indicating that the Agenda Wizard has all the information it needs. Click **Yes** or **No** depending on whether or not you want help as you complete the agenda.
- Click the **Finish command button.**
- Save the document as **ELVAGNDA.DOC.**

Step 6: Complete the Agenda

- Figure 3.10g displays the agenda created by the Agenda Wizard based on the answers you supplied.
- Complete the Agenda by entering the additional information, such as the names of the attendees and the specifics of what to read or bring, as shown in the figure.
- Change to the **Page Layout** view. Zoom to **Whole Page** to see the document you have created.
- Save the file.

Indicates active document

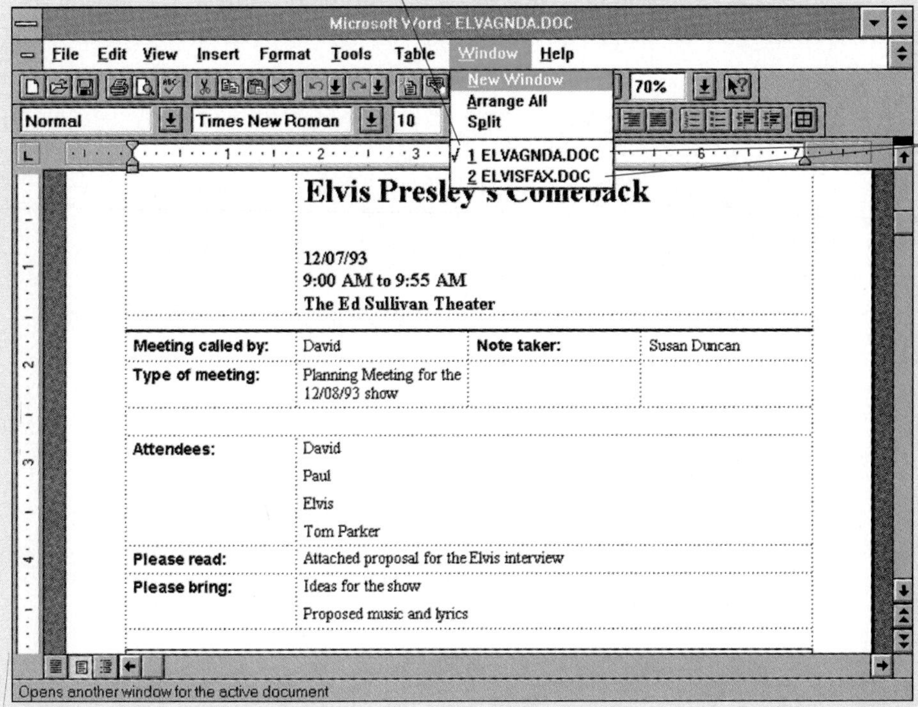

Two documents are currently open

(g) Complete the Agenda (step 6)

FIGURE 3.10 Hands-on Exercise 2 (continued)

> **AWARD YOURSELF**
>
> Use the ***Award Wizard*** to create a certificate for yourself citing the outstanding work you have done so far. The Award Wizard lets you choose one of four styles (formal, modern, decorative, or jazzy) in either portrait or landscape orientation. It's fun, it's easy, and you deserve it!

Step 7: View both documents simultaneously

- Pull down the **Window menu** to see the names of the open documents: Document1, ELVAGNDA.DOC, and ELVISFAX.DOC.
- Click **Document1** to switch to this document. (Document1 is an empty document that is opened when Word is loaded.) Pull down the **File menu.** Click **Close.**
- Pull down the **Window menu** a second time as shown in Figure 3.10g. This time, two documents are open, ELVISFAX.DOC and ELVAGNDA.DOC, although only one (ELVAGNDA.DOC) is visible on the screen. The check mark next to ELVAGNDA.DOC indicates that it is the active document.
- Click the **Print button** on the Standard toolbar to print ELVAGNDA.DOC.
- Pull down the **Window menu.** Click **ELVISFAX.DOC** to switch to this document. Click the **Print button** on the Standard toolbar to print it.
- Pull down the **Window menu** a final time. Click **Arrange All** to display open

windows simultaneously as shown in Figure 3.10h. Click in either window to change the active document, then scroll or edit the document in that window.

- Pull down the **File menu** and exit Word.

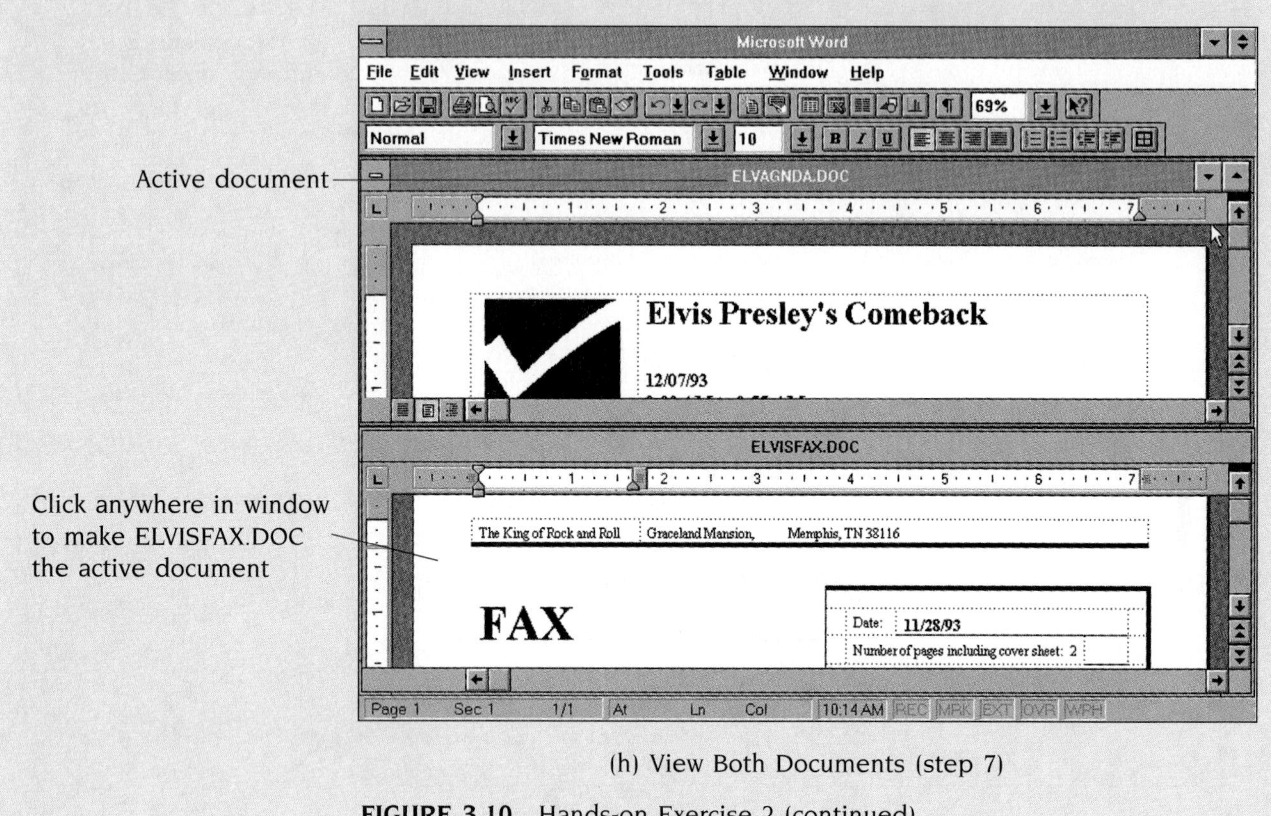

(h) View Both Documents (step 7)

FIGURE 3.10 Hands-on Exercise 2 (continued)

MAIL MERGE

A ***mail merge*** takes the tedium out of sending form letters, as it creates the same letter many times, changing the name, address, and other information as appropriate from letter to letter. You might use the mail merge capability to look for a job upon graduation, when you send essentially the same letter to many different people. The concept is illustrated in Figure 3.11, where Elvis drafts a form letter describing his comeback, then merges that letter with a set of names and addresses, to produce the individual letters.

A mail merge requires the creation of two separate files: the ***main document*** in Figure 3.11a and the ***data source*** in Figure 3.11b. The main document contains standardized text together with one or more merge fields to indicate where variable information is to be inserted in the individual letters. The data source contains the information that varies from letter to letter—for example, an addressee's title, name, and address.

Word organizes the data source as a table. The first row is called the header row and identifies the fields in the remaining rows. Every other row contains the information needed to create one letter and is called a data ***record.*** Every data record contains the same fields in the same order—for example, Title, FirstName, LastName, and so on.

ELVIS PRESLEY

Graceland Mansion
Memphis, TN 38116
(901) 332-3322

November 28, 1993

«Title» «FirstName» «LastName»
«Address1»
«City», «State» «Zipcode»

Dear «Title» «LastName»,

I am seeking an engagement as the lead act at a Las Vegas night club. I have extensive experience both in private clubs and road tours throughout the United States, and have enclosed my résumé for your review.

It has been some time since I have been in the public eye, but I have never stopped singing or living my music. I am well aware of current trends and have many new songs that will, without question, catch the public's imagination. Everyone needs a gimmick in today's market and I have several extraordinary ideas in mind.

I would welcome the opportunity to meet you to discuss my ideas and audition my new act. Please contact me at the above address or call me at 1-800-HOUND-DOG. I look forward to hearing from you.

Sincerely,

Elvis

(a) The Main Document

Title	FirstName	LastName	Address1	City	State	Zipcode
Mr.	David	Letterman	1697 Broadway	New York	NY	10019
Mr.	Arsenio	Hall	5555 Melrose Avenue	Hollywood	CA	90038
Mr.	Jay	Leno	3000 West Alameda Avenue	Burbank	CA	91523

(b) The Data Source

FIGURE 3.11 The Mail Merge

The main document and the data source are created in conjunction with one another, with the ***merge codes*** in the main document referencing the corresponding fields in the data source. The first line in the address contains three entries in angled brackets, *<<Title>> <<FirstName>> <<LastName>>*; these entries are not typed explicitly but are entered through special commands described in the hands-on exercise.

The merge process examines each record in the data source and substitutes the appropriate field values for the corresponding merge codes as it creates the individual form letters. For example, the first three fields in the first record will produce *Mr. David Letterman*; the same fields in the second record will produce, *Mr. Jay Leno,* and so on.

In similar fashion, the second line in the address of the main document contains the *<<Address1>>* field, and the third line *<<City>>*, *<<State>>*, and <<Zipcode>> fields. The salutation repeats the *<<Title>>* and *<<LastName>>* fields. The mail merge prepares the letters one at a time, with one letter created for every record in the data source until the file of names and addresses is exhausted. The individual letters are shown in Figure 3.11c. Each letter begins on a new page.

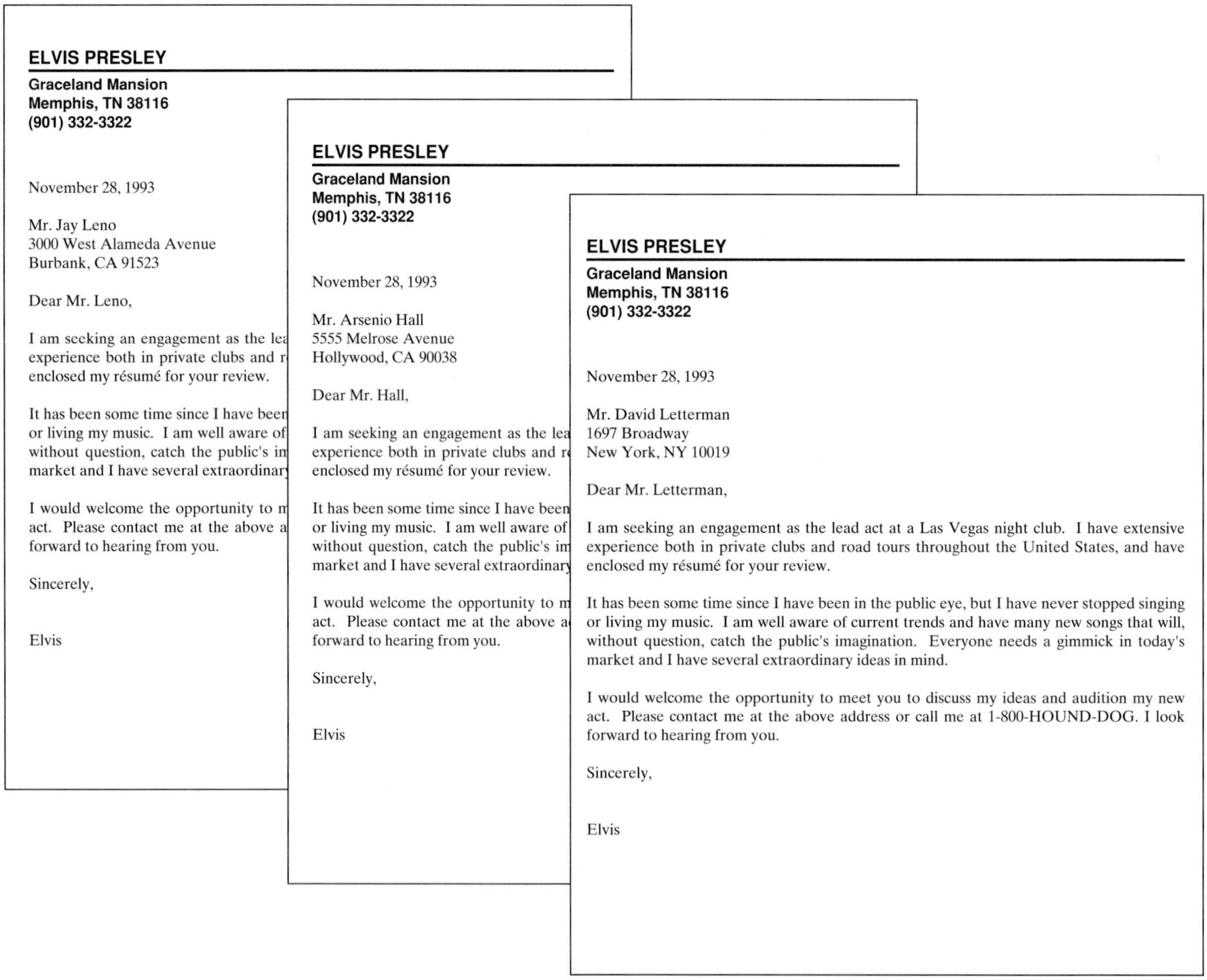

ELVIS PRESLEY

Graceland Mansion
Memphis, TN 38116
(901) 332-3322

November 28, 1993

Mr. Jay Leno
3000 West Alameda Avenue
Burbank, CA 91523

Dear Mr. Leno,

I am seeking an engagement as the le
experience both in private clubs and r
enclosed my résumé for your review.

It has been some time since I have bee
or living my music. I am well aware of
without question, catch the public's in
market and I have several extraordinar

I would welcome the opportunity to m
act. Please contact me at the above a
forward to hearing from you.

Sincerely,

Elvis

ELVIS PRESLEY

Graceland Mansion
Memphis, TN 38116
(901) 332-3322

November 28, 1993

Mr. Arsenio Hall
5555 Melrose Avenue
Hollywood, CA 90038

Dear Mr. Hall,

I am seeking an engagement as the lea
experience both in private clubs and r
enclosed my résumé for your review.

It has been some time since I have been
or living my music. I am well aware of
without question, catch the public's im
market and I have several extraordinary

I would welcome the opportunity to m
act. Please contact me at the above a
forward to hearing from you.

Sincerely,

Elvis

ELVIS PRESLEY

Graceland Mansion
Memphis, TN 38116
(901) 332-3322

November 28, 1993

Mr. David Letterman
1697 Broadway
New York, NY 10019

Dear Mr. Letterman,

I am seeking an engagement as the lead act at a Las Vegas night club. I have extensive experience both in private clubs and road tours throughout the United States, and have enclosed my résumé for your review.

It has been some time since I have been in the public eye, but I have never stopped singing or living my music. I am well aware of current trends and have many new songs that will, without question, catch the public's imagination. Everyone needs a gimmick in today's market and I have several extraordinary ideas in mind.

I would welcome the opportunity to meet you to discuss my ideas and audition my new act. Please contact me at the above address or call me at 1-800-HOUND-DOG. I look forward to hearing from you.

Sincerely,

Elvis

(c) The Printed Letters

FIGURE 3.11 The Mail Merge (continued)

> **FILE DESIGN**
>
> The zip code should be defined as a separate field in the data source in order to sort on zip code and take advantage of bulk mail. A person's first and last name should also be defined separately, so that you have access to either field, perhaps to create a friendly salutation such as Dear Joe or to sort on last name.

Implementation in Word

The implementation of a mail merge in Word is easy, provided you understand the basic concept. In essence there are three things you must do:

1. Create and save the main document
2. Create and save the data source
3. Merge the main document and data source to create the individual letters

The Mail Merge command is located in the Tools Menu. Execution of the command displays the Mail Merge Helper, which lists the steps in the mail merge process and guides you every step of the way.

The screen in Figure 3.12 shows the Mail Merge Helper as it would appear after steps 1 and 2 have been completed. The main document has been created and saved as FORMLET.DOC. The data source has been created and saved as NAMES.DOC. All that remains is to merge the files and create the individual form letters. The options in effect indicate that the letters will be created in a new document. (The Query Options command button enables you to select and/or sort the records in the data source prior to the merge; these options are discussed after the hands-on exercise.)

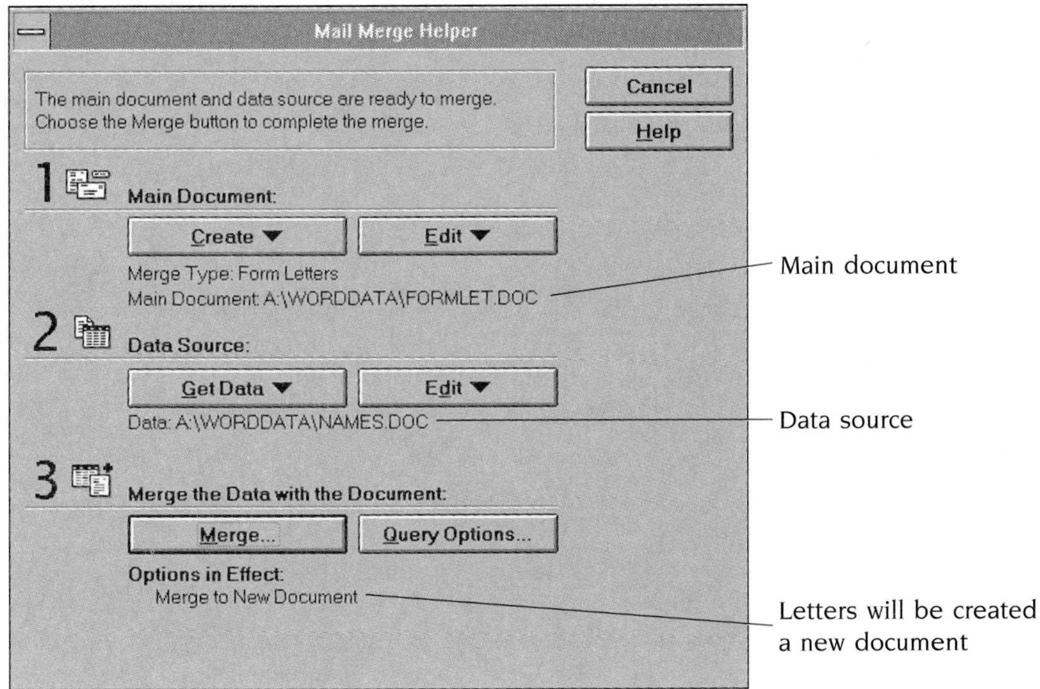

FIGURE 3.12 Mail Merge Helper

MAIL MERGE HELP

Pull down the Help menu, search on Mail Merge, then select Mail Merge: Step by Step. Click the maximize button to maximize the help window and increase the amount of information displayed on the screen. Press the Tab key to jump from one highlighted topic to the next, or press the enter key to display the highlighted topic. Press Alt+Tab to move back and forth between the open applications, which include Word Help, How To, and Word itself (with the edited document).

HANDS-ON EXERCISE 3:

Mail Merge

Objective To create a main document and associated data source; to implement a mail merge and produce a set of form letters.

Step 1: Retrieve the cover letter

- Pull down the **File menu.** Click **Open.**
- Double click **ELVISAFT.DOC** to open the edited version of the cover letter from the first exercise.
- Pull down the **File menu.** Save the document as **FORMLET.DOC.**
- Pull down the **View menu** and click **Page Layout** (or click the **Page Layout button** on the status bar).
- Click the **Zoom control arrow** on the Standard toolbar and select **Two Pages.** Release the mouse to see the envelope and letter as in Figure 3.13a.
- The merge could be developed to print envelopes in addition to form letters, but we will omit the envelope from the exercise. Click and drag to select the envelope, then press the **Del key** to delete the envelope from the document.

Step 2: Create the Main Document

- Click the **Zoom control arrow** to change to **Page Width.**
- Delete David Letterman's address at the beginning of the letter as well as the salutation so that your letter matches Figure 3.13b.
- Save the letter.
- Pull down the **Tools menu.** Click **Mail Merge.** Click the **Create command button** to create the main document as shown in Figure 3.13b.
- Click **Form Letters,** then click **Active Window** to indicate that you will use FORMLET.DOC (in the active window) as the main document.

Step 3: Create the Data Source

- Click **Get Data,** then click **Create Data Source** to produce the dialog box in Figure 3.13c.
- Word provides commonly used field names for the data source, but not all of the data fields are necessary.
- Click **JobTitle,** then click the **Remove Field Name** command button. Delete the Company, Address2, PostalCode, Country, HomePhone, and WorkPhone fields in similar fashion.

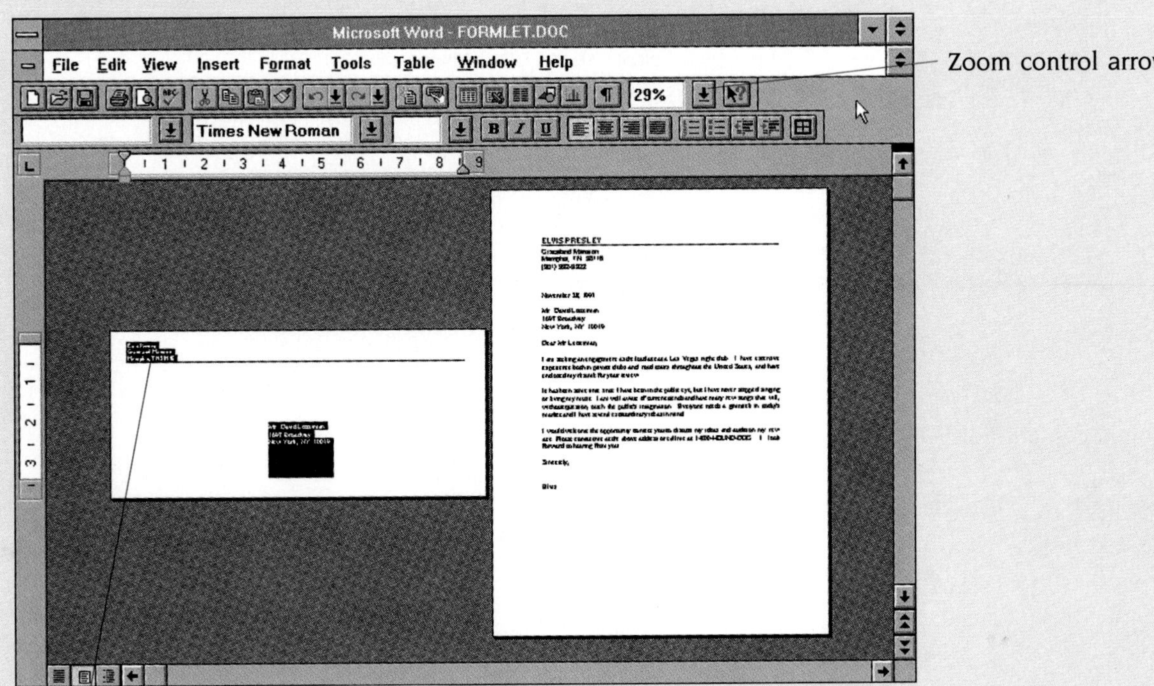

(a) Delete the Envelope (step 1)

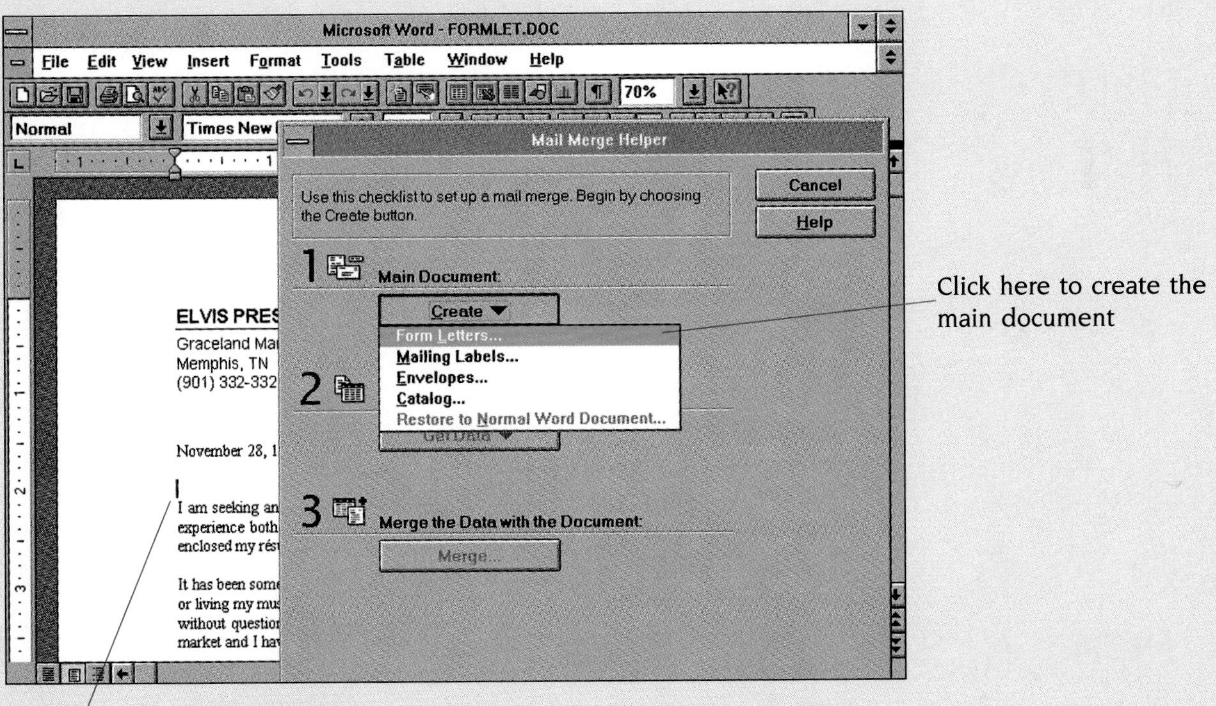

(b) Create the Form Letter (step 2)

FIGURE 3.13 Hands-on Exercise 3

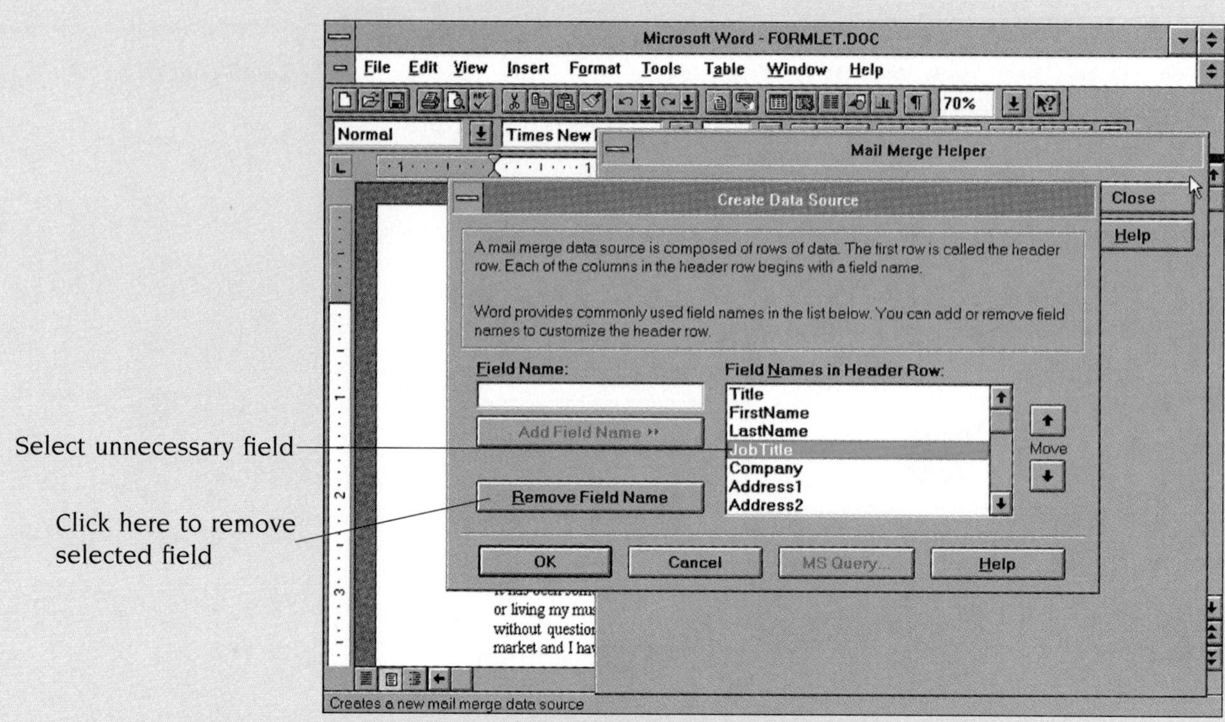

(c) Create the Data Source (step 3)

FIGURE 3.13 Hands-on Exercise 3 (continued)

- Click in the **Field Name** text box. Type **Zipcode.** Click the **Add Field Name** command button to add this field.
- Click **OK** to end the definition of the data source. Type **NAMES** in the File Name text box as the name of the data source. Click **OK** to save the file.
- You will see a message indicating that the data source does not contain any records. Click **Edit Data Source.**

Step 4: Add the Data

- Enter data for the first record. Type **Mr.** in the Title field. Press **Tab** to move to the next (FirstName) field and type **David.** Continue in this fashion until you have completed the first record as shown in Figure 3.13d.
- Click **Add New** to enter the data for Arsenio Hall:
  — Mr. Arsenio Hall
  — 5555 Melrose Avenue
  — Hollywood, CA 90038
- Click **Add New** to enter the data for Jay Leno:
  — Mr. Jay Leno
  — 3000 West Alameda Avenue
  — Burbank, CA 91523
- Click **OK** to end the data entry and return to the main document.

Step 5: Add the merge fields

- Click in the main document immediately below the date. Press **enter** to leave a blank line between the date and the first line of the address.
- Click the **Insert Merge Field** button on the Merge toolbar. Click **Title** from the list of fields within the data source. The title field is inserted into the main document and enclosed in angled brackets as shown in Figure 3.13e.

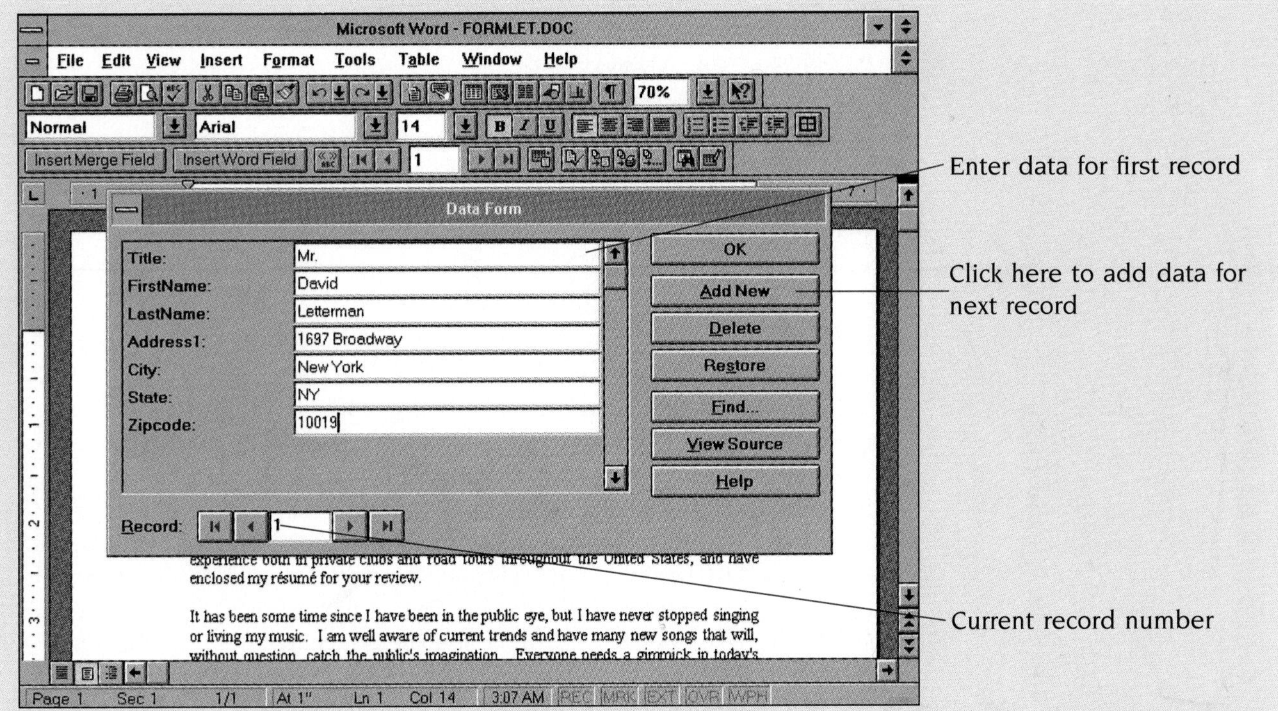

(d) Adding Data (step 4)

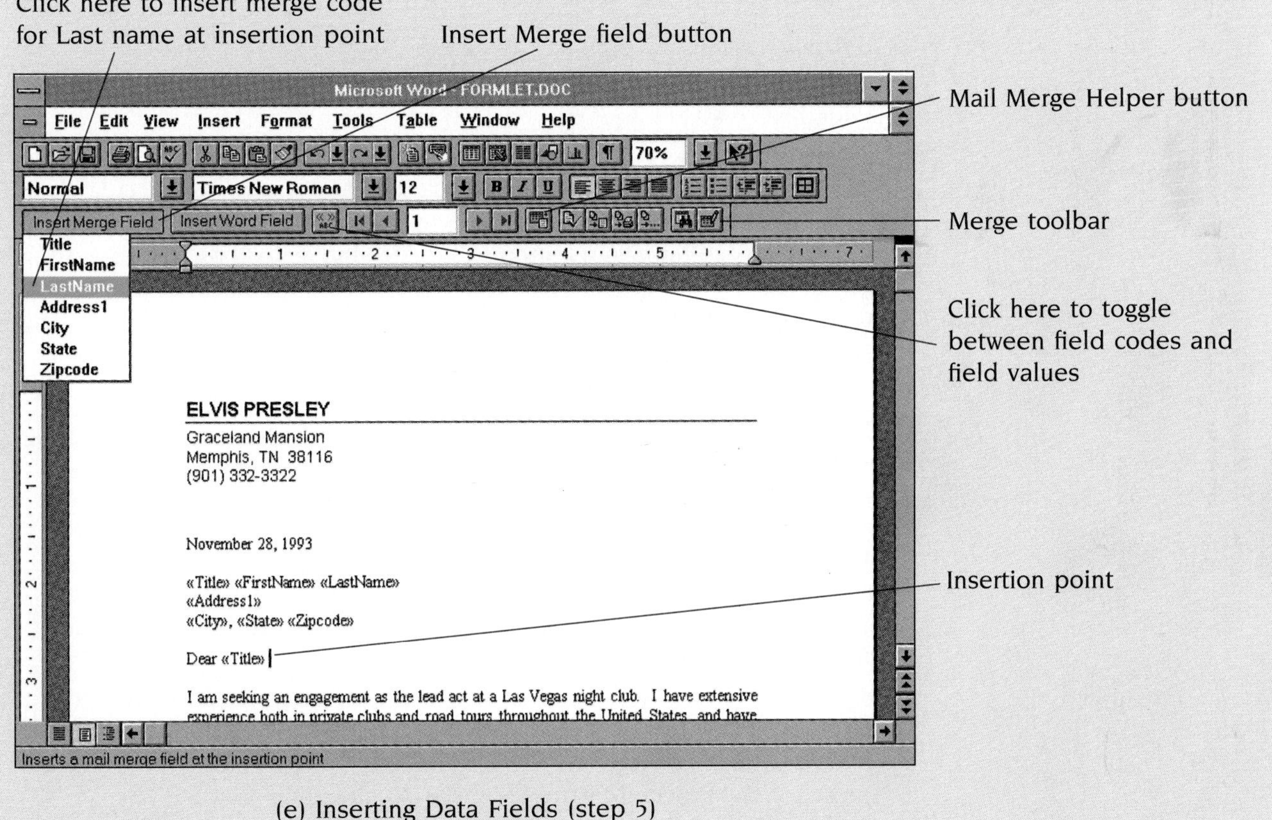

(e) Inserting Data Fields (step 5)

FIGURE 3.13 Hands-on Exercise 3 (continued)

- Press the **space bar.** Click the **Insert Merge Field** button a second time. Click **FirstName.** Press the **space bar.**
- Click the **Insert Merge Field** button again. Click **LastName.**
- Press **enter** to move to the next line in the address. Enter the remaining fields in the address as shown in Figure 3.13e. Enter the merge fields for the salutation as well. Type a **comma** after the salutation.
- Save the main document.

Step 6: The Mail Merge toolbar

- The Mail Merge toolbar enables you to preview the form letters before they are created.
- Click the **<<abc>> button** on the Merge toolbar to display field values rather than field codes; you will see Mr. David Letterman instead of <<Title>> <<FirstName>> <<LastName>>, etc.
- The **<<abc>> button** functions as a toggle switch; click it once and you switch from field codes to field values; click it a second time and you go from field values back to field codes. Display the field values.
- Look at the text box on the Merge toolbar, which displays the number 1 to indicate the first record. Click the **▶ button** to display the form letter for the next record (Arsenio Hall).
- Click the **▶ button** again to display the form letter for the next record (Jay Leno). The toolbar indicates you are on the third record. Click the **◀ button** to return to the previous (second) record.
- Click the |◀ button to move directly to the first record (David Letterman). Click the ▶| button to display the form letter for the last record (Jay Leno).

Step 7: The Mail Merge Helper

- Click the **Mail Merge Helper button** on the Merge toolbar to display the dialog box in Figure 3.13f.
- The Mail Merge Helper shows your progress thus far:
  - — The main document has been created and saved as FORMLET.DOC.
  - — The data source has been created and saved as NAMES.DOC.
- Click the Merge command button to produce the dialog box in Figure 3.13g.

EDIT THE DATA SOURCE

Click the Mail Merge Helper button to display a dialog box with information about the mail merge, click the Edit command button under Data Source, then click the file containing the data source. Click the View Source command button to see multiple records in the data source displayed within a table; the first row contains the field names and each succeeding row contains a data record. Edit the data source, then pull down the Window menu and click the name of the file containing the main document to continue working on the mail merge.

Step 8: The merge

- The selected options in Figure 3.13g should already be set:
  - — If necessary, click the arrow in the Merge To list box and select New Document.

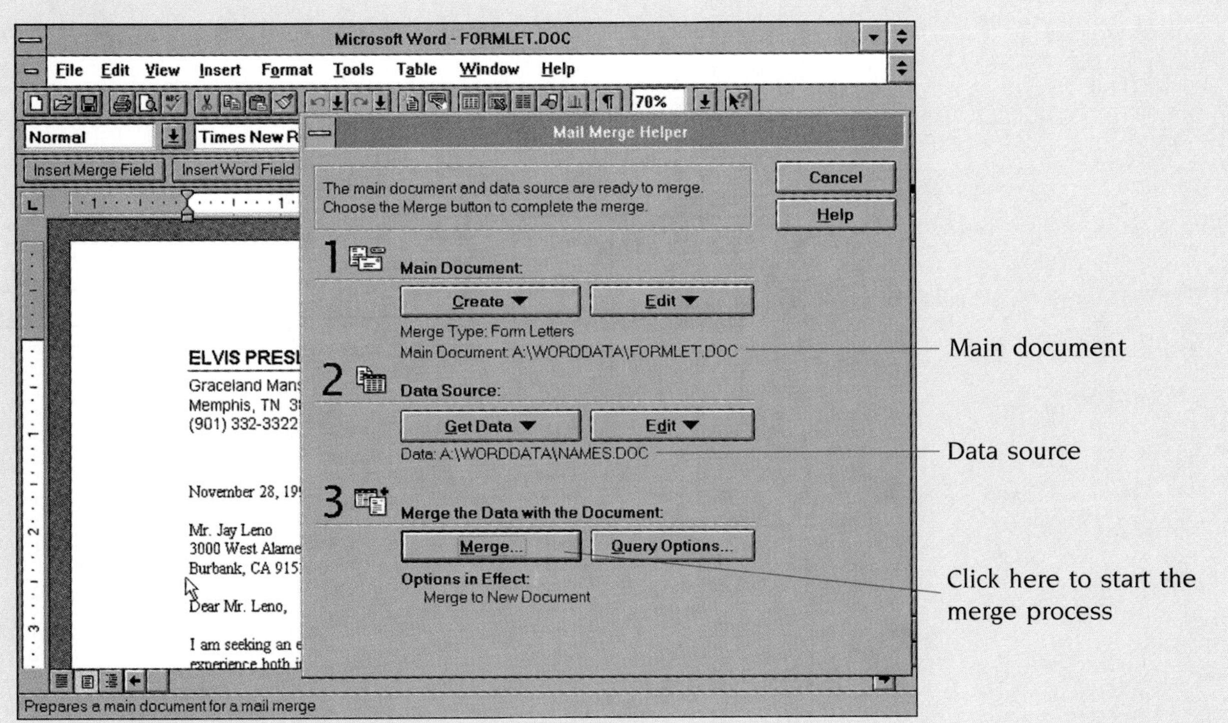

(f) Mail Merge Toolbar (steps 6 and 7)

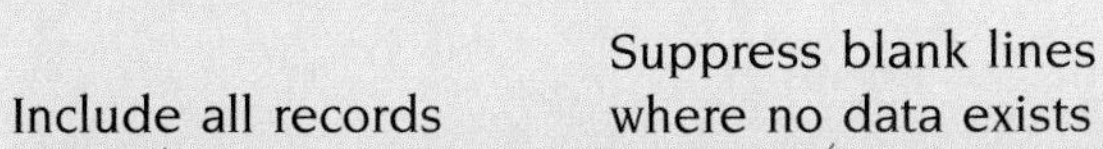

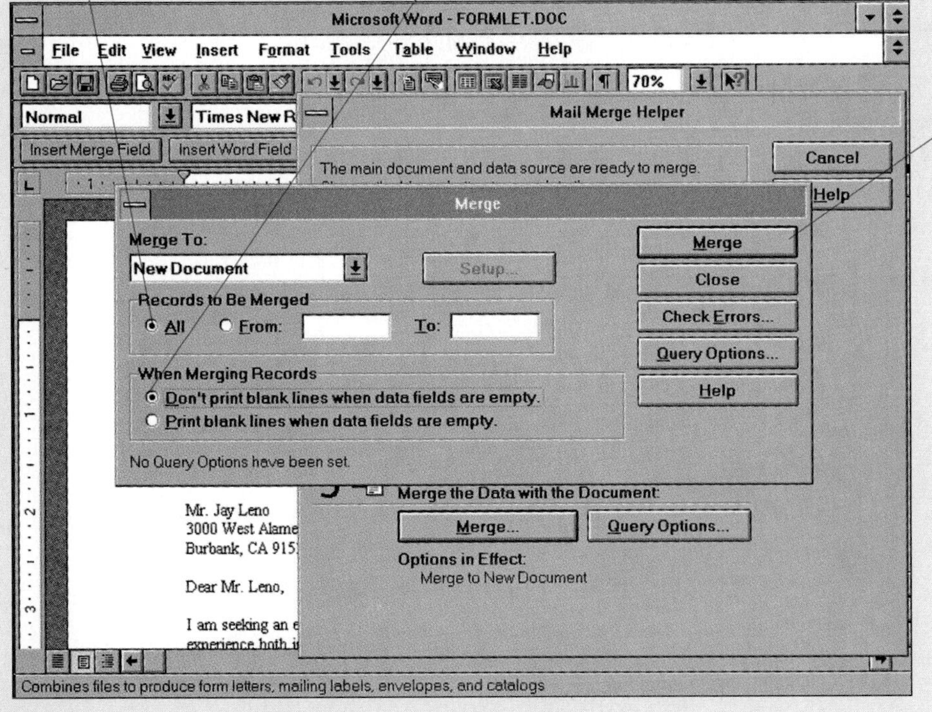

(g) Merge (step 8)

FIGURE 3.13 Hands-on Exercise 3 (continued)

— If necessary, click the All option button to include all records in the data source.

— If necessary, click the option button to suppress blank lines if data fields are empty.

➤ Click the **Merge command button.** Word pauses momentarily, then generates the three form letters in a new document.

Step 9: The form letters

➤ The title bar of the active window changes to Form Letters1.

➤ Pull down the **View menu.** Click **Zoom.** Click **Many Pages.** Click the monitor icon and drag to display three pages side by side. Click **OK.**

➤ You should see the three form letters as shown in Figure 3.13h.

Step 10: Exit Word

➤ Double click the **control-menu box** in the application window for Word to exit the program.

➤ Pay close attention to the informational messages that ask whether to save the modified file(s). There is no need to save the merged document (Form Letters1) because you can always recreate the merged letters provided you have the main document and data source.

➤ Save the files FORMLET.DOC and NAMES.DOC if you are prompted to do so.

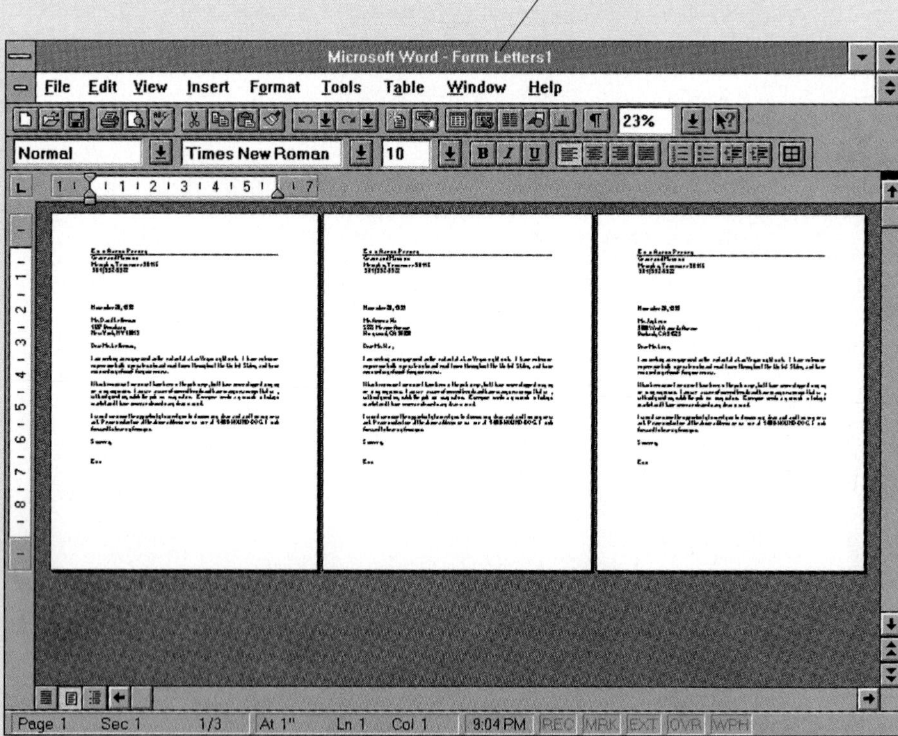

(h) The Individual Form Letters (step 8)

FIGURE 3.13 Hands-on Exercise 3 (continued)

FINER POINTS OF MAIL MERGE

The hands-on exercise just completed acquaints you with the basics of a mail merge, but there is much more that you can do. You can, for example, sort the data source so that the form letters are printed in a different sequence—for example, by zip code to take advantage of bulk mail. You can also select the records that are to be included in the mail merge; that is, a letter need not be sent for every record in the data source.

Figure 3.14 illustrates both options and is accessed through the Query Options command button in the Mail Merge Helper window. The records in the data source may be sorted on as many as three fields, as indicated in Figure 3.14a, which sorts the records by zip code, and by last name within zip code. Both fields are in ascending (low-to-high) sequence.

The dialog box in Figure 3.14b lets you specify which records in the data source will receive an individual letter by establishing selection criteria; for example, letters will be sent only to those persons living in California. The implemen-

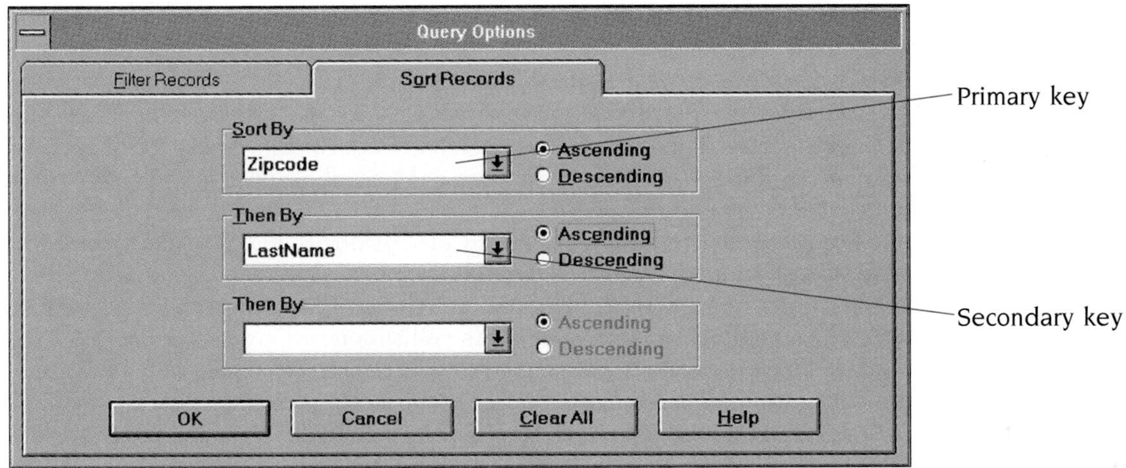

(a) Sorting Records

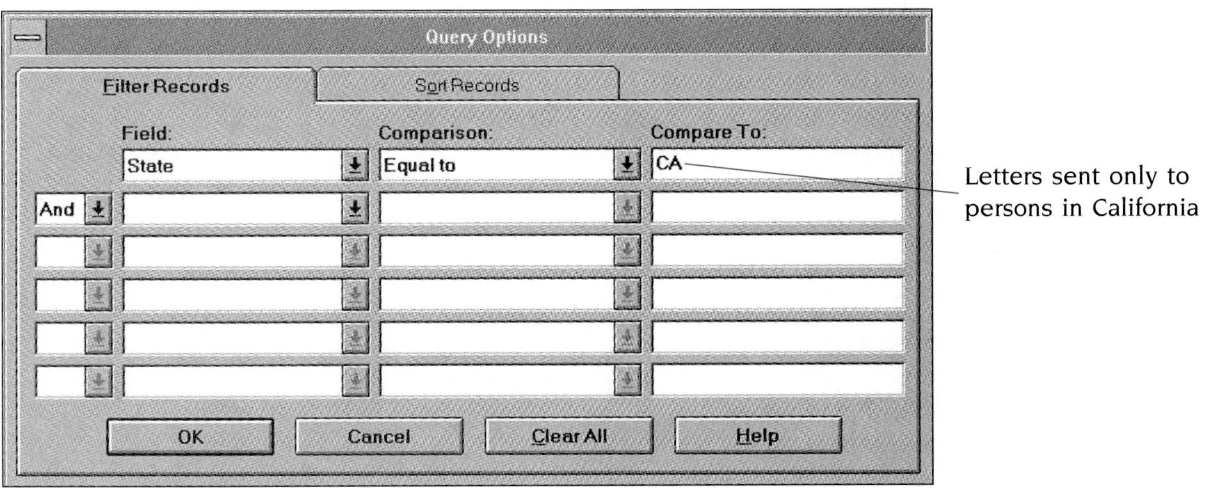

(b) Selecting Records

FIGURE 3.14 Finer Points of Mail Merge

tation is straightforward and you can impose additional rules or clear an existing rule by clicking the appropriate command button.

SUMMARY

The spelling checker compares the words in a document to those in a standard and/or custom dictionary. It will detect misspellings, duplicated phrases, and/or irregular capitalization, but will not flag properly spelled words that are used incorrectly.

The AutoCorrect feature corrects predefined spelling errors and/or mistakes in capitalization automatically as the words are entered. The feature can also be used to create a personal shorthand as it will expand abbreviations as they are typed.

The thesaurus suggests synonyms and/or antonyms. It can also recognize multiple forms of a word (noun, verb, and adjective) and offers suggestions for each.

The grammar checker searches for mistakes in punctuation, writing style, and word usage, by comparing strings of text within a document to a series of predefined rules.

The Insert Date command puts a date code into a document that is updated automatically whenever the document is retrieved. The date can be displayed as either a field code or field result during editing.

The Insert Symbol command provides easy access to special characters, making it easy to place typographic characters into a document. Many special symbols are found in the Normal text, Wingdings, and Symbol fonts. All TrueType fonts are scalable from 4 to 127 points.

Wizards and templates help create professionally designed documents with a minimum of time and effort. A template is a partially completed document that contains formatting and other information. A wizard is an interactive program that creates a template based on the answers you supply.

A mail merge creates the same letter many times, changing only the variable data—for example, the addressee's name and address as appropriate—from letter to letter. It is performed in conjunction with a main document and a data source, both of which exist as separate documents. The mail merge can be used to create a form letter for only selected records. It may print those letters in a sequence different from the way the records are stored in the data source.

Key Words and Concepts

- Agenda wizard
- Antonym
- AutoCorrect feature
- Award wizard
- Change command button
- Custom dictionary
- Data source
- Date field
- Date text
- Envelopes and Labels command
- Fax wizard
- Field
- Field code
- Field result
- Grammar checker
- Insert Date command
- Insert Symbol command
- Look Up button
- Mail merge
- Main document
- Merge code
- Record
- Replace button
- Résumé Wizard
- Spelling checker
- Synonym
- Template
- Thesaurus
- Wizard

Multiple Choice

1. Which of the following will be detected by the spelling checker?
   (a) Duplicate words
   (b) Irregular capitalization
   (c) Both (a) and (b)
   (d) Neither (a) nor (b)

2. Which of the following is true about the thesaurus program?
   (a) It recognizes different forms of the same word—for example, a noun and a verb
   (b) It generally offers antonyms as well as synonyms
   (c) Both (a) and (b)
   (d) Neither (a) nor (b)

3. Which of the following are unlikely to be found in a custom dictionary?
   (a) Proper names
   (b) Words related to the user's particular application
   (c) Acronyms created by the user for his or her application
   (d) Standard words of English usage

4. Ted and Sally both use Word but on different computers. Both have written a letter to Dr. Joel Stutz and have run a spelling check on their respective documents. Ted's program flags *Stutz* as a misspelling, whereas Sally's accepts it as written. Why?
   (a) The situation is impossible; if they use identical word processing programs they should get identical results
   (b) Ted has added *Stutz* to his custom dictionary
   (c) Sally has added *Stutz* to her custom dictionary
   (d) All of the above reasons are equally likely as a cause of the problem

5. The spelling checker will do all of the following *except*:
   (a) Flag properly spelled words used incorrectly
   (b) Identify misspelled words
   (c) Accept (as correctly spelled) words that are in the custom dictionary
   (d) Suggest alternatives to misspellings it identifies

6. Assume that your document contains the character string T??T, and that you invoke the spelling checker in Word. The program will:
   (a) Return an error message
   (b) Display all four-letter words in its dictionary that start and end with T
   (c) Locate all occurrences of the character string in the document
   (d) Do nothing because you have not typed in a replacement string

7. The names and addresses of the individuals slated to receive a form letter are found in:
   (a) The main document and the data source
   (b) The main document only
   (c) The data source only
   (d) Neither the main document nor the data source

8. A person's first name, last name, and street address in a mail merge operation are known as
   (a) Characters
   (b) Fields
   (c) Records
   (d) Files

9. Which of the following is true about the Insert Symbol command?
   (a) It can insert a symbol in any size from 4 to 127 points
   (b) It can access any TrueType font
   (c) Both (a) and (b)
   (d) Neither (a) nor (b)

10. The AutoCorrect feature will:
   (a) Correct errors in capitalization as they occur during typing
   (b) Expand user-defined abbreviations as the entries are typed
   (c) Both (a) and (b)
   (d) Neither (a) nor (b)

11. Which of the following is a *false* statement about the date field?
   (a) It is updated automatically whenever the document is printed
   (b) It may be displayed during editing as either a field code or a field result
   (c) It may be displayed in a variety of different formats
   (d) It is the exact equivalent of manually typing the current date into a document except that it is faster

12. Which of the following is a true statement about wizards?
   (a) They are accessed through the New command in the File menu
   (b) They always produce a completely finished document
   (c) Both (a) and (b)
   (d) Neither (a) nor (b)

13. Which of the following best describes how files are saved and printed within the mail merge operation?
   (a) The main document and data source are printed but not saved
   (b) The individual form letters are saved in a separate file but are not printed
   (c) Both (a) and (b)
   (d) Neither (a) nor (b)

14. Which of the following is true about the mail merge operation?
   (a) A letter must be created for every record in the data source but the letters can be printed in a different sequence
   (b) A letter can be created for only a subset of records but the letters must be printed in the same sequence as the data source
   (c) A letter must be created for every record in the data source and the letters must be printed in the same sequence as the data source
   (d) A letter can be created for only a subset of records and the letters may be printed in a different sequence from the records in the data source

15. Which of the following is true regarding the main document and data source associated with the mail merge operation?
   (a) They are stored in the same document
   (b) They are stored in separate documents, but only one can be open at a time

(c) They are stored in separate documents; both can be open at the same time, but only one document can be visible

(d) They are stored in separate documents, both can be open at the same time, and both can be visible at the same time

ANSWERS

1. c	**6.** b	**11.** d
2. c	**7.** c	**12.** a
3. d	**8.** b	**13.** d
4. c	**9.** c	**14.** d
5. a	**10.** c	**15.** d

EXPLORING WORD

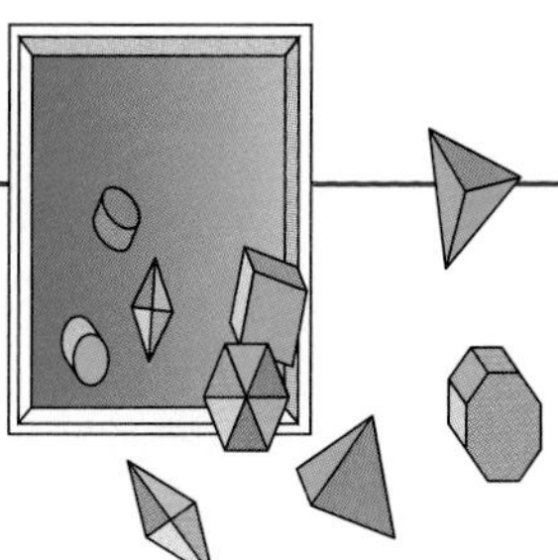

1. Use Figure 3.15 to match each action with its result; a given action may be used more than once.

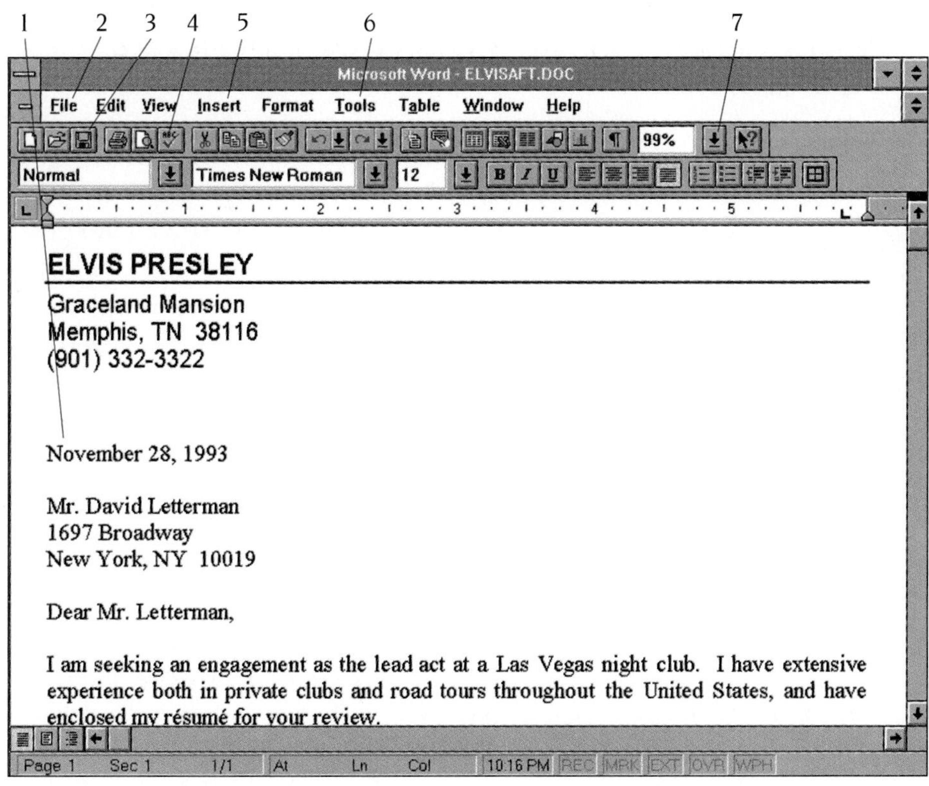

FIGURE 3.15 Figure for Problem 1

Action		**Result**
a. Click at 1, click at 5	___	Change the format of the date field
b. Click at 2	___	Spell check the current document
c. Click at 3	___	Change the AutoCorrect options in effect
d. Click at 4	___	Save the document
e. Click at 5	___	Use the current document to create a mail merge main document

f. Click at 6 ___ Insert a ♥ into the document

g. Click at 7 ___ Change to view two pages side by side

___ Create an envelope

___ Grammar check the current document

___ Create a fax cover sheet

2. Figure 3.16 contains the draft version of the PROB0302.DOC document contained on the data disk.

a. Proofread the document and circle any mistakes in spelling, grammar, capitalization, or punctuation.

b. Load the document into Word and run the spelling checker. Did Word catch any mistakes you missed? Did you find any errors that were missed by the program?

c. Use the thesaurus to come up with alternate words for *document,* which appears entirely too often within the paragraph.

d. Run the grammar checker on the revised document. Did the program catch any grammatical errors you missed? Did you find any mistakes that were missed by the program?

e. Add your name to the revised document, save it, print it, and submit the completed document to your instructor.

All documents should be thoroughly proofed before they be printed and distributed.This means that documents, at a minimum should be spell cheked,, grammar cheked, and proof read by the author. A documents that has spelling errors and/or grammatical errors makes the Author look unprofessional and illiterate and their is nothing worse than allowing a first impression too be won that makes you appear slopy and disinterested, and a document full or of misteakes will do exactly that. Alot of people do not not realize how damaging a bad first impression could be, and documents full of misteaks has cost people oppurtunities that they trained and prepared many years for.

FIGURE 3.16 Screen for Problem 2

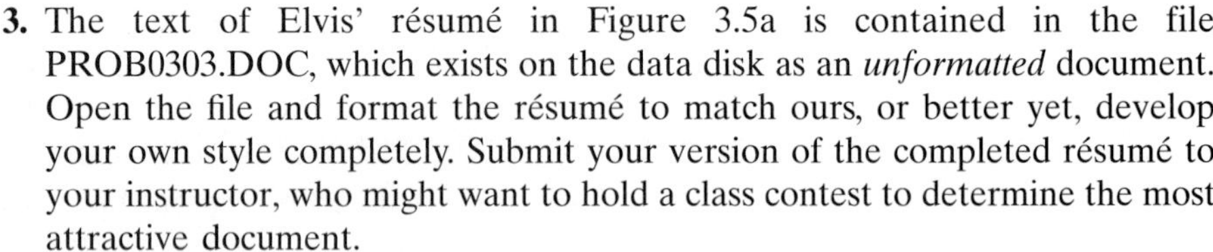

3. The text of Elvis' résumé in Figure 3.5a is contained in the file PROB0303.DOC, which exists on the data disk as an *unformatted* document. Open the file and format the résumé to match ours, or better yet, develop your own style completely. Submit your version of the completed résumé to your instructor, who might want to hold a class contest to determine the most attractive document.

4. The letterhead in the cover letter of Figure 3.5b is simple and open to improvement. Design your own letterhead for Elvis, including an address, telephone, and whatever other information you think appropriate. Use different fonts and/or the Format Border command to introduce horizontal lines to your letterhead. You might also want to decrease the top margin so that your letterhead prints closer to the top of the page. Submit the completed letterhead for entry into a class contest.

5. Exploring mail merge: Create two different letters for members of the ΦΔΓ sorority. The first letter is to be sent to all members, welcoming them for the semester and asking that they be on campus no later than August 25th; the second will be mailed to just the members living in the sorority house, detailing the house rules for the coming year. In addition, modify the data source in Figure 3.17 as follows:

a. Add Anne Green to the file MEMBER.DOC on the data disk, as she has decided to return to school after all. Anne is a junior who will be living in the house, and whose permanent address is 567 West Flagler Street, Tampa, FL 33065.

b. Delete Jackie St. Clair from the file, as she has become inactive.

c. Edit the file to indicate that Jamie Metzger and Francine Blum will be living in the house after all.

Both sets of letters are to be printed in alphabetical order by last name. As previously noted, the welcome back letter is to be sent to everyone, whereas the second letter is only for those members living in the sorority house.

FirstName	LastName	Address1	City	State	Zipcode	Year	House	Dues
Andrea	Lalji	1234 Delaware Avenue	Ft. Lauderdale	FL	33312	Sr	Yes	$350
Francine	Blum	278 West 77 Terrace	Chicago	IL	60620	Jr	No	$200
Lien	Le	9807 S.W. 152 Street	Miami	FL	33157	So	Yes	$350
Sylvia	Gudat	426 Savona Avenue	Minneapolis	MN	55476	Sr	Yes	$350
Debbie	Rowe	8900 W. Jamaica Avenue	New York	NY	10020	So	No	$200
Tiffany	Bost	900 Hurricane Drive	Miami	FL	33124	Jr	No	$200
Kim	Zimmerman	8344 N.W. 74 Street	Gainesville	FL	32601	Sr	Yes	$350
Jackie	St. Clair	456 Ryder Road	Boston	MA	02190	Jr	Yes	$350
Beth Ann	King	900 Mahoney Drive	Buffalo	NY	14203	So	No	$200
Joan	Rhyne	2500 Freshman Way	Miami	FL	33157	Sr	Yes	$200
Carol	Villar	234 Rivo Alto	Miami Beach	FL	33139	Jr	Yes	$350
Lori	Pryor	8976 S.W. 75 Street	San Francisco	CA	94114	So	Yes	$350
Claudia	Moore	3456 Robertson Avenue	Denver	CO	80228	Sr	No	$200
Jessica	Kinzer	7177 Hall Avenue	Atlanta	GA	30316	Jr	Yes	$350
Jennie	Lee	987 Best Street	Charleston	SC	29410	So	Yes	$350
Bianca	Costo	8765 S.W. 79 Court	Miami	FL	33143	Sr	Yes	$350
Jamie	Metzger	5660 N.W. 145 Terrace	Baltimore	MD	21224	So	No	$200
Jennifer	Vedo	8765 Jackson Manor	Santa Rosa	CA	95405	Jr	Yes	$350
Cori	Rice	2980 S.W. 75 Street	Coral Gables	FL	33134	Sr	Yes	$350
Lynda	Black	7500 Reno Road	Houston	TX	77090	So	No	$200

FIGURE 3.17 Data File for Problem 5

6. Answer the following with respect to the screens in Figure 3.18:
   a. What is the name of the file containing the main document? In which subdirectory is it stored?
   b. What is the name of the file containing the data source? In which subdirectory is it stored?
   c. Will every record in the data source be included in the merge?
   d. How would you print the merged letters in zip code order?

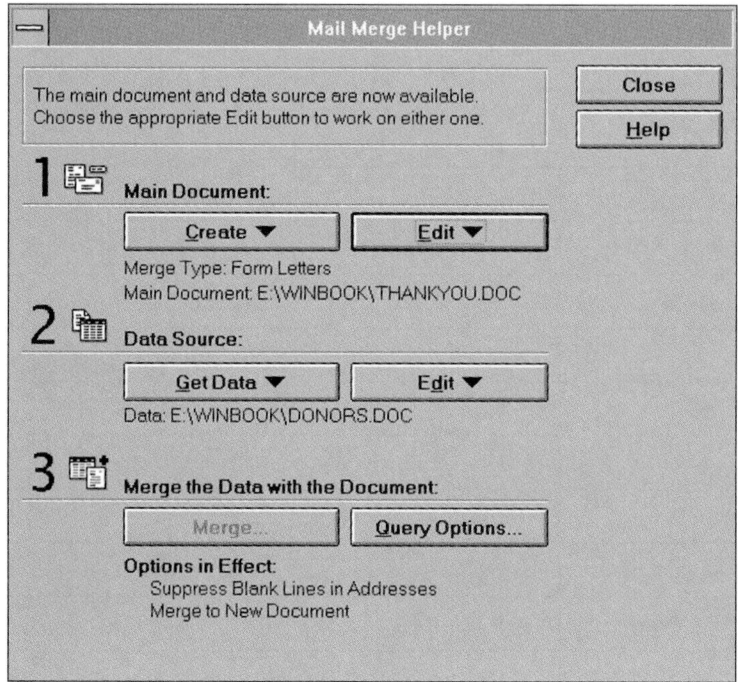

(a) Mail Merge Helper

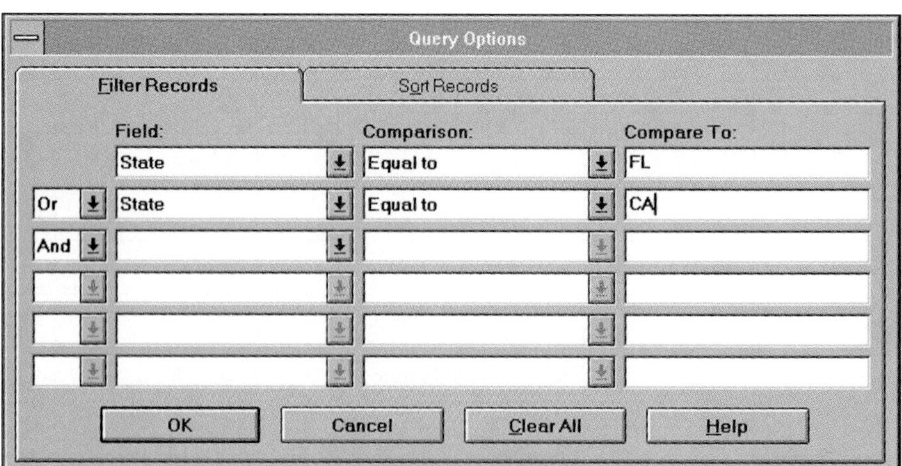

(b) Query Options

FIGURE 3.18 Mail Merge Helper for Problem 6

7. Exploring TrueType: Windows 3.1 includes a total of 14 TrueType fonts, which are accessible from any application. Two of these, Symbols and Wingdings, contain a variety of special characters that can be used to create some unusual documents. Use the Insert Symbol command, your imagination, and the fact that TrueType fonts are scalable from 4 to 127 points, to recreate the documents in Figure 3.19. Better yet, use your imagination to create your own documents.

Valentine's Day

We'll serenade your sweetheart

Call 284–LOVE

(a) Using the Symbol Font

STUDENT COMPUTER LAB

Fall Semester Hours

(b) Using the Wingding Font

FIGURE 3.19 Insert Symbol Command

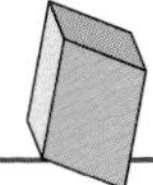

Case Studies

What Else Can Go Wrong?

You don't know how it happened, but your secretary used an old version of both the main document and data source for the most important mail merge of your career. The good news is that it was only a trial effort (only four letters were created) and the real mailing did not go out. There are so many problems that it's hard to describe them all, but there were mistakes in both the main document and data source. You won't even be able to read the main document unless you change the font size. Give this your immediate attention as the mailing is already late; your instructor needs to see the four letters first thing in the morning. Start with the OLDLETER.DOC and OLDDATA.DOC files on the data disk.

A Junior Year Abroad

How lucky can you get? You are spending the second half of your junior year in Paris. The problem is you will have to submit your work in French, and the English version of Word for Windows won't do. Is there a foreign language version available? What about the dictionary and thesaurus? How do you enter the accented characters that occur so frequently? You are leaving in two months so you had better get busy. What are your options? Bon voyage.

A Better Printer

The 200 cps dot matrix printer that has served you (and your brother before you) so well is on its last legs and it's just as well. It's too slow, too noisy, and the output is nowhere as crisp as that of your classmates. You are considering a laser printer and your parents have agreed to help, provided you keep the price down. What are the most important factors in the purchase of a laser printer? How important are speed, resolution, and memory? Are there other types of printers you should consider beside the dot matrix and laser? Summarize your findings in a one-page document to share with your classmates.

Looking for Business

Every business needs customers and one way of finding customers is through the mail. The mechanics of a mail merge are easy. The hard part is obtaining and then maintaining a suitable mailing list. Mailing lists are for sale, however, just like anything else. The hard part is knowing where to look and you are on your own, other than our suggestion to start with the yellow pages. Obtain genuine prices and descriptions for lists that you think will be suitable for your business.

4

The Professional Document: Headers, Footers, Styles, and Tables

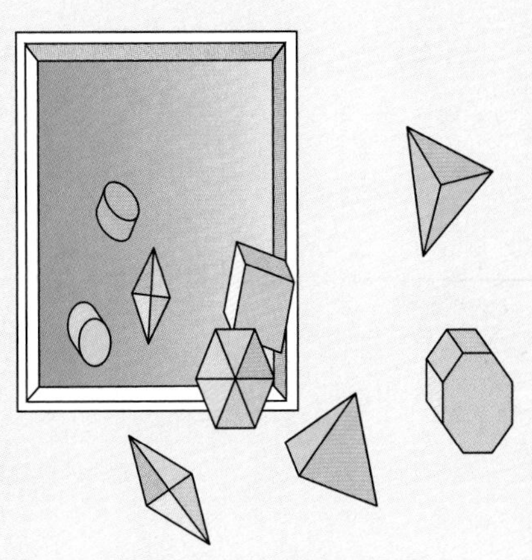

CHAPTER OBJECTIVES

After reading this chapter you will be able to:

1. Explain in general terms how styles automate the formatting process and provide a consistent appearance in a document.
2. Create and/or modify a style; apply existing styles to selected elements of a document.
3. Use the AutoFormat command.
4. Define a section and explain how section formatting differs from character and paragraph formatting.
5. Create a header and/or a footer; establish different headers or footers for the first, odd, or even pages in the same document.
6. Insert page numbers into a document; use the Go To command to move directly to a specific page in a document.
7. Create and update a table of contents.
8. Explain in general terms the use of the tables feature; create a table and insert it into a document.

OVERVIEW

This chapter presents a series of features to give a document a professional look. We begin with the concept of a style, or set of formatting instructions that provide a consistent appearance to similar elements within a document. We describe the AutoFormat command that applies styles to a document and greatly simplifies the formatting process.

The chapter covers several items associated with longer documents such as page numbers, headers and footers, and a table of contents. We also introduce the concept of a section, and describe how section formatting differs from character and paragraph formatting with which you are already familiar.

The last portion of the chapter introduces the tables feature, which is one of the most powerful features in Word. Tables provide an easy way to arrange text, numbers, and/or graphics.

STYLES

A characteristic of professional documents is the use of uniform formatting for each element. Different elements can have different formatting; for example, headings may be set in one font and the text under those headings in a different font. You may want the headings centered and the text fully justified.

If you are like most people, you will change your mind several times before arriving at a satisfactory design; then you will want consistent formatting for each occurrence of that element. You can use the Format Painter (see page 59) to copy the formatting from one occurrence of an element to another, but it still requires you to select the individual elements and paint each one whenever formatting changes.

A much easier way to achieve uniformity is to store the formatting information as a ***style,*** then apply that style to multiple occurrences of the same element within the document. Change the style and you automatically change all text defined by that style.

Styles are created on the character or paragraph level. A ***character style*** stores character formatting (font, size, and style) and affects only the selected text. A ***paragraph style*** stores paragraph formatting (alignment, line spacing, borders and shading, and also the font, size, and style of the text in the paragraph). A paragraph style affects the current paragraph or multiple paragraphs if several paragraphs are selected. The ***Styles command*** in the Format menu creates and/or modifies either type of style, then enables you to apply that style within a document.

Execution of the Styles command displays the dialog box shown in Figure 4.1, which lists the styles available within a document. The ***Normal Style*** is defined in every document and contains default paragraph settings (left justified, single spacing, and a default font). The Normal Style is automatically assigned to every paragraph unless a different style is specified. The Heading 1 and Body Text styles are other predefined styles.

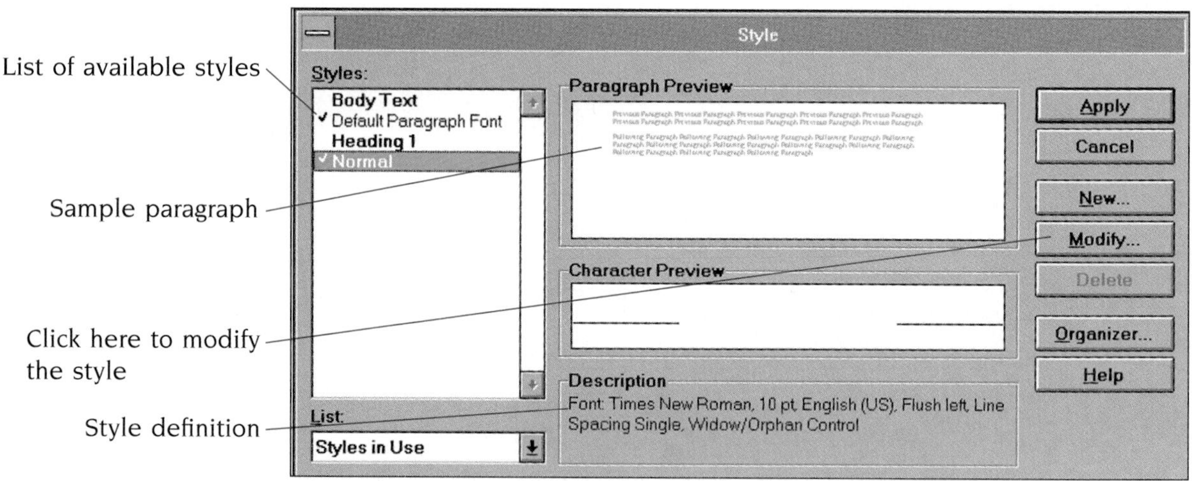

FIGURE 4.1 The Normal Style

The Description box displays the style definition—for example, Times New Roman, 10 point, flush left, single spacing, and widow/orphan control. The Paragraph Preview box shows how paragraphs formatted in that style will appear. The Modify command button provides access to the Format Paragraph and Format Font commands to change the characteristics of the selected style. The New command button enables you to define a new style.

Styles automate the formatting process and provide a consistent appearance to a document. Any type of character or paragraph formatting can be stored within a style, and once a style has been defined, it can be applied to multiple occurrences of the same element within a document to produce identical formatting.

> **STYLES AND PARAGRAPHS**
>
> A paragraph style affects the entire paragraph; that is, you cannot apply a paragraph style to only part of a paragraph. To apply a style to an existing paragraph, place the insertion point anywhere within the paragraph, pull down the Style list box on the Formatting toolbar, then click the name of the style you want.

The AutoFormat Command

The ***AutoFormat command*** enables you to format lengthy documents quickly, easily, and in a consistent fashion. In essence, the command analyzes a document and formats it for you. Its most important capability is the application of styles to individual paragraphs. The command goes through an entire document, determines how each paragraph is used, then applies an appropriate style to each paragraph. The formatting process assumes that one-line paragraphs are headings and applies the predefined ***Heading 1 style*** to those paragraphs. It applies a ***Body Text style*** to ordinary paragraphs and can also detect lists and apply a numbered or bullet style to those lists.

The AutoFormat command will also add special touches to a document if you request those options. It can replace ordinary quotation marks (″ ″) with ***smart quotation marks*** (“ ”) that curl and face each other. It replaces (C), (R), and (TM) with ©, ®, and ™, respectively, to indicate the copyright, registered trademark, and trademark symbols. The command can adjust tabs and spaces by substituting tab characters for multiple spaces and/or eliminate unnecessary tabs in favor of a first-line indent. It can also remove empty paragraphs by deleting blank lines (extra paragraph marks) between heading and body styles.

Options in the AutoFormat command are accessed from the dialog box shown in Figure 4.2. Once the options have been set, all formatting is done auto-

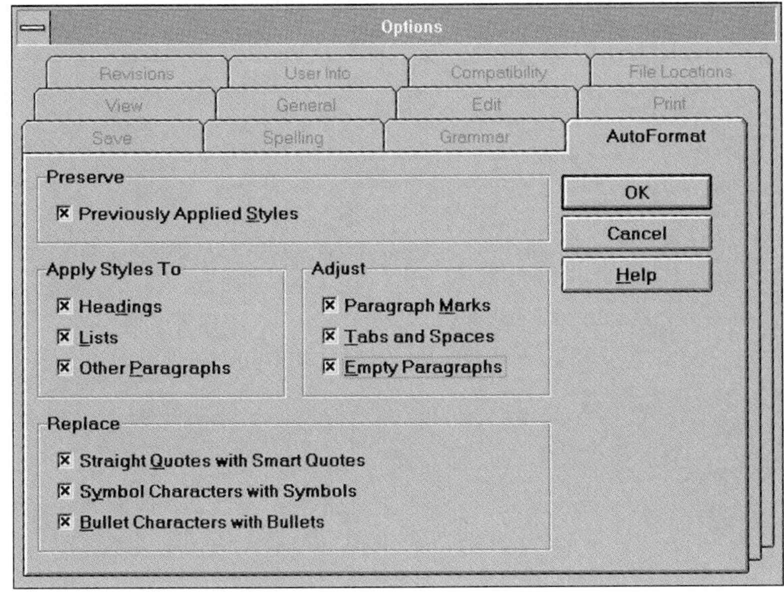

FIGURE 4.2 The AutoFormat Command

matically by selecting the AutoFormat command from the Format menu. The changes are not final, however, as the command gives you the opportunity to review each formatting change individually, then accept the change or reject it as appropriate.

HANDS-ON EXERCISE 1:

Styles

Objective To use the AutoFormat command on an existing document; to modify existing styles; to create a new style. Use Figure 4.3 as a guide for the exercise.

Step 1: Load the practice document

- Load Word. Pull down the **File menu.** Click **Open.**
- Double click **WORDTIPS.DOC** to retrieve the unformatted document that will be used in the exercise. The document consists of 55 tips for Word that have appeared throughout the text.
- Save the document as **STYLES.DOC** so that you can return to the original WORDTIPS.DOC if necessary.
- Click anywhere in the document. The Style box on the Formatting toolbar displays Normal, indicating that the default style is in effect.

Step 2: Establish the view

- Pull down the **View menu** and click **Normal** (or click the **Normal icon** at the left of the status bar).
- Pull down the **View menu** a second time, click **Zoom,** click **Page Width,** and click **OK** (or click the arrow on the **Zoom control box** on the Standard toolbar and select **Page Width**).

Step 3: The AutoFormat command

- Press **Ctrl+Home** to move to the beginning of the document.
- Pull down the **Format menu.** Click **AutoFormat** to produce the dialog box in Figure 4.3a.
- Click the **Options command button.** Be sure that the following options are set: Apply Styles to Headings, Apply Styles to Other Paragraphs, Adjust Paragraph Marks, and Adjust Empty Paragraphs. Click **OK** to accept the options.
- Click **OK** a second time to format the document. You will see a message at the left side of the status bar as the formatting is taking place, then you will see a newly formatted document behind a dialog box.
- Click the **Accept command button** to accept the formatting changes.
- Save the document.

Step 4: Style assignments

- Click anywhere in the heading of the first tip. The Style list box on the Formatting toolbar displays Heading 1 to indicate that this style has been applied to the title of the tip.

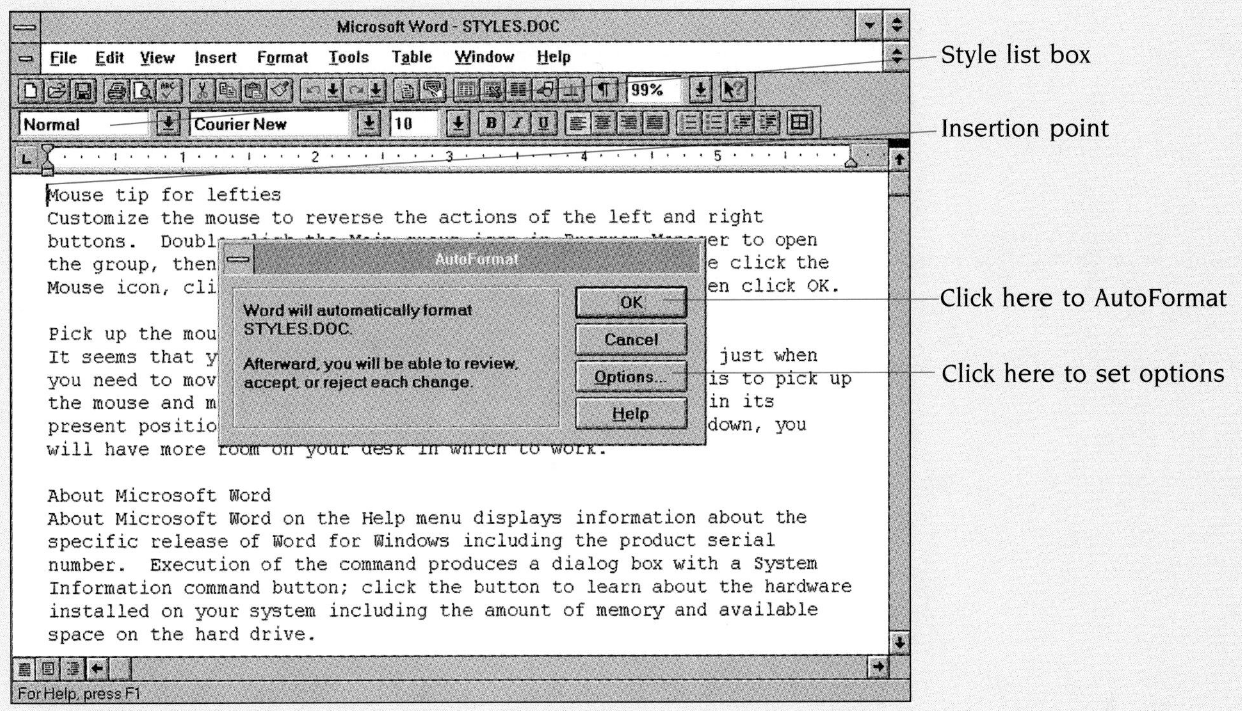

(a) AutoFormat Command (step 3)

FIGURE 4.3 Hands-on Exercise 1

- Click anywhere in the text of the first tip. The Style list box on the Formatting toolbar displays Body Text to indicate that this style has been applied to the current paragraph.
- Click the title of any tip and you will see the Heading 1 style in the Style box.
- Click the text of any tip and you will see the Body Text style in the Style box.

Step 5: Modify the Body Text style

- Press **Ctrl+Home** to move to the beginning of the document. Click anywhere in the text of the first tip.
- Pull down the **Format menu.** Click **Style.** The Body Text Style is automatically selected and its characteristics are displayed within the dialog box.
- Click the **Modify command button** to produce the Modify Style dialog box in Figure 4.3b.
- Click the **Format command button.**
  - Click **Paragraph** to produce the Paragraph dialog box.
  - Click the arrow on the **Alignment** list box. Click **Justified.**
  - Change the **Spacing After** to **12.**
  - Click the **Text Flow tab** on the Paragraph dialog box.
  - Click the **Keep Lines Together** check box so that text of an individual tip will not be broken over two pages. Click **OK** to close the Paragraph dialog box.
- Click **OK** to close the Modify Style dialog box. Click the **Close command button** to return to the document.
- Save the document.

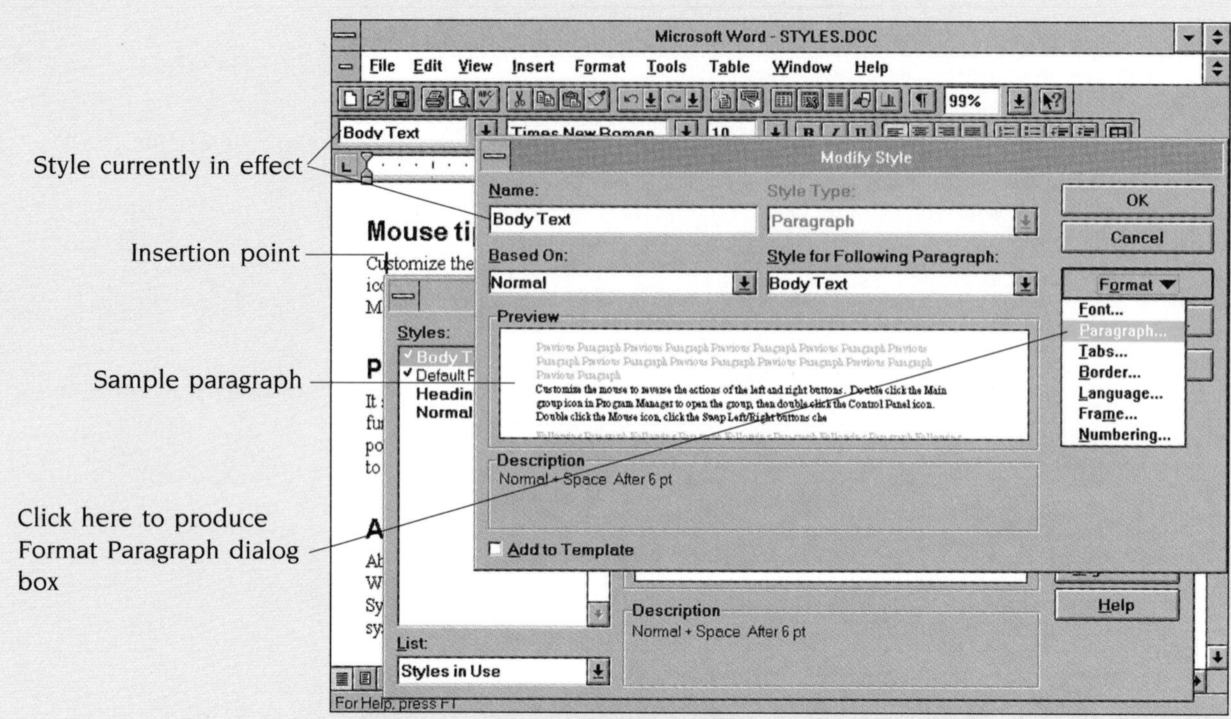

(b) Modify the Body Text (step 5)

FIGURE 4.3 Hands-on Exercise 1 (continued)

Step 6: Review the formatting

- All paragraphs in the document change automatically to reflect the new definition of the Body Text style.
- Click the **Help button** on the Standard toolbar; the mouse pointer changes to a large question mark. Click in any paragraph to display the formatting in effect for that paragraph as shown in Figure 4.3c.
- You will see formatting specifications for the Body Text style (Indent: Left 0," Justified, Space After 12 pt, Keep Lines Together, Font Times New Roman, 10pt, and English (US).) Click the **Help button** to resume editing.

Step 7: Modify the Heading 1 style

- Click anywhere in the title of the first tip. The Style box on the Formatting toolbar contains Heading 1 to indicate that this style has been applied to the current paragraph.
- Pull down the **Format menu.** Click **Style.** The Heading 1 style is automatically selected and its characteristics are displayed within the dialog box.
- Click the **Modify command button** to produce the Modify Style dialog box.
- Click the **Format command button.**
  - Click **Paragraph** to produce the Paragraph dialog box. Click the **Indents and Spacing tab.**
  - Change the **Spacing After** to **0** (there should be no space separating the heading and the paragraph).
  - Change the **Spacing Before** to **0** (since there are already 12 points after the Body Text style as per the settings in step 5).
  - Click **OK.**
- Click the **Format command** button a second time.

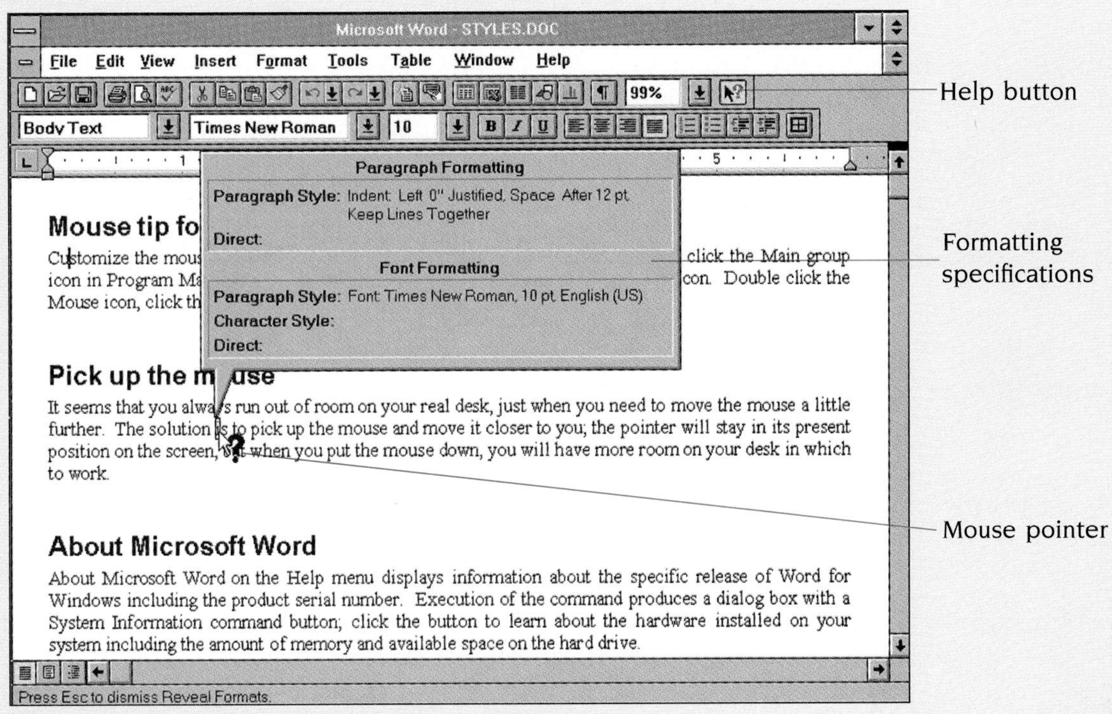

(c) Review Formatting (step 6)

FIGURE 4.3 Hands-on Exercise 1 (continued)

— Click **Font** to produce the Font dialog box.
— Click **10** in the Font size box. Click **OK.**

- Click **OK** to close the Modify Style dialog box. Click the **Close command button** to return to the document and view the changes.
- Save the document.

MODIFY STYLES BY EXAMPLE

The Modify command button in the ***Format Style command*** is one way to change a style, but it prevents the use of the toolbar icons. It is often easier to modify an existing style by example. Select any text that is defined by the style you want to modify, then reformat that text using the toolbar, shortcut keys, or pull-down menus. Click the Style box on the Formatting toolbar and press enter, then click OK when asked if you want to redefine the style.

Step 8: Create a new style

- Press **Ctrl+Home** to move to the beginning of the document.
- Press **Ctrl+Enter** to create a page break for the title page.
- Move the insertion point above the page break. Press the **enter key** five to ten times to move to an appropriate position for the title.
- Click the **Show/Hide** ¶ icon on the Standard toolbar to display the nonprinting characters. Select the paragraph marks, pull down the **Style list** on the Formatting toolbar, and click **Normal.**

➤ Enter the title, **55 Tips in Word for Windows** in **28 Point Arial Bold** as shown in Figure 4.3d.
➤ Click the **Centering button** on the Formatting toolbar.
➤ Check that the title is still selected, then click the **Styles List box** on the Formatting toolbar. The style name, Normal, is highlighted.
➤ Type **Mystyle** (the name of the new style). Press **enter.**
➤ You have just created a new style that we will use in the next exercise.
➤ Save the document.

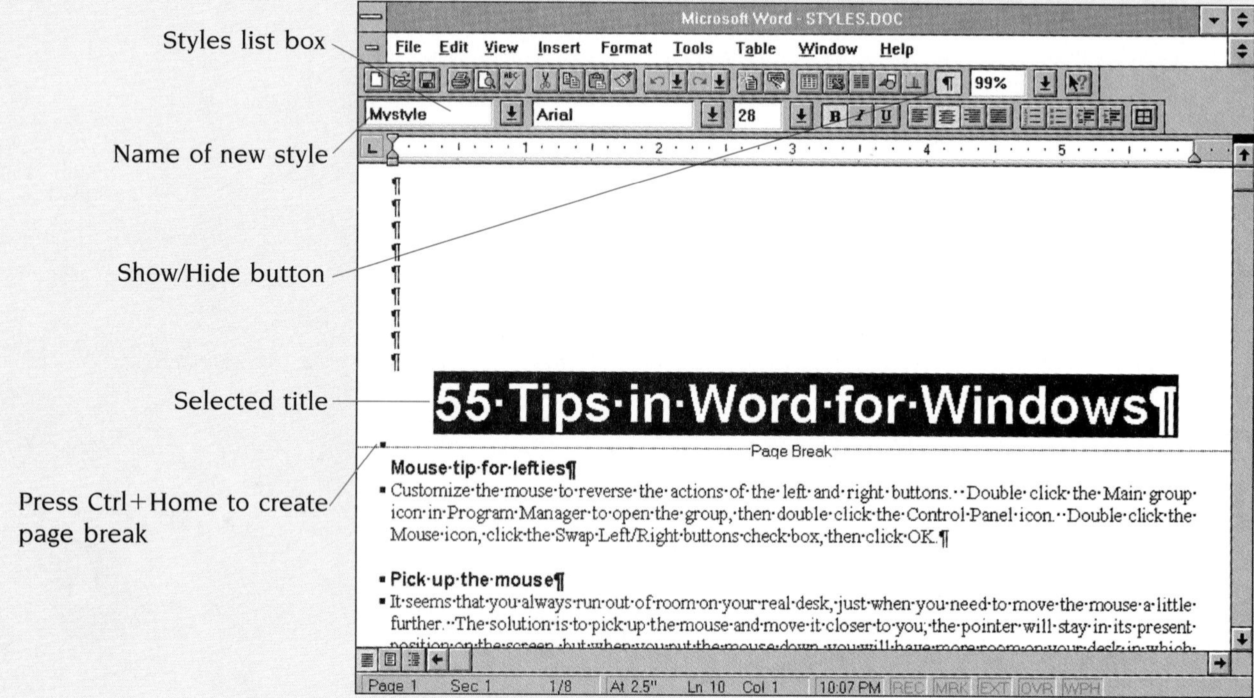

(d) Create a New Style (step 8)

FIGURE 4.3 Hands-on Exercise 1 (continued)

MORE FONTS

We have restricted our design to the Arial and Times New Roman fonts because they are supplied with Windows and hence are always available. In all likelihood you will have several additional fonts available, in which case you can modify the fonts in the Heading 1 and/or Body Text styles to create a completely different design.

Step 9: Complete the title page

➤ Click the **Page Layout icon** on the status bar. Click the arrow on the **Zoom Control box** on the Standard toolbar. Click **Two Pages.**
➤ Complete the title page as shown in Figure 4.3e.
  — Click immediately to the left of the ¶ after the title to deselect the text. Press **enter** once or twice.

— Click the arrow on the **Font Size box** on the Formatting toolbar. Click **12.**
— Type **by Robert Grauer and Maryann Barber.** Press **enter.**

➤ Save the document. Print the document. Exit Word.

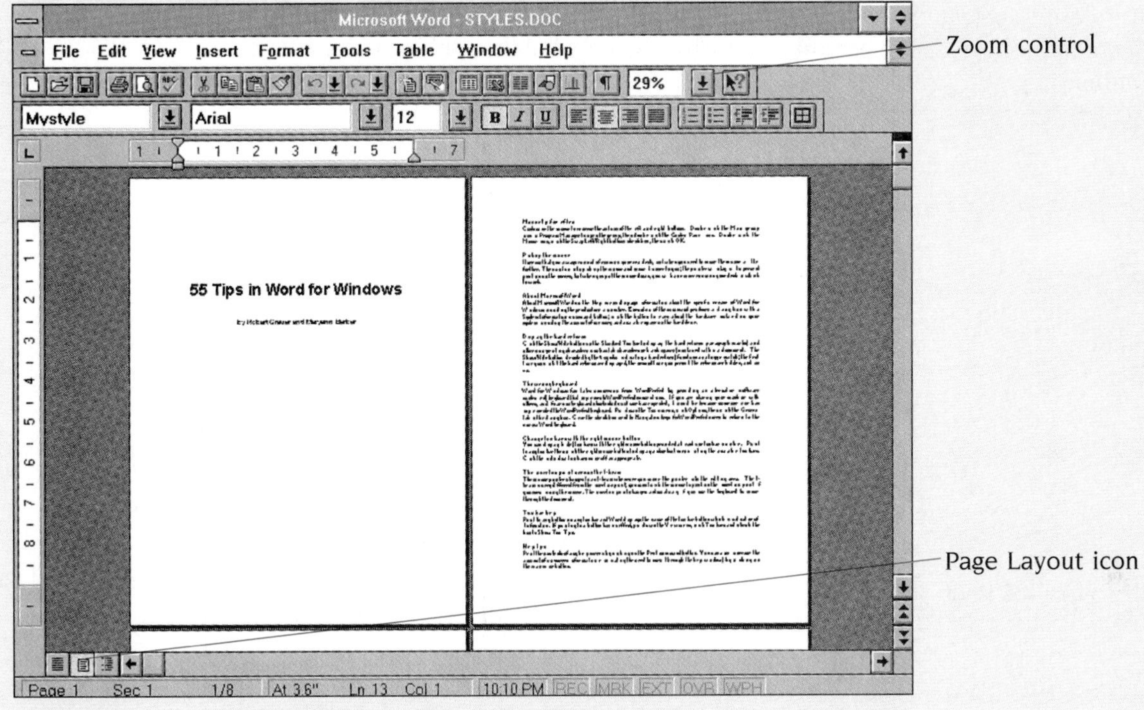

(e) The Completed Document (step 9)

FIGURE 4.3 Hands-on Exercise 1 (continued)

WORKING WITH LONGER DOCUMENTS

Long documents such as term papers or reports require additional formatting for better organization. These documents typically contain ***page numbers,*** headers and/or footers, and a table of contents. Each of these elements is discussed in turn.

Page Numbers

The ***Insert Page Number*** command is the easiest way to place page numbers into a document and is illustrated in Figure 4.4. The page numbers can appear at the top or bottom of a page, and can be left, centered, or right justified. Additional flexibility is provided as shown in Figure 4.4b; you can use Roman rather than Arabic numerals and you need not start at page number one.

The Insert Page Number command is limited in two ways. It does not provide for additional text next to the page number, nor does it allow for different placements on the odd and even pages of a document as in a book or newsletter. Both restrictions are overcome by modifying the header or footer that contains the page number.

Headers and Footers

Headers and footers give a professional appearance to a document. A ***header*** consists of one or more lines that appear at the top of every page. A ***footer*** is printed

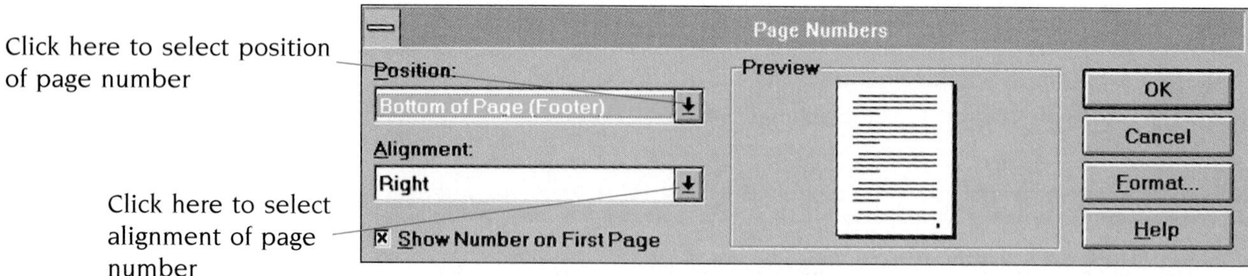

(a) Placement

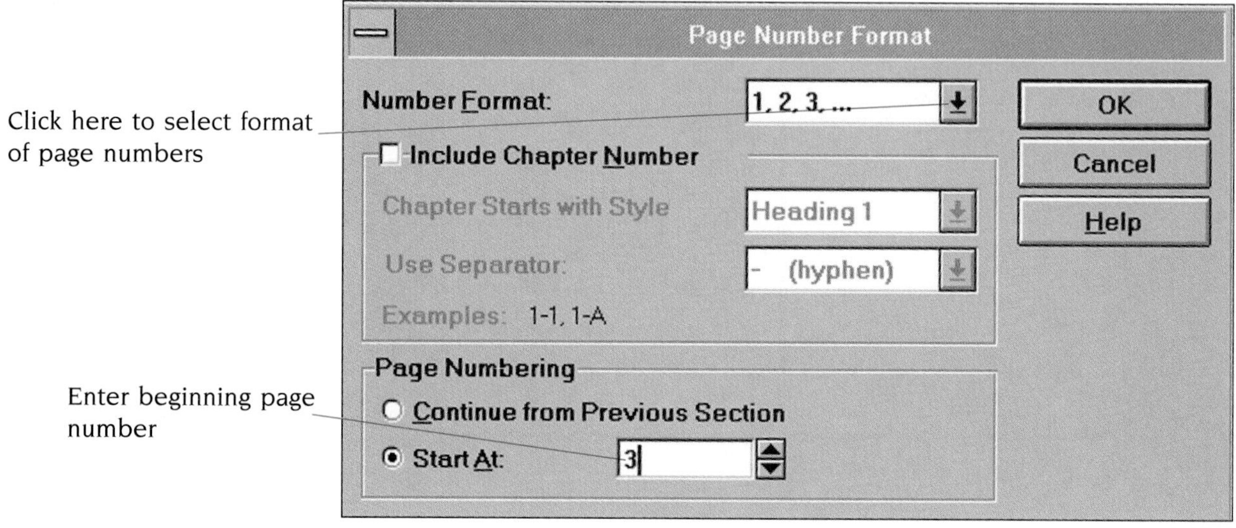

(b) Format

FIGURE 4.4 Page Numbers

at the bottom of the page. A document may contain headers but not footers, footers but not headers, or both headers and footers.

Headers and footers are created from the View menu. (A header or footer is also created automatically by the Insert Page Number command, depending on whether the page number is at the top or bottom of a page.) Headers and footers are formatted like any other paragraph and can be centered, left or right justified. They can be formatted in any typeface or point size and can include special codes to automatically insert the page number, date, and/or time a document is printed.

The advantage of using a header or footer (over typing the text yourself at the top or bottom of every page) is that you type the text only once, after which it appears automatically according to your specifications. The placement of the headers and footers is adjusted for changes in page breaks caused by the insertion or deletion of text in the body of the document.

Headers and footers can change continually throughout a document. You can specify a different header or footer for the first page, and/or specify different headers and footers for the odd or even pages.

Sections

Formatting in Word occurs on three levels: the character and paragraph levels with which you are already familiar and the section level, which controls headers and footers, page numbers, margins, and page orientation. All of the documents created so far have consisted of a single ***section*** and any section formatting (headers and footers, margins, and page numbering) applied to the entire document. You can, however, divide a document into any number of sections and format each section independently.

You determine where one section ends and another begins by using the Insert menu to create a ***section break.*** You also have the option of deciding how the section break will be implemented on the printed page; that is, you can specify that the new section continue on the same page, that it begin on a new page, or that it begin on the next odd or even page even if a blank page has to be inserted.

Word stores the formatting characteristics of each section in the section break at the end of a section. Thus deleting a section break also deletes the section formatting, causing the text above the break to assume the formatting characteristics of the next section.

Figure 4.5 displays a multipage view of a nine-page document. The document has been divided into two sections, and the insertion point is currently on the fourth page of the document (page four of nine), which is also the first page of the second section. Note the corresponding indications on the status bar and the position of the headers and footers throughout the document.

Figure 4.5 also displays the Headers and Footers toolbar, which contains various icons associated with these elements. As indicated, a header or footer may contain text and/or special codes—for example, the word *page* followed by a code for the page number. The latter is inserted into the header by clicking the appropriate icon on the Headers and Footers toolbar.

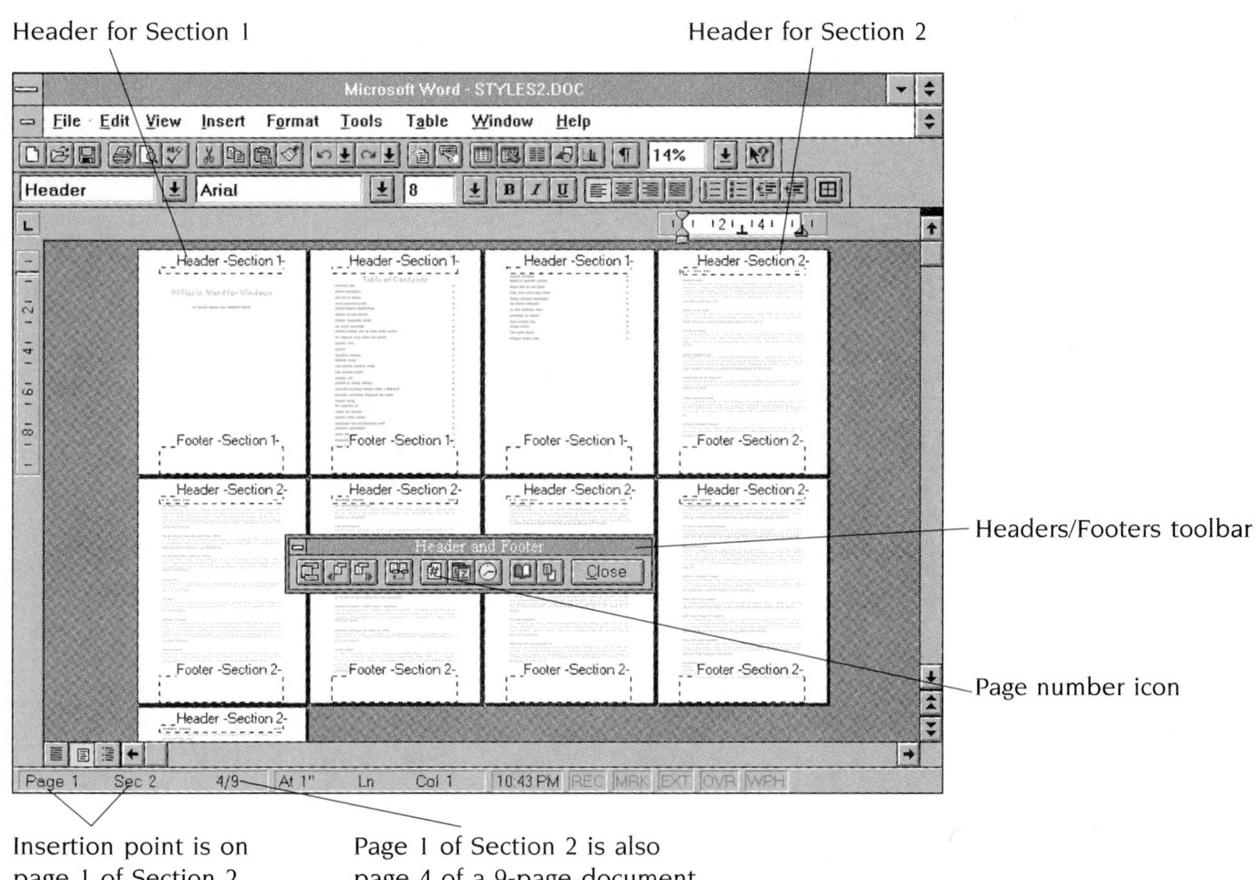

FIGURE 4.5 Headers and Footers

> ### THE SECTION VERSUS THE PARAGRAPH
>
> Line spacing, alignment, tabs, and indents are stored at the paragraph level; that is, change any of these parameters anywhere within a paragraph and you change the entire paragraph, but *only* that paragraph. Margins, headers and footers, page size and orientation, and newspaper columns are stored at the section level; change these parameters anywhere within a section and you change the characteristics of every paragraph within that section.

Table of Contents

A ***table of contents*** lists headings in the order they appear in a document and the page numbers where the entries begin. Word will create the table of contents automatically, provided you have identified each heading in the document with a built-in heading style (Heading 1 through Heading 9). Word will also update the table automatically to accommodate the addition or deletion of headings and/or changes in page numbers brought about through changes in the document.

The table of contents is created through the ***Index and Tables command*** from the Insert menu as shown in Figure 4.6. You have your choice of several predefined formats and the number of levels within each format. The latter correspond to the heading styles used within the document. You can also choose the ***leader character*** and whether or not to right align the page numbers.

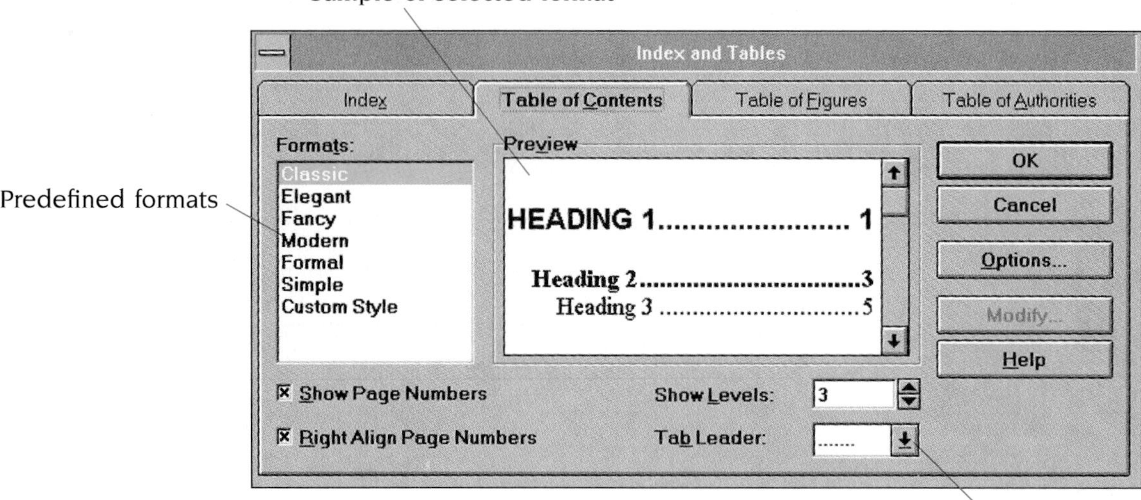

FIGURE 4.6 Index and Tables Command

The Go To Command

The ***Go To command*** moves the insertion point to the top of a designated page. The command is accessed from the Edit menu, or by pressing the **F5** function key, or by double clicking the page number on the status bar. After the command has been executed, you are presented with a dialog box in which you enter the desired page number. You can also specify a relative page number—for example, **P+2** to move forward two pages, or **P-1** to move back one page.

HANDS-ON EXERCISE 2:

Working with Longer Documents

Objective To create a header (footer), which includes page numbers; to insert and update a table of contents; to insert a section break and demonstrate the Go To command; to view multiple pages of a document. Use Figure 4.7 as a guide for the exercise.

Step 1: Load the practice document

- Load Word. Pull down the **File menu.** Click **Open.**
- Double click **STYLES.DOC** to retrieve the document from the first exercise.
- The document should already be in the Page Layout view with two pages displayed; if necessary, change the view so that it matches Figure 4.7a.
- Save the document as **STYLES2.DOC** so that you can return to the original document if necessary.

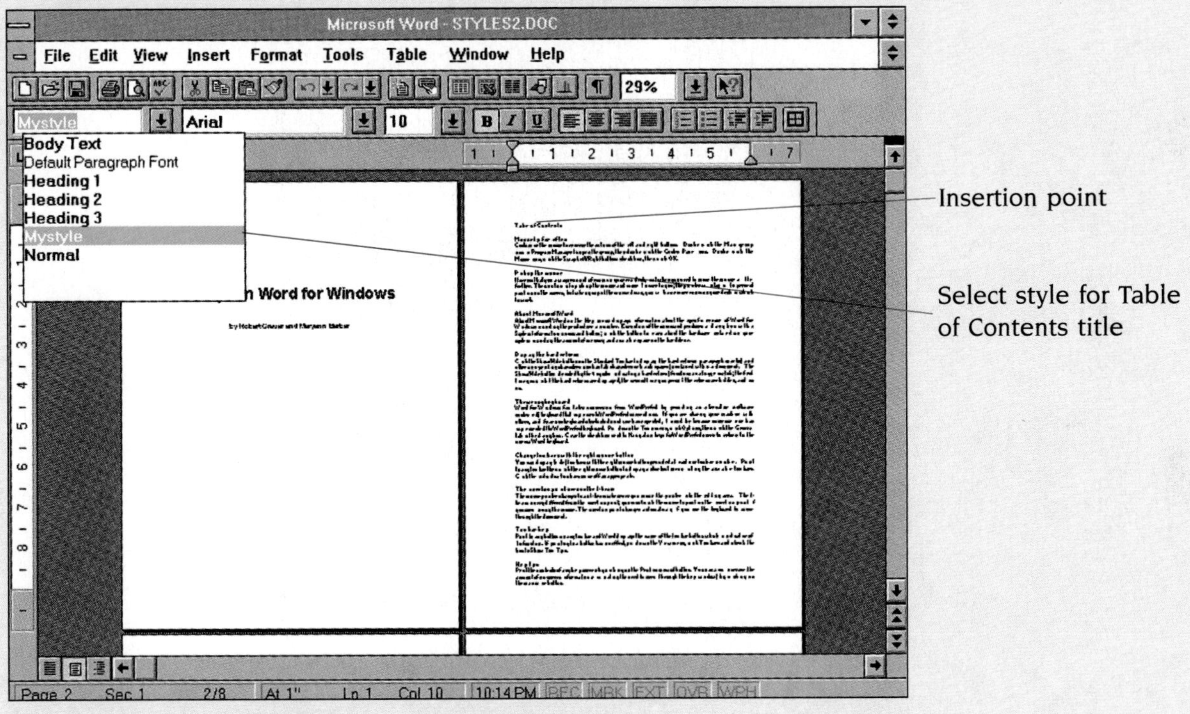

(a) Applying a Style (step 2)

FIGURE 4.7 Hands-on Exercise 2

Step 2: Applying a style

- Click at the beginning of the second page. Type **Table of Contents.** Press the **enter key** two times.
- Click anywhere within the phrase **Table of Contents.**
- Click the **arrow** on the **Style list box** to pull down the styles for this document as shown in Figure 4.7a.
- Click **Mystyle** (the style you created at the end of the previous exercise). The text is centered in 28 point Arial bold according to the definition of Mystyle.

Step 3: View many pages

- Pull down the **View menu.** Click **Zoom** to produce the dialog box in Figure 4.7b.
- Click **Many Pages.** Click the monitor icon and drag to display two pages down by five pages across as shown in the figure. Release the mouse.
- Click **OK.**

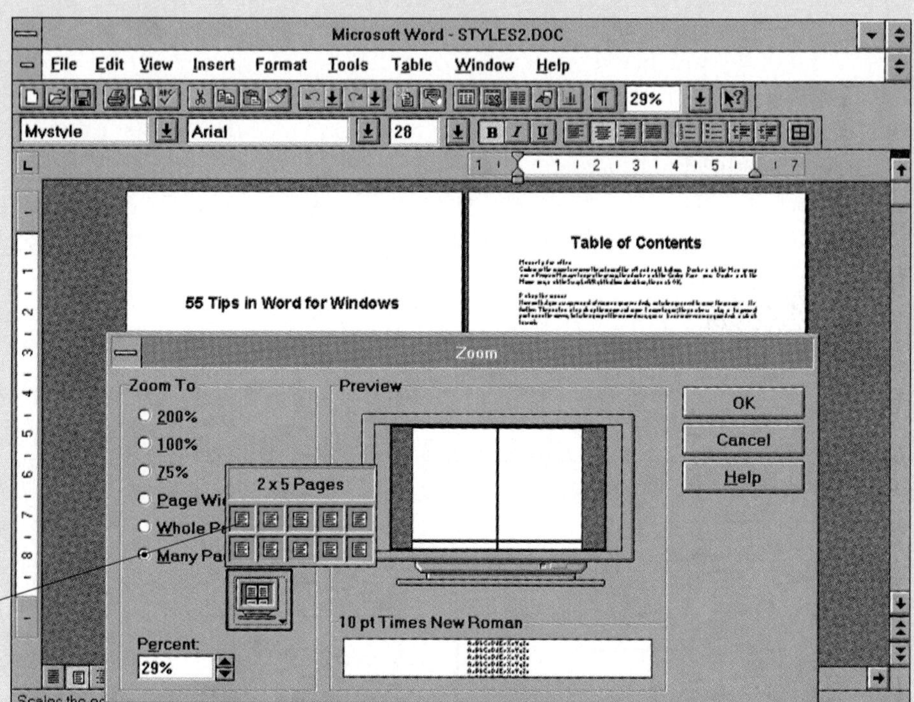

(b) View Zoom Command (step 3)

FIGURE 4.7 Hands-on Exercise 2 (continued)

AUTOFORMAT AND THE TABLE OF CONTENTS

Word will create a table of contents automatically provided you use the built-in ***heading styles*** to define the items for inclusion. If you have not applied the heading styles to the document, the AutoFormat command will do it for you. Once the heading styles are in the document, pull down the Insert command, click Index and Tables, then click the Table of Contents command.

Step 4: Create the table of contents

- Click under the heading for the Table of Contents.
- Pull down the **Insert menu.** Click **Index and Tables.** If necessary, click the **Table of Contents tab** to produce the dialog box in Figure 4.7c.
- Click **Elegant** in the **Formats list box.** Click the arrow in the **Tab Leader box.** Choose an appropriate leader. Click **OK.** Word takes a moment to create the table of contents, which extends to two pages.

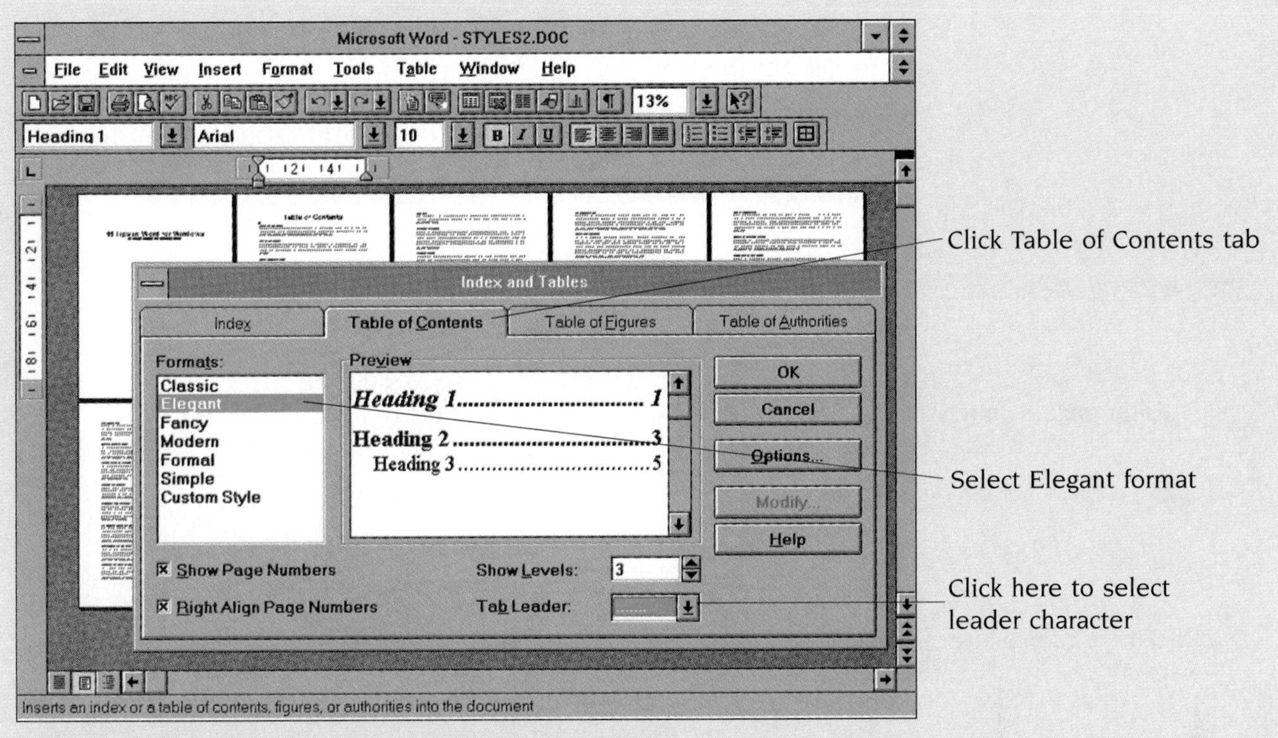

(c) Table of Contents (step 4)

FIGURE 4.7 Hands-on Exercise 2 (continued)

MOVING WITHIN LONG DOCUMENTS

Double click the page indicator on the status bar to display the dialog box for the Edit Go To command. You can also double click a page number in the table of contents (created through the Index and Tables command in the Insert menu) to go directly to the associated entry.

Step 5: Field codes versus field text

- Click on the table of contents, which assumes a gray background.
- Click the arrow on the **Zoom Control box** on the Standard toolbar. Click **Page Width** in order to read the table of contents as in Figure 4.7d.
- Press **Shift+F9.** The entire table of contents is replaced by an entry similar to {TOC\o "1/3"} to indicate a field code; the exact code depends on your selections in step 4.
- Make sure the table of contents code is selected. Press **Shift+F9** a second time. The field code for the table of contents is replaced by text.
- Pull down the **Edit menu.** Click **Go To** to produce the dialog box in Figure 4.7d.
- Type **3** and press the **enter key** to go to page 3.
- Click **Close.**

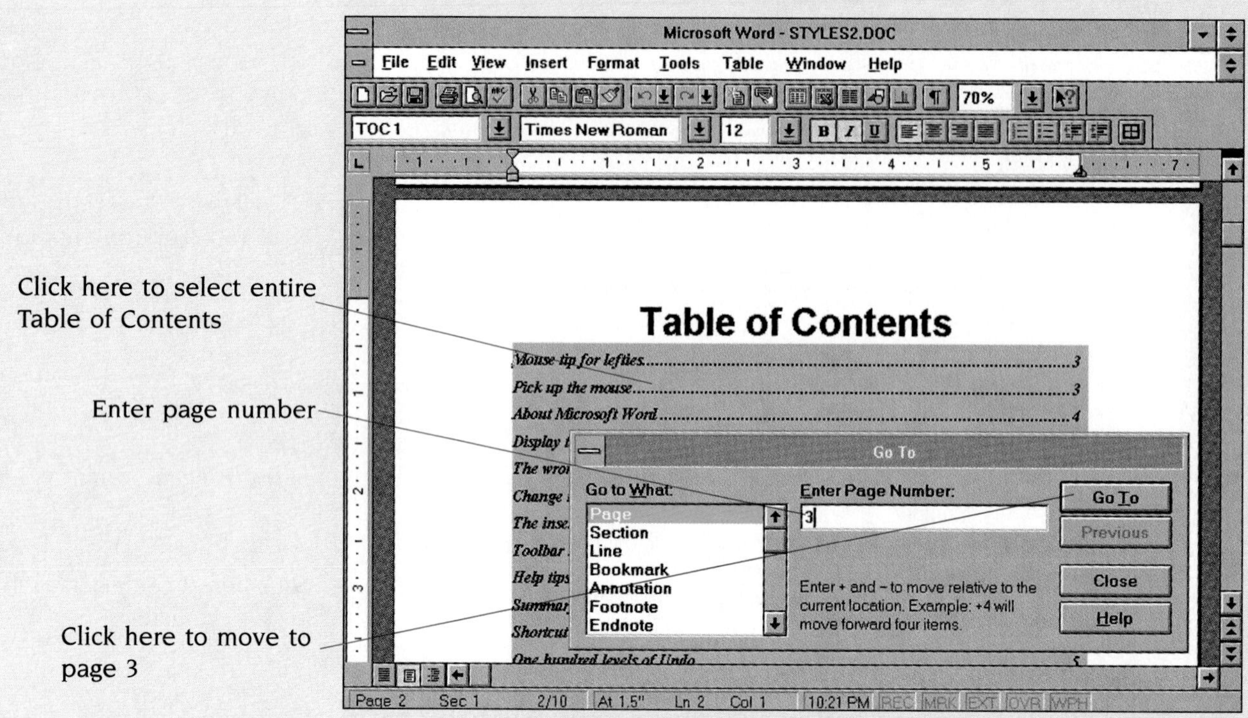

(d) Field Codes versus Field Text (step 5)

FIGURE 4.7 Hands-on Exercise 2 (continued)

THE GO TO AND GO BACK COMMANDS

The F5 key is the shortcut equivalent of the Edit Go To command and produces a dialog box to move to a specific location within a document. The Shift+F5 combination executes the Go Back command and returns to a previous location of the insertion point; press Shift+F5 repeatedly to cycle through the last three locations of the insertion point.

Step 6: Insert a section break

- Scroll down page three until you are at the end of the table of contents. Click to the left of the first tip heading as shown in Figure 4.7e.
- Pull down the **Insert menu.** Click **Break** to produce the dialog box in Figure 4.7e.
- Click the **Next Page button** under Section Breaks. Click **OK** to create a section break, simultaneously forcing the first tip to begin on a new page.
- The status bar displays Page 1 Sec 2 to indicate you are on page one in the second section. The entry 4/10 indicates that you are physically on the fourth page of a ten-page document.

Step 7: Create the header

- Pull down the **File menu.** Click **Page Setup.** If necessary, click the **Layout tab** to display the dialog box in Figure 4.7f.
- If necessary, clear the box for Different Odd and Even pages and for Different First Page, as all pages are to have the same header. Click **OK.**

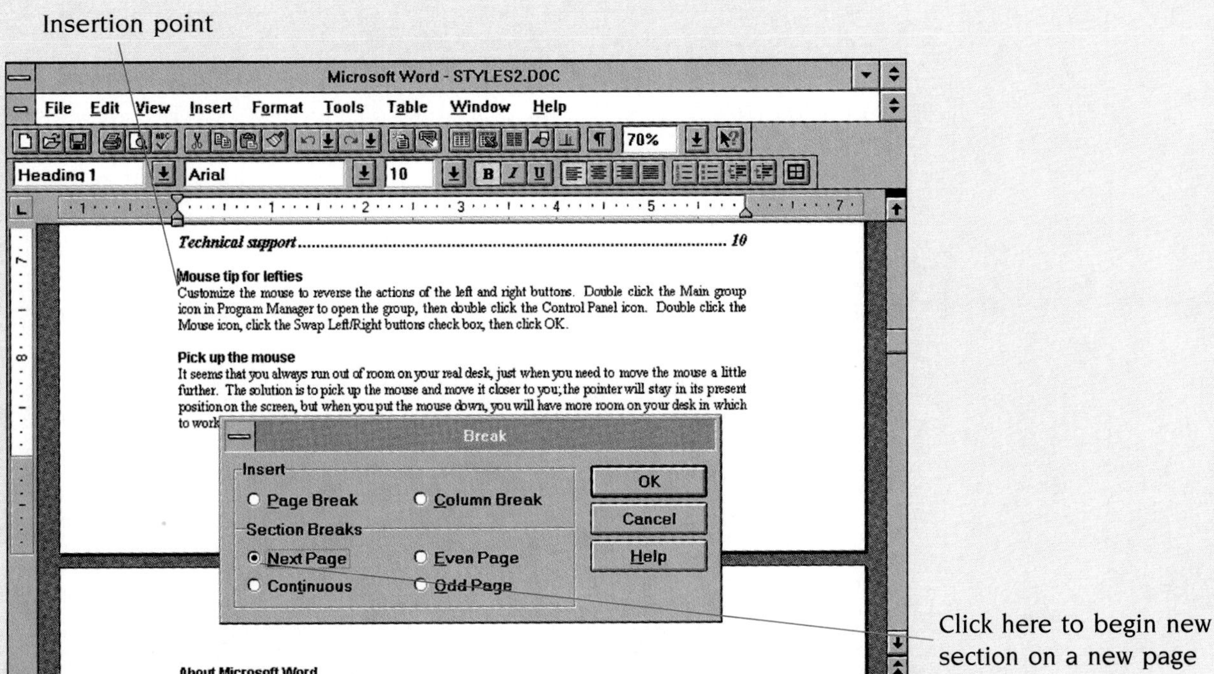

(e) Inserting a Section Break (step 6)

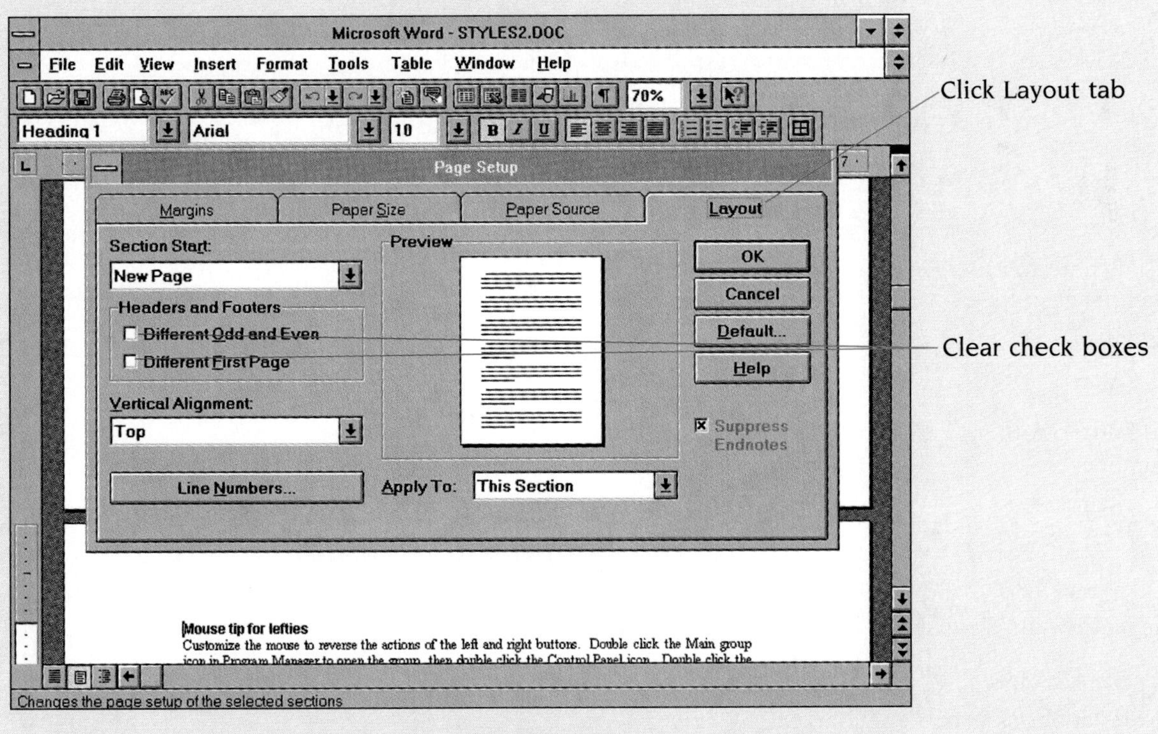

(f) Page Setup Command (step 7)

FIGURE 4.7 Hands-on Exercise 2 (continued)

SECTIONS AND THE GO TO COMMAND

Press the F5 key to display the dialog box for the Edit Go To command. Enter the section number and the page number in the dialog box—for example, S2P1 to move to the first page in the second section.

Step 8: Create the header (continued)

- Pull down the **View menu.** Click **Header and Footer** to produce the screen in Figure 4.7g.
- The Header and Footer toolbar appears in the middle of the screen. The text in the document is faded to indicate that you are editing the header as opposed to the document. The phrase "Same as Previous" appears to the right of the Header line.
- Click the **Same as Previous icon** (fourth from the left) on the Header and Footer toolbar. The "Same as Previous" indicator will disappear from the header. The header will appear only in section two.
- Click in the Header. Click the **arrow** on the Font list box on the Formatting toolbar. Click **Arial.** Click the **arrow** on the Font size box. Click **8.** Type **55 TIPS IN WORD FOR WINDOWS.**
- Press the **Tab key** twice. Type **Page.** Press the **space bar.** Click the **Page Numbers icon** on the Header and Footer toolbar to insert a code for the page number. Press the **enter key** to insert a blank line in the header.
- Click the **Close button.** The header is faded and the document text is available for editing.
- Save the document.

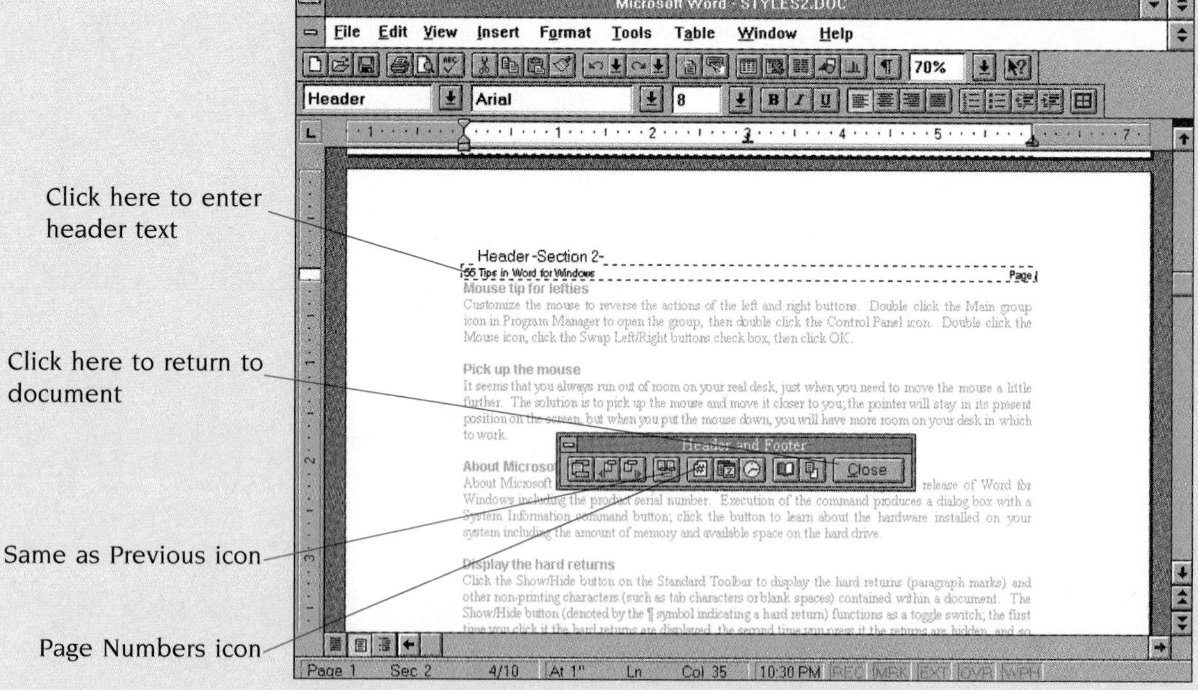

(g) Create the Header (step 8)

FIGURE 4.7 Hands-on Exercise 2 (continued)

HEADERS AND FOOTERS

If you do not see a header or footer, it is most likely because you are in the wrong view. Headers and footers are displayed in the Page Layout view but not in the Normal view. (Click the Page Layout icon on the status bar to change the view.) Even in the Page Layout view the header (footer) is faded, indicating that it cannot be edited unless it is selected (opened) by double clicking.

Step 9: Update the table of contents

- Press **Ctrl+Home** to move to the beginning of the document. The status bar indicates Page 1, Sec 1.
- Click the **Next Page icon** on the vertical scroll bar to move to the page containing the table of contents.
- Click anywhere in the table of contents, which assumes a gray background. The first tip, Mouse Tip for Lefties, is shown to begin on page 3.
- Press the **F9** key to update the table of contents. If necessary, click the **Update Entire Table** button, then click **OK.**
- The pages are renumbered to reflect the actual page numbers in the second section.

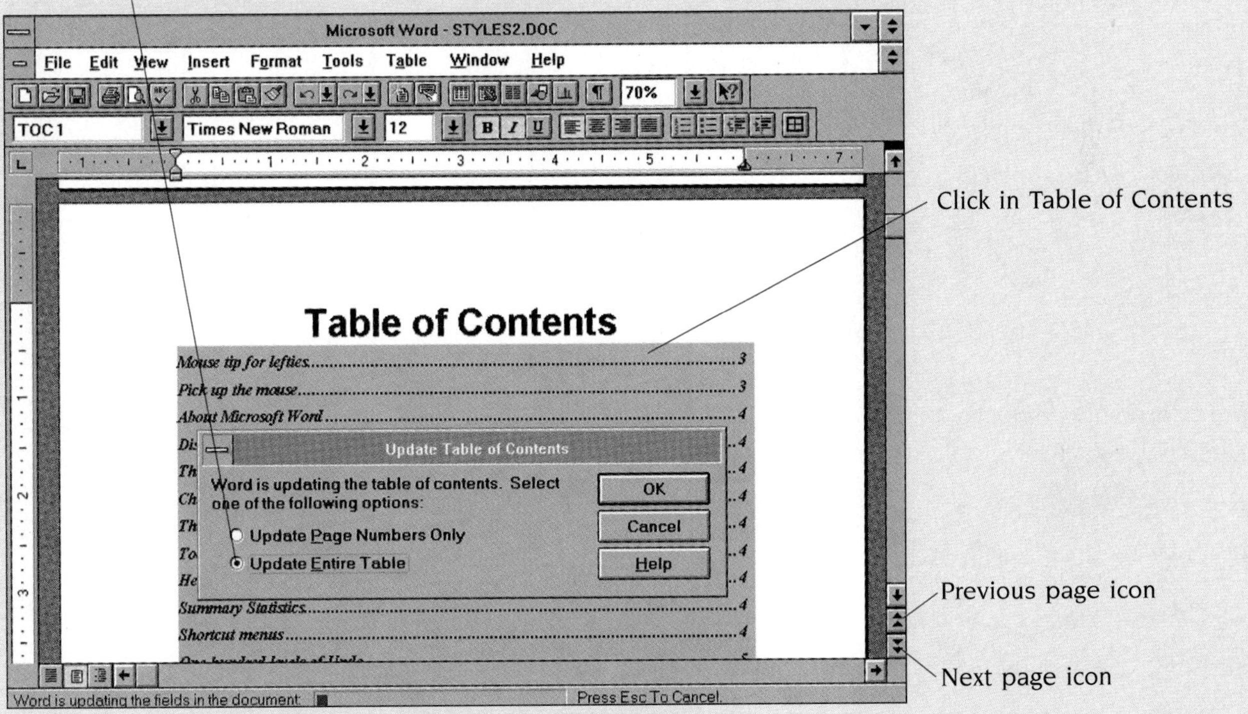

(h) Update the Table of Contents (step 9)

FIGURE 4.7 Hands-on Exercise 2 (continued)

UPDATING THE TABLE OF CONTENTS

Use a Shortcut menu to update the table of contents. Point anywhere in the table of contents, then press the right mouse button to display a Shortcut menu. Click Update Field, click the Update Entire Table command button, and click OK. The table of contents will be adjusted automatically to reflect page number changes as well as the addition or deletion of any items defined by any built-in heading style.

Step 10: The completed document

- Pull down the **View menu.** Click **Zoom.** Click **Many Pages.**
- Click and drag the monitor icon to display two pages down by five pages. Release the mouse. Click **OK.**
- The completed document is shown in Figure 4.7i.
- Press **Ctrl+End** to move to the last page in the document.
- The Status Bar displays Page 7, Sec 2, 10/10 to indicate the seventh page in the second section, which is also the tenth page in the ten-page document.
- Save the document. Print the entire document. Exit Word.

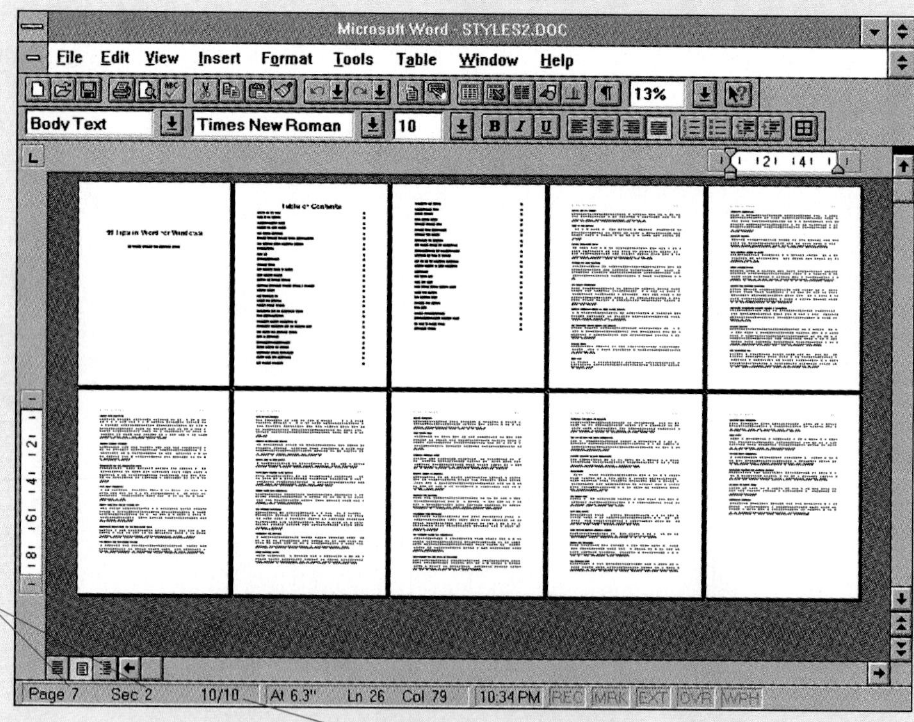

(i) The Completed Document (step 10)

FIGURE 4.7 Hands-on Exercise 2 (continued)

BOOKMARKS

A ***bookmark*** is a predefined place in a document that is accessible through the Edit Go To command. Place the insertion point where you want the bookmark, pull down the Edit menu, click Bookmark, enter a name for the bookmark (40 characters or less consisting of letters, numbers, and/or the underscore), and click the Add command button. To return to the bookmark when subsequently editing the document, press the F5 key to display the dialog box for the Go To command, click Bookmark, choose the name of the bookmark from the displayed list, then click the Go To command button.

TABLES

The ***tables feature*** is one of the most powerful in Word and is the basis for an almost limitless variety of documents. The study schedule in Figure 4.8a, for example, is actually a 12 × 8 (12 rows and 8 columns) table as can be seen from the underlying structure in Figure 4.8b.

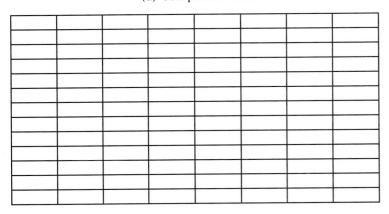

Weekly Class and Study Schedule							
	Monday	Tuesday	Wednesday	Thursday	Friday	Saturday	Sunday
8:00AM							
9:00AM							
10:00AM							
11:00AM							
12:00PM							
1:00PM							
2:00PM							
3:00PM							
4:00PM							
Notes							

(a) Completed Table

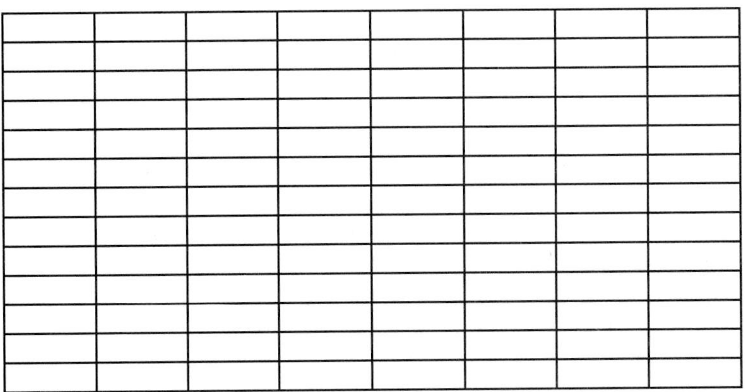

(b) Underlying Structure

FIGURE 4.8 The Tables Features

The rows and columns in a table intersect to form ***cells,*** which contain text, numbers, and/or graphics. Commands operate on one or more cells. Individual cells can be joined together to form a larger cell as was done in the first and last rows of Figure 4.8. The rows within a table can be different heights, and each row may contain a different number of columns.

A table is created through the ***Insert Table command*** in the Table menu. The command produces a dialog box in which you enter the number of rows and columns. Once a table has been defined, you enter text in individual cells. Text wraps as it is entered within a cell, so that you can add or delete text in a cell without affecting the text in other cells. You can format the contents of an individual cell the same way you format an ordinary paragraph; that is, you can change the font, use boldface or italics, change the justification, or apply any other formatting command. You can also select multiple cells and apply the formatting to all selected cells.

The Insert and Delete commands in the Table menu enable you to add new rows or columns, or delete existing rows or columns. You can invoke other commands to shade and/or border selected cells or the entire table. It's easy, and as you may have guessed, it's time for another hands-on exercise.

LEFT ALIGNED	CENTERED	RIGHT JUSTIFIED

Many documents call for left-aligned, centered, and/or right-justified text on the same line, an effect that is easily accomplished through a table. To achieve the effect shown in the first line of this tip, create a 1 × 3 table (one row and three columns), type the text in the three cells, then use the icons on the toolbar to left align, center, and right align the respective cells.

HANDS-ON EXERCISE 3:

Tables

Objective To create a table; to change row heights and column widths; to join cells together; to apply borders and shading to selected cells. Use Figure 4.9 as a guide.

Step 1: Page Setup

- Pull down the **File menu.** Click **Page Setup**. If necessary, click the **Paper Size tab** to produce the dialog box in Figure 4.9a. Click the **Landscape** option button.
- Click the **Margins tab.** Change the left and right margins to **.5** inch each. Change the top and bottom margins to **.75** inch.
- Click **OK** to accept the settings and close the dialog box.
- Change to the **Page Layout** view. Zoom to **Page Width.**
- Save the document as **STUDY.DOC.**

Step 2: Create the table

- Pull down the **Table menu.** Click **Insert Table** to produce the dialog box in Figure 4.9b.

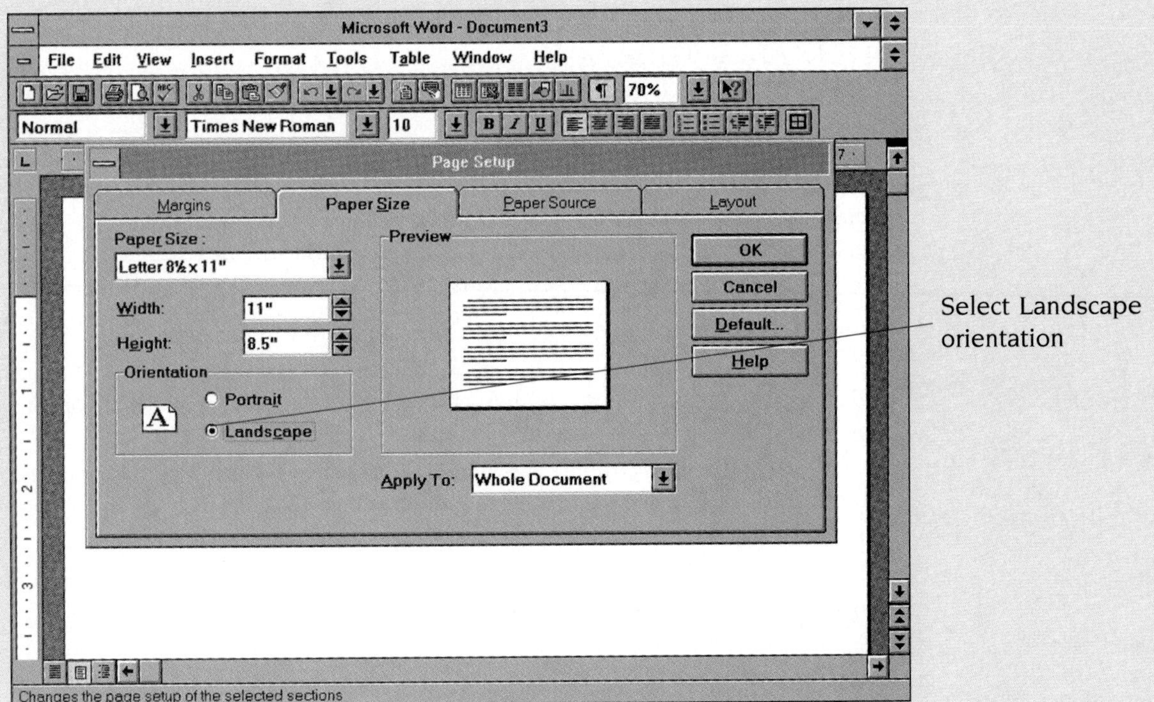

(a) Change the Orientation (step 1)

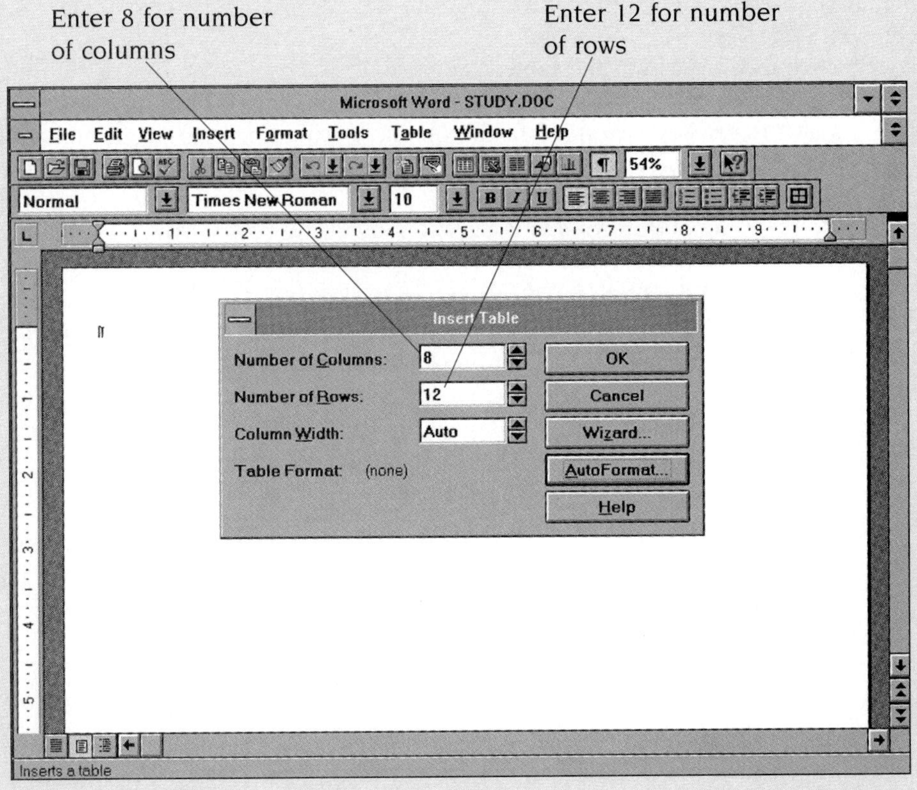

(b) Create the Table (step 2)

FIGURE 4.9 Hands-on Exercise 3

THE TABLE TOOL

The fastest way to create a table is to use the Table button on the Standard toolbar. Click the Table icon to display a grid, then drag the mouse across and down the grid until you have the desired number of rows and columns. Release the mouse to create the table.

- ➤ Enter **8** as the number of columns. Enter **12** as the number of rows.
- ➤ Click **OK** and the table will be inserted into the document. The cells in a table are separated by dotted lines known as ***gridlines,*** which appear on the monitor, but not in the printed document.
- ➤ If you do not see the table, it is probably because the gridlines have been suppressed. Pull down the **Table menu** and click **Gridlines.**

TABLES AND THE SHOW/HIDE BUTTON

The Show/Hide icon can be toggled on (off) to display (hide) the non-printing characters associated with a table. The ¤ symbol indicates the end-of-cell (or end-of-row) marker and is analogous to the ¶ symbol at the end of a paragraph in a regular document.

Step 3: Table Basics

- ➤ Practice moving within the table:
  - — If the cells in the table are empty (as they are now), press the **left and right arrow keys** to move from column to column. If the cells contain text (as they will later in the exercise), you must press **Tab** and **Shift+Tab** to move from column to column.
  - — Press the **up and down arrow keys** to move from row to row. This works for both empty cells and cells with text.
- ➤ Select a cell row, column, or block of contiguous cells:
  - — To select a single cell, click immediately to the right of the left grid line (the pointer changes to an arrow when you are in the proper position).
  - — To select a row, click outside the table to the left of the first cell in that row.
  - — To select a column, click just above the top of the column.
  - — To select adjacent cells, drag the mouse over the cells.
  - — To select the entire table, drag the mouse over the table.

TABS AND TABLES

The Tab key functions differently in a table than in a regular document. Press the Tab key to move to the next cell in the current row (or to the first cell in the next row if you are at the end of a row). Press Shift+Tab to move to the previous cell in the current row (or to the last cell in the previous row). You must press Ctrl+Tab to insert a regular tab character within a cell.

Step 4: Merge the cells

- Click outside the table to the left of the first cell in the first row to select the entire first row as shown in Figure 4.9c.
- Pull down the **Table menu.** Click **Merge Cells.**
- Type **Weekly Class and Study Schedule** and format the text in 24 point Arial bold. Center the text within the cell.
- Click outside the table to the left of the first cell in the last row to select the entire row.
- Pull down the **Table menu.** Click **Merge Cells** to join the cells into a single cell.
- Type **Notes** and format the entry in 12 point Arial Bold.
- Save the table.

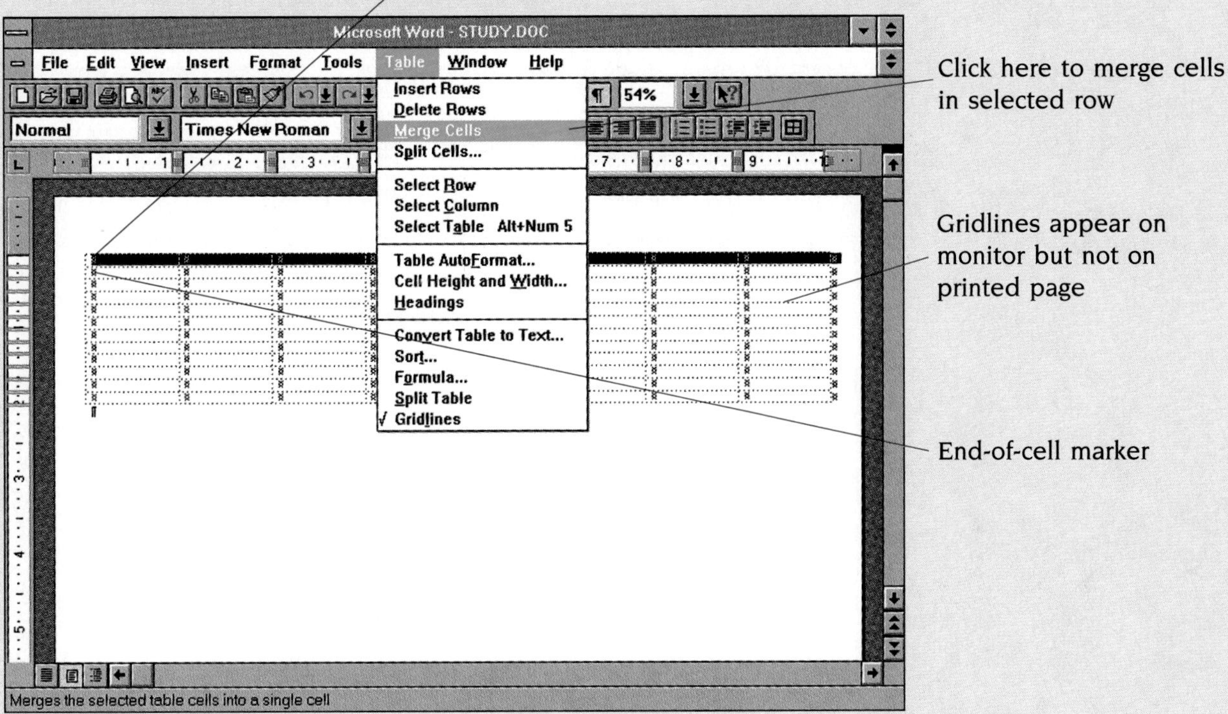

(c) Merge the Cells (step 4)

FIGURE 4.9 Hands-on Exercise 3 (continued)

> **TABLES AND THE SHORTCUT MENU**
>
> Point to any cell in a table, then click the right mouse button to produce a Shortcut menu listing the available commands from the Table menu.

Step 5: Enter the days and hours

- Click the second cell in the second row. Type **Monday.**
- Press the **Tab** (or **right arrow**) **key** to move to the next cell. Type **Tuesday.** Continue until the days of the week have been entered.

- Use the Formatting toolbar to change the font and justification for the days of the week:
  - — Select the entire row.
  - — Click the **Font List box** to choose an appropriate font, such as **Arial.**
  - — Click the **Font List box** to choose an appropriate size, such as **10** point.
  - — Click the **Justification icon** and **center** the text.
  - — Click anywhere in the table to deselect the text and see the effect of the formatting change.
- Click the first cell in the third row. Type **8:00AM.** Press the **down arrow key** to move to the first cell in the fourth row. Type **9:00AM.**
- Continue in this fashion until you have entered the hourly periods up to 4:00PM. Format as appropriate. Your table should match Figure 4.9d.
- Save the table.

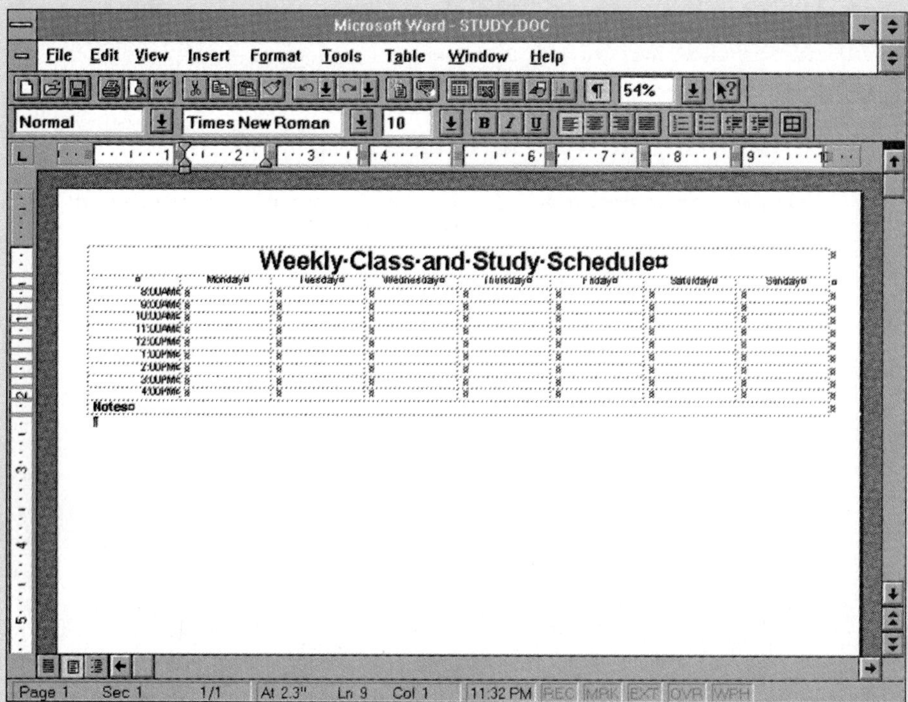

(d) Enter the Days and Hours (step 5)

FIGURE 4.9 Hands-on Exercise 3 (continued)

TABLES AND STYLES

Each cell within a table may be formatted differently. All cells assume the style of the paragraph containing the insertion point when the Table command was executed. Use the Styles List box on the Formatting toolbar to apply existing styles to one or more cells within a table.

Step 6: Change the row heights

- Click immediately after the word *Notes.* Press the **enter key** five times. The height of the cell increases automatically to accommodate the additional carriage returns.
- Select the cells containing the hours of the day. Pull down the **Table menu.** Click **Cell Height and Width** to produce the dialog box in Figure 4.9e.
- If necessary, click the **Row tab.** Click the arrow for the Height of Rows list box. Click **Exactly,** then enter **36** (36 points is equal to 1/2 an inch) in the At text box.
- Click **OK.** Click anywhere to deselect the text and see the new row heights.
- Save the table.

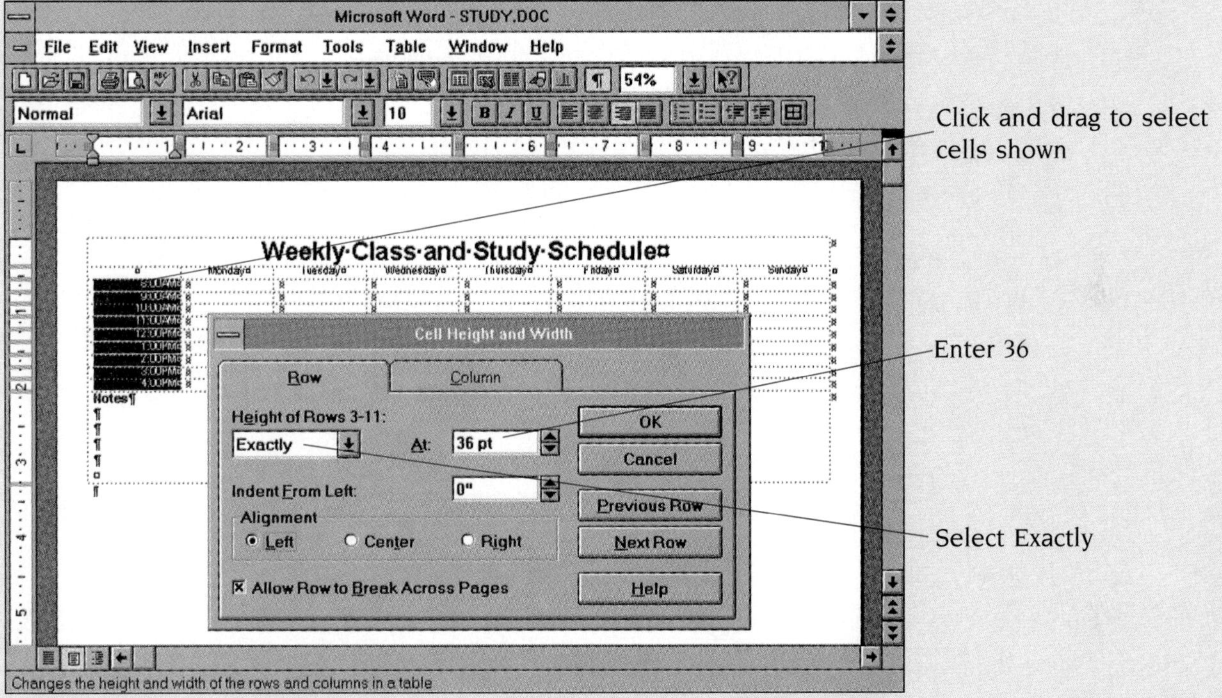

(e) Change the Row Height (step 6)

FIGURE 4.9 Hands-on Exercise 3 (continued)

Step 7: Borders and Shading

- Pull down the **Table menu** and click **Select Table** (or drag the mouse over the entire table).
- Pull down the **Format menu.** Click **Borders and Shading** to produce the dialog box in Figure 4.9f.
- If necessary, click the **Borders Tab.** Click **Grid** in the **Presets** area.
- Click **OK** to close the dialog box. Click anywhere in the table to deselect the table and see the effect of the Borders command.
- Select the first row in the table. Pull down the **Format menu** a second time. Click **Borders and Shading.**
- Click the **Shading Tab.** Click **10%** in the Shading list box. Click **OK.**
- Save the table.

Step 8: The completed table

➤ The completed schedule is shown in Figure 4.9g.

➤ Print the table. Exit Word.

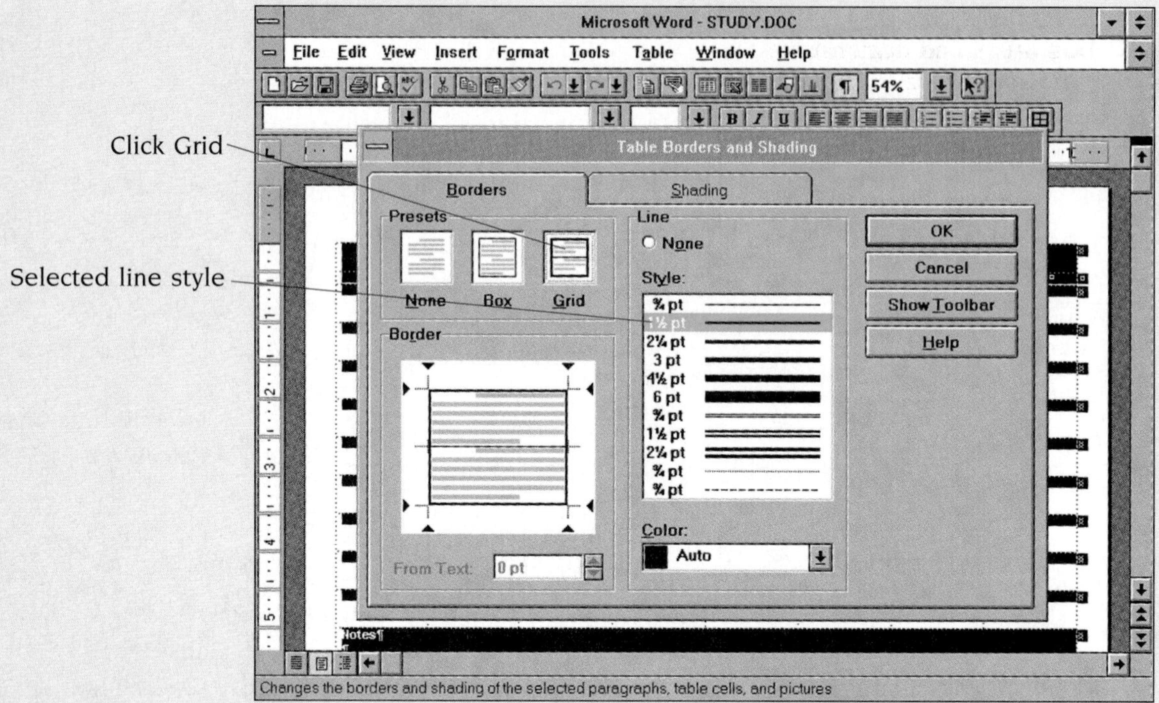

(f) Borders and Shading (step 7)

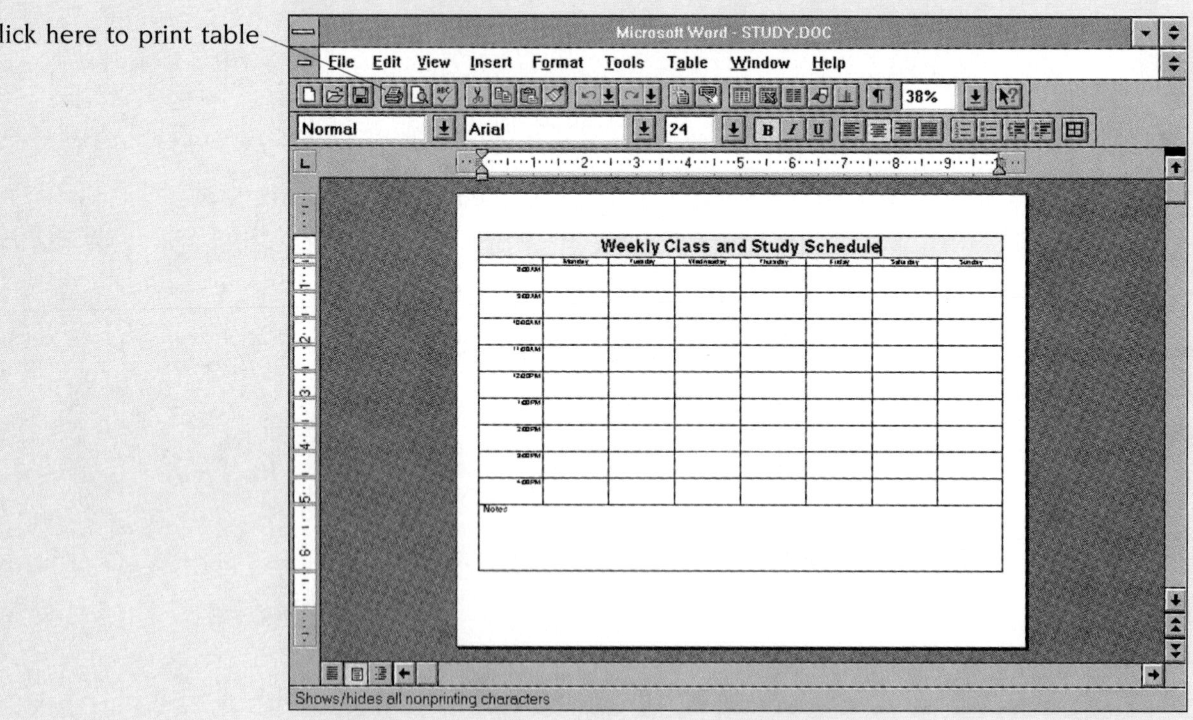

(g) The Completed Table (step 8)

FIGURE 4.9 Hands-on Exercise 3 (continued)

SUMMARY

A style is a set of formatting instructions that has been saved under a distinct name. Styles are created at the character or paragraph level and provide a consistent appearance to similar elements throughout a document. Existing styles can be modified to change the formatting of all text defined by that style.

The AutoFormat command analyzes a document and formats it for you. The command goes through an entire document, determines how each paragraph is used, then applies an appropriate style to each paragraph.

Formatting occurs at the character, paragraph, or section level. Section formatting controls margins, columns, page orientation and size, and headers and footers. A header consists of one or more lines that appear at the top of every (designated) page in a document. A footer is text that is displayed at the bottom of the pages. Page numbers may be added to either a header or footer.

A table of contents lists headings in the order they appear in a document. It can be created automatically provided the built-in heading styles were previously applied to the items for inclusion. The Go To command enables you to move directly to a specific page, section, or bookmark within a document.

Tables represent a very powerful capability within Word and are created through the Insert Table command in the Table menu or by using the table icon on the Standard toolbar. The cells in a table can contain text, numbers and/or graphics. The cells in the table are separated by dotted lines known as gridlines, which appear on the monitor but not in the printed document.

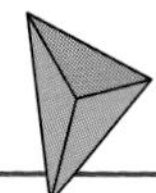

Key Words and Concepts

AutoFormat command
Body Text style
Bookmark
Cell
Character style
Footer
Format Style command
Go Back command
Go To command
Gridline
Header
Heading style
Index and Tables command
Insert Page Number command
Insert Table command
Leader character
Normal style
Page numbers
Paragraph style
Section
Section break
Smart quotation marks
Style
Styles command
Table of contents
Tables feature

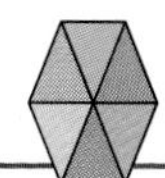

Multiple Choice

1. Which of the following can be stored within a paragraph style?
   (a) Tabs and indents
   (b) Line spacing and justification
   (c) Shading and borders
   (d) All of the above

2. What is the easiest way to change the justification of five paragraphs scattered throughout a document, each of which has been formatted according to the same style?
   (a) Select the paragraphs individually, then click the icons on the tool bar to change the formatting

(b) Select the paragraphs at the same time, then click the icons on the toolbar to change the formatting
(c) Change the format of the existing style, which changes the paragraphs
(d) Retype the paragraphs according to the new specifications

3. The AutoFormat command will do all of the following except:
(a) Apply styles to individual paragraphs
(b) Apply boldface italics to terms that require additional emphasis
(c) Replace ordinary quotes with smart quotes
(d) Substitute typographic symbols for ordinary letters—for example, © for (C) and ™ for (TM)

4. The AutoFormat command
(a) Enables you to review its formatting changes individually and accept or reject the changes one at a time
(b) Enables you to select which formatting options will be in effect
(c) Both (a) and (b)
(d) Neither (a) nor (b)

5. In which view do you see headers and/or footers?
(a) Page Layout view
(b) Normal view
(c) Both (a) and (b)
(d) Neither (a) nor (b)

6. Which of the following numbering schemes can be used with page numbers?
(a) Roman numerals (I, II, III . . . or i, ii, iii)
(b) Regular numbers (1, 2, 3 . . .)
(c) Letters (A, B, C . . . or a, b, c)
(d) All of the above

7. Which of the following is true regarding headers and footers within a document?
(a) Every document must have at least one header
(b) Every document must have at least one footer
(c) Both (a) and (b)
(d) Neither (a) nor (b)

8. Which of the following is true regarding headers and footers within a document?
(a) A different header (footer) can be established for odd and even pages
(b) A different header (footer) can be established for the first page
(c) Both (a) and (b)
(d) Neither (a) nor (b)

9. Page numbers can be specified in:
(a) A header but not a footer
(b) A footer but not a header
(c) A header or a footer
(d) Neither a header nor a footer

10. Which of the following is true regarding the formatting within a document?
(a) Line spacing and alignment are implemented at the section level
(b) Margins, headers, and footers are implemented at the paragraph level
(c) Both (a) and (b)
(d) Neither (a) nor (b)

11. What happens when you press the Tab key from within a table?
(a) A Tab character is inserted just as it would be for ordinary text
(b) The insertion point moves to the next column in the same row or the first column in the next row if you are at the end of the row
(c) Both (a) and (b)
(d) Neither (a) nor (b)

12. Which of the following is true, given that the status bar displays Page 1, Section 3, followed by 7/9?
(a) The document has a maximum of three sections
(b) The third section begins on page 7
(c) The insertion point is on the very first page of the document
(d) All of the above

13. The Go To command enables you to move the insertion point to:
(a) A specific page
(b) A relative page forward or backward from the current page
(c) A specific section
(d) Any of the above

14. Once a table of contents has been created and inserted into a document,
(a) Any subsequent page changes arising from the insertion or deletion of text to existing paragraphs must be entered manually
(b) Any additions to the entries in the table arising due to the insertion of new paragraphs defined by a heading style must be entered manually
(c) Both (a) and (b)
(d) Neither (a) nor (b)

15. What must be done to print the lines separating the cells within a table in the printed document?
(a) Select the Gridlines option from the Table menu
(b) Use the Format Border command
(c) Either (a) or (b) but not both
(d) Both (a) and (b) must be in effect at the same time

ANSWERS

1. d
2. c
3. b
4. c
5. a
6. d
7. d
8. c
9. c
10. d
11. b
12. b
13. d
14. d
15. b

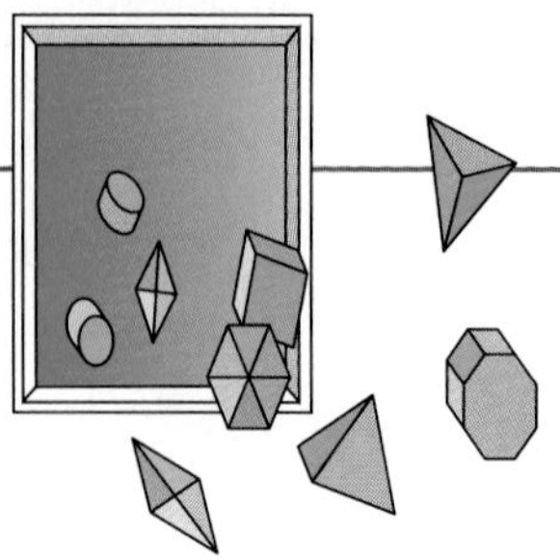

1. Use Figure 4.10 to match each action with its result; a given action may be used more than once.

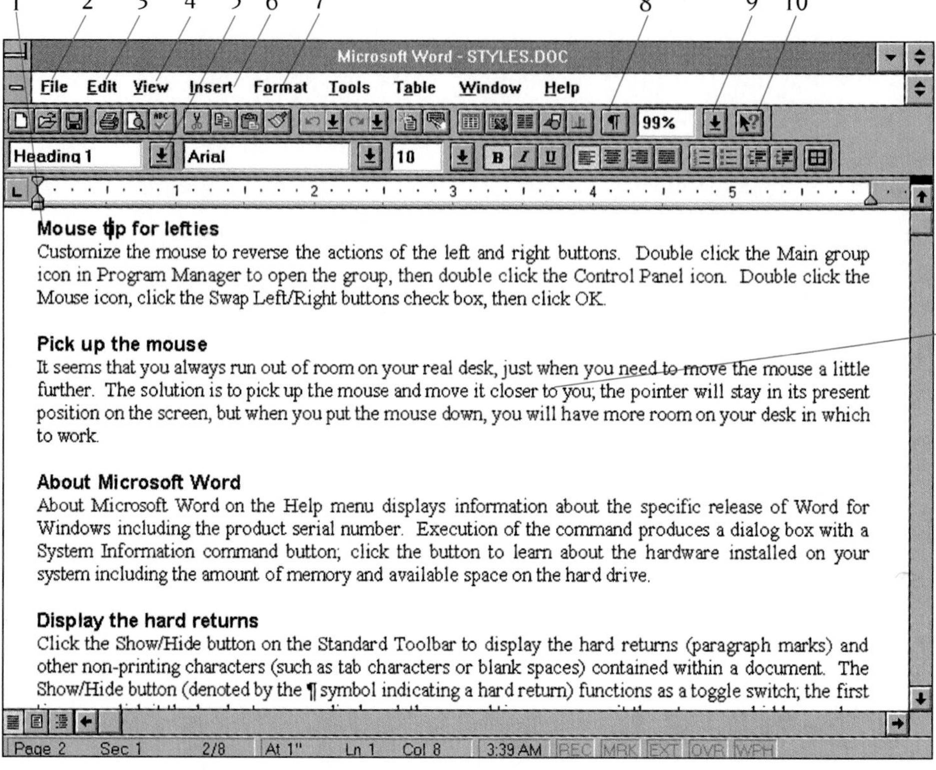

FIGURE 4.10 Screen for Problem 1

Action		Result
a. Click at 1, click at 7	___	Change to landscape orientation
b. Click at 2	___	Insert page numbers into the document
c. Click at 3	___	View the list of existing styles
d. Click at 4	___	Show the paragraph marks
e. Click at 5	___	Create a table of contents
f. Click at 6	___	Zoom to two pages
g. Click at 7	___	Go to page six
h. Click at 8	___	Edit the existing style
i. Click at 9	___	View the paragraph's formatting specifications
j. Click at 10, click at 11	___	Create a header

2. Adding emphasis: Figure 4.11 illustrates the use of a pull quote to add emphasis to a paragraph within a document. Figure 4.11a displays a paragraph set to the specifications of the style in Figure 4.11b.

Horizontal rules are effective to separate one topic from another, emphasize a subhead, or call attention to a pull quote (a phrase or sentence taken from an article to emphasize a key point).

(a) Printed Paragraph

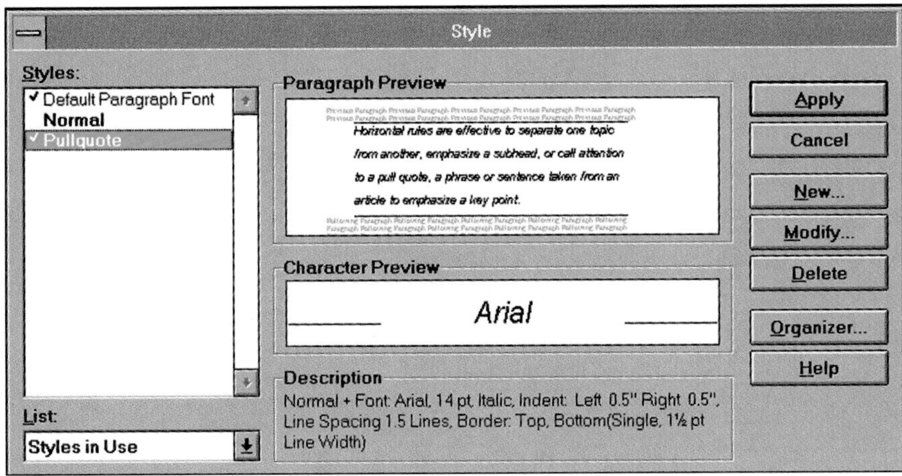

(b) Style Specifications

FIGURE 4.11 Pull Quotes

a. What is the name of the style?
b. Which typeface, point size, and other font attributes are specified?
c. Which paragraph attributes are specified?
d. Which border attributes are specified?
e. What is the easiest way to create the style; that is, should the style be created before or after the commands in parts b through d were executed?
f. How would you modify the style to use a drop shadow rather than the parallel lines at the top and bottom?
g. How would you modify the style so that the text is shaded?

3. Modifying styles: Retrieve the STYLES2.DOC document as it existed at the end of the second exercise and modify it as follows:
   a. Delete the first tip in the document, which is titled Microsoft Tools. Move the next two tips, Mouse Tip for Lefties and Pick up the Mouse, to the end of the document.
   b. Change the Heading 1 style to 12 point Times New Roman (bold).
   c. Change the Body Text style to left justification.
   d. Update the table of contents to reflect all changes to the document.
   e. Add your name somewhere on the title page.
   f. Print the revised document and submit it to your instructor.
4. For the health conscious: Figure 4.12 displays the first five tips in a document describing tips for healthier living. Retrieve the document HEALTHY.DOC from the data disk, then modify it as follows:

Start a Diet Journal

Keep a daily record of your weight and the foods you've eaten. Study your journal to become aware of your eating behavior. It will tell you when you're eating too much or if you're eating the wrong foods.

Why Do You Want to Lose Weight?

Write a list of reasons in your diet journal and refer to it often to sustain your motivation. Good health, good looks, more self-confidence, and new romantic possibilities are only the beginning.

Fighting Fatigue

Paradoxically, the more you do, the less tired you'll feel. Regular balanced exercise will speed up your metabolism, burn calories more efficiently, raise your energy level, and uplift your spirits.

You Are What You Eat

Foods laden with fat, salt, and sugar leave you feeling lethargic and depressed. They set you up for more overeating. A nutritious low-fat diet has the opposite effect. You feel energized, revitalized, and happier.

"Water is the only drink for a wise man." Thoreau

Water is the perfect weight loss beverage. It fills your stomach, curbs your appetite, and cleanses your entire system. Add a twist of lemon or lime to improve the taste and drink eight glasses every day.

FIGURE 4.12 Tips for the Health Conscious

a. Use the AutoFormat command to apply the Heading 1 and Body Text styles throughout the document.

b. Change the specifications for the Body Text and Heading 1 styles so that your document matches the document in the figure.

c. Create a table of contents for the document.

d. Create a header for the document consisting of the title, *Tips for the Health Conscious,* and the author, *Marion B. Grauer.* The header is not to appear on the title page or on the table of contents page.

d. Create a simple footer for the document consisting of the word *Page,* followed by the page number, centered on the bottom of the page. The footer is not to appear on the title page or on the table of contents page.

5. Windows tips: Use the WINDTIPS.DOC document on the data disk as the basis for this exercise:

a. What is the name of the style in effect for the text of the individual tips? What are the specifications for this style? Change the specifications to include a different typeface and/or a different type size.

b. What is the name of the style in effect for the tip headings? What are the current specifications for this style? Change the specifications for the style to include a different typeface, boldface or italics as appropriate, and/or a different type size.

c. Create different headers for the even and odd pages; the even header is to left justify the title of the document, *55 Windows Tips,* whereas the odd header should right justify the authors' names, *Grauer and Barber.* Both headers are to be set in 8 point capital letters. Change the top margin to .75 inch to accommodate the header.

d. Create a title page, 55 Windows Tips by Grauer and Barber. Add a second line somewhere on the page indicating that the tips were prepared for you (and include your name) so that the instructor will know the assignment came from you. Do not print a header on the title page.

e. Include page numbers at the beginning (end) of the header similar to the way the page numbers appear in a book; that is, the page number is to appear before the text of the header on an even page and after it on an odd page.

6. Excel tips: Open the EXCELTIP.DOC document on the data disk and use it as the basis for the following document.

a. Use the AutoFormat command to apply the Heading 1 and Body Text styles throughout the document.

b. Modify the Body Text and Heading 1 styles to your own specifications.

c. Create a title page.

d. Create a table of contents.

e. Create different headers for the left and right pages in the document; do not use a header for the title page or the table of contents page.

7. Sports fans: The tables feature is perfect to display the standings of any league, be it amateur or professional. Figure 4.13, for example, shows hypothetical standings of the NFL and was a breeze. Pick any sport or league that you like and create a table with the standings as of today.

American Conference Standings as of December 5, 1993				
East	Wins	Losses	Ties	Percent
Miami	9	2	0	.818
Buffalo	8	3	0	.727
N.Y. Jets	7	4	0	.636
Indianapolis	3	8	0	.273
New England	1	10	0	.091
Central	Wins	Losses	Ties	Percent
Houston	7	4	0	.636
Pittsburgh	6	5	0	.545
Cleveland	5	6	0	.455
Cincinnati	1	10	0	.091
West	Wins	Losses	Ties	Percent
Kansas City	8	3	0	.727
Denver	7	4	0	.636
L.A. Raiders	6	5	0	.545
San Diego	5	6	0	.455
Seattle	5	6	0	.455

FIGURE 4.13 Table for Problem 7

8. Form design: The tables feature is ideal to create forms as shown by the document in Figure 4.14, which displays an employment application. Reproduce the document shown in the figure or design your own application. Submit the completed document to your instructor.

<table>
<tr><td colspan="4">Computer Consultants, Inc
Employee Application Form</td></tr>
<tr><td>Last Name:</td><td colspan="2">First Name</td><td>Middle Initial:</td></tr>
<tr><td colspan="4">Address:</td></tr>
<tr><td>City:</td><td>State:</td><td>Zip Code:</td><td>Telephone:</td></tr>
<tr><td>Date of Birth:</td><td colspan="2">Place of Birth:</td><td>Citizenship:</td></tr>
<tr><td>Highest Degree Attained:
High School Diploma
Bachelor's Degree
Master's Degree
Ph.D.</td><td colspan="3">List Schools Attended (include years attended):</td></tr>
<tr><td colspan="4">List Specific Computer Skills:</td></tr>
<tr><td colspan="4">List Relevant Computer Experience:</td></tr>
<tr><td colspan="4">References (list name, title, and current mailing address):
1.
2.
3.</td></tr>
</table>

FIGURE 4.14 Table for Problem 8

9. Graphics: A table may contain anything—text, graphics, or numbers—as shown by the document in Figure 4.15, which displays a hypothetical computer ad. Follow the steps below:
   a. Create a 7 × 4 table.
   b. Merge the cells in row one and type the heading. Merge the cells in row two and type the text describing the sale.
   c. Use the Insert Picture command to bring the monitor into the cell in row one, column one. The monitor is found in the file COMPUTER.WMF in the \WINWORD\CLIPART directory.

   d. Enter the sales data in rows three through seven of the table; all entries are centered within the respective cells.
   e. Use the Format Borders command to implement lines and shading, then print the completed document.

   Of course, it isn't quite as simple, but we think you get the idea. Good luck and feel free to improve on our design.

Computers To Go

Our tremendous sales volume enables us to offer the fastest, most powerful series of 486 computers at prices almost too good to be true. Each microprocessor is offered in a variety of configurations so that you get exactly what you need. All configurations include a local bus video, a 15-inch monitor, a mouse, Windows 3.1 and DOS 6.2.

	Configuration 1 4Mb RAM 130 Mb Hard Drive	Configuration 2 8Mb RAM 245 Mb Hard Drive	Configuration 3 16Mb RAM 540 Mb Hard Drive
486SX-25Mz	$1695	$1695	$2295
486DX-33Mz	$1895	$2195	$2495
486DX2-50Mz	$2095	$2395	$2695
486DX2-66Mz	$2295	$2595	$2895

FIGURE 4.15 Table for Problem 9

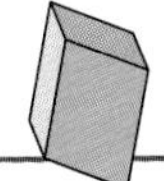

Case Studies

Milestones in Communications

We take for granted immediate news of everything that is going on in the world, but it was not always that way. Did you know, for example, that it took five months for Queen Isabella to hear of Columbus' discovery, or that it took two weeks for Europe to learn of Lincoln's assassination? We've done some research on milestones in communications and left the file for you (COMMUN.DOC). It runs for two, three, or four pages, depending on the formatting, which we leave to you. We would like you to include a header, and we think you should box the quotations that appear at the end of the document (it's your call as to whether to separate the quotations or group them together). Please be sure to number the pages. Don't forget a title page.

The Term Paper

Go to your most demanding professor and obtain the formatting requirements for the submission of a term paper. Be as precise as possible; for example, ask about margins, type size, and so on. What are the requirements for a title page? Is there a table of contents? Are there footnotes or endnotes, headers or footers? What is the format for the bibliography? Summarize the requirements, then indicate the precise means of implementation within Word for Windows.

Forms, Forms, and More Forms

Every business uses a multitude of forms. Job applicants submit an employment application, sales personnel process order forms, and customers receive invoices. Even telephone messages have a form of their own. The office manager needs forms for everything and she has come to you for help. You remember reading something about a tables feature and suggest that as a starting point. She needs more guidance so you sit down with her and quickly design two forms that meet with her approval. Bring the two forms to class and compare your work with that of your classmates.

The Shareholders' Meeting

Your job as CEO also includes the requirement to address the stockholders at the annual meeting. You'll need some charts with the equivalent information as an annual report (use your imagination) but in bulleted form with a much more limited amount of text. The charts should have a consistent look, be done in a larger type size, and be printed with landscape orientation. Use Word for Windows to create a suitable presentation (six charts will do). You might also explore the availability of presentation graphic programs to achieve the same result.

5

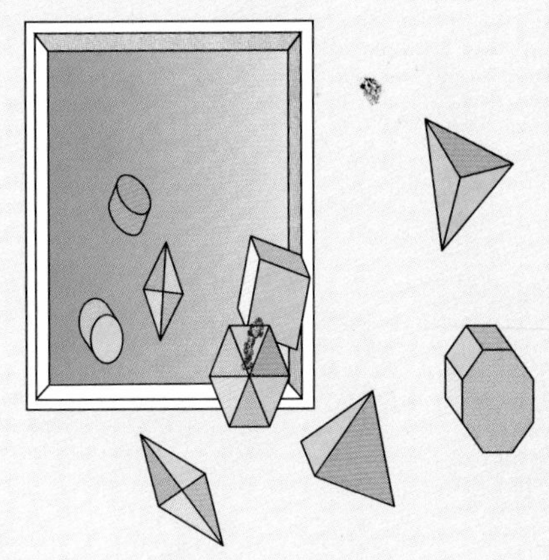

Desktop Publishing: Creating a Newsletter

CHAPTER OBJECTIVES

After reading this chapter you will be able to:

1. Create a multicolumn document; explain how sections are used to vary the number of columns in a document.
2. Use the Format Borders command to create boxes, shading, and reverses within a newsletter.
3. Create a bulleted or numbered list; change the default character for either type of list.
4. Insert a picture into a document; explain how frames are used to move the graphic.
5. Differentiate between clicking and double clicking an object; modify a picture using the drawing tools within Word for Windows.
6. Discuss the importance of a grid in the design of a document; describe the use of white space as a design element.

OVERVIEW

Desktop publishing evolved through a combination of technologies including faster computers, laser printers, and sophisticated page composition software to manipulate text and graphics. Today's generation of word processors has matured to such a degree that it is difficult to tell where word processing ends and desktop publishing begins. Word for Windows is, for all practical purposes, a desktop publishing program that can be used to produce all types of documents.

The essence of desktop publishing is the merging of text with graphics to produce a professional-looking document without reliance on external services. Desktop publishing will save you time and money because you are doing work that used to be done by others. In practice, it is not so easy because you are doing work that was done by others who were skilled in their respective areas. Thus, in addition to learning the commands within Word to implement desktop publishing, you need to learn the basics of graphic design.

The chapter focuses on desktop publishing as it is implemented in Word, followed by a brief introduction to graphic design. We show you how to create a multicolumn document, how to import graphic images, and how to edit those images as embedded objects. We review material from earlier chapters on the Borders and Shading command and section formatting, both of which are used in desktop publishing. We also include several guidelines to help you create a more polished document.

THE NEWSLETTER

The entire chapter is driven by the newsletter of Figure 5.1, which illustrates the most basic capabilities of desktop publishing. These include the ability to:

- Switch fonts within a document
- Use newspaper-style columns
- Include graphic elements
- Preview the document on the screen and manipulate its various elements

The hands-on exercises in this chapter help you create the newsletter(s) in the figure. We think you will be pleased at how easy the process is and hope that you go on to create more sophisticated designs.

Figure 5.1a shows the newsletter as it exists on the data disk. We supply the text, but the formatting is up to you. Figure 5.1b shows the newsletter at the end of the first hands-on exercise. It contains balanced newspaper columns, a masthead within thick parallel lines, and a bulleted list.

Figure 5.1c displays a more interesting design that contains a graphic, columns of different widths, and a vertical line to separate the columns. The figure also uses shading to emphasize a specific paragraph and a ***reverse*** (white text on a black background) in the masthead.

> **ADDING INTEREST**
>
> Boxes, shading, and reverses (light text on a dark background) add interest to a document. Horizontal (vertical) lines are also effective in separating one topic from another, emphasizing a subhead, or calling attention to a ***pull quote*** (a phrase or sentence taken from the article to emphasize a key point).

Typography

Typography, the process of selecting typefaces, styles, and sizes, is a critical element in the design of any document. The basics were presented in Chapter 2, where we distinguished between a serif and a sans-serif typeface, indicated that serif typefaces were preferable for large amounts of text, and that sans serif was preferable for headings and titles. We said that type size was measured in points and that there were 72 points to the inch.

Typography influences the appearance of a document more than any other element. Good typography goes almost unnoticed. Poor typography calls attention to itself and distracts from the document. There are no hard and fast rules, only guidelines and common sense. What works in one instance may not work in another.

One generally accepted guideline is to limit the number of typefaces in a document to two, but to use multiple styles and sizes of those typefaces. Use

Contest Winner
Congratulations to Carol Vazquez Villar, who submitted the winning entry for our logo. Carol wins a pair of running shoes, which she promises to show off at the upcoming Jungle Jog.

Warming Up
Ever pull a muscle running your first mile or playing your first game of tennis? You should have stretched before you started -- right? Not according to a panel of sports medicine experts put together by the National Strength and Conditioning Association.

Warming up, not stretching, is the most important thing you can do to prevent injuries. Muscles that are cold are not very pliable and thus are susceptible to injury. Even stretching should be put off until you warm up with a few minutes of light jogging to increase your metabolic rate and raise your body's core temperature. When should you stretch? After your exercise -- when your muscles are warm.

Cold muscles injure easily
Begin with light jogging
Stretch after exercising
Be kind to your muscles!

Better Fit Than Fat
There is nothing like finishing a meal with a delicate French pastry or a luscious chocolate mousse, but how much will that indulgence cost in calories? And what will you look like on the beach if you keep treating yourself to such delights?

Exercise is important to weight control, giving you more caloric leeway in your diet and suppressing your appetite. The number of calories burned during physical exercise depends on many factors -- how big you are (thinner, smaller people burn fewer calories at the same activity level as heavier, larger people), how hard or fast you work out (the harder the labor or faster the speed, the more calories you burn per minute), the air temperature (the colder the weather, the more calories you burn), the clothes you wear, the type of activity you choose and the amount of time you spend doing it.

Some sports burn more fat than others. Start-Stop activities, such as tennis or sprinting, are primarily carbohydrate burning activities and use 60-70% carbohydrates and only 30-40% fat. Continuous sports, on the other hand, such as walking or jogging, consume 50-60% fat and 40-50% carbohydrates.

Any strenuous workout, be it jogging, energetic walking, biking, or swimming, is fine. The important thing is to make a commitment to exercise regularly, at least three to five times a week, every week. If you haven't exercised in a while, start off slowly and gradually build up to the level that you desire.

Exercise and Income
According to a recent Gallup poll, the higher a person's income, the more likely he or she is to exercise; for example, in households with an income over $30,000, 68% of the men and 60% of the women exercise regularly. In addition, people with college degrees are more likely to exercise than those with only high school diplomas.

The Sun and Your Skin
If you have blond or red hair and your eyes are blue, green, or gray, you are more prone to skin cancer. The harmful rays of the sun are the ultra-violet (UV) ones. Unlike the infrared rays that are screened by the clouds, the UV rays go right through. So even on overcast days you need to protect your skin with a sunscreen with a high SPF factor. The best sunscreens are those that contain PABA esters and benzophenones that protect against both UVA and UVB rays.

As a precaution against skin cancer, examine brown spots, birth marks, moles, and sores that don't heal within two weeks. See your doctor immediately if you notice any change in shape or color.

Jungle Jog
Run the trails at the City Zoo on Saturday, March 15th at 7:00 AM, then meet at the Pavilion for breakfast among the beasts. Robert Plant will defend his title from last year. 35:55 is the time to beat.

(a) Text for Newsletter

The Athlete's Hi

Contest Winner
Congratulations to Carol Vazquez Villar, who submitted the winning entry for our logo. Carol wins a pair of running shoes, which she promises to show off at the upcoming Jungle Jog.

Warming Up
Ever pull a muscle running your first mile or playing your first game of tennis? You should have stretched before you started -- right? Not according to a panel of sports medicine experts put together by the National Strength and Conditioning Association.

Warming up, not stretching, is the most important thing you can do to prevent injuries. Muscles that are cold are not very pliable and thus are susceptible to injury. Even stretching should be put off until you warm up with a few minutes of light jogging to increase your metabolic rate and raise your body's core temperature. When should you stretch? After your exercise -- when your muscles are warm.

- Cold muscles injure easily
- Begin with light jogging
- Stretch after exercising
- Be kind to your muscles!

Better Fit Than Fat
There is nothing like finishing a meal with a delicate French pastry or a luscious chocolate mousse, but how much will that indulgence cost in calories? And what will you look like on the beach if you keep treating yourself to such delights?

Exercise is important to weight control, giving you more caloric leeway in your diet and suppressing your appetite. The number of calories burned during physical exercise depends on many factors -- how big you are (thinner, smaller people burn fewer calories at the same activity level as heavier, larger people), how hard or fast you work out (the harder the labor or faster the speed, the more calories you burn per minute), the air temperature (the colder the weather, the more calories you burn), the clothes you wear, the type of activity you choose and the amount of time you spend doing it.

Some sports burn more fat than others. Start-Stop activities, such as tennis or sprinting, are primarily carbohydrate burning activities and use 60-70% carbohydrates and only 30-40% fat. Continuous sports, on the other hand, such as walking or jogging, consume 50-60% fat and 40-50% carbohydrates.

Any strenuous workout, be it jogging, energetic walking, biking, or swimming, is fine. The important thing is to make a commitment to exercise regularly, at least three to five times a week, every week. If you haven't exercised in a while, start off slowly and gradually build up to the level that you desire.

Exercise and Income
According to a recent Gallup poll, the higher a person's income, the more likely he or she is to exercise; for example, in households with an income over $30,000, 68% of the men and 60% of the women exercise regularly. In addition, people with college degrees are more likely to exercise than those with only high school diplomas.

The Sun and Your Skin
If you have blond or red hair and your eyes are blue, green, or gray, you are more prone to skin cancer. The harmful rays of the sun are the ultra-violet (UV) ones. Unlike the infrared rays that are screened by the clouds, the UV rays go right through. So even on overcast days you need to protect your skin with a sunscreen with a high SPF factor. The best sunscreens are those that contain PABA esters and benzophenones that protect against both UVA and UVB rays.

As a precaution against skin cancer, examine brown spots, birth marks, moles, and sores that don't heal within two weeks. See your doctor immediately if you notice any change in shape or color.

Jungle Jog
Run the trails at the City Zoo on Saturday, March 15th at 7:00 AM, then meet at the Pavilion for breakfast among the beasts. Robert Plant will defend his title from last year. 33:55 is the time to beat.

(b) At End of Exercise 1

The Athlete's Hi

Contest Winner
Congratulations to Carol Vazquez Villar, who submitted the winning entry for our logo. Carol wins a pair of running shoes, which she promises to show off at the upcoming Jungle Jog.

Warming Up
Ever pull a muscle running your first mile or playing your first game of tennis? You should have stretched before you started -- right? Not according to a panel of sports medicine experts put together by the National Strength and Conditioning Association.

Warming up, not stretching, is the most important thing you can do to prevent injuries. Muscles that are cold are not very pliable and thus are susceptible to injury. Even stretching should be put off until you warm up with a few minutes of light jogging to increase your metabolic rate and raise your body's core temperature. When should you stretch? After your exercise -- when your muscles are warm.

- Cold muscles injure easily
- Begin with light jogging
- Stretch after exercising
- Be kind to your muscles!

Better Fit Than Fat
There is nothing like finishing a meal with a delicate French pastry or a luscious chocolate mousse, but how much will that indulgence cost in calories? And what will you look like on the beach if you keep treating yourself to such delights?

Exercise is important to weight control, giving you more caloric leeway in your diet and suppressing your appetite. The number of calories burned during physical exercise depends on many factors -- how big you are (thinner, smaller people burn fewer calories at the same activity level as heavier, larger people), how hard or fast you work out (the harder the labor or faster the speed, the more calories you burn per minute), the air temperature (the colder the weather, the more calories you burn), the clothes you wear, the type of activity you choose and the amount of time you spend doing it.

Some sports burn more fat than others. Start-Stop activities, such as tennis or sprinting, are primarily carbohydrate burning activities and use 60-70% carbohydrates and only 30-40% fat. Continuous sports, on the other hand, such as walking or jogging, consume 50-60% fat and 40-50% carbohydrates.

Any strenuous workout, be it jogging, energetic walking, biking, or swimming, is fine. The important thing is to make a commitment to exercise regularly, at least three to five times a week, every week. If you haven't exercised in a while, start off slowly and gradually build up to the level that you desire.

Exercise and Income
According to a recent Gallup poll, the higher a person's income, the more likely he or she is to exercise; for example, in households with an income over $30,000, 68% of the men and 60% of the women exercise regularly. In addition, people with college degrees are more likely to exercise than those with only high school diplomas.

The Sun and Your Skin
If you have blond or red hair and your eyes are blue, green, or gray, you are more prone to skin cancer. The harmful rays of the sun are the ultra-violet (UV) ones. Unlike the infrared rays that are screened by the clouds, the UV rays go right through. So even on overcast days you need to protect your skin with a sunscreen with a high SPF factor. The best sunscreens are those that contain PABA esters and benzophenones that protect against both UVA and UVB rays.

As a precaution against skin cancer, examine brown spots, birth marks, moles, and sores that don't heal within two weeks. See your doctor immediately if you notice any change in shape or color.

Jungle Jog
Run the trails at the City Zoo on Saturday, March 15th at 7:00 AM, then meet at the Pavilion for breakfast among the beasts. Robert Plant will defend his title from last year. 35:55 is the time to beat.

(c) At End of Exercise 2

FIGURE 5.1 The Newsletter

boldface and/or italics for emphasis. Vary the type size to distinguish between headings, subheadings, and text.

You should also choose a type size that is consistent with the column width. The larger the type size, the longer the line, or conversely, the shorter the line, the smaller the type size. Avoid very narrow columns because they are choppy and difficult to read. Overly wide columns can be just as bad because they seem to go on indefinitely.

Columns

The ***Columns command*** in the Format menu enables you to define ***newspaper-style columns*** in which text flows continuously from the bottom of one column to the top of the next. You specify the number of columns and optionally the space between columns. Word does the rest. It calculates the width of each column according to the left and right margins on the page and the specified (default) space between columns.

The dialog box in Figure 5.2 specifies three equal columns with .25 inch between each column. The two-inch width of each column is computed automatically based on left and right margins of one inch each and the one-quarter inch spacing between columns. The margins and the space between the columns, a total of 2½ inches in this example, is subtracted from the page width of 8½ inches. The remaining 6 inches is divided by three, resulting in a column width of two inches.

The number of columns can vary within a document. The newsletter, for example, uses a single column at the top of the page for the masthead and multiple columns on the rest of the page. Columns are implemented at the section level and thus a section break must be inserted whenever the column specification changes. (Section formatting was described in Chapter 4, where sections were used to change margins, headers and/or footers, and page numbering.)

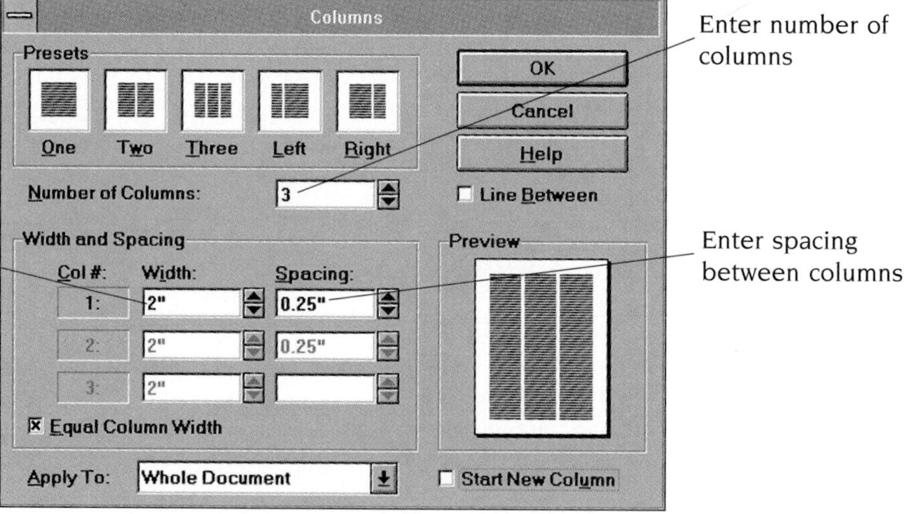

FIGURE 5.2 The Columns Command

UNEQUAL COLUMNS

Add interest to a document by creating columns of different widths. Pull down the Format menu, click Columns, then click the Left or Right icon in the Presets area. Change the number, width, and/or spacing between columns, and Word automatically changes the other parameters to match.

Lists

Three types of lists are built into Word. A ***bulleted list*** emphasizes (and separates) the items. A ***numbered list*** sequences (and prioritizes) the items and is automatically updated to accommodate additions or deletions to the list. A ***multilevel list*** implements an outline and is not discussed further. Any of the lists are created by selecting the items, then executing the ***Bullets and Numbering command*** in the Format menu.

The tabs within the Bullets and Numbering dialog box enable you to modify the style of any list as shown in Figure 5.3. Different bullets may be chosen as shown in Figure 5.3a, or different numbering schemes as in Figure 5.3b. A hanging indent may be specified for either type of list. Additional flexibility is provided by clicking the Modify command button in either dialog box to change the distance between the numbers or bullets and the associated text.

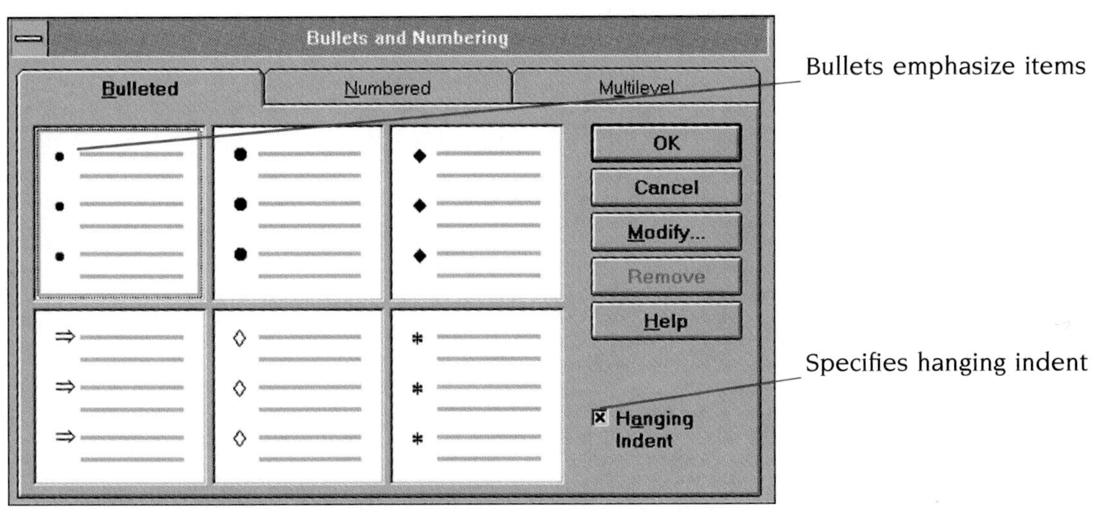

(a) Bulleted List

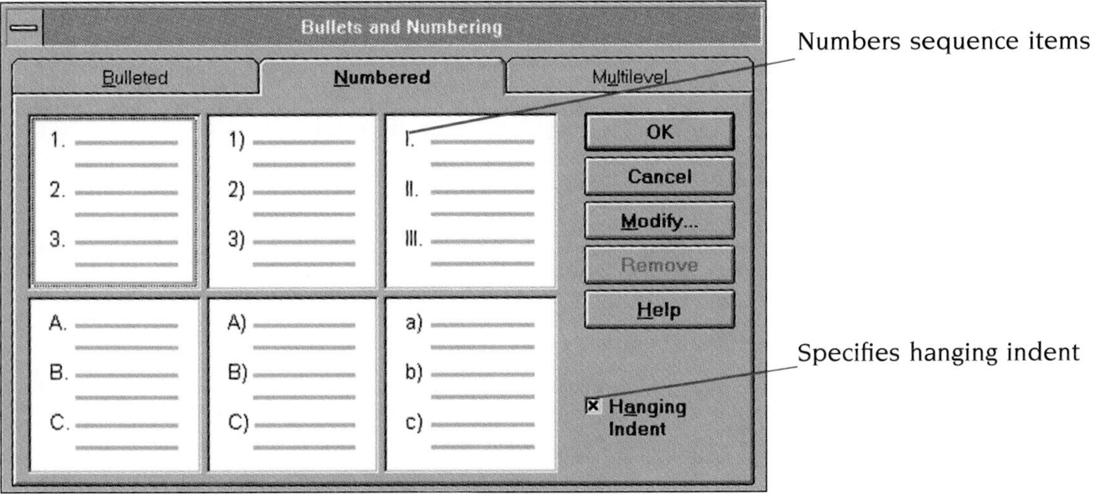

(b) Numbered List

FIGURE 5.3 Lists

HANDS-ON EXERCISE 1:

Newspaper Columns

Objective To create a multicolumn document with equal text in each column, to create a masthead, and to implement a bulleted or numbered list. The exercise uses earlier material on sections, views, and the Borders and Shading command. Use Figure 5.4 as a guide for the exercise.

Step 1: Load the practice document

- Load Word. Pull down the **File menu** and click **Open** (or click the **File Open button** on the toolbar). Double click **NEWSTEXT.DOC** to retrieve the text of the newsletter.
- If necessary, click the **Page Layout icon** on the status bar. Set the magnification (zoom) to **Page Width** to match the document in the figure.
- Save the document as **MYNEWS.DOC** so that you can return to the original NEWSTEXT.DOC if necessary.

Step 2: Newspaper columns

- Pull down the **Format menu.** Click **Columns** to produce the dialog box in Figure 5.4a.
- Click the **Presets icon** for **Two.** The column width for each column and the spacing between columns will be determined automatically from the existing margins and number of columns.
- If necessary, clear the **Line Between** box. Click **OK** to accept the settings and exit the dialog box. The text of the newsletter should be displayed in two columns.

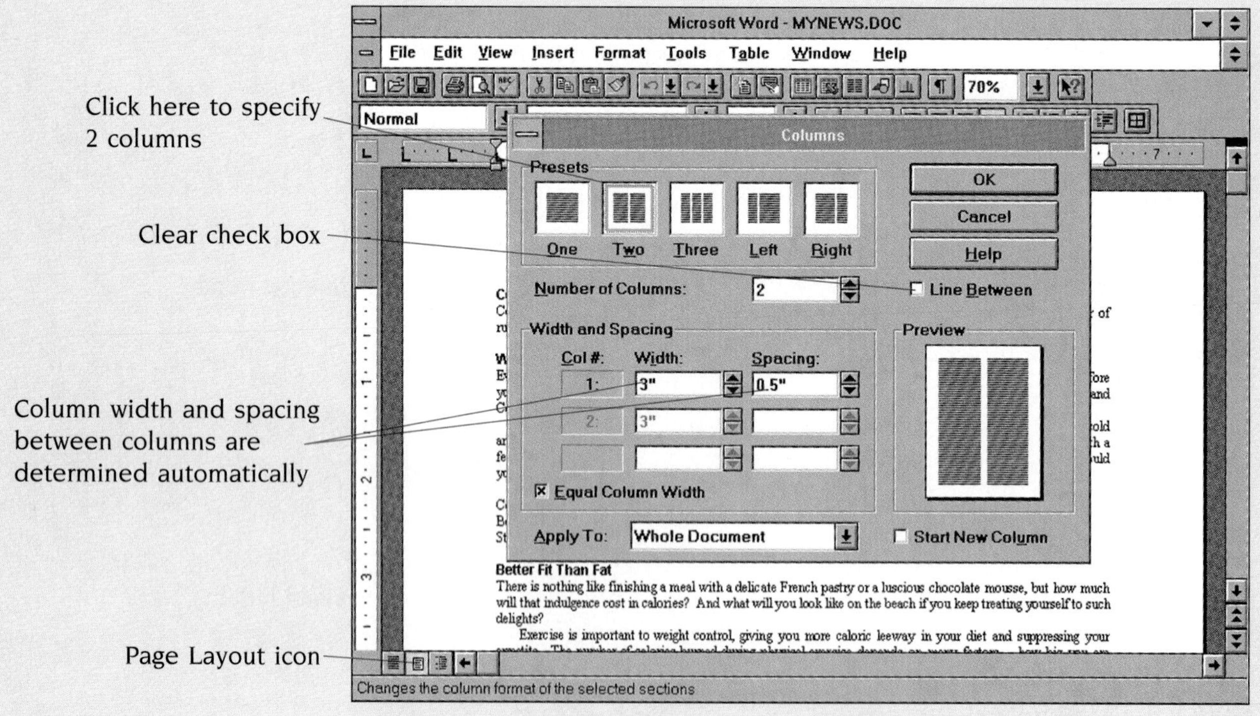

(a) Newspaper Columns (steps 1 and 2)

FIGURE 5.4 Hands-on Exercise 1

VIEWS AND COLUMNS

You must be in the Page Layout view, not the Normal view, in order to see columns displayed side-by-side within a document. Thus, if you do not see columns, it is probably because you are in the wrong view. Click the Page Layout icon on the status bar to change the view, then click the arrow on the Zoom control box on the Standard toolbar to see more or less of the page as necessary.

Step 3: Balance the columns

- Use the **Zoom control box** on the Standard toolbar to zoom to **Whole Page** to see the entire newsletter as in Figure 5.4b. Do not be concerned if the columns are of different lengths.
- Press **Ctrl+End** to move to the end of the document.
- Pull down the **Insert Menu.** Click **Break** to produce the dialog box of Figure 5.4b.
- Click the **Continuous button** under Section Breaks. Click **OK.** The columns should be balanced although one column may be a line longer (shorter) than the other.

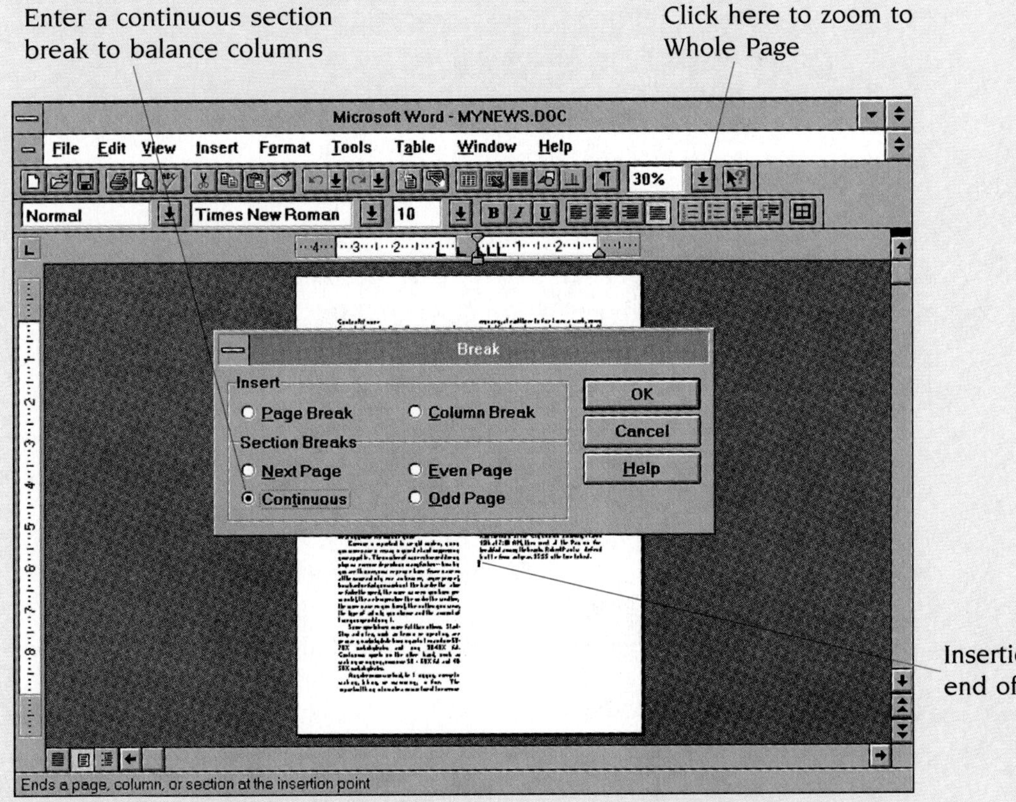

(b) Balance the Columns (step 3)

FIGURE 5.4 Hands-on Exercise 1 (continued)

THE COLUMN ICON

The **Column icon** on the Standard toolbar is the fastest way to create columns in a document. Click the icon, drag the mouse to choose the number of columns, then release the mouse to create the columns. The toolbar lets you change the number of columns, but not the spacing between columns. The toolbar is also limited in that you cannot create columns of different widths.

Step 4: Create the masthead

- Use the **Zoom control box** on the Standard toolbar to change to **Page Width.** Click the **Show/Hide icon** to display the paragraph (and section) marks.
- Press **Ctrl+Home** to move to the beginning of the document.
- Pull down the **Insert menu.** Click **Break.** Click **Continuous button.** Click **OK** to produce a double dotted line indicating a section break as shown in Figure 5.4c.
- Click above the dotted line, which will place the insertion point to the left of the line. Check the status bar to be sure you are in Section 1, then format this section as a single column as follows:
  - — Pull down the **Format menu,** click **Columns,** choose **One** from the Presets column formats, and click **OK.**
  - — *Or* click the **Column icon** on the Standard toolbar and select one column.
- Type **The Athlete's Hi** and press **enter** twice. Select the newly entered text as shown in Figure 5.4c. Click the **Center icon** on the Formatting toolbar. Change the font to **60 pt Arial Bold.**
- Save the newsletter.

COLUMNS AND SECTIONS

Columns are implemented at the section level and thus a new section is required whenever the number of columns changes within a document. Select the text that is to be formatted in columns, click the Columns icon on the toolbar, then drag the mouse to set the desired number of columns. Word will automatically insert the section breaks before and after the selected text.

Step 5: Add lines to the masthead

- Press **Ctrl+Home** to move to the beginning of the newsletter. Click anywhere within the paragraph containing **The Athlete's Hi.**
- Pull down the **Format menu.** Click **Borders and Shading.** If necessary, click the **Borders tab** to produce the dialog box in Figure 5.4d.
- Click the **None icon** in the Presets area. Click the **top line** of the border model to apply a top border. Click the **4½** point line style. Click the **bottom line** in the Border box to apply the same line to the bottom border.
- Click **OK** to return to the document. The masthead should be enclosed in parallel horizontal lines.
- Save the newsletter.

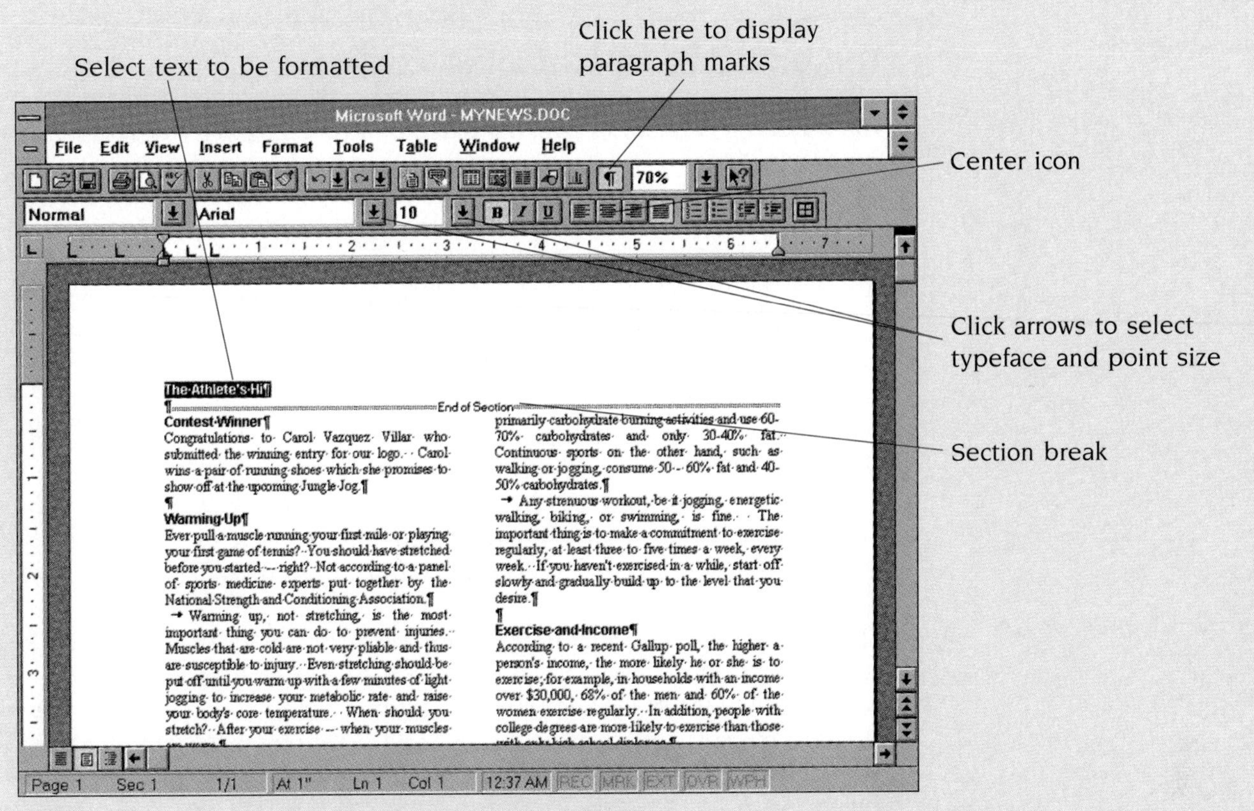

(c) Create the Masthead (step 4)

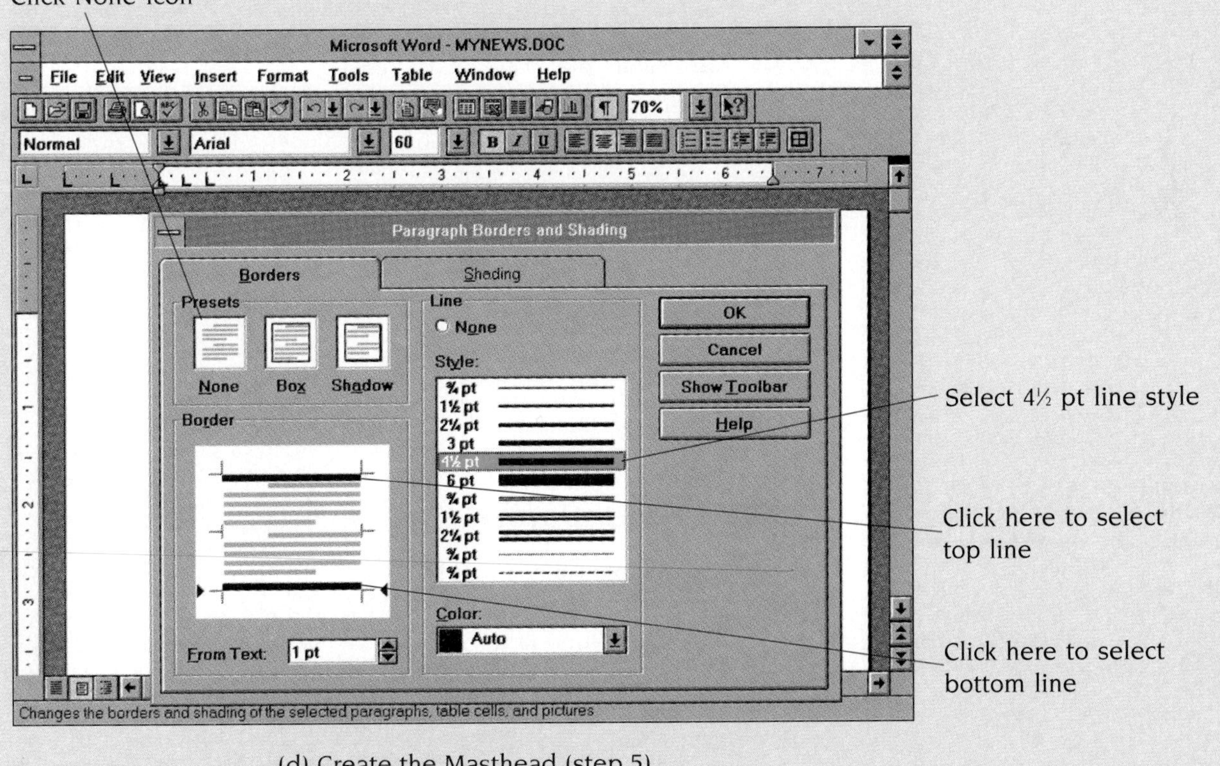

(d) Create the Masthead (step 5)

FIGURE 5.4 Hands-on Exercise 1 (continued)

THE BORDERS AND SHADING COMMAND

The ***Borders and Shading command*** takes practice, but once you get used to it, you will love it. To place a border around multiple paragraphs, select the paragraphs *prior* to execution of the Borders and Shading command, which treats the selected text as a single block. To select an individual side within the Border box, click along the desired side (*not* at the border marker), then select the desired line style.

Step 6: Bulleted and Numbered lists

- Scroll in the document until you come to the list at the end of the Warming Up paragraph. Select the entire list as shown in Figure 5.4e.
- Pull down the **Format menu.** Click **Bullets and Numbering.** If necessary, click the **Numbered tab** to produce the dialog box in the figure.
- Choose a number style. Click **OK** to return to the document, which now contains a numbered list.
- Click at the end of the first item on the list. Press the **enter key** to begin a new line and enter a new item, **Begin with light jogging.** Word automatically renumbers the list to include the item you just typed.
- Drag the mouse to select all four items on the list (the numbers will not be highlighted). Click the **Bullet icon** on the Formatting toolbar to change to a bulleted list.
- Click the **Increase Indent icon** on the Formatting toolbar to indent the entire list to the next tab stop. Click the **Decrease Indent icon** to move the list to

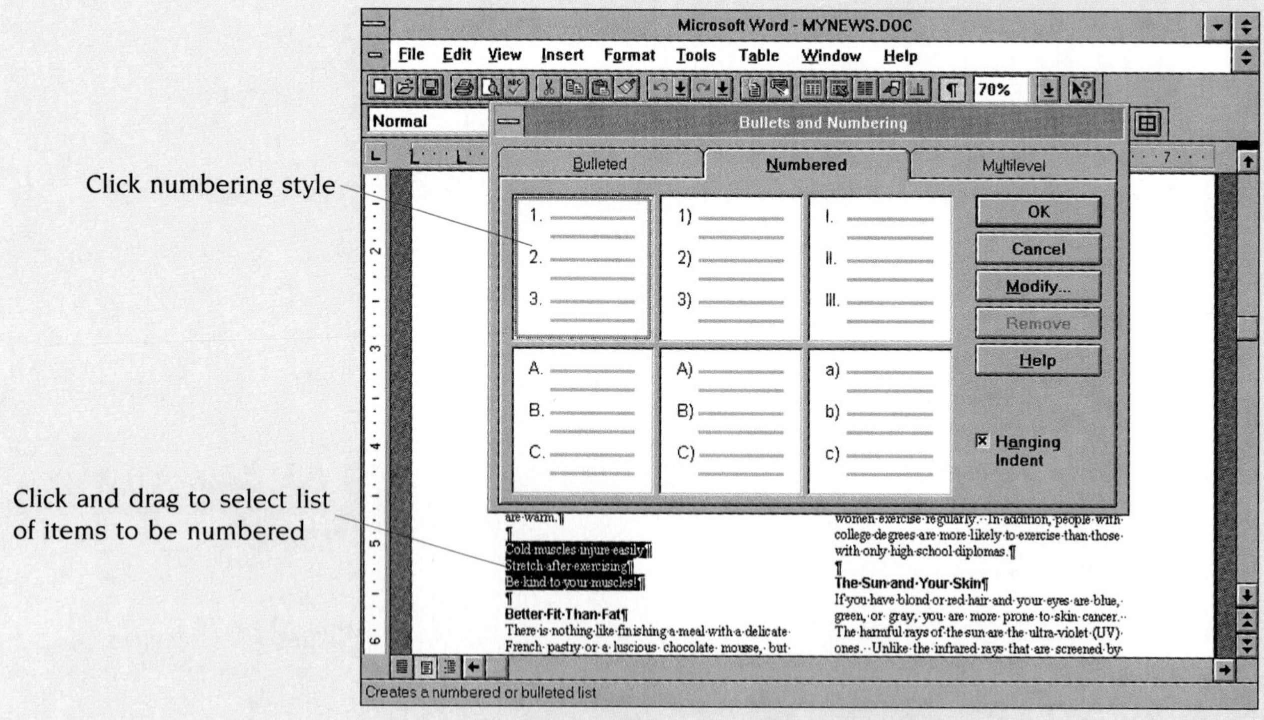

(e) Bullets and Numbering (step 6)

FIGURE 5.4 Hands-on Exercise 1 (continued)

the previous tab stop. Click the **Increase Indent button** a second time to end with the bulleted items indented one tab stop.

➤ Save the newsletter.

LISTS AND THE FORMATTING TOOLBAR

The Formatting toolbar contains four buttons for use with bulleted and numbered lists. The Increase Indent and Decrease Indent buttons move the selected items one tab stop to the right and left, respectively. The Bullets icon creates a bulleted list from unnumbered items or converts a numbered list to a bulleted list. The Numbering icon creates a numbered list or converts a bulleted list to numbers. The Bullets and Numbering icons also function as toggle switches; for example, clicking the Bullets icon when a bulleted list is already in effect will remove the bullets.

Step 7: The completed newsletter

➤ Use the **Zoom control box** on the Standard toolbar to zoom to **Whole Page** to see the entire newsletter as in Figure 5.4f.

➤ Click the **Show/Hide icon** to suppress the paragraph markers.

➤ Pull down the **File menu** and **Close** the document.

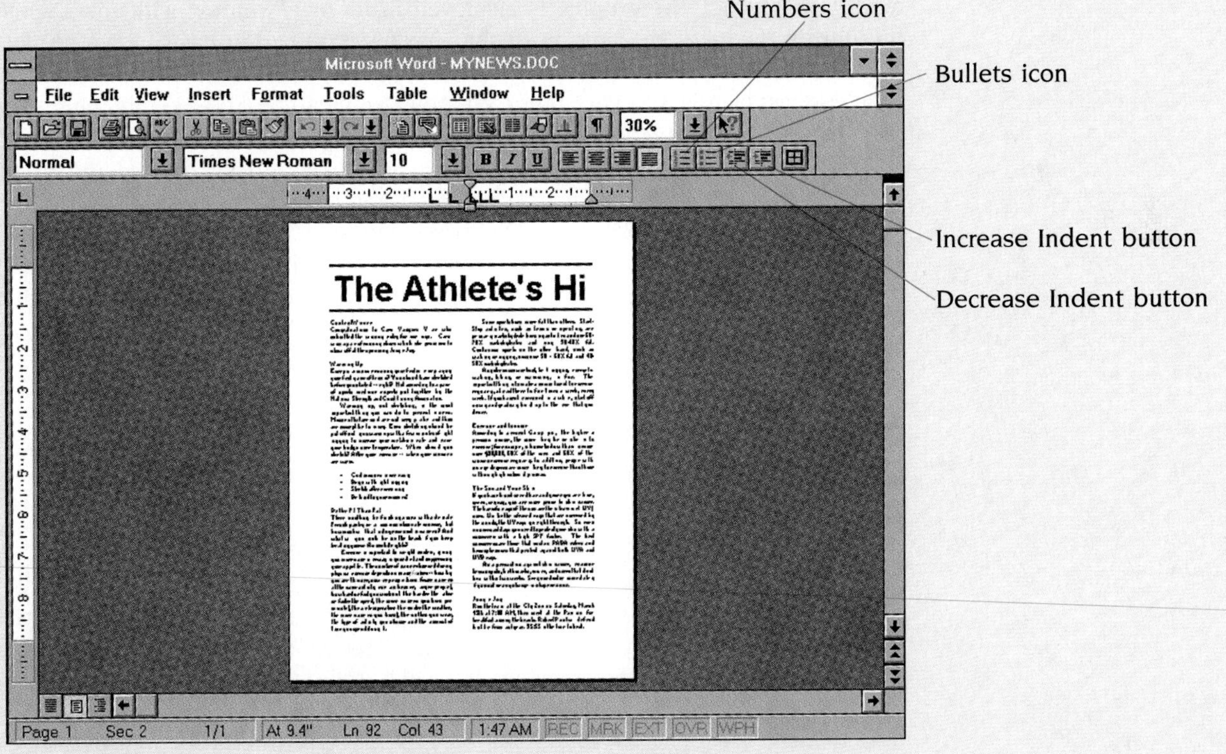

(f) The Completed Newsletter (step 7)

FIGURE 5.4 Hands-on Exercise 1 (continued)

PAGE BREAKS VERSUS COLUMN BREAKS

Press Ctrl+Enter to create a hard page break in order to begin the next line on a new page. Press Ctrl+Shift+Enter to create a ***column break*** and begin the next line in a new column.

GRAPHICS

The right picture adds immeasurably to a document. ***Clip art*** (graphic images) is available from a variety of sources including Word for Windows. The pictures provided with Word are stored in a separate subdirectory that is created automatically when Word is installed. Clip art from other applications can be located anywhere on your disk.

The ***Insert Picture command*** is the first step in placing a picture into a document. Execution of the command produces the dialog box of Figure 5.5a, which lets you preview a picture prior to inserting it. The available graphics are displayed in the File Name list box. All you do is select (click) a graphic, then click the OK command button to insert the graphic into the document.

Once a graphic has been inserted into a document, you can change its size, change its position, or even modify its content. Clicking the object selects it and lets you move or size the object within the document. Double clicking the object loads the drawing portion of Word for Windows in order to modify the picture as shown in Figure 5.5b.

Word for Windows includes a complete set of drawing tools to create and/or modify a graphic. The graphic is displayed in its own window with the ***Drawing toolbar*** displayed at the bottom of the window. You can point to any tool to display the name of the tool just as you can with any other toolbar. On-line help is available just as it is for every other Windows application. So too is the Undo command, which we find invaluable.

The complete capabilities of the drawing program are beyond the present discussion, but you will be surprised at what you can do with a little bit of experimentation. We modified the Dancers graphic by selecting the woman, clicking the tool to rotate her about the vertical axis, then dragging her away from her partner. We also added a text box in which the man asks her to come back. You can experiment with grouping and ungrouping the parts of the figure. You can also add color.

DROP CAPS

D***rop caps*** add interest to a document and are created through the Drop Cap command in the Format menu. Click at the beginning of a paragraph (where the drop cap is to appear), pull down the Format Menu, and click Drop Cap. Choose the type of Drop Cap you want, its font, and the point size (lines to drop), then click OK; the Drop Cap will be inserted into a frame in the document.

Clip art directory
Selected picture
Click here to preview picture

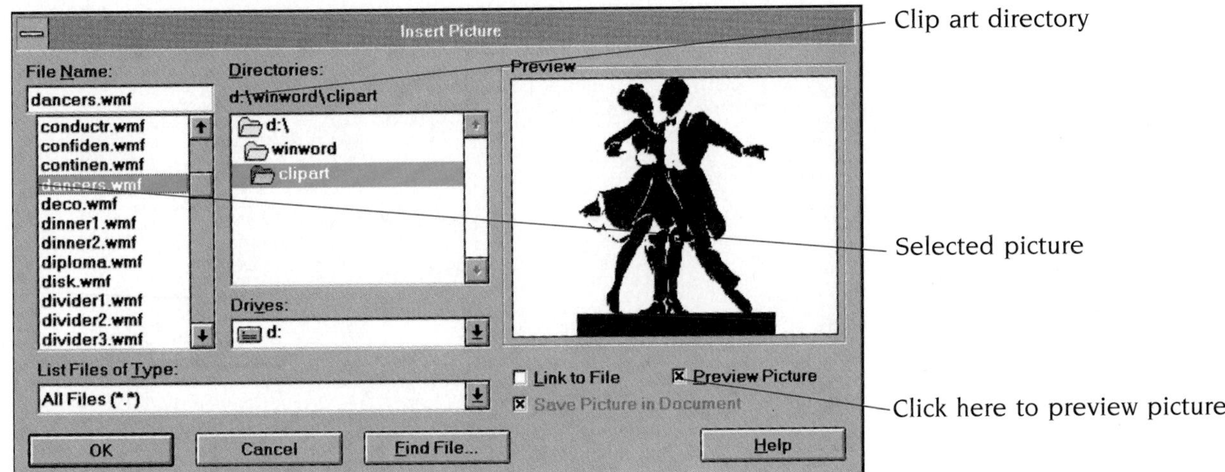

(a) Insert Picture Command

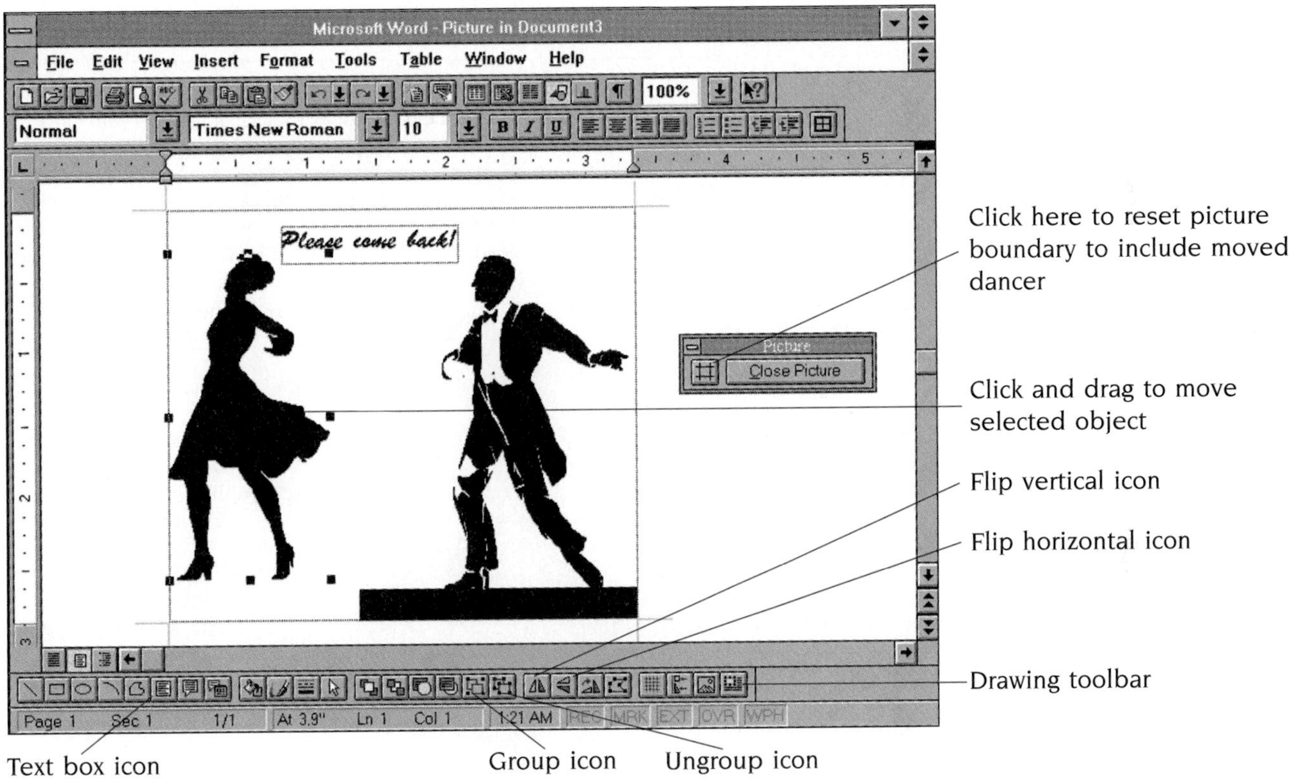

Click here to reset picture boundary to include moved dancer
Click and drag to move selected object
Flip vertical icon
Flip horizontal icon
Drawing toolbar
Text box icon
Group icon
Ungroup icon

(b) Modifying a Picture

FIGURE 5.5 Graphics (continued)

Frames

After a picture has been placed into a document, it should be inserted into a frame. A ***frame*** is a container that holds an object, and it provides the easiest way to position the object within a document. Anything at all can be placed in a frame: a picture, a dropped capital letter, or an object created by another application.

A frame (and its contents) can be positioned using the mouse or aligned more precisely with the ***Format Frame command*** shown in Figure 5.5c. The command enables you to specify the precise horizontal and vertical location of the frame. It also determines whether or not text is to wrap around the frame.

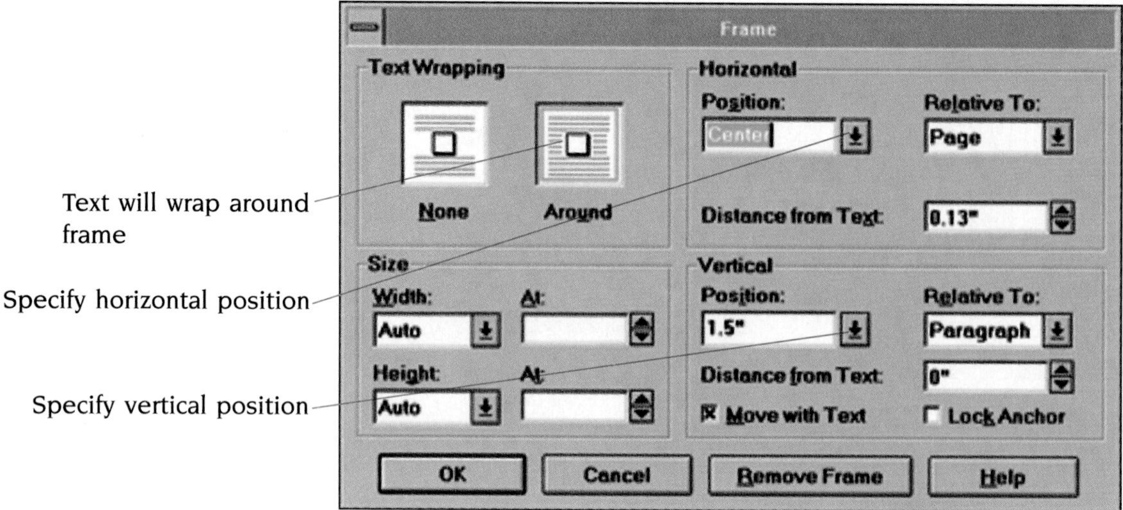

(c) Format Frame Command

Once a graphic has been inserted into a document, you can change its size, change its position, or even modify its content. Clicking the object selects it and lets you move or size the object within the document. Double clicking the object loads the drawing portion of Word for Windows in order to modify the picture. Once a graphic has been inserted into a document, you can change its size, change its position, or even modify its content. Clicking the object selects it and lets you to move or size the object within the document. Double clicking the object loads the drawing portion of Word for Windows in order to modify the picture. Once a graphic has been inserted into a document, you can change its size, change its position, or even modify its content. Clicking the object selects it and lets you move or size the object within the document. Double clicking the object loads the drawing portion of Word for Windows in order to modify the picture. Once a graphic has been inserted into a document, you can change its size, change its position, or even modify its content. Clicking the object selects it and lets you move or size the object within the document. Double clicking the object loads the drawing portion of Word for Windows in order to modify the picture. Once a graphic has been inserted into a document, you can change its size, change its position, or even modify its content. Clicking the object selects it and lets you move or size the object within the document. Double clicking the object loads the drawing portion of Word for Windows in order to modify the picture. Once a graphic has been inserted into a document, you can change its size, change its position, or even modify its content. Clicking the object selects it and lets you move or size the object within the document. Double clicking the object loads the drawing portion of Word for Windows in order to modify the picture. Once a graphic has been inserted into a document, you can change its size, change its position, or even modify its content.

(d) The Completed Document

FIGURE 5.5 Graphics (continued)

Figure 5.5d displays a document containing text and the Dancers graphic. (We decided to reunite our dancers and use the original picture.) The text wraps around the graphic in accordance with the specifications in the Format Frame command of Figure 5.5c. The horizontal and vertical placement of the graphic are also consistent with the placement options within the command.

TO FRAME OR NOT TO FRAME

Enclosing an object in a frame enables you to position it freely on the page and/or wrap text around the object. Without a frame, the object is treated as an ordinary paragraph and movement is restricted to one of three positions (left, center, or right). Text cannot be wrapped around an unframed object.

HANDS-ON EXERCISE 2:

Graphics

Objective Insert a picture into a document, then modify the picture to include your initials; frame the picture, then size and move the graphic within the document; create a drop cap, boxed text, and reverse for emphasis. The end result of this exercise is the newsletter of Figure 5.1c. Use Figure 5.6 as a guide.

Step 1: Load the newsletter

- Pull down the **File menu** and click **Open** (or click the **File Open icon** on the toolbar). Double click **MYNEWS.DOC** to retrieve the newsletter from the first exercise.
- Save the document as **MYNEWS2.DOC** so that you can always return to the newsletter as it existed at the end of the first exercise.
- If necessary, change to the **Page Layout** view and zoom to **Page Width.**
- Pull down the **File menu,** click **Page Setup,** and if necessary, click the **Margins tab** to produce the dialog box in Figure 5.6a.
- Change the top and bottom margins to **.75** and **.75,** respectively, as shown in the figure. Click the arrow in the **Apply To** list box and select **Whole Document.** Click **OK.**

Step 2: Add the graphic

- Click in the blank line at the end of the paragraph announcing the contest winner.
- Pull down the **Insert menu.** Click **Picture** to produce the dialog box of Figure 5.6b.
- The clip art directory should already be selected, but if not, you must indicate to Word where the clip art can be found:
  - Click the appropriate drive—for example, drive C—then scroll in the directory list box until you come to the root directory (C:\). Double click **C:\.**
  - Scroll down the list box until you come to the **WINWORD** directory. Double click **WINWORD**.
  - Double click the **CLIPART** subdirectory.
- The list of available figures is contained within the File Name list box. Scroll

down and click **SPORTS.WMF.** If necessary, click the **Preview Picture check box** to see the graphic. Click **OK** to insert the figure into the document.

➤ Save the document.

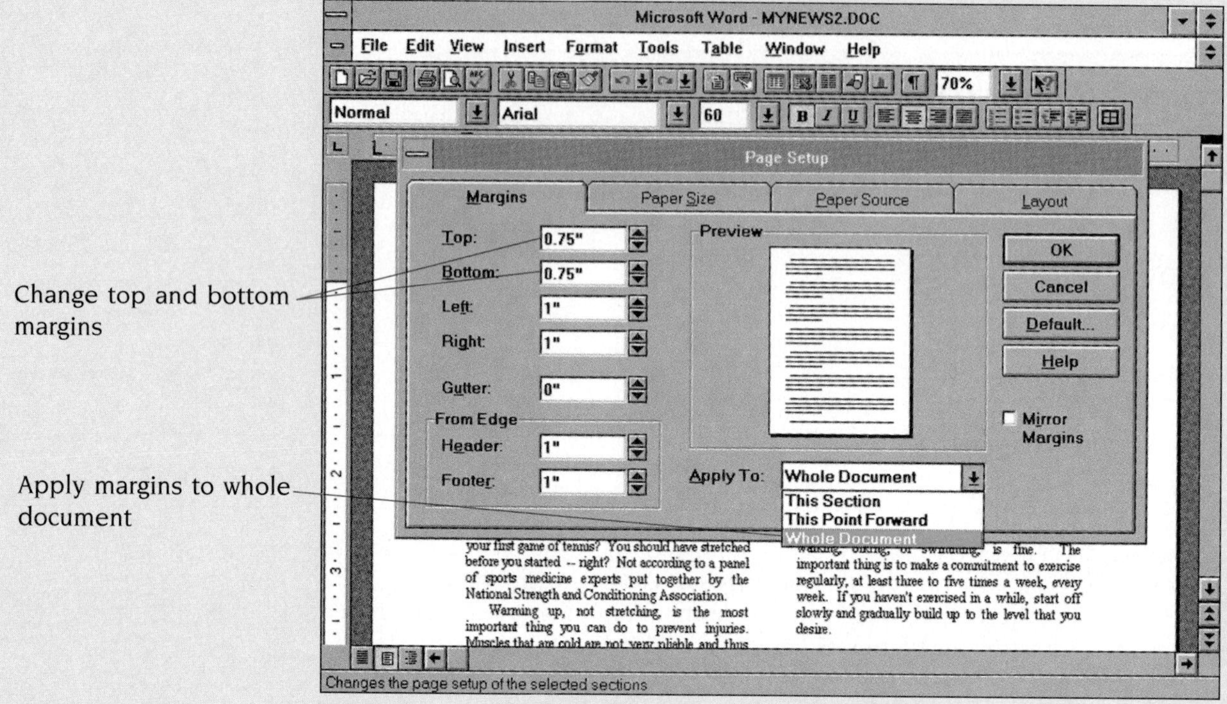

(a) Page Setup Command (step 1)

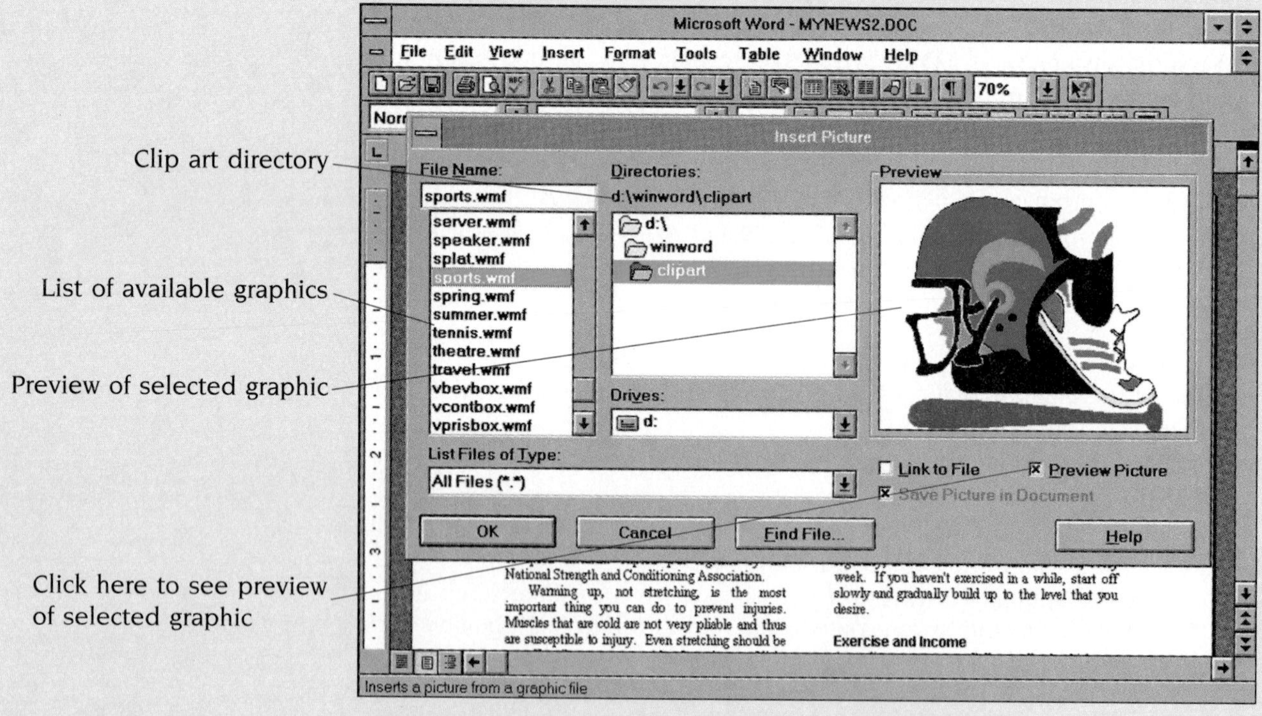

(b) Insert the Picture (step 2)

FIGURE 5.6 Hands-on Exercise 2

Step 3: Size the graphic

- Use the **Zoom control box** on the Standard toolbar to change to **Two Pages** as shown in Figure 5.6c; the newsletter may or may not spill to the second page, depending on the precise content of your document.
- Point to the graphic, then click the left mouse button to select the graphic and enclose it within the sizing handles. Experiment with the graphic:
  - — Drag a corner handle (the mouse pointer changes to a double arrow) to change the length and width simultaneously and keep the graphic in proportion.
  - — Drag a handle on the horizontal or vertical border to change one dimension only, which distorts the graphic.
  - — Drag any handle outward to increase the size of the picture or inward to shrink it.
  - — Press and hold the **Shift key** as you drag a handle to crop (hide) a portion of the figure.
  - — To undo a sizing operation, click outside the graphic to deselect it, then click the **Undo icon** on the Standard toolbar.
- Size the graphic so that the newsletter fits on a single page. Save the document.

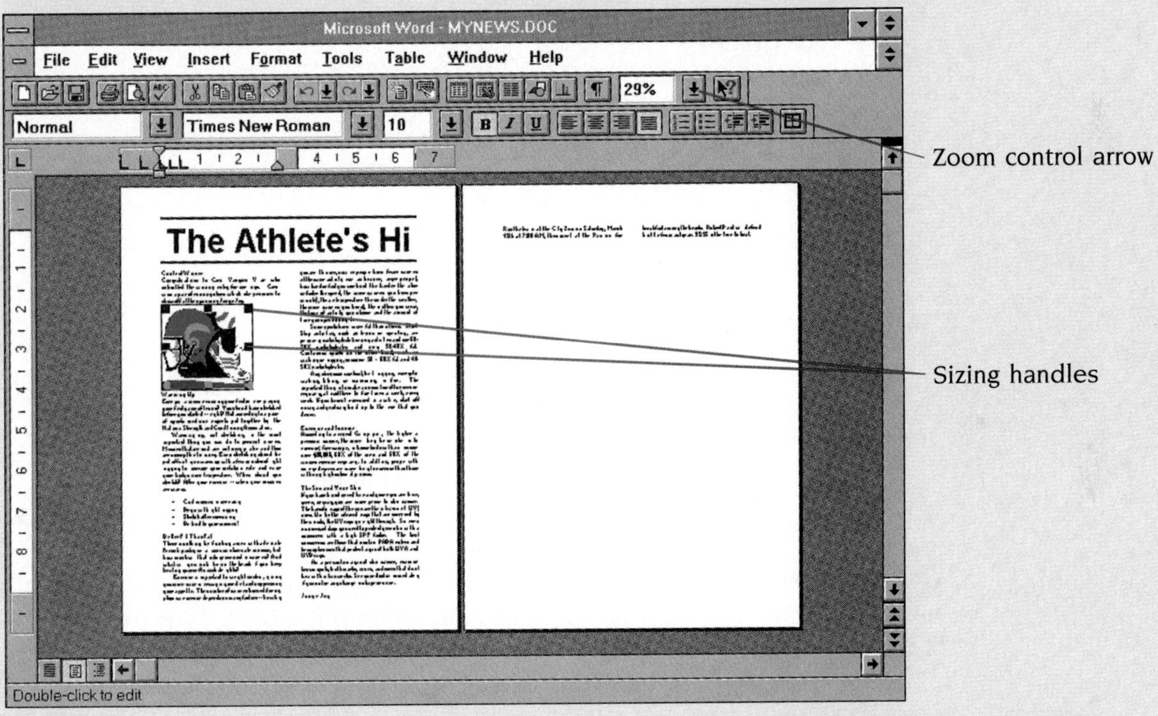

(c) Size the Graphic (step 3)

FIGURE 5.6 Hands-on Exercise 2 (continued)

PICTURE RESET COMMAND

The ***Picture Reset command*** restores a graphic to its original dimensions and is helpful when you size or crop a picture beyond recognition. Select the object, pull down the Format menu, click Picture, click the Reset command button, then click OK to restore the graphic.

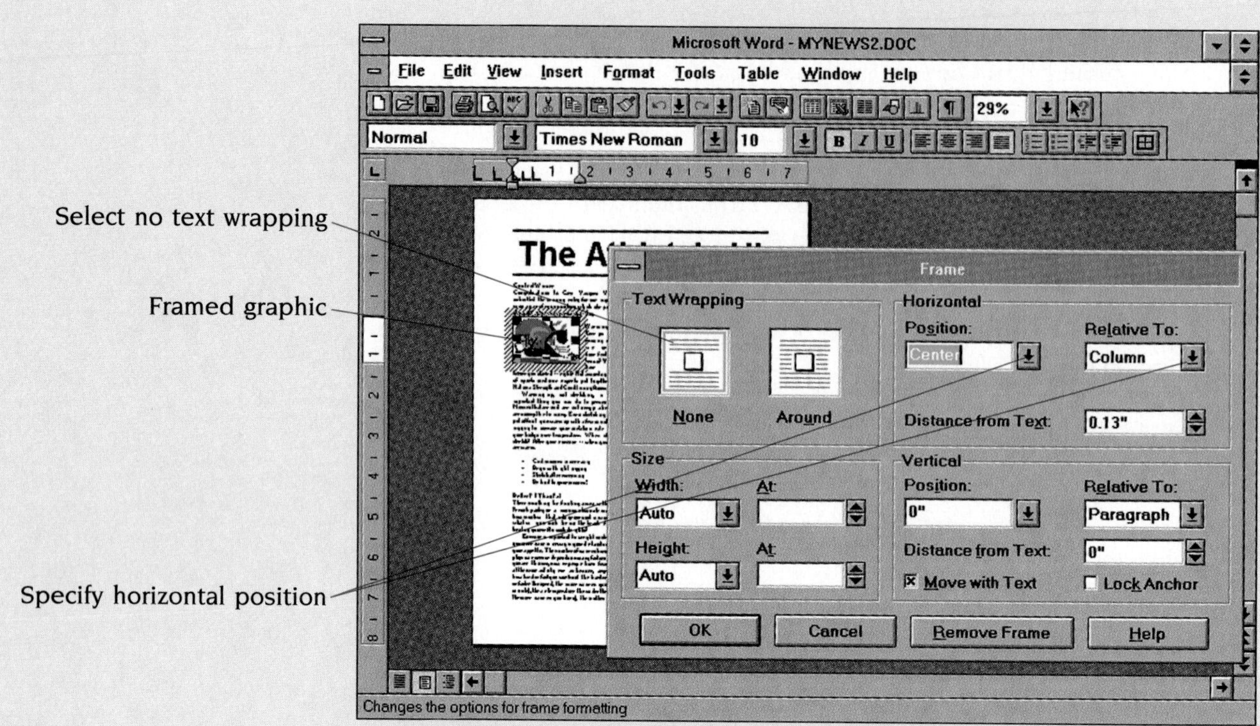

(d) Format the Frame (step 4)

FIGURE 5.6 Hands-on Exercise 2 (continued)

Step 4: Frame the graphic

- Select the graphic. Pull down the **Insert menu.** Click **Frame;** the picture is now enclosed within a shaded border to indicate a frame.
- Check that the frame is still selected. Pull down the **Format menu.** Click **Frame** to produce the dialog box in Figure 5.6d.
- The text in the newsletter may or may not wrap around the picture, depending on the size of the picture and the options in effect. (Word requires a minimum of one inch of text in order for the text to wrap.)
- Click the arrow on the **Horizontal Position box.** Click **Center.**
- Click the arrow on the **Horizontal Relative To box.** Click **Column.**
- If necessary, click the icon to indicate **None** for Text Wrapping. Click **OK.** The sports picture should be centered within the column.
- Save the newsletter.

Step 5: Modify the graphic

- Double click the sports graphic in order to edit the picture in its own window as shown in Figure 5.6e.
- Click the arrow on the **Zoom control box** on the toolbar and zoom to **200%.**
- Click the **Text Box icon** on the Drawing toolbar at the bottom of the window. Click the helmet in the drawing (the mouse pointer changes to a tiny cross) and drag the mouse to create a text box as shown in Figure 5.6e.

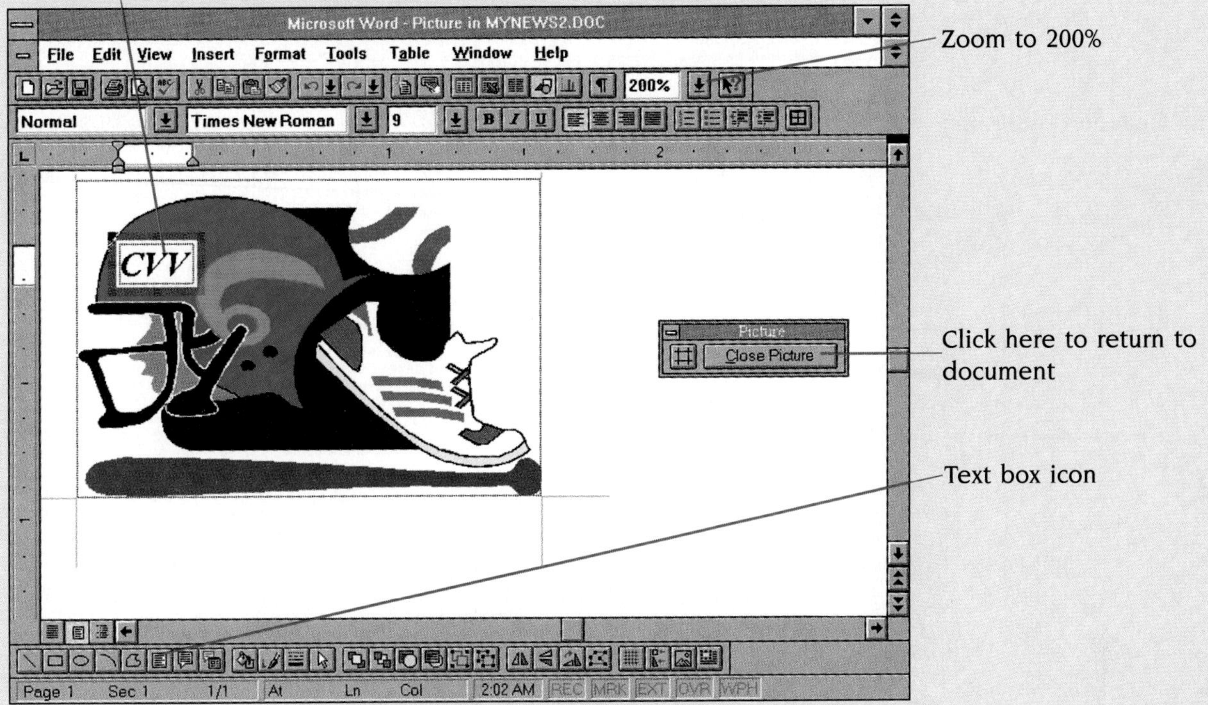

(e) Modify the Picture (step 5)

FIGURE 5.6 Hands-on Exercise 2 (continued)

- Click in the text box. Click the **Boldface** and **Italics** icons on the Formatting toolbar, then type your initials.
- Click the **Close Picture** command button to exit the drawing and return to the newsletter.
- Use the **Zoom control Box** to change to **Page Width.**
- Save the newsletter.

PICTURES, FRAMES, AND SHORTCUT MENUS

Point to a picture, then click the right mouse button to produce a Shortcut menu. The commands in the menu will be appropriate for the selected object; that is, the menu will contain either the Frame Picture or the Format Frame command, depending on whether or not the graphic has already been framed.

Step 6: The Masthead

- Press **Ctrl+Home** to move to the beginning of the document.
- Click the **Borders button** on the Formatting toolbar to display the ***Borders toolbar*** shown in Figure 5.6f.
- Click the arrow on the **Shading box** on the Borders toolbar. Choose **Solid (100%)** shading.

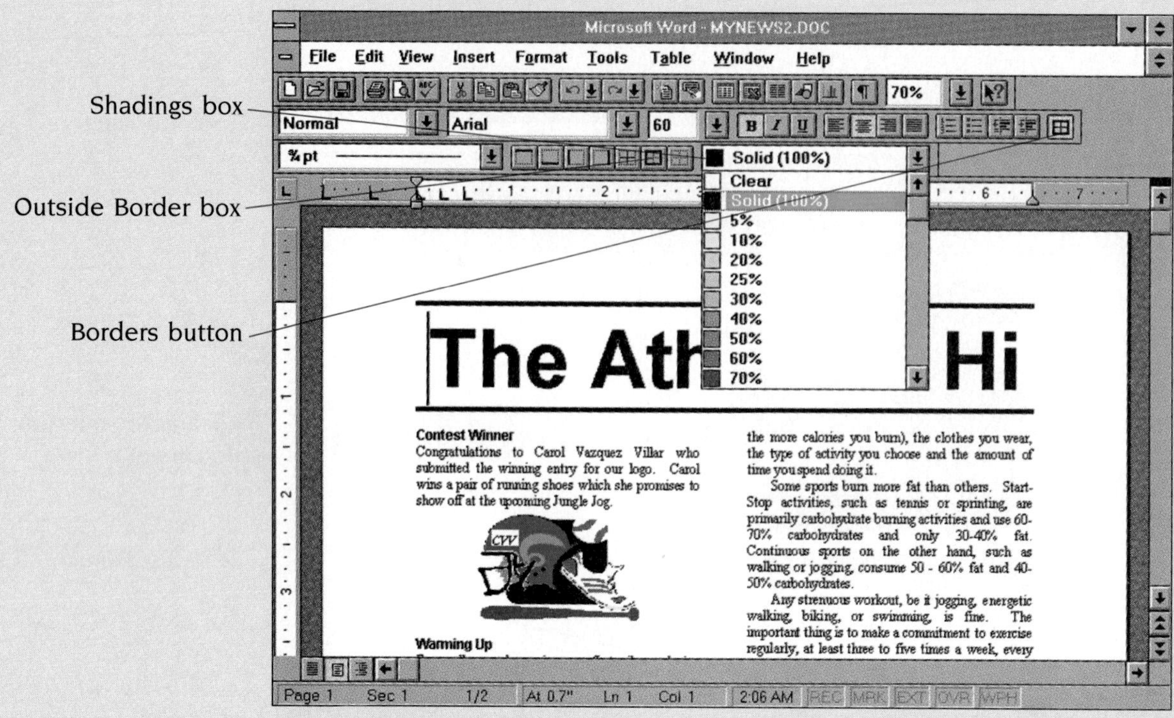

(f) Borders and Shading (step 6)

FIGURE 5.6 Hands-on Exercise 2 (continued)

- ➤ Click outside the masthead to see the results. You should see white letters on a solid background.
- ➤ Save the newsletter.

> **TO CLICK OR DOUBLE CLICK**
>
> Clicking an object selects the object and produces the sizing handles to move and/or size the object. Double clicking an object loads the application that created it and enables you to modify the object using that application.

Step 7: Boxed and shaded text

- ➤ Press **Ctrl+End** to move to the end of the newsletter. Select the paragraphs containing the Jungle Jog announcement along with its title.
- ➤ Click the arrow in the **Shading box** on the Borders toolbar. Choose **10%** shading.
- ➤ Click the **Outside border button** on the Borders toolbar to apply a border around the selected paragraphs. Click the arrow on the **Line style list** box to increase (decrease) the thickness of the line as you see fit.
- ➤ Click outside the selected text to see the results. Save the newsletter.

Step 8: Add a Drop Cap

- ➤ Scroll to the beginning of the newsletter. Click immediately before the C in "Congratulations."

- Pull down the **Format menu.** Click **Drop Cap** to produce the dialog box in Figure 5.6g.
- Click the **Position icon** for **Dropped** as shown in the figure. You can also change the font, size (lines to drop), or distance from the text by clicking the arrow on the appropriate list box.
- Click **OK** to create the drop cap, exit the dialog box, and return to the document. Click outside the frame around the drop cap.
- Save the newsletter.

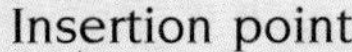

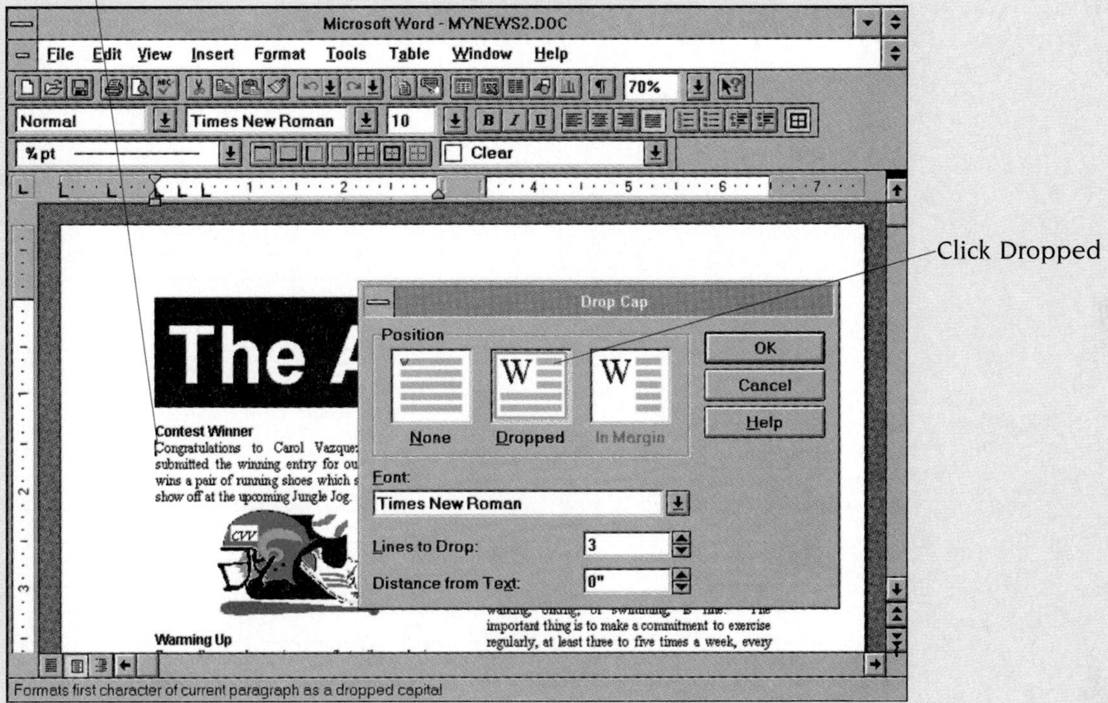

(g) Drop Cap (step 8)

FIGURE 5.6 Hands-on Exercise 2 (continued)

Step 9: Change column formatting

- Click anywhere in the body of the newsletter, making sure you are in the second section.
- Pull down the **Format menu.** Click **Columns** to produce the dialog box in Figure 5.6h.
- Click the **Left Preset icon.** Change the width of the first column to **2″**, which automatically changes the width of the second column to 4″.
- Click the **Lines Between box.** Click **OK.**
- Use the **Zoom control box** to zoom to **Whole Page** to display the completed newsletter as shown in Figure 5.6i. If necessary, size the graphic so that the newsletter fits on one page.
- Save the document a final time, then print the newsletter.

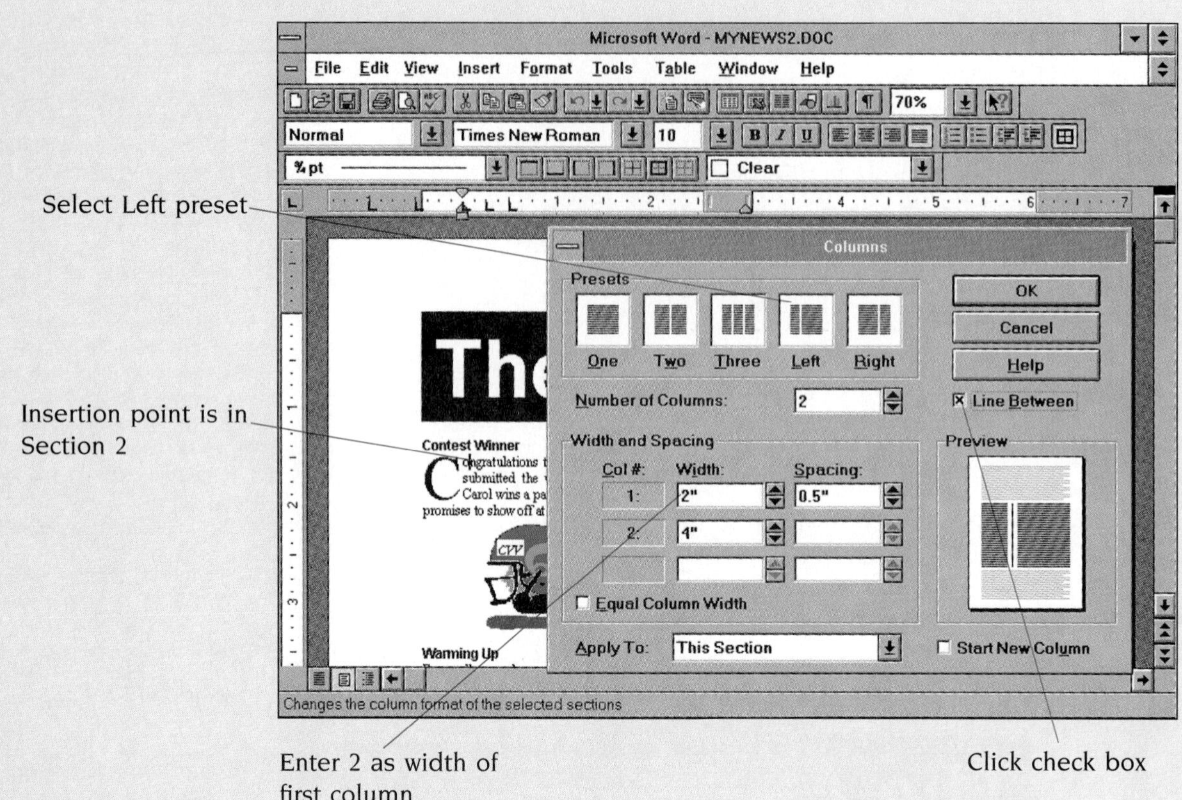

(h) Change Column Formatting (step 9)

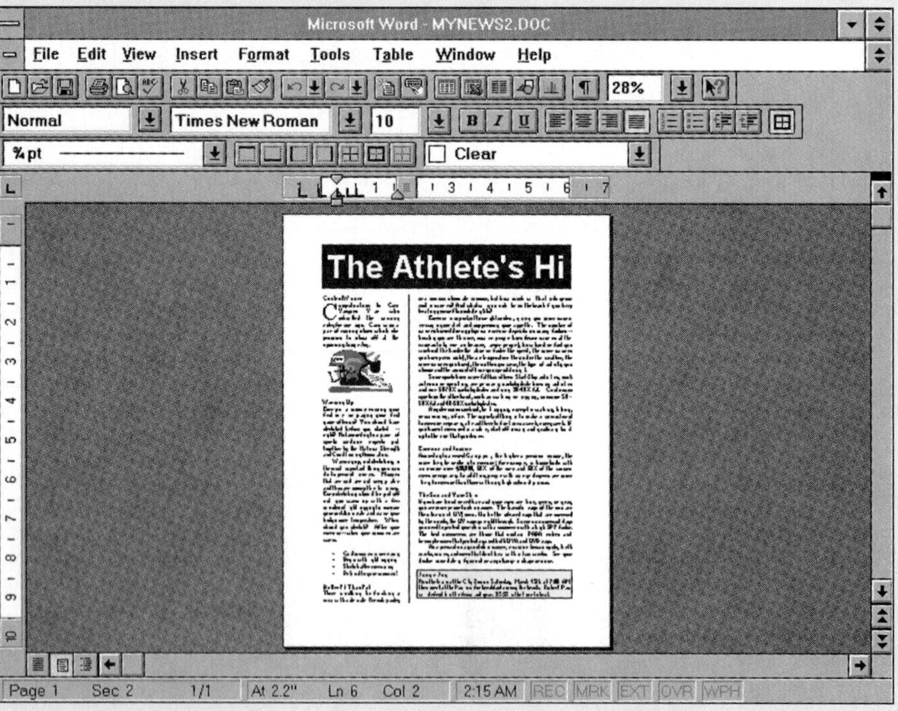

(i) The Completed Document (step 9)

FIGURE 5.6 Hands-on Exercise 2 (continued)

We trust you have completed the hands-on exercises without difficulty and that you were able to reproduce the newsletter. Realize, however, that the mere availability of Word and a laser printer does not guarantee success in desktop publishing, any more than a word processor turns its author into a Shakespeare or a Hemingway. Other skills are necessary and so we conclude with an introduction to basic principles of graphic design.

Much of what we say is subjective, and what works in one situation will not necessarily work in another. Your eye is the best judge of all and you should stick to your own instincts. Experiment freely and realize that successful design is the result of trial and error. Seek inspiration from others by maintaining a file of publications, with examples of both good and bad design, and use the file as the basis for your own publications.

The Grid

The design of a document should be developed on a ***grid,*** an underlying, but *invisible,* set of horizontal and vertical lines that determine the placement of the major elements. A grid establishes the overall structure of a document by indicating the number of columns, the space between columns, the size of the margins, the placement of headlines, art, and so on. The grid does *not* appear in the printed document nor on the screen.

A grid may be simple or complex, but is always distinguished by the number of columns it contains. The three-column grid of Figures 5.7a and 5.7b is one

(a) Empty Three-column Grid

No can do

He felt more and more pressure to play the game of not playing. Maybe that's why he stepped in front of that truck.

People wonder why people do things like this, but all you have to do is look around and see all the stress and insanity each person in responsibility is required to put up with. There is no help or end in sight. It seems that managers are managing less and shoveling the workloads on to their underlings. This seems to be the overall response to the absence of raises or benefit packages they feel are their entitlement. Something must be done now!

People wonder why people do things like this, but all you have to do is look around and see all the stress and insanity each person in responsibility is required to put up with. There is no help or end in sight. It seems that managers are managing less and shoveling the workloads on to their underlings. This seems to be the overall response to the absence of raises or benefit packages they feel are their entitlement. Something must be done now!

People wonder why people do things like this, but all you have to do is look around and see all the stress and insanity each person in responsibility is required to put up with. There is no help or end in sight. It seems that managers are managing less and shoveling the workloads on to their underlings. This seems to be the overall response to the absence of raises or benefit packages they feel are their entitlement.

People wonder why people do things like this, but all you have to do is look around and see all the stress and insanity each person in responsibility is required to put up with. There is no help or end in sight. It seems that managers are managing less and shoveling the workloads on to their underlings. This seems to be the overall response to the absence of raises or benefit packages they feel are their entitlement. Something must be done now!

People wonder why people do things like this, but all you have to do is look around and see all the stress and insanity each person in responsibility is required to put up with. There is no help or end in sight. It seems that managers are managing less.

Something must be done now! ▼

(b) Three-column Grid

FIGURE 5.7 The Grid System of Design

He felt more and more pressure to play the game of not playing. Maybe that's why he stepped in front of that truck.

People wonder why people do things like this, but all you have to do is look around and see all the stress and insanity each person in responsibility is required to put up with. There is no help or end in sight. It seems that managers are managing less and shoveling the workloads on to their underlings. This seems to be the overall response to the absence of raises or benefit packages they feel are their entitlement. Something must be done !

People wonder why people do things like this, but all you have to do is look around and see all the stress and insanity each person in responsibility is required to put up with. There is no help or end in sight. It seems that managers are managing less and shoveling the workloads on to their underlings. This seems to be the overall response to the absence of raises or benefit packages they feel are their entitlement. Something must be done now!

People wonder why people do things like this, but all you have to do is look around and see all the stress and insanity each person in responsibility is required to put up with. There is no help or end in sight. It seems that managers are managing less and shoveling the workloads on to their underlings. This seems to be the overall response to the absence of raises or benefit packages they feel are their entitlement.

People wonder why people do things like this, but all you have to do is look around and see all the stress and insanity each person in responsibility is required to put up with. There is no help or end in sight. It seems that managers are managing less and shoveling the workloads on to their underlings. This seems to be the overall response to the absence of raises or benefit packages they feel are their entitlement. Something must be done now!

People wonder why people do things like this, but all you have to do is look around and see all the stress and insanity each person in responsibility is required to put up with. There is no help or end in sight. This seems to be the overall response to the absence of raises or benefit packages they feel are their entitlement. Something must be done!

People wonder why people do things like this, but all you have to do is look around and see all the stress and insanity each person in responsibility is required to put up with. There is no help or end in sight. Solving the problem now is easily said but it will take willingness and creativity for a permanent solution! ▼

(c) Four-column Grid

People wonder why people do things like this, but all you have to do is look around and see all the stress and insanity each person in responsibility is required to put up with. There is no help or end in sight. It seems that managers are managing less and shoveling the workloads on to their underlings. This seems to be the overall response to the absence of raises or benefit packages they feel are their entitlement. Something must be done!

People wonder why people do things like this, but all you have to do is look around and see all the stress and insanity each person in responsibility is required to put up with. There is no help or end in sight. It seems that managers are managing less and shoveling the workloads on to their underlings. This seems to be the overall response to the absence of raises or benefit packages they feel are their entitlement. Something must be done now!

People wonder why people do things like this, but all you have to do is look around and see all the stress and insanity each person in responsibility is required to put up with. There is no help or end in sight. It seems that managers are managing less and shoveling the workloads on to their underlings. This seems to be the overall response to the absence of raises or benefit packages they feel are their entitlement. Something must be done now!

He felt more and more pressure to play the game of not playing. Maybe that's why he stepped in front of that truck.

People wonder why people do things like this, but all you have to do is look around and see all the stress and insanity each person in responsibility is required to put up with. There is no help or end in sight. It seems that managers are managing less and shoveling the workloads on to their underlings. This seems to be the overall response to the absence of raises or benefit packages they feel are their entitlement. Something must be done now!

People wonder why people do things like this, but all you have to do is look around and see all the stress and insanity each person in responsibility is required to put up with. There is no help or end in sight. It seems that managers are managing less and shoveling the workloads on to their underlings. This seems to be the overall response to the absence of raises or benefit packages they feel are their entitlement. Something must be done!

People wonder why people do things like this, but all you have to do is look around and see all the stress and insanity each person in responsibility is required to put up with. There is no help or end in sight. It seems that managers are managing less and shoveling the workloads on to their underlings. This seems to be the overall response to the absence of raises or benefit packages they feel are their entitlement. Something must be done!

People wonder why people do things like this, but all you have to do is look around and see all the stress and insanity each person in responsibility is required to put up with. There is no help or end in sight. It seems that managers are managing less and shoveling the workloads on to their underlings. Something must be done now! ▼

(d) Five-column Grid

FIGURE 5.7 The Grid System of Design (continued)

of the most common and utilitarian designs. Figure 5.7c shows a four-column design for the same document, with unequal column widths to provide interest. Figure 5.7d illustrates a five-column grid that is often used with large amounts of text. Many other designs are possible as well. A one-column grid is used for term papers and letters. A two-column, wide-and-narrow format is appropriate for textbooks and manuals. Two- and three-column formats are used for newsletters and magazines.

The simple concept of a grid should make the underlying design of any document obvious, which in turn gives you an immediate understanding of page composition. Moreover, the conscious use of a grid will help you organize your material and result in a more polished and professional-looking publication. It will also help you to achieve consistency from page to page within a document (or from issue to issue of a newsletter). Indeed, much of what goes wrong in desktop publishing stems from failing to follow or use the underlying grid.

White Space

White space, or space that is free of text and art, is underutilized by most newcomers to graphic design. White space is essential, however, to provide contrast, and to give the eye a place to rest. Conversely, the lack of white space makes a document crowded and difficult to read as seen in Figure 5.8a.

White space is introduced into a document in several ways, but not every document will use every technique. White space will appear:

- Around a headline; surrounding a headline with white space gives it additional emphasis.

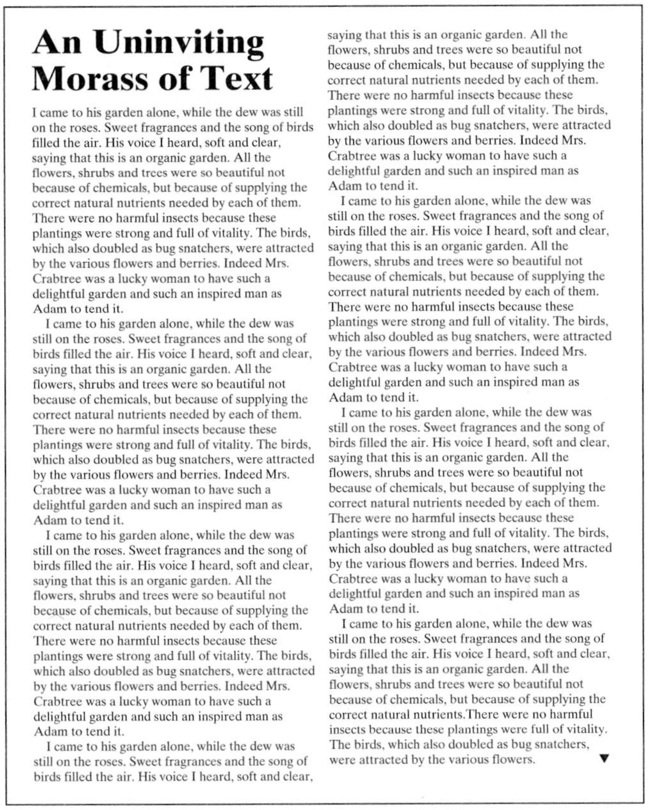

An Uninviting Morass of Text

I came to his garden alone, while the dew was still on the roses. Sweet fragrances and the song of birds filled the air. His voice I heard, soft and clear, saying that this is an organic garden. All the flowers, shrubs and trees were so beautiful not because of chemicals, but because of supplying the correct natural nutrients needed by each of them. There were no harmful insects because these plantings were strong and full of vitality. The birds, which also doubled as bug snatchers, were attracted by the various flowers and berries. Indeed Mrs. Crabtree was a lucky woman to have such a delightful garden and such an inspired man as Adam to tend it.

I came to his garden alone, while the dew was still on the roses. Sweet fragrances and the song of birds filled the air. His voice I heard, soft and clear, saying that this is an organic garden. All the flowers, shrubs and trees were so beautiful not because of chemicals, but because of supplying the correct natural nutrients needed by each of them. There were no harmful insects because these plantings were strong and full of vitality. The birds, which also doubled as bug snatchers, were attracted by the various flowers and berries. Indeed Mrs. Crabtree was a lucky woman to have such a delightful garden and such an inspired man as Adam to tend it.

I came to his garden alone, while the dew was still on the roses. Sweet fragrances and the song of birds filled the air. His voice I heard, soft and clear, saying that this is an organic garden. All the flowers, shrubs and trees were so beautiful not because of chemicals, but because of supplying the correct natural nutrients needed by each of them. There were no harmful insects because these plantings were strong and full of vitality. The birds, which also doubled as bug snatchers, were attracted by the various flowers and berries. Indeed Mrs. Crabtree was a lucky woman to have such a delightful garden and such an inspired man as Adam to tend it.

I came to his garden alone, while the dew was still on the roses. Sweet fragrances and the song of birds filled the air. His voice I heard, soft and clear, saying that this is an organic garden. All the flowers, shrubs and trees were so beautiful not because of chemicals, but because of supplying the correct natural nutrients needed by each of them. There were no harmful insects because these plantings were strong and full of vitality. The birds, which also doubled as bug snatchers, were attracted by the various flowers and berries. Indeed Mrs. Crabtree was a lucky woman to have such a delightful garden and such an inspired man as Adam to tend it.

I came to his garden alone, while the dew was still on the roses. Sweet fragrances and the song of birds filled the air. His voice I heard, soft and clear, saying that this is an organic garden. All the flowers, shrubs and trees were so beautiful not because of chemicals, but because of supplying the correct natural nutrients needed by each of them. There were no harmful insects because these plantings were strong and full of vitality. The birds, which also doubled as bug snatchers, were attracted by the various flowers and berries. Indeed Mrs. Crabtree was a lucky woman to have such a delightful garden and such an inspired man as Adam to tend it.

I came to his garden alone, while the dew was still on the roses. Sweet fragrances and the song of birds filled the air. His voice I heard, soft and clear, saying that this is an organic garden. All the flowers, shrubs and trees were so beautiful not because of chemicals, but because of supplying the correct natural nutrients needed by each of them. There were no harmful insects because these plantings were strong and full of vitality. The birds, which also doubled as bug snatchers, were attracted by the various flowers and berries. Indeed Mrs. Crabtree was a lucky woman to have such a delightful garden and such an inspired man as Adam to tend it.

I came to his garden alone, while the dew was still on the roses. Sweet fragrances and the song of birds filled the air. His voice I heard, soft and clear, saying that this is an organic garden. All the flowers, shrubs and trees were so beautiful not because of chemicals, but because of supplying the correct natural nutrients needed by each of them. There were no harmful insects because these plantings were strong and full of vitality. The birds, which also doubled as bug snatchers, were attracted by the various flowers and berries. Indeed Mrs. Crabtree was a lucky woman to have such a delightful garden and such an inspired man as Adam to tend it.

I came to his garden alone, while the dew was still on the roses. Sweet fragrances and the song of birds filled the air. His voice I heard, soft and clear, saying that this is an organic garden. All the flowers, shrubs and trees were so beautiful not because of chemicals, but because of supplying the correct natural nutrients.There were no harmful insects because these plantings were full of vitality. The birds, which also doubled as bug snatchers, were attracted by the various flowers. ▼

(a) Crowded Page

A Page Should Leave a Place for the Bird to Fly

I came to his garden alone, while the dew was still on the roses. Sweet fragrances and the song of birds filled the air. His voice I heard, soft and clear, saying that this is an organic garden. All the flowers, shrubs and trees were so beautiful not because of chemicals, but because of supplying the correct natural nutrients needed by each of them. There were no harmful insects because these plantings were strong and full of vitality. The birds, which also doubled as bug snatchers, were attracted by the various flowers and berries. Indeed Mrs. Crabtree was a lucky woman and to have such a delightful garden and such an inspired man as Adam to tend it.

I came to his garden alone, while the dew was still on the roses. Sweet fragrances and the song of birds filled the air. His voice I heard, soft and clear, saying that this is an organic garden. All the flowers, shrubs and trees were so beautiful not because of chemicals, but because of supplying the correct natural nutrients needed by each of them. There were no harmful insects because these plantings were strong and full of vitality. The birds, which also doubled as bug snatchers, were attracted by the various flowers and berries. Indeed Mrs. Crabtree was a lucky woman and to have such a delightful garden and such an inspired man as Adam to tend it.

I came to his garden alone, while the dew was still on the roses. Sweet fragrances and the song of birds filled the air. His voice I heard, soft and clear, saying that this is an organic garden. All the flowers, shrubs and trees were so beautiful not because of chemicals, but because of supplying the correct natural nutrients needed by each of them. There were no harmful insects because these plantings were strong and full of vitality. The birds, which also doubled as bug snatchers, were attracted by the various flowers and berries. Indeed Mrs. Crabtree was a lucky woman and to have such a delightful garden and such an inspired man as Adam to tend it.

I came to his garden alone, while the dew was still on the roses. Sweet fragrances and the song of birds filled the air. His voice I heard, soft and clear, saying that this is an organic garden. Indeed Mrs. Crabtree was a lucky woman to have such a delightful garden and such an inspired man as Adam to tend it. ▼

(b) White Space

FIGURE 5.8 White Space as a Design Element

- In the page margins (left, right, top, and bottom); a minimum of one inch all around is a generally accepted guideline.
- Between columns in a multicolumn layout; the wider the columns, the more space is required between the columns.
- Between lines of text through adequate space between the lines.
- In paragraph indents and/or the ragged line endings of left-aligned type.
- Around a figure to emphasize the art.
- Between paragraphs through use of a paragraph spacing command. This subtlety increases the space after a hard carriage return and gives a more professional appearance than double spacing between paragraphs, which adds too much space.

White space can be used as a design element by leaving a column empty (or almost empty) as was done in Figures 5.8b and 5.8c. The use of vertical white space in this fashion is a very effective tool. White space is *not* attractive, however, when it is trapped in the middle of a page as in Figure 5.8d.

Emphasis

Good design makes it easy for the reader to determine what is important. ***Emphasis*** is achieved in several ways, the easiest being variations in type size and/or type style. Headings should be set in type sizes larger than the subheadings, which in turn should be larger than body copy. The use of **boldface** is effective as are *italics,* but both should be done in moderation. Shading, reverses (white letters on a black background), or boxes are also effective.

Picking Flowers from Mrs. Crabtree's Garden

I came to his garden alone, while the dew was still on the roses. Sweet fragrances and the song of birds filled the air. His voice I heard, soft and clear, saying that this is an organic garden. All the flowers, shrubs and trees were so beautiful not because of chemicals, but because of supplying the correct natural nutrients needed by each of them. There were no harmful insects because these plantings were strong and full of vitality. The birds, which also doubled as bug snatchers, were attracted by the various flowers and berries. Indeed Mrs. Crabtree was a lucky woman to have such a delightful garden and such an inspired man as Adam to tend it.

I came to his garden alone, while the dew was still on the roses. Sweet fragrances and the song of birds filled the air. His voice I heard, soft and clear, saying that this is an organic garden. All the flowers, shrubs and trees were so beautiful not because of chemicals, but because of supplying the correct natural nutrients needed by each of them. There were no harmful insects because these plantings were strong and full of vitality. The birds, which also doubled as bug snatchers, were attracted by the various flowers and berries. Indeed Mrs. Crabtree was a lucky woman to have such a delightful garden and such an inspired man as Adam to tend it.

I came to his garden alone, while the dew was still on the roses. Sweet fragrances and the song of birds filled the air. His voice I heard, soft and clear, saying that this is an organic garden. Indeed Mrs. Crabtree was a lucky woman to have such a delightful garden and such an inspired man as Adam to tend it. Sweet fragrances and the song of birds filled the air. The birds, which also doubled as bug snatchers, were attracted by the various flowers and berries. Indeed Mrs. Crabtree was a lucky woman to have such a delightful garden and such an inspired man as Adam to tend it. All of the flowers, shrubs and trees were so beautiful because of the special nutrients carefully supplied to them. ▼

(c) Emphasis

Picking Flowers from Mrs. Crabtree's Garden

I came to his garden alone, while the dew was still on the roses. Sweet fragrances and the song of birds filled the air. His voice I heard, soft and clear, saying that this is an organic garden. All the flowers, shrubs and trees were so beautiful not because of chemicals, but because of supplying the correct natural nutrients needed by each of them. There were no harmful insects because these plantings were strong and full of vitality. The birds, which also doubled as bug snatchers, were attracted by the various flowers and berries. Indeed Mrs. Crabtree was a lucky woman to have such a delightful garden and such an inspired man as Adam to tend it.

I came to his garden alone, while the dew was still on

the roses. Sweet fragrances and the song of birds filled the air. His voice I heard, soft and clear, saying that this is an organic garden. All the flowers, shrubs and trees were so beautiful not because of chemicals, but because of supplying the correct natural nutrients needed by each of them. There were no harmful insects because these plantings were strong and full of vitality. The birds, which also doubled as bug snatchers, were attracted by the various flowers and berries. Indeed Mrs. Crabtree was a lucky woman to have such a delightful garden and such an inspired man as Adam to tend it.

I came to his garden alone, while the dew was still on the roses. Sweet fragrances and the song of birds filled the air. His voice I heard, soft and clear, saying that this is an organic garden. All the flowers, shrubs and trees were so beautiful not because of chemicals, but because of supplying the correct natural nutrients needed by each of them. There were no harmful insects because these plantings were strong and full of vitality. The birds, which also doubled as bug snatchers, were attracted by the various flowers and berries. Indeed Mrs. Crabtree was a lucky woman to have such a delightful garden and such an inspired man as Adam to tend it.

I came to his garden alone, while the dew was still on the roses. Indeed Mrs. Crabtree was a lucky woman to have such a delightful garden and such an inspired man as Adam to tend it. ▼

(d) Trapped White Space

FIGURE 5.8 White Space as a Design Element (continued)

DO NOT, HOWEVER, EMPHASIZE LARGE AMOUNTS OF TEXT WITH ALL UPPERCASE LETTERS BECAUSE THE READER GETS LOST TOO EASILY. Underlining is usually ineffective, primarily because the underline interferes with the descenders on lowercase letters extending below the baseline.

Facing Pages

A multipage document such as a manual, newsletter, or brochure is typically viewed two pages at a time by the reader. If this is true for your publication, it makes sense to develop ***facing pages*** as a unit, as opposed to creating the pages individually. This is illustrated by Figure 5.9a, which shows individually balanced pages that do not look very well together. Figure 5.9b rearranges the same material in a more appealing fashion. Use the Page Layout view in Word and zoom to two pages to work on your document.

SUMMARY

The essence of desktop publishing is the merging of text with graphics to produce a professional-looking document. Proficiency in desktop publishing requires not only knowledge of Word, but familiarity with the basics of graphic design.

A document can be divided into any number of newspaper-style columns in which text flows from the bottom of one column to the top of the next. Columns are implemented by clicking the Column icon on the Standard toolbar or by selecting the Columns command from the Format menu. Sections are required if

Tall Ships and Iron Horses: The Golden Age of Transportation?

It is interesting that during the same period of time two vitally needed forms of transportation were developed. One, on the sea, working with nature's best principles to create a totally eco-friendly means of transportation, and the other, on land, working against established social systems, the ecology of land and air using combustion, land acquisitions, and the power of the bullet to subdue nature and the native societies. It takes time to learn from our mistakes, and even more time to repair the damage done to man and nature.

It is interesting that during the same period of time two vitally needed forms of transportation were developed. One, on the sea, working with nature's best principles to create a totally eco-friendly means of transportation, and the other, on land, working against established social systems, the ecology of land and air using combustion, land acquisitions, and the power of the bullet to subdue nature and the native societies. It takes time to learn from our mistakes, and even more time to repair the damage done to man and nature.

It is interesting that during the same period of time two vitally needed forms of transportation were developed. One, on the sea, working with nature's best principles to create a totally eco-friendly means of transportation, and the other, on land, working against established social systems, the ecology of land and air using combustion, land acquisitions, and the power of the bullet to subdue nature and the native societies. It takes time to learn from our mistakes, and even more time to repair the damage done to man and nature.

It is interesting that during the same period of time two vitally needed forms of transportation were developed. One, on the sea, working with nature's best principles to create a totally eco-friendly means of transportation, and the other, on land, working against established social systems, the ecology of land and air using combustion, land acquisitions, and the power of the bullet to subdue nature and the native societies. It takes time to learn from our mistakes, and even more time to repair the damage done to man and nature.

It is interesting that during the same period of time two vitally needed forms of transportation were developed. It takes time to learn from our mistakes, and even more time to repair the damage done to man and nature. ▼

In the days when travel was a real adventure, the journey was as important as the destination.

It is interesting that during the same period of time two vitally needed forms of transportation were developed. One, on the sea, working with nature's best principles to create a totally eco-friendly means of transportation, and the other, on land, working against established social systems, the ecology of land and air using combustion, land acquisitions, and the power of the bullet to subdue nature and the native societies. It takes time to learn from our mistakes, and even more time to repair the damage done to man and nature.

It is interesting that during the same period of time two vitally needed forms of transportation were developed. One, on the sea, working with nature's best principles to create a totally eco-friendly means of transportation, and the other, on land, working against established social systems, the ecology of land and air using combustion, land acquisitions, and the power of the bullet to subdue nature and the native societies. It takes time to learn from our mistakes, and even more time to repair the damage done to man and nature.

It is interesting that during the same period of time two vitally needed forms of transportation were developed. One, on the sea, working with nature's best principles to create a totally eco-friendly means of transportation, and the other, on land, working against established social systems, the ecology of land and air using combustion, land acquisitions, and the power of the bullet to subdue nature and the native societies. It takes time to learn from our mistakes, and even more time to repair the damage done to man and nature.

It is interesting that during the same period of time two vitally needed forms of transportation were developed. One, on the sea, working with nature's best principles to create a totally eco-friendly means of transportation, and the other, on land, working against established social systems, the ecology of land and air using combustion, land acquisitions, and the power of the bullet to subdue nature and the native societies. It takes time to learn from our mistakes, and even more time to repair the damage done to man and nature.

It is interesting that during the same period of time two vitally needed forms of transportation were developed. It takes time to learn from our mistakes, and even more time to repair the damage done to man and nature.

It is interesting that during the same period of time two vitally needed forms of transportation were developed. One, on the sea, working with nature's best principles to create a totally eco-friendly means of transportation, and the other, on land, working against established social systems, the ecology of land and air using combustion, land acquisitions, and the power of the bullet to subdue nature and the native societies. It takes time to learn from our mistakes, and even more time to repair the damage done to man and nature. ▼

(a) Pages Balanced Individually

Tall Ships and Iron Horses: The Golden Age of Transportation?

In the days when travel was a real adventure, the journey was as important as the destination.

It is interesting that during the same period of time two vitally needed forms of transportation were developed. One, on the sea, working with nature's best principles to create a totally eco-friendly means of transportation, and the other, on land, working against established social systems, the ecology of land and air using combustion, land acquisitions, and the power of the bullet to subdue nature and the native societies. It takes time to learn from our mistakes, and even more time to repair the damage done to man and nature.

It is interesting that during the same period of time two vitally needed forms of transportation were developed. One, on the sea, working with nature's best principles to create a totally eco-friendly means of transportation, and the other, on land, working against established social systems, the ecology of land and air using combustion, land acquisitions, and the power of the bullet to subdue nature and the native societies. It takes time to learn from our mistakes, and even more time to repair the damage done to man and nature. It takes time to learn from our mistakes, and even more time to repair the damage done to man and nature. It takes time to learn from our mistakes.

It is interesting that during the same period of time two vitally needed forms of transportation were developed. One, on the sea, working with nature's best principles to create a totally eco-friendly means of transportation, and the other, on land, working against established social systems, the ecology of land and air using combustion, land acquisitions, and the power of the bullet to subdue nature and the native societies. One, on the sea, working with nature's best principles to create a totally eco-friendly means of transportation, and the other, on land, working against established social systems, the ecology of land and air using combustion, land acquisitions, and the power of the bullet to subdue nature and the native societies. It takes time to learn from our mistakes, and even more time to repair the damage done to man and nature.

It is interesting that during the same period of time two vitally needed forms of transportation were developed. It takes time to learn from our mistakes, and even more time to repair the dam-age done to man and nature. It takes time to learn from our mistakes.

It is interesting that during the same period of time two vitally needed forms of transportation were developed. One, on the sea, working with nature's best principles to create a totally eco-friendly means of transportation, and the other, on land, working against established social systems, the ecology of land and air using combustion, land acquisitions, and the power of the bullet to subdue nature and the native societies. It takes time to learn from our mistakes, and even more time to repair the damage done to man and nature. It takes time to learn. ▼

(b) Pages Balanced as a Unit

FIGURE 5.9 Balance Facing Pages

different column arrangements are present in the same document. The Page Layout view is required to see the columns displayed side-by-side.

A bulleted or numbered list can be created by clicking the appropriate icon on the Formatting toolbar or by executing the Bullets and Numbering command in the Format menu.

The Insert Picture command places a picture into a document that can subsequently be modified using the drawing tools within Word for Windows. A frame facilitates moving and/or sizing the picture.

The successful use of desktop publishing requires knowledge of graphic design in addition to proficiency in Word. The use of a grid, white space, and appropriate emphasis are basic design techniques.

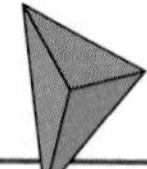

Key Words and Concepts

Borders toolbar
Borders and Shading command
Bulleted list
Bullets and Numbering command
Clip art
Column break
Columns command
Crop
Desktop publishing
Drawing toolbar
Drop cap
Emphasis
Facing pages
Format Frame command
Frame
Grid
Insert Picture command
Masthead
Multilevel list
Newspaper-style columns
Numbered list
Picture Reset command
Reverse
Section break
Section formatting
Typography
White space

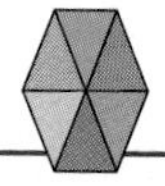

Multiple Choice

1. Which of the following *must* be specified by the user in the Column command?
   (a) The number of columns
   (b) The width of each column
   (c) Both (a) and (b)
   (d) Neither (a) nor (b)
2. Which view enables you to see a multicolumn document as it will appear on the printed page?
   (a) Normal view at any magnification
   (b) Page Layout view at any magnification
   (c) Normal or Page Layout view at 100% magnification
   (d) Normal or Page Layout view at Full Page magnification
3. Which of the following is a *false* statement regarding lists?
   (a) A bulleted list can be changed to a numbered list and vice versa
   (b) The symbol for the bulleted list can be changed to a different character
   (c) The numbers in a numbered list can be changed to letters or roman numerals
   (d) The bullets or numbers cannot be removed

4. Where (in which subdirectory) can you find the clip art supplied with Word?
   (a) In the same subdirectory as the document you are editing
   (b) In the WINWORD subdirectory
   (c) In the CLIPART subdirectory under the WINWORD subdirectory
   (d) In the WINDOWS subdirectory
5. What is the difference between clicking and double clicking an object such as the sports graphic in the newsletter?
   (a) Clicking selects the object; double clicking enables you to edit the object
   (b) Double clicking selects the object; clicking enables you to edit the object
   (c) Clicking changes to Normal view; double clicking changes to Page Layout view
   (d) Double clicking changes to Normal view; clicking changes to Page Layout view
6. Which of the following is correct with respect to page and column breaks?
   (a) Press Ctrl+Enter to create a page break
   (b) Press Ctrl+Shift+Enter to create a column break
   (c) Both (a) and (b)
   (d) Neither (a) nor (b)
7. Which of the following can be placed into a frame?
   (a) A picture or dropped capital letter
   (b) An object created by another application
   (c) Both (a) and (b)
   (d) Neither (a) nor (b)
8. Which of the following is controlled by the Format Frame command?
   (a) The horizontal and/or vertical placement of the frame
   (b) Wrapping (not wrapping) text around the framed object
   (c) Both (a) and (b)
   (d) Neither (a) nor (b)
9. What is the effect of dragging one of the four corner handles on a selected object?
   (a) The length of the object is changed but the width remains constant
   (b) The width of the object is changed but the length remains constant
   (c) The length and width of the object are changed in proportion to one another
   (d) Neither the length nor width of the object is changed
10. Which type size is the most reasonable for columns of text, such as those appearing in the newsletter created in the chapter?
    (a) 6 point
    (b) 10 point
    (c) 14 point
    (d) 18 point
11. A grid is applicable to the design of
    (a) Documents with one, two, or three columns and moderate clip art
    (b) Documents with four or more columns and no clip art
    (c) Both (a) and (b)
    (d) Neither (a) nor (b)

12. Which of the following is *not* an appropriate place to introduce white space in a document?
    (a) Between columns of a multicolumn document
    (b) Trapped in the middle of a page
    (c) In the page margins
    (d) Between paragraphs

13. Which of the following can be used to add emphasis to a document in the absence of clip art?
    (a) Boxes
    (b) Shading
    (c) Both (a) and (b)
    (d) Neither (a) nor (b)

14. Which of the following is a recommended guideline in design?
    (a) Use underlining and/or all uppercase letters to achieve emphasis
    (b) Use at least three different typefaces in a document to maintain interest
    (c) Use wider columns for larger type sizes
    (d) Use the same type size for the heading and text of an article

15. Which of the following are implemented at the section level?
    (a) Columns
    (b) Margins
    (c) Both (a) and (b)
    (d) Neither (a) nor (b)

ANSWERS

1. a	**4.** c	**7.** c	**10.** b	**13.** c
2. b	**5.** a	**8.** c	**11.** c	**14.** c
3. d	**6.** c	**9.** c	**12.** b	**15.** c

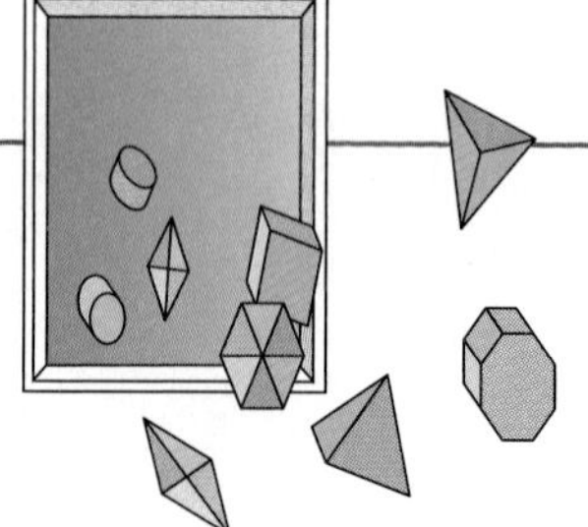

EXPLORING WORD

1. Use Figure 5.10 to match each action with its result; a given action may be used more than once.

Action		Result
a. Click at 1, click at 6	___	Size the graphic
b. Double click at 2	___	Allow text to wrap around the graphic
c. Click at 2, drag a handle	___	Change the newsletter to three columns
d. Click at 2, click at 5	___	Modify the picture
e. Click at 2, click at 6	___	Insert the picture in a frame
f. Click at 2, click at 7	___	Put a border around the picture
g. Click at 3, click at 8	___	Shade the masthead
h. Click at 4	___	Add a drop cap for the second article

i. Click at 6 ___ Change the zoom to Whole Page

j. Click at 9 ___ Change the top and bottom margins

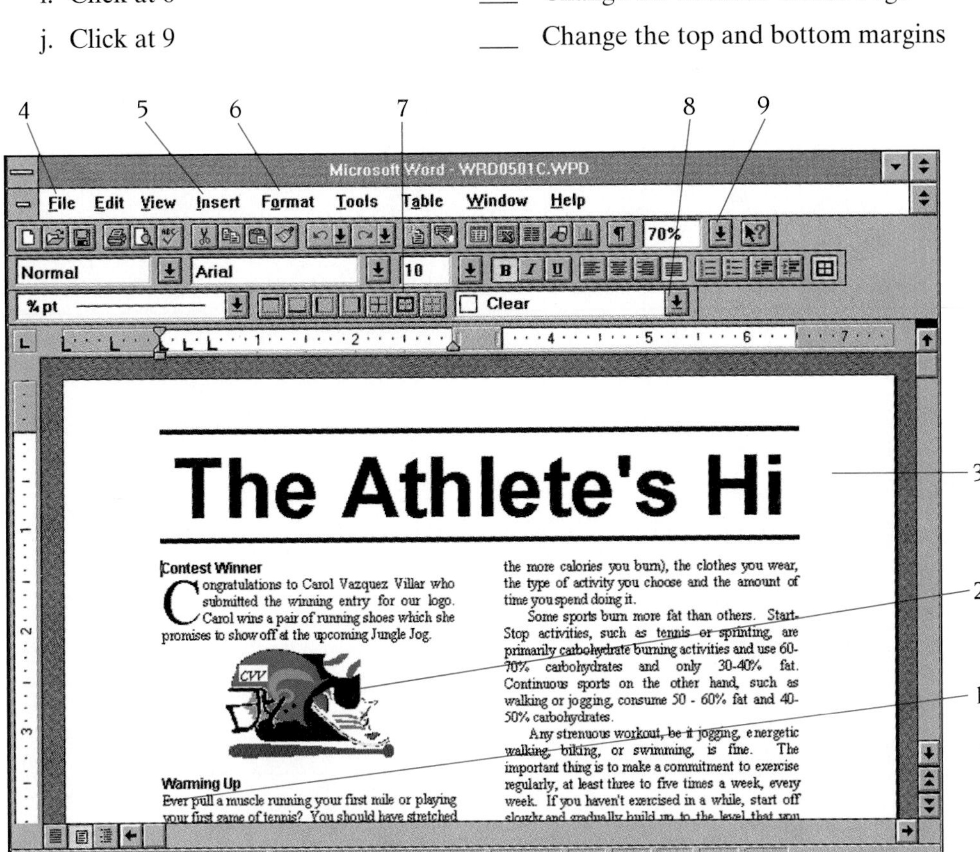

FIGURE 5.10 Screen for Problem 1

2. Each part of Figure 5.11 contains two versions of the same page, one of which violates basic rules of design and one of which follows them. List several problems in the poorly designed page, then indicate how they were corrected in the revised version.
3. Typography: The best way to practice design and type selection is to create a simple document, then set that document in a variety of typefaces, type sizes, and column arrangements. Accordingly, create a one-paragraph document containing the text below, then copy the paragraph several times until it takes at least a page.

   There is a definite relationship between type size and column width; that is, the smaller the type, the shorter the line; or conversely, the larger the type, the longer the line. In other words, the line length of a document set in 8 point type should be shorter than one set in 10 point type, which in turn should be shorter than one set in 12 point type.

   Experiment with some (or all) of the following designs suggested below:

   a. A two-column grid in various type sizes—for example, in 8, 10, and 12 point type. Use a serif typeface such as Times New Roman. Choose the type size you think most appropriate, then experiment with different alignments (left and full justification) and the use (omission) of a vertical line between columns. Vary the space between columns and/or the left and right margins until you arrive at a satisfactory design.

A Special Report: Living Latin

Latin was one of the subjects which I really enjoyed in high school. Many people laugh at it because they say it is a useless, dead language. Churches do not even use it any more in their services, pity. Something like eighty-five percent of the English language is derived from a mere ninety latin root words. I cannot express how useful it was to have an understanding of latin when it came to memorizing the order, phylum and classification of organisms in zoology class, later on in college. My creative writing classes also got a shot in the arm because of it. It was also interesting to find out the toll that the dark ages took on the European civilization which the Romans had established for centuries. Latin is indeed living. But it is living quietly in the essence of western civilization.

Latin was one of the subjects which I really enjoyed in high school. Many people laugh at it because they say it is a useless, dead language. Churches do not even use it any more in their services, pity. Something like eighty-five percent of the English language is derived from a mere ninety latin root words. I cannot express how useful it was to have an understanding of latin when it came to memorizing the order, phylum and classification of organisms in zoology class, later on in college. My creative writing classes also got a shot in the arm because of it. It was also interesting to find out the toll that the dark ages took on the European civilization which the Romans had established for centuries.

Latin is indeed living. But it is living quietly in the essence of western civilization.

Latin was one of the subjects which I really enjoyed in high school. Many people laugh at it because they say it is a useless, dead language. Churches do not even use it any more in their services, pity. Something like eighty-five percent of the English language is derived from a mere ninety latin root words. I cannot express how useful it was to have an understanding of latin when it came to memorizing the order, phylum and classification of organisms in zoology class, later on in college. My creative writing classes also got a shot in the arm because of it. It was also interesting to find out the toll that the dark ages took on the European civilization which the Romans had established for centuries. Latin is indeed living. But it is living quietly in the essence of western civilization.

Latin was one of the subjects which I really enjoyed in high school. Many people laugh at it because they say it is a useless, dead language. Churches do not even use it any more in their services, pity. Something like eighty-five percent of the English language is derived from a mere ninety latin root words.

I cannot express how useful it was to have an understanding of latin when it came to memorizing the order, phylum and classification of organisms in zoology class, later on in college. My creative writing classes also got a shot in the arm because of it. It was also interesting to find out the toll that the dark ages took on the European civilization which the Romans had established for centuries. Latin is indeed living. But it is living quietly in the essence of western civilization.

Latin was one of the subjects which I really enjoyed in high school. Many people laugh at it because they say it is a useless, dead language. Churches do not even use it any more in their services, pity. Something like eighty-five percent of the English language is derived from a mere ninety latin root words. I cannot express how useful it was to have an understanding of latin when it came to memorizing the order, phylum and classification of organisms in zoology class, later on in college. My creative writing classes also got a shot in the arm because of it. It was also interesting to find out the toll that the dark ages took on the European civilization which the Romans had established for centuries. Latin is indeed living. But it is living quietly in the essence of western civilization. It was also interesting to find out the toll that the dark ages took on the European civilization which the Romans had established for centuries.

Latin is indeed living. But it is living quietly in the essence of western civilization. It was also interesting to find out the toll that the dark ages took on the European civilization which the Romans had established for centuries. It was also interesting to find out the toll that the dark ages took on the European civilization. Latin is indeed living. But it is living quietly, living very well, in the essence of western civilization.▼

A Special Report: Living Latin

Latin was one of the subjects which I really enjoyed in high school. Many people laugh at it because they say it is a useless, dead language. Churches do not even use it any more in their services, pity. Something like eighty-five percent of the English language is derived from a mere ninety latin root words.

I cannot express how useful it was to have an understanding of latin when it came to memorizing the order, phylum and classification of organisms in zoology class, later on in college. My creative writing classes also got a shot in the arm because of it. It was also interesting to find out the toll that the dark ages took on the European civilization which the Romans had established for centuries. Latin is indeed living. But it is living quietly in the essence of western civilization.

Latin was one of the subjects which I really enjoyed in high school. Many people laugh at it because they say it is a useless, dead language. Churches do not even use it any more in their services, pity. Something like eighty-five percent of the English language is derived from a mere ninety latin root words. I cannot express how useful it was to have an understanding of latin when it came to memorizing the order, phylum and classification of organisms in zoology class, later on in college. My creative writing classes also got a shot in the arm because of it.

It was also interesting to find out the toll that the dark ages took on the European civilization which the Romans had established for centuries. Latin is indeed living. But it is living quietly in the essence of western civilization. It was also interesting to find out the toll that the dark ages took on the European civilization which the Romans had established for centuries.

I cannot express how useful it was to have an understanding of latin when it came to memorizing the order, phylum and classification of organisms in zoology class, later on in college. My creative writing classes also got a shot in the arm because of it. It was also interesting to find out the toll that the dark ages took on the European civilization which the Romans had established for centuries. Latin is indeed living. But it is living quietly in the essence of western civilization.

Latin was one of the subjects which I really enjoyed in high school. Many people laugh at it because they say it is a useless, dead language. Churches do not even use it any more in their services, pity. Something like eighty-five percent of the English language is derived from a mere ninety latin root words.▼

(a)

A Special Report: Living Latin

Something like eighty-five percent of the English language is derived from a mere ninety latin root words.

Latin was one of the subjects which I really enjoyed in high school. Many people laugh at it because they say it is a useless, dead language. Churches do not even use it any more in their services, pity. Something like eighty-five percent of the English language is derived from a mere ninety latin root words. I cannot express how useful it was to have an understanding of latin when it came to memorizing the order, phylum and classification of organisms in zoology class, later on in college. My creative writing classes also got a shot in the arm because of it. It was also interesting to find out the toll that the dark ages took on the European civilization which the Romans had established for centuries. Latin is indeed living. But it is living quietly in the essence of western civilization.

Many people laugh at it because they say it is a useless, dead language. Churches do not even use it any more in their services, pity. Something like eighty-five percent of the English language is derived from a mere ninety latin root words.

I cannot express how useful it was to have an understanding of latin when it came to memorizing the order, phylum and classification of organisms in zoology class, later on in college. My creative writing classes also got a shot in the arm because of it. It was also interesting to find out the toll that the dark ages took on the European civilization which the Romans had established for centuries. Latin is indeed living. But it is living quietly in the essence of western civilization.

Latin was one of the subjects which I really enjoyed in high school. Many people laugh at it because they say it is a useless, dead language. Churches do not even use it any more in their services, pity. Something like eighty-five percent of the English language is derived from a mere ninety latin root words. I cannot express how useful it was to have an understanding of latin when it came to memorizing the order, phylum and classification of organisms in zoology class, later on in college. My creative writing classes also got a shot in the arm because of it. It was also interesting to find out the toll that the dark ages took on the European civilization which the Romans had established. My creative writing classes also got a shot in the arm because of it.

It was also interesting to find out the toll that the dark ages took on the European civilization which the Romans had established for centuries. Latin is indeed living. But it is living quietly in the essence of western civilization. I cannot express how useful it was to have an understanding of latin when it came to memorizing the order, phylum and classification of organisms in zoology class, later on in college. My creative writing classes also got a shot in the arm because of it. Latin is indeed living. But it is living quietly in western civilization. ▼

Latin is indeed living. But it is living quietly in the essence of western civilization.

A Special Report: Living Latin

Latin was one of the subjects which I really enjoyed in high school. Many people laugh at it because they say it is a useless, dead language. Churches do not even use it any more in their services, pity. Something like eighty-five percent of the English language is derived from a mere ninety latin root words. I cannot express how useful it was to have an understanding of latin when it came to memorizing the order, phylum and classification of organisms in zoology class, later on in college. My creative writing classes also got a shot in the arm because of it. It was also interesting to find out the toll that the dark ages took on the European civilization which the Romans had established for centuries. Latin is indeed living. But it is living quietly in the essence of western civilization.

Many people laugh at it because they say it is a useless, dead language. Churches do not even use it any more in their services, pity. Something like eighty-five percent of the English language is derived from a mere ninety latin root words.

I cannot express how useful it was to have an understanding of latin when it came to memorizing the order, phylum and classification of organisms in zoology class, later on in college. My creative writing classes also got a shot in the arm because of it. It was also interesting to find out the toll that the dark ages took on the European civilization which the Romans had established for centuries. Latin is indeed living. But it is living quietly in the essence of western civilization.

Latin was one of the subjects which I really enjoyed in high school. Many people laugh at it because they say it is a useless, dead language. Churches do not even use it any more in their services, pity. Something like eighty-five percent of the English language is derived from a mere ninety latin root words. I cannot express how useful it was to have an understanding of latin when it came to memorizing the order, phylum and classification of organisms in zoology class, later on in college. My creative writing classes also got a shot in the arm because of it. It was also interesting to find out the toll that the dark ages took on the European civilization which the Romans had established. My creative writing classes also got a shot in the arm because of it.

It was also interesting to find out the toll that the dark ages took on the European civilization which the Romans had established for centuries. I cannot express how useful it was to have understanding of latin when it came to memorizing the order, phylum and classification of organisms in zoology class, later on in college. My creative writing classes also got a shot in the arm because of it. Latin was one of the subjects which I really enjoyed in high school. ▼

Latin is indeed living. But it is living quietly in the essence of western civilization.

(b)

FIGURE 5.11 Pages for Problem 2

(Adapted from Burns, Diane, and Venit, S., "What's Wrong with this Page?", PC *Magazine*, October 13, 1987)

Living Latin Bulletin

Published by The Romulus and Remus Society of Southern California — Januarious MXMXCIV

Managers Required to Study Roman Classics

Latin was one of the subjects which I really enjoyed in high school. Many people laugh at it because they say it is a useless, dead language. Churches do not even use it any more in their services, pity. Something like eighty-five percent of the English language is derived from a mere ninety latin root words. I cannot express how useful it was to have an understanding of latin when it came to memorizing the order, phylum and classification of organisms in zoology class, later on in college. My creative writing classes also got a shot in the arm because of it. It was also interesting to find out the toll that the dark ages took on the European civilization which the Romans had established for centuries. Latin is indeed living. But it is living quietly in the essence of western civilization. ▼

Group to Attend Archeological Dig

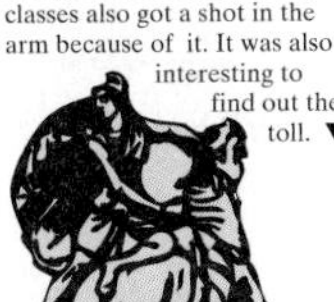

Latin was one of the subjects which I really enjoyed in high school. Many people laugh at it because they say it is a useless, dead language. Churches do not even use it any more in their services, pity. Something like eighty-five percent of the English language is derived from a mere ninety latin root words. I cannot express how useful it was to have an understanding of latin when it came to memorizing the order, phylum and classification of organisms in zoology class, later on in college. My creative writing classes also got a shot in the arm because of it. ▼

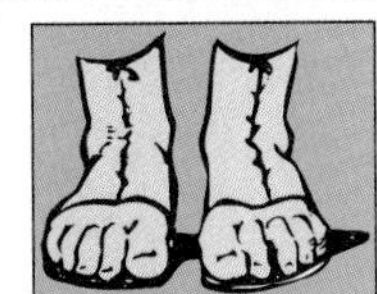

These Boots Were Made for Walkin'

Latin was one of the subjects which I really enjoyed in high school. Many people laugh at it because they say it is a useless, dead language. Churches do not even use it any more in their services, pity. Something like eighty-five percent of the English language is derived from a mere ninety latin root words. I cannot express how useful it was to have an understanding of latin when it came to memorizing the order, phylum and classification of organisms in zoology class, later on in college. My creative writing classes also got a shot in the arm because of it. It was also interesting to find out the toll. ▼

Living Latin Bulletin

Published by The Romulus and Remus Society of Southern California — Januarious MXMXCIV

Managers Required to Study Roman Classics

Latin was one of the subjects which I really enjoyed in high school. Many people laugh at it because they say it is a useless, dead language. Churches do not even use it any more in their services, pity. Something like eighty-five percent of the English language is derived from a mere ninety latin root words. I cannot express how useful it was to have an understanding of latin when it came to memorizing the order, phylum and classification of organisms in zoology class, later on in college. My creative writing classes also got a shot in the arm because of it. It was also interesting to find out the toll that the dark ages took on the European civilization which the Romans had established for centuries. Latin is indeed living. But it is living quietly in the essence of western civilization.

Latin was one of the subjects which I really enjoyed in high school. Many people laugh at it because they say it is a useless, dead language. Churches do not even use it any more in their services, pity. Something like eighty-five percent of the English language is derived from a mere ninety latin root words. I cannot express how useful it was to have an understanding of latin when it came to memorizing the order, phylum and classification of organisms in zoology class, later on in college. My creative writing classes also got a shot in the arm because of it. It was also interesting to find out the toll that the dark ages took on the European civilization which the Romans had established for centuries. Latin is indeed living. But it is living quietly in the essence of western civilization. ▼

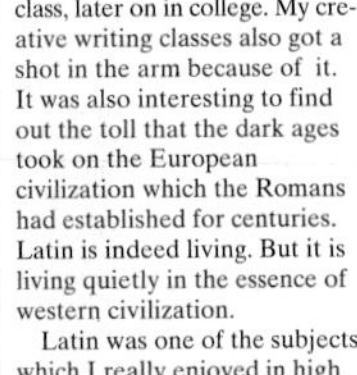

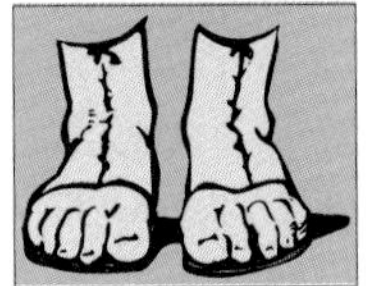

These Boots Were Made for Walkin'

Latin was one of the subjects which I really enjoyed in high school. Many people laugh at it because they say it is a useless, dead language. Churches do not even use it any more in their services, pity. Something like eighty-five percent of the English language is derived from a mere ninety latin root words. I cannot express how useful it was to have an understanding of latin when it came to memorizing the order, phylum and classification of organisms in zoology class, later on in college. My creative writing classes also got a shot in the arm because of it. It was also interesting to find out the toll that the dark ages took on the European civilization which the Romans had established for centuries. Latin is indeed living. But it is living quietly in the essence of western civilization. Latin is indeed living. It is living quietly in the essence of western civilization. ▼

(c)

FIGURE 5.11 Pages for Problem 2 (continued)

b. Use a three- (rather than two-) column grid and vary all of the design parameters from part a—that is, justification, type size, and the use (omission) of a vertical line between columns.

c. Add a sans serif heading to randomly selected paragraphs from part a or part b. Use a larger type size and/or boldface for the heading(s).

d. Create a masthead using the Borders and Shading command to add horizontal line(s) as appropriate.

e. Redo the design using columns of different widths.

f. Choose the design you like best. Add your name to the completed document and submit it to your instructor. Hold a contest in class to select the best document.

4. The flyers in Figure 5.12 were created from a graphic in the CLIPART directory that was imported into a document and sized (and moved) appropriately. It's easy provided you remember to click the frame icon immediately after capturing the graphic. Reproduce either or both of our flyers, or better yet, create your own.

5. Design your own letterhead containing your name, address, telephone number, hypothetical fax number and Email address, and any other text you want to include (e.g, Attorney at Law). You may also want to consider the use of horizontal lines to offset the letterhead and/or a graphical logo.

(a) UM Jazz Band

CIS 120 Study Sessions

For those who don't know a bit from a byte
Come to Mahoney Hall this Tuesday night
We'll study the concepts that aren't always clear
And memorize terms that hackers hold dear

We'll hit the books from 7 til 10
And then on Thursday we'll do it again
It can't hurt you to try us - so come on by
And give the CIS tutors that old college try!

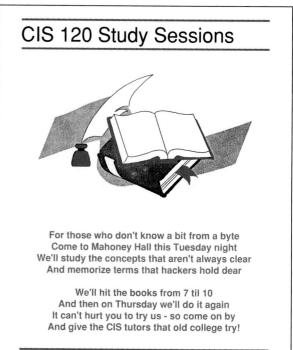

(b) CIS 120 Study Sessions

FIGURE 5.12 Flyers for Problem 4

6. Figure 5.13 displays three additional mastheads suitable for the newsletter that was developed in the chapter. Each masthead was created as follows:
   a. A one-by-two table was used in Figure 5.13a to right justify the date of the newsletter. The use of a table to right align text was suggested in the tip on page 160.
   b. A different font was used for the masthead in Figure 5.13b. The border around the masthead is a drop shadow.
   c. Microsoft WordArt (see problem 7) was used to create the masthead in Figure 5.13c.

   Choose the masthead you like best, then modify the newsletter as it existed at the end of the second hands-on exercise to include the new masthead.
7. Create a complete multicolumn newsletter containing at least one graphic from the clip art subdirectory. The intent of this problem is simply to provide practice in graphic design; that is, there is no requirement to write meaningful text, but the headings in the newsletter should follow the theme of the graphic.
   a. Select a graphic from the clip art directory, then write one or two sentences in support of that graphic. If, for example, you choose BOOKS.WMF, you could write a sentence describing how you intend to hit the books in an effort to boost your GPA and make the Dean's List.
   b. As indicated, there is no requirement to write meaningful text for the newsletter; just copy the sentences from part a once or twice to create a paragraph, then copy the paragraph several times to create the newsletter. You should, however, create meaningful headings to add interest to the document.

The Athlete's Hi

Volume 1 November 1994

(a) With Volume Number and Date

The Athlete's Hi

(b) Alternate Font and Drop Shadow

The Athlete's Hi

(c) Microsoft WordArt

FIGURE 5.13 The Masthead (problem 6)

c. Develop an overall design away from the computer—that is, with pencil and paper. Use a grid to indicate the placement of the articles, headings, clip art, and masthead. You may be surprised to find that it is easier to master commands in Word than it is to design the newsletter; do not, however, underestimate the importance of graphic design in the ultimate success of your document.

d. More is not better; and you should not use too many fonts, styles, sizes, and clip art just because they are there. Don't crowd the page, and remember that white space is a very effective design element. There are no substitutes for simplicity and good taste.

8. Exploring Word Art: The right clip art image adds immeasurably to a document, but what if you cannot find an appropriate graphic? Word for Windows anticipates this situation and includes a delightful application, ***WordArt,*** that enables you to create special effects with text. It lets you rotate and/or flip text, display it vertically on the page, shade it, slant it, arch it, or even print it upside down. Create a document in the usual fashion, then pull down the Insert menu, click Object, and select WordArt from the Object Type list. It's fun, it's easy, and you can create some truly dynamite documents.

Figure 5.14 contains several samples of WordArt. Try to recreate our examples, or better yet, create an entirely different document. One suggestion is to create a cover page that you can use for all future assignments with your name, the date, and the title of the assignment.

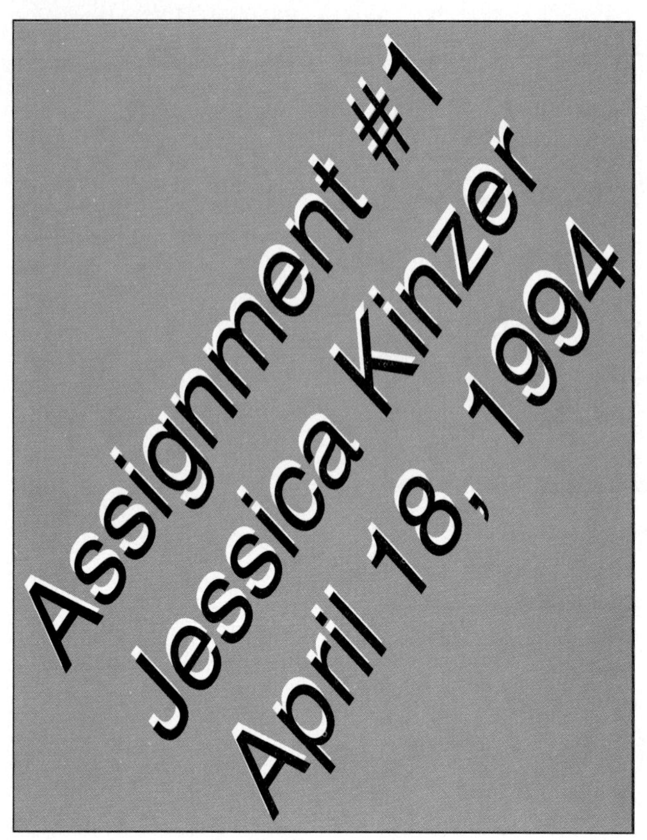

(a) WordArt Example 1

(b) WordArt Example 2

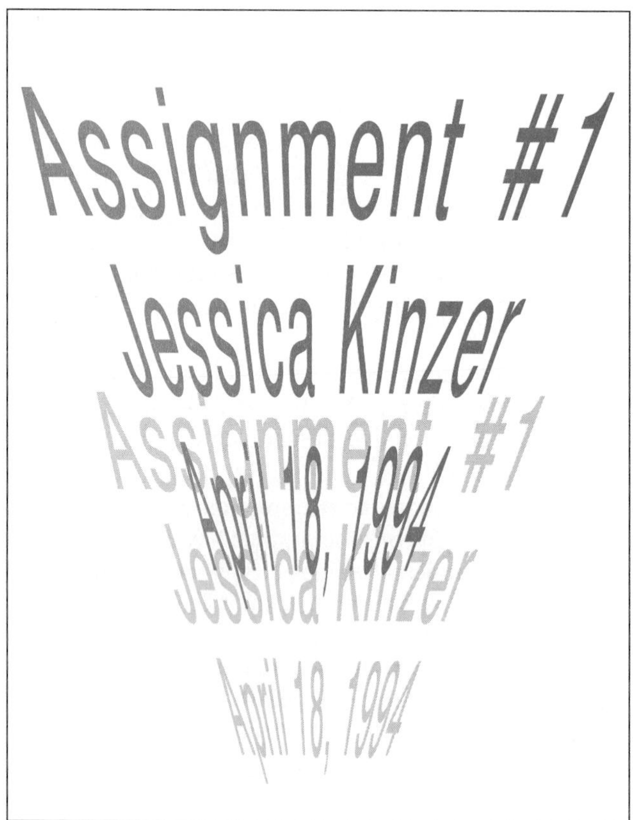

(c) WordArt Example 3

FIGURE 5.14 WordArt (problem 8)

9. A guide to smart shopping: This problem is more challenging than the previous exercises in that you are asked to consider content as well as design. The objective is to develop a one- (or two-) page document with helpful tips to the novice on buying a computer. We have, however, written the copy for you and put the file on the data disk.

   a. Open the file BUYING.DOC and print the document, which takes approximately a page and a half as presently formatted. Read our text and determine the tips you want to retain and those you want to delete. Add other tips as you see fit.
   b. Examine the available clip art by previewing the files in the clip art subdirectory. There is no requirement to include a graphic. Use clip art only if you think it will enhance the document.
   c. Consult a current computer magazine (or another source) to determine actual prices for one or more configurations, then include this information prominently in your document.
   d. Create the masthead for the document, then develop with pencil and paper a rough sketch of the completed document showing the masthead, the placement of the text, clip art, and special of the month (the configuration in part c).
   e. Return to the computer and implement the design of part d. Create a balanced publication that completely fills the space allotted; that is, your document should take exactly one or two pages (rather than the page and a half in the original BUYING.DOC on the data disk).

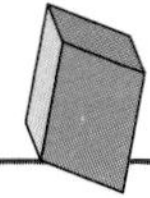

Case Studies

Before and After

The best way to learn about the do's and don'ts of desktop publishing is to study the work of others. Choose a particular type of document—for example, a newsletter, résumé, or advertising flyer—then collect samples of that document. Choose one sample that is particularly bad and redesign the document. You need not enter the actual text, but you should keep all of the major headings so that the document retains its identity. Add or delete clip art as appropriate. Bring the before and after samples to class and hold a contest to determine the most radical improvement.

Clip Art

Clip art—you see it all the time, but where do you get it, and how much does it cost? Some images are supplied with a word processor, but you grow tired of these and yearn for more. Scan the computer magazines and find at least two sources for additional clip art. Return to class with specific information on price and the nature of the clip art. Be sure to determine in advance how much disk space the clip art will require; the answer may surprise you.

The Invitation

Choose an event and produce the perfect invitation. The possibilities are endless and limited only by your imagination. You can invite people to your wedding or to a fraternity party. Your laser printer and abundance of fancy fonts enable you to do anything a professional printer can do. Clip art and/or special paper will add the finishing touch. Go to it—this assignment is a lot of fun.

The Flyer

It's rush week and you're the publicity chairperson for your fraternity or sorority. Needless to say, it's highly competitive, and you need effective flyers to attract new members. This is an absolutely critical assignment, and people are counting on you. Don't blow it!

Paper Makes a Difference

Most of us take paper for granted, but the right paper can make a significant difference in the effectiveness of the document. Reports and formal correspondence are usually printed on white paper, but you would be surprised how many different shades of white there are. Other types of documents lend themselves to color paper for additional impact. In short, the paper you use is far from an automatic decision. Research the subject and tell us what you find.

Countries of the World

Presentation programs such as Freelance and PowerPoint supply clip art that includes maps and flags of foreign countries. Design a one-page travel brochure for a country you would like to visit. Open the presentation program, copy the appropriate clip art image(s) to the Windows clipboard, then paste it into the word processing document.

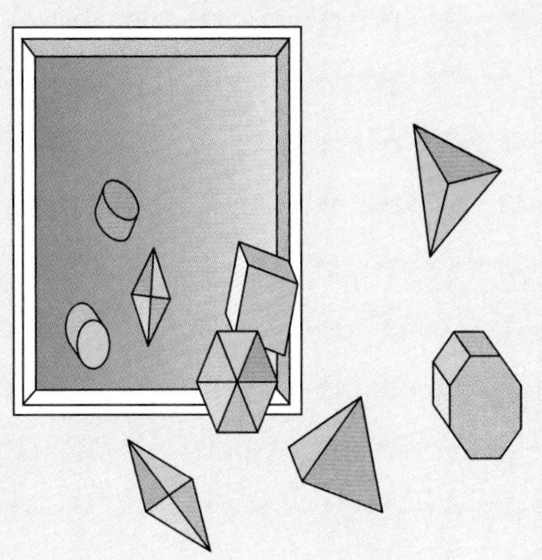

Appendix A: Object Linking and Embedding 2.0: Sharing Data Among Programs

OVERVIEW

One of the primary advantages of Windows is the ability to create a ***compound document***—that is, a document containing data from multiple applications. There are three different ways this can be accomplished: pasting, linking, and embedding.

Pasting is the simplest operation and is done with the cut, copy, and paste commands present in all Windows applications. You cut or copy data onto the ***clipboard,*** then paste it elsewhere into the same application, or into a different application to produce a compound document. There are two disadvantages to the simple paste operation. First, it is a static connection meaning that if the data is subsequently changed in the original document, the change is not reflected in the compound document. Second, once data has been pasted into a compound document, it can no longer be edited using the original application.

Object Linking and Embedding (OLE) offers a superior way to share data between documents. In actuality, there are two separate techniques, linking and embedding, and each will be illustrated in its own exercise. The following terminology is essential to the discussion:

- An ***object*** is any piece of data created by a Windows application, such as a spreadsheet created in Excel or a document created in Word.
- The ***source document*** is the place where the object originates. The source document—for example, an Excel spreadsheet—is created by the ***server application,*** Excel 5.0.
- The ***destination document*** is the file into which the object is placed. The destination document (for example, a Word document) is created by the ***client application,*** Word for Windows.

Figure A.1 displays the compound document that will be created in the first hands-on exercise, in which an Excel spreadsheet is ***embedded*** into a Word document. Excel is the server application and Word is the client application. The exercise uses the ***Insert Object command*** in Word to place a copy of the spreadsheet into the Word document, then modifies the (copy of the) spreadsheet through

in-place editing. In-place editing requires the application to support the Microsoft specification for Object Linking and Embedding 2.0. Both Excel 5.0 and Word for Windows 6.0 support this standard.

In-place editing enables you to double click an embedded object (the spreadsheet) and change it, using the tools of the server application (Excel). In other words, you remain in the client application (Word for Windows in this example) but you have access to the Excel toolbar and pull-down menus. In-place editing modifies the copy of the embedded object in the destination document. It does *not* change the original object because there is no connection between the source and destination documents.

Lionel Douglas

402 Mahoney Hall • Coral Gables, Florida 33124

May 10, 1994

Dear Folks,

I heard from Mr. Black, the manager at University Commons, and the apartment is a definite for the Fall. Manny and I are very excited, and can't wait to get out of the dorm. The food is poison, not that either of us are cooks, but anything will be better than this! I have been checking into car prices (we are definitely too far away from campus to walk!), and have done some estimating on what it will cost. The figures below are for a Jeep Wrangler, the car of my dreams:

Price of car	$11,995			
Manufacturer's rebate	$1,000			
Down payment	$3,000		**My assumptions**	
Amount to be financed	$7,995		Interest rate	7.90%
Monthly payment	$195		Term (years)	4
Gas	$40			
Maintenance	$50			
Insurance	$100			
Total per month	$385			

My initial estimate was $471 based on a $2,000 down payment and a three-year loan at 7.9%. I know this is too much so I plan on earning an additional $1,000 and extending the loan to four years. If that won't do it, I'll look at other cars.

Lionel

FIGURE A.1 A Compound Document

HANDS-ON EXERCISE 1:

Embedding

Objective To embed an Excel spreadsheet into a Word document; to use in-place editing to modify the spreadsheet. The exercise requires both Word 6.0 and Excel 5.0; the faster your computer, the better.

Step 1: Open the Word document

- Pull down the **File menu** and click **Open** (or click the **File Open button** on the toolbar).
- If you have not yet changed the default directory:
  - — Click the **drop-down list box** to specify the appropriate drive, which is the same drive you have been using throughout the text.
  - — Scroll through the directory list box until you come to the **WORDDATA** directory. Double click this directory to make it the active directory.
- Double click **CAR.DOC** to open the document.
- Pull down the **File menu.** Click the **Save As** command to save the document as **MYCAR.DOC.**
- The title bar reflects **MYCAR.DOC,** but you can always return to the original document if you edit the duplicated file beyond redemption.
- If necessary, change to the **Page Layout view** at **Page Width.**

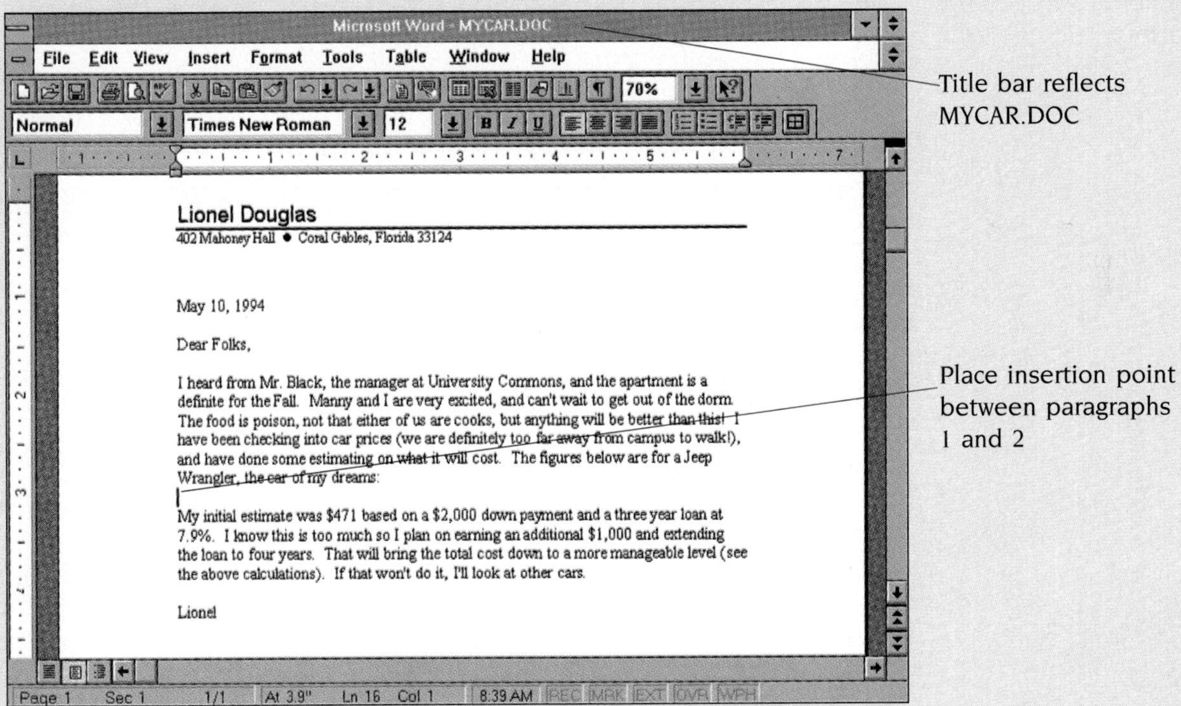

(a) The Word Document (step 1)

FIGURE A.2 Hands-on Exercise 1

Step 2: Embed the Excel spreadsheet

- Click the blank line between paragraphs one and two, the place in the document where the spreadsheet is to go.

- Pull down the **Insert menu,** click **Object,** then click the **Create from File** tab as shown in Figure A.2b.
  - Click the **drop-down list box** to specify the appropriate drive, which is the same drive you are using for the Word for Windows files.
  - Scroll through the directory list box until you come to the **EXCLDATA** directory. Double click this directory to make it the active directory.
- Click **CAR.XLS,** then click the **OK** command button to bring the spreadsheet into the document.

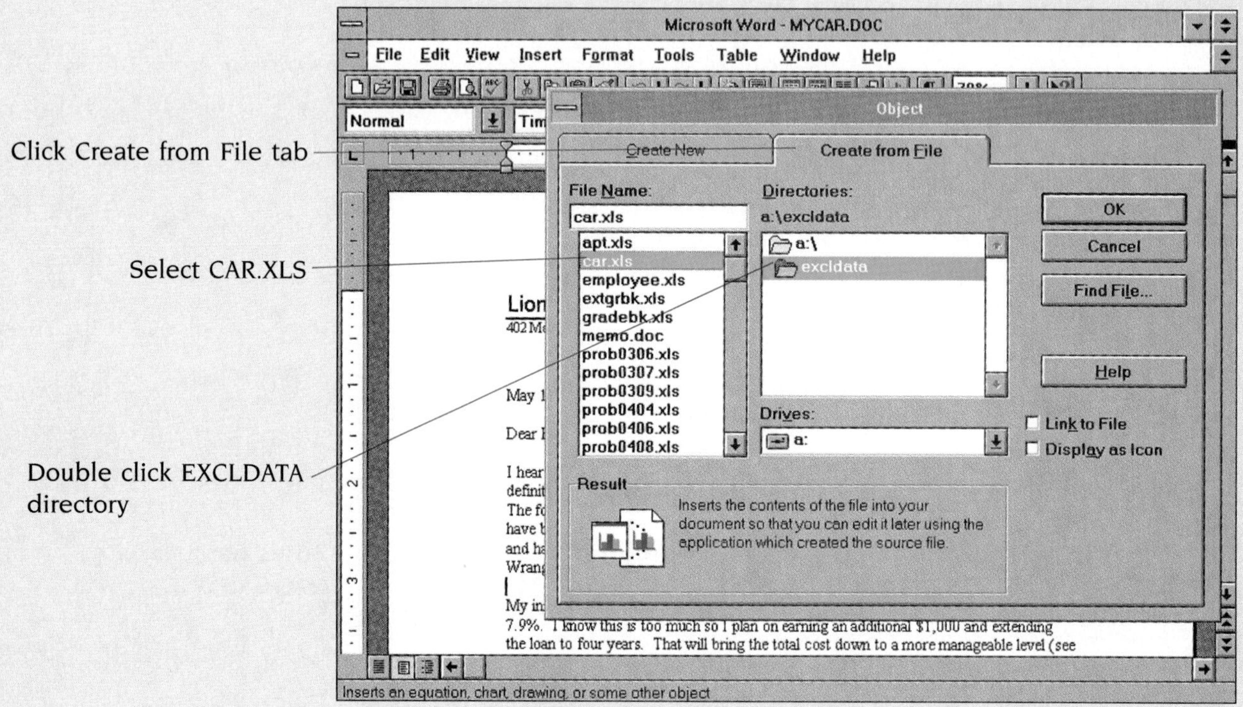

(b) Insert Object Command (step 2)

FIGURE A.2 Hands-on Exercise 1 (continued)

Step 3: Frame the spreadsheet

- Point to the spreadsheet, then click the **right mouse button** to produce a Shortcut menu.
- Click **Frame Picture** to frame the spreadsheet in order to position it more easily within the document.
- Drag the spreadsheet so that it is centered within the memo as shown in Figure A.2c. You may want to enter a blank line(s) between the paragraphs to give the spreadsheet more room.

Step 4: In-place editing

- Double click the spreadsheet in order to edit it in place as shown in Figure A.2d. Be patient as this step takes a while, even on a fast machine. Soon the Excel grid, the row and column labels, will appear around the spreadsheet as shown in Figure A.2d.
- You are still in Word as indicated by the title bar (Microsoft Word - MYCAR.DOC), but the Excel 5.0 toolbars are displayed in the document window.

- ➤ Click in cell **B3** and change the down payment to **$3,000.**
- ➤ Click in cell **E5** and change the years to **4.** The Monthly payment and Total per month drop to $195 and $385, respectively.

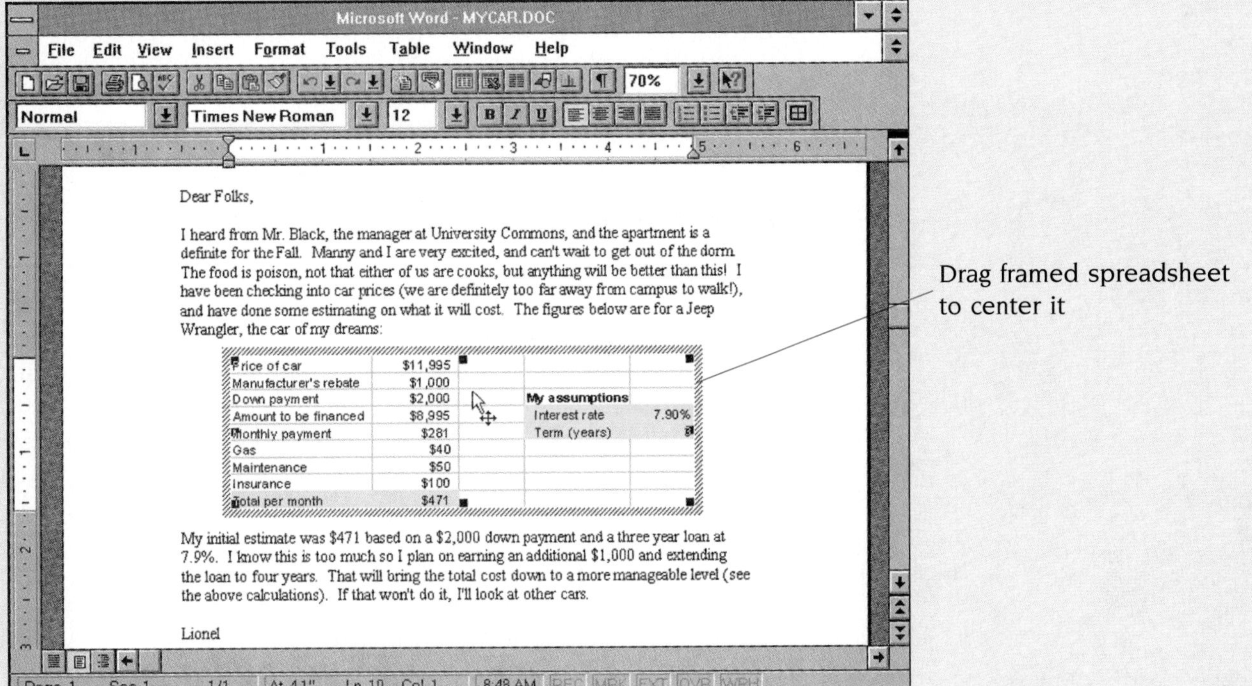

(c) Moving the Spreadsheet (step 3)

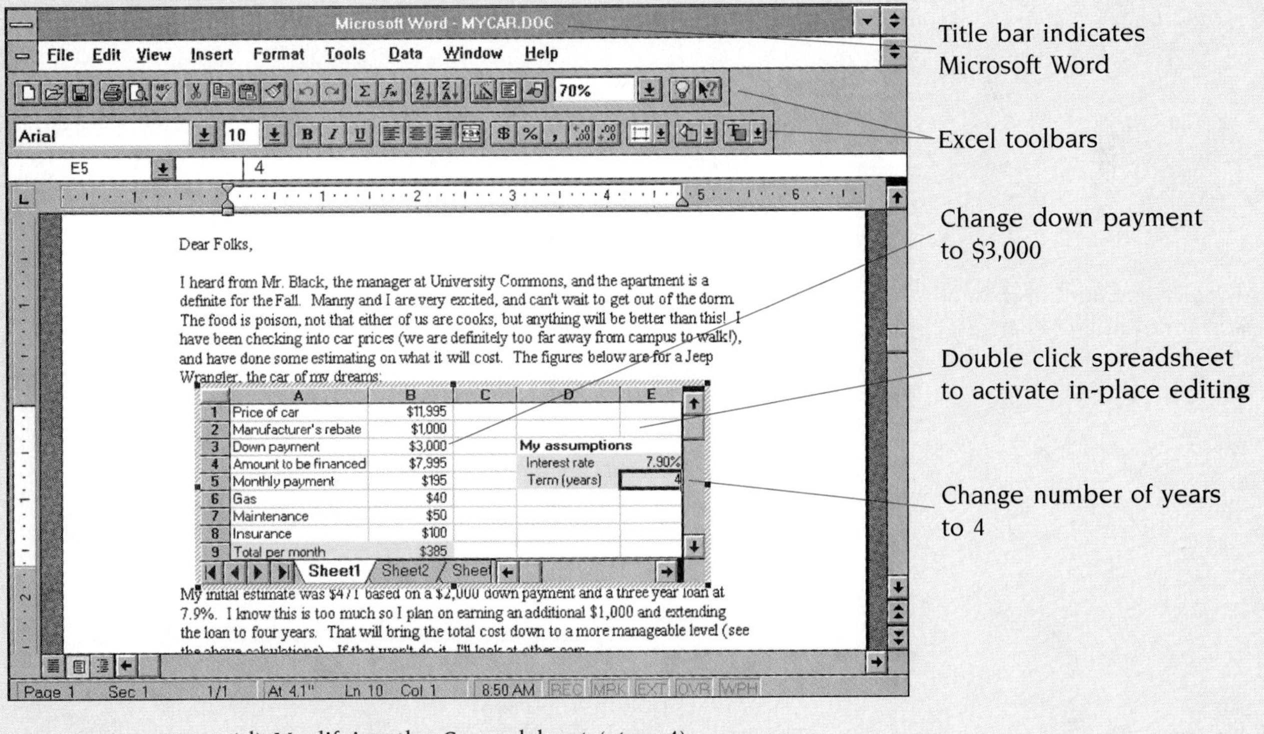

(d) Modifying the Spreadsheet (step 4)

FIGURE A.2 Hands-on Exercise 1 (continued)

IN-PLACE EDITING

In-place editing is implemented in Microsoft's Object Linking and Embedding 2.0 specification and provides access to the toolbar and pull-down menus of the server application. Thus when editing an Excel spreadsheet embedded into a Word document, the title bar is that of the client application (Word for Windows), but the toolbar and pull-down menus reflect the server application (Excel). There are, however, two exceptions; the File and Window menus are those of the client application (Word) so that you can save the compound document and/or arrange multiple documents within the client application.

Step 5: Save the Word document

- Click anywhere outside the spreadsheet to deselect it and view the completed Word document as shown in Figure A.2e.
- Pull down the **File menu** and click **Save** (or click the **Save button** on the Standard toolbar).
- Exit Word, which returns you to Program Manager.

Step 6: View the original object

- If necessary, open the group window that contains Excel 5.0, then double click the **Excel 5.0 program icon** to load Excel.
- The ***common user interface*** imposed on all Windows applications implies

Monthly Payment and Total per month reflect changes made

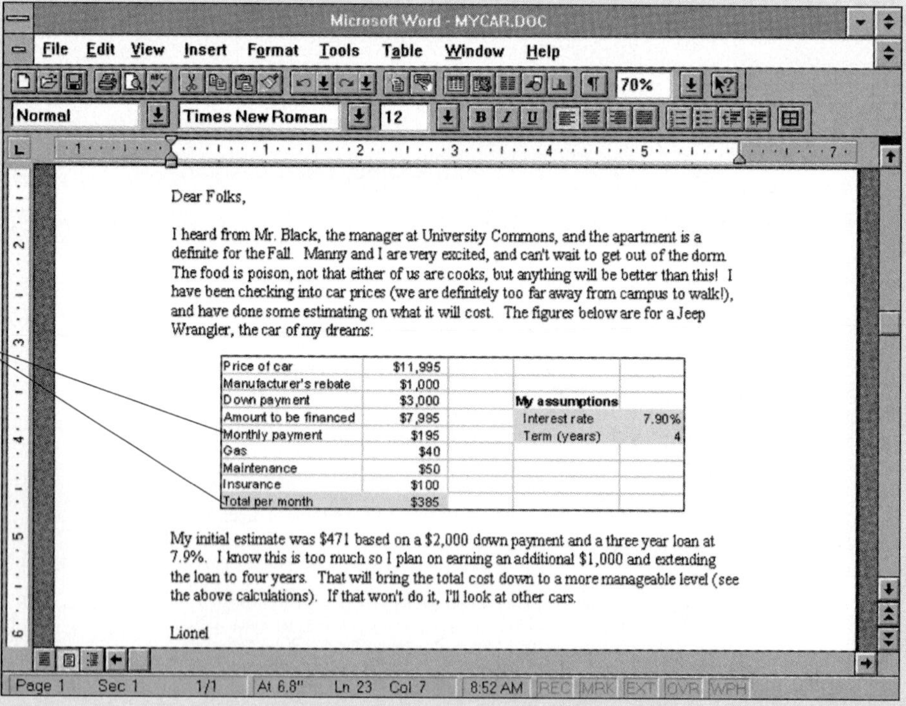
Dear Folks,

I heard from Mr. Black, the manager at University Commons, and the apartment is a definite for the Fall. Manny and I are very excited, and can't wait to get out of the dorm. The food is poison, not that either of us are cooks, but anything will be better than this! I have been checking into car prices (we are definitely too far away from campus to walk!), and have done some estimating on what it will cost. The figures below are for a Jeep Wrangler, the car of my dreams:

Price of car	$11,995			
Manufacturer's rebate	$1,000			
Down payment	$3,000		**My assumptions**	
Amount to be financed	$7,995		Interest rate	7.90%
Monthly payment	$195		Term (years)	4
Gas	$40			
Maintenance	$50			
Insurance	$100			
Total per month	$385			

My initial estimate was $471 based on a $2,000 down payment and a three year loan at 7.9%. I know this is too much so I plan on earning an additional $1,000 and extending the loan to four years. That will bring the total cost down to a more manageable level (see the above calculations). If that won't do it, I'll look at other cars.

Lionel

(e) Completed Word Document (step 5)

FIGURE A.2 Hands-on Exercise 1 (continued)

that the procedure to open a file in Excel will be similar (virtually identical) to the procedure in Word:

- — Pull down the **File menu** and click **Open** (or click the **File Open button** on the toolbar).
- — Click the **drop-down list box** to specify the appropriate drive, which is the same drive you have been using throughout the text.
- — Scroll through the directory list box until you come to the **EXCLDATA** directory. Double click this directory to make it the active directory.
- — Double click **CAR.XLS** to open the spreadsheet shown in Figure A.2f; this is the original (unmodified) spreadsheet, with a down payment of $2,000 and a three-year loan, that was first inserted into the Word document. The Monthly payment and Total per month are $281 and $471, respectively.

➤ Pull down the **File menu.** Click **Exit,** which returns you to Program Manager.

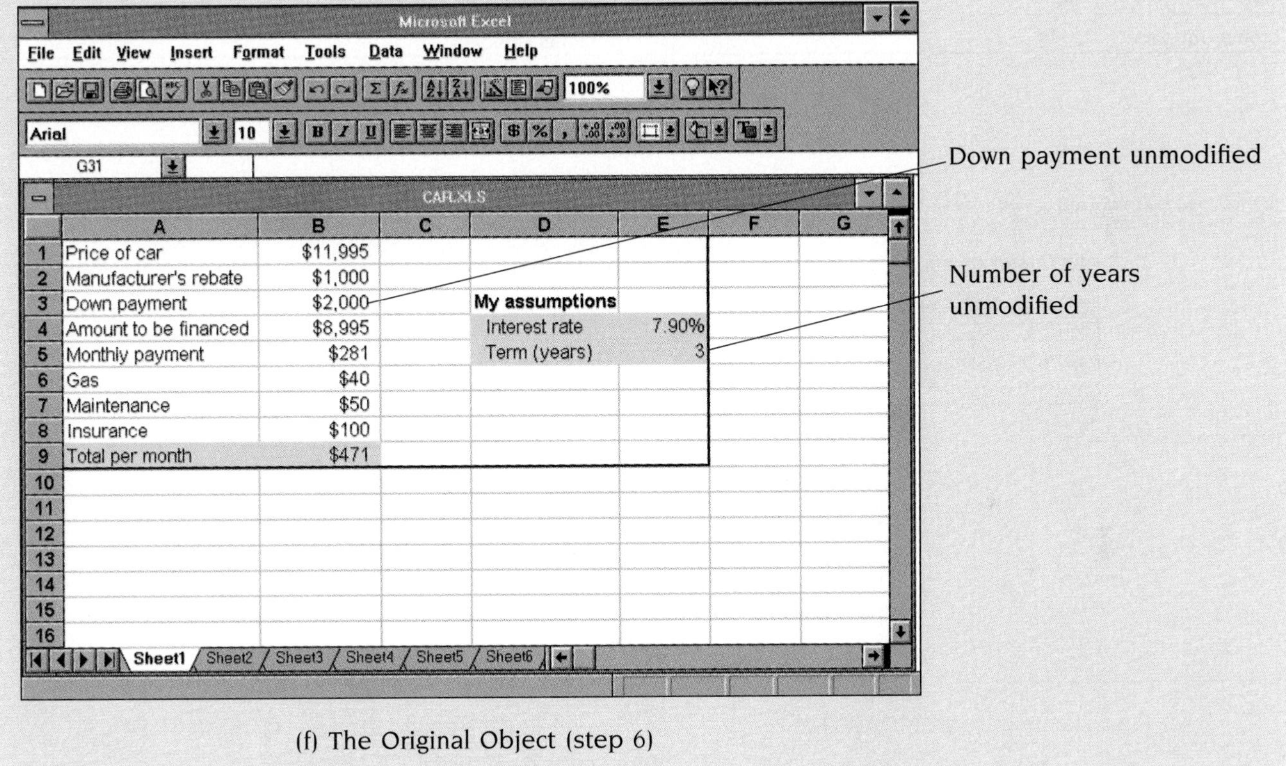

(f) The Original Object (step 6)

FIGURE A.2 Hands-on Exercise 1 (continued)

Linking

Linking is very different from embedding. Linking provides a dynamic connection between the source and destination documents; embedding does not. With linking, the source document (e.g., an Excel spreadsheet) is tied to the destination document (e.g., a Word document) in such a way that any changes in the Excel spreadsheet are automatically reflected in the Word document. The destination document contains a representation of the spreadsheet, as well as a pointer (that is, a link) to the file containing the spreadsheet.

Linking requires that the object be saved to disk prior to establishing the link. Embedding, on the other hand, lets you embed an object *without* saving it as a separate file. (The embedded object simply becomes part of the compound document.)

Consider now Figure A.3, in which the same spreadsheet is linked to two different documents. Both documents contain a pointer to the spreadsheet. In-place editing is not used as in the first exercise, which focused on an embedded object. Instead changes to the spreadsheet are made directly in the source document in Excel so that every document linked to the spreadsheet will reflect these changes.

The following exercise links a single Excel spreadsheet to two different Word documents. During the course of the exercise both applications (client and server) will be explicitly open, and it will be necessary to switch back and forth between the two. Thus the exercise also demonstrates the ***multitasking*** capability within Windows and the use of the ***task list*** to display the open applications. (See pages 53-75 in Grauer and Barber, *Exploring Windows,* Prentice Hall, 1994, for additional information on object linking and embedding, multitasking, and the common user interface.)

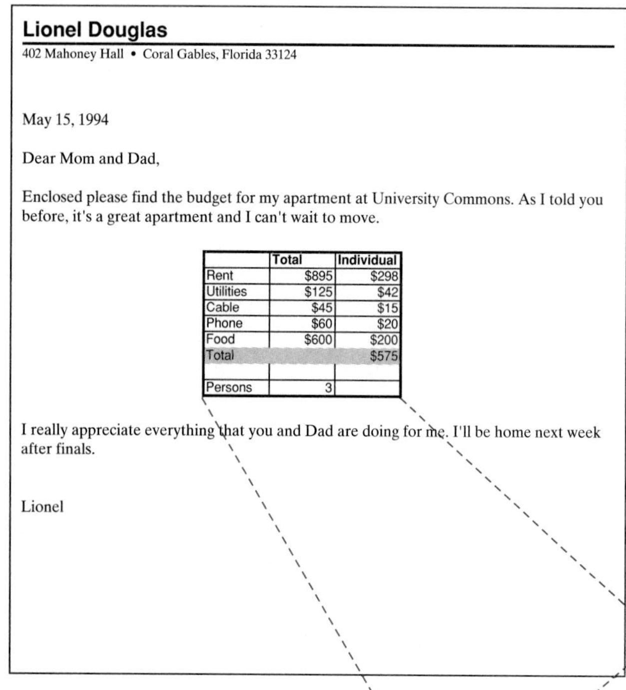

Lionel Douglas

402 Mahoney Hall • Coral Gables, Florida 33124

May 15, 1994

Dear Mom and Dad,

Enclosed please find the budget for my apartment at University Commons. As I told you before, it's a great apartment and I can't wait to move.

	Total	Individual
Rent	$895	$298
Utilities	$125	$42
Cable	$45	$15
Phone	$60	$20
Food	$600	$200
Total		$575
Persons	3	

I really appreciate everything that you and Dad are doing for me. I'll be home next week after finals.

Lionel

(a) First Document (MOMDAD.DOC)

Lionel Douglas

402 Mahoney Hall • Coral Gables, Florida 33124

May 15, 1994

Dear Manny,

I just got the final figures for our apartment next year and am sending you an estimate of our monthly costs. I included the rent, utilities, phone, cable, and food. I figure that food is the most likely place for the budget to fall apart, so learning to cook this summer is critical. I'll be taking lessons from the Galloping Gourmet, and suggest you do the same.

	Total	Individual
Rent	$895	$298
Utilities	$125	$42
Cable	$45	$15
Phone	$60	$20
Food	$600	$200
Total		$575
Persons	3	

Guess what - the three bedroom apartment just became available, which saves us more than $100 per month over the two bedroom we had planned to take. Jason Adler has decided to transfer and he can be our third roommate.

We should have a great year!

Lionel

(b) Second Document (MANNY.DOC)

	A	B	C
1		Total	Individual
2	Rent	$895	$298
3	Utilities	$125	$42
4	Cable	$45	$15
5	Phone	$60	$20
6	Food	$600	$200
7	Total		$575
8			
9	Persons	3	

(c) Spreadsheet (APT.XLS)

FIGURE A.3 Linking

Hands-On Exercise 2:

Linking

Objective To demonstrate multitasking and the ability to switch between applications; to link an Excel spreadsheet to multiple Word documents. The exercise requires both Word 6.0 and Excel 5.0.

Step 1: Open the Word document

- Load Word. Pull down the **File menu** and click **Open** (or click the **File Open button** on the toolbar).
- If you have not yet changed the default directory:
  - Click the **drop-down list box** to specify the appropriate drive, which is the same drive you have been using throughout the text.
  - Scroll through the directory list box until you come to the **WORDDATA** directory. Double click this directory to make it the active directory.
- Double click **MOMDAD.DOC** to open this document.
- If necessary, change to the **Page Layout view** at **Page Width.**

Step 2: Load Excel

- Press **Ctrl+Esc** to display the task list as in Figure A.4a. The contents of the task list depend on the applications open on your system, but you should see Microsoft Word and Program Manager.
- Double click **Program Manager** to switch to Program Manager.
- If necessary, open the group window that contains Excel 5.0 (for example, Microsoft Office), then double click the **Excel 5.0 program icon** to load Excel.

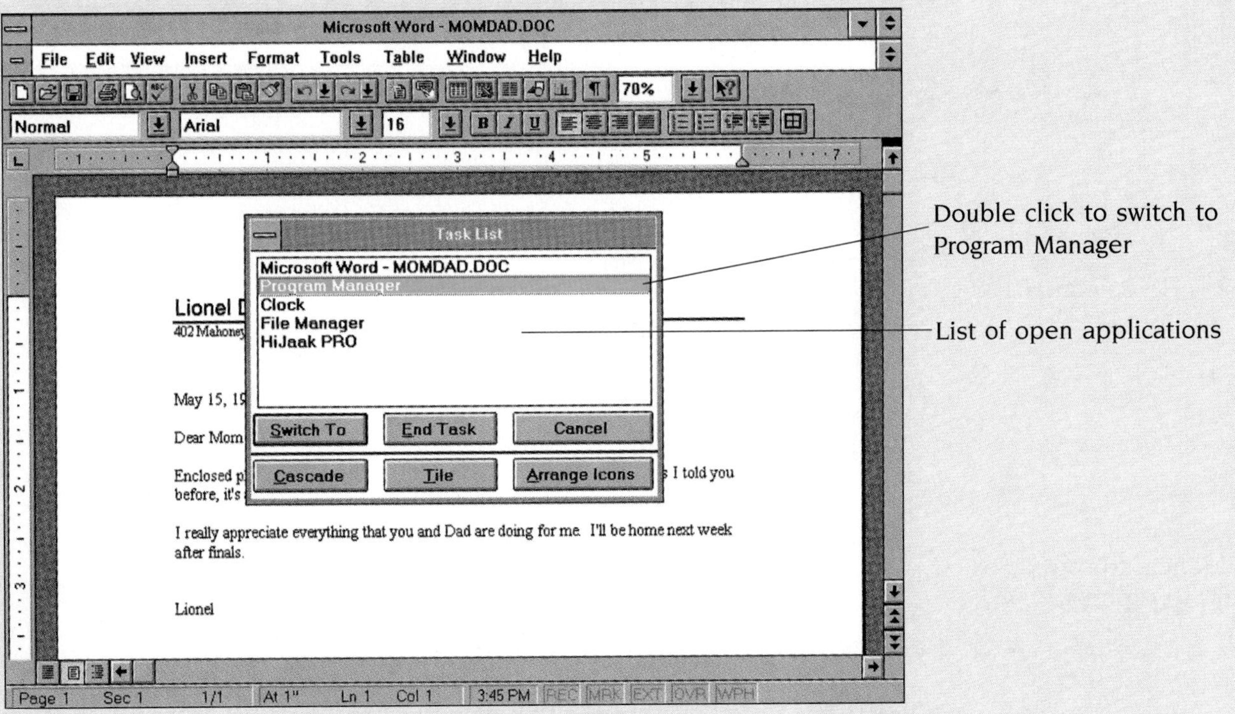

(a) Display the Task List (step 2)

FIGURE A.4 Hands-on Exercise 2

USE ALT+TAB TO SWITCH BETWEEN APPLICATIONS

Press and hold the Alt key while you press and release the Tab key repeatedly to cycle through the open applications. Release the Alt key when you see the title bar of the application you want.

Step 3: Open the APT.XLS spreadsheet

- Pull down the **File menu** and click **Open** (or click the **File Open button** on the toolbar).
- Click the **drop-down list box** to specify the appropriate drive.
- Scroll through the directory list box until you come to the **EXCLDATA** directory. Double click this directory to make it the active directory.
- Double click **APT.XLS** to open the spreadsheet.

Step 4: Copy the spreadsheet to the clipboard

- Click in cell **A1.** Drag the mouse over cells **A1 through C9** so that the entire spreadsheet is selected as shown in Figure A.4b.
- Point to the selected area, then press the **right mouse button** to display a Shortcut menu as shown in the figure. Click **Copy.** A flashing dashed line (known as a marquee) appears around the entire spreadsheet, indicating that the spreadsheet has been copied to the clipboard.
- Press **Ctrl+Esc** to display the task list. Double click **Microsoft Word - MOMDAD.DOC** to return to the Word document.

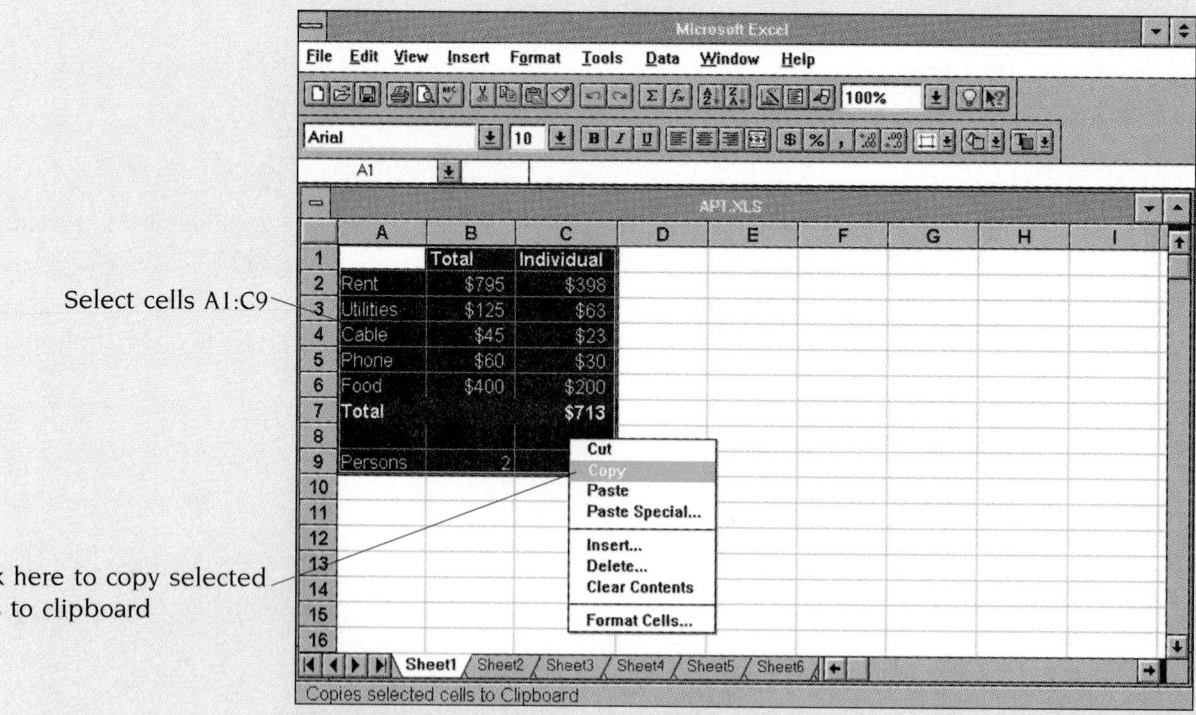

(b) Copying to the Clipboard (step 4)

FIGURE A.4 Hands-on Exercise 2 (continued)

Step 5: Create the Link

- Click in the document where you want the spreadsheet.
- Pull down the **Edit menu.** Click **Paste Special** to produce the dialog box in Figure A.4c.
- Click the **Paste Link** option button. Click **Microsoft Excel 5.0 Worksheet Object.** Click **OK** to insert the spreadsheet into the document as shown in Figure A.4d. You may want to insert a blank line before and after the spreadsheet to make it easier to read.
- Save the document containing the letter to Mom and Dad.

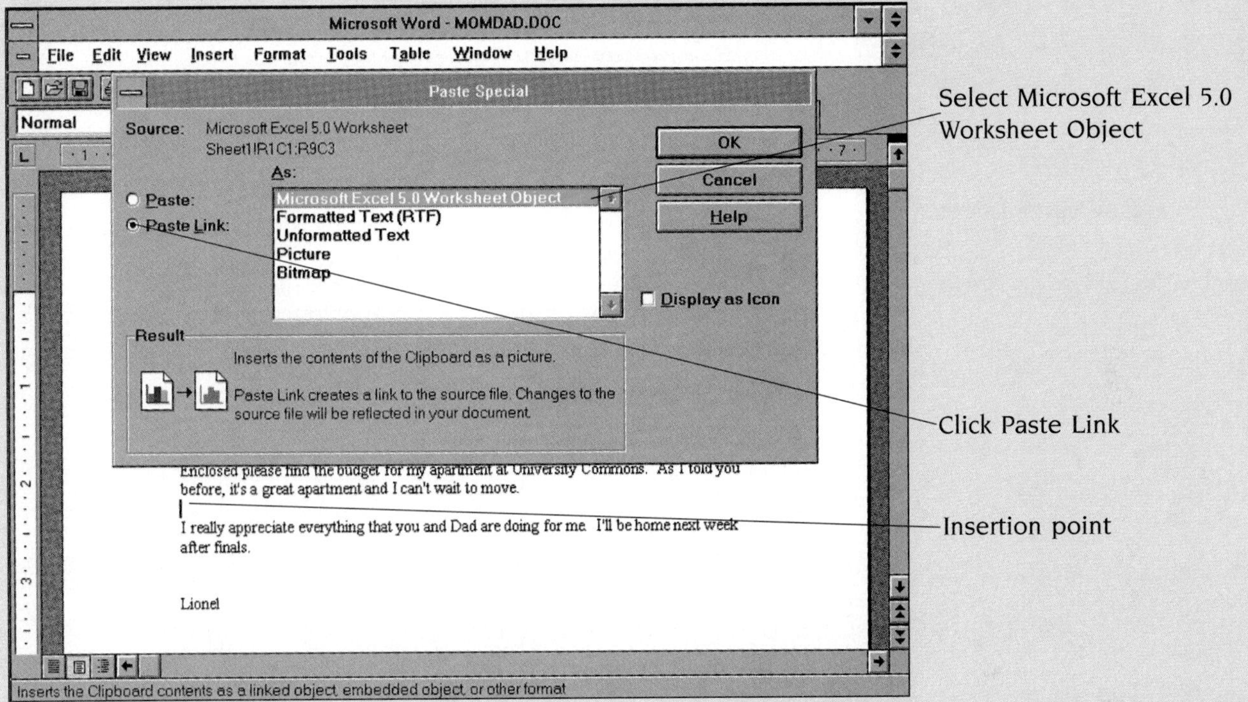

(c) Create the Link (step 5)

FIGURE A.4 Hands-on Exercise 2 (continued)

Step 6: Open the second Word document.

- Pull down the **File menu** and click **Open** (or click the **File Open button** on the toolbar).
- Double click **MANNY.DOC** to open the *second* document as shown in Figure A.4e, but without the spreadsheet.
- The spreadsheet is still in the clipboard. Click in the document where you want the spreadsheet to go.
- Pull down the **Edit menu.** Click **Paste Special.** Click the **Paste Link** option button. Click **Microsoft Excel 5.0 Worksheet Object.** Click **OK** to insert the spreadsheet into the document.
- Save the document containing the letter to Manny.

Step 7: Modify the spreadsheet

- Double click the spreadsheet in order to change it; the system pauses as it switches to Excel and returns to the source document APT.XLS, as shown in Figure A.4f.

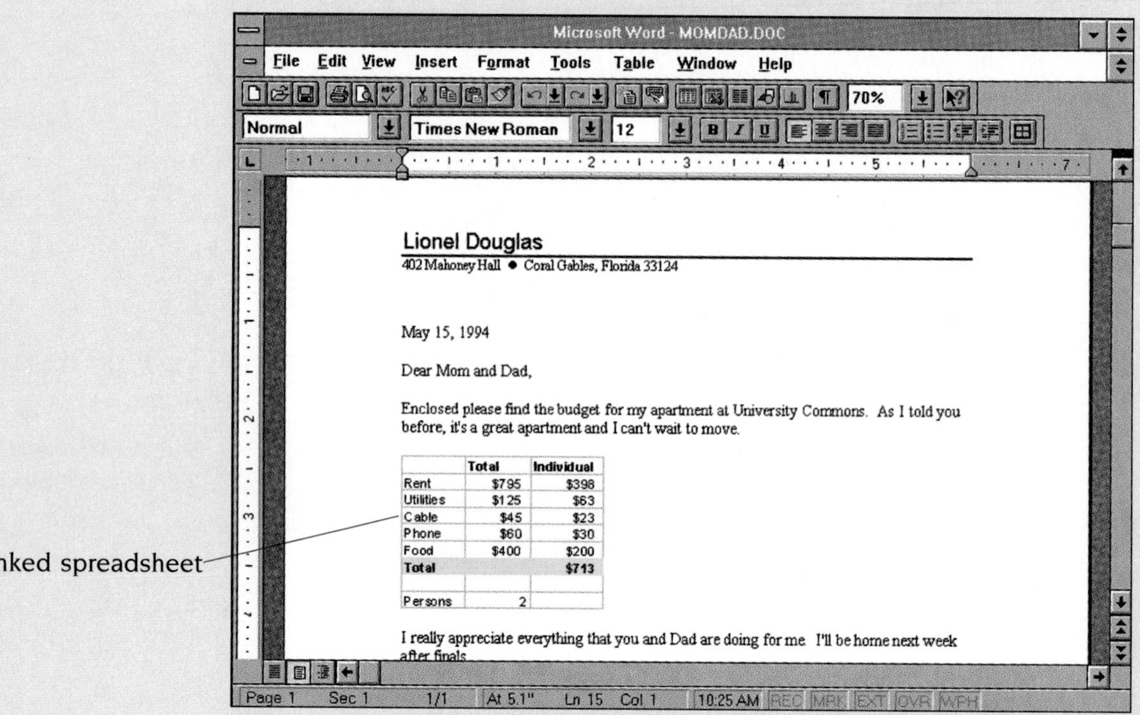

(d) Create the Link (step 5)

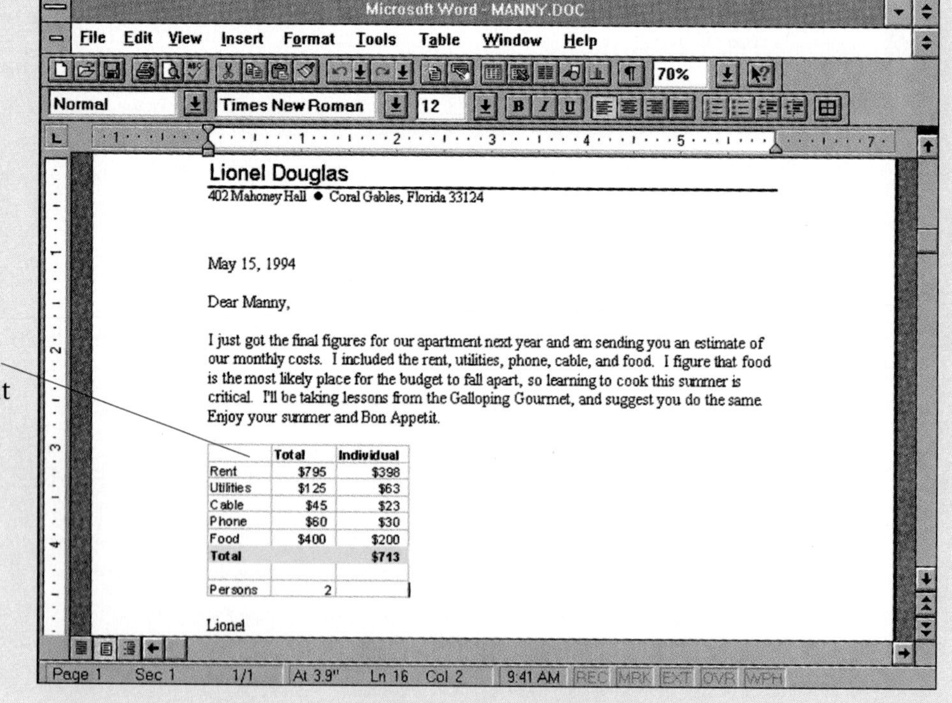

(e) The Second Document (step 6)

FIGURE A.4 Hands-on Exercise 2 (continued)

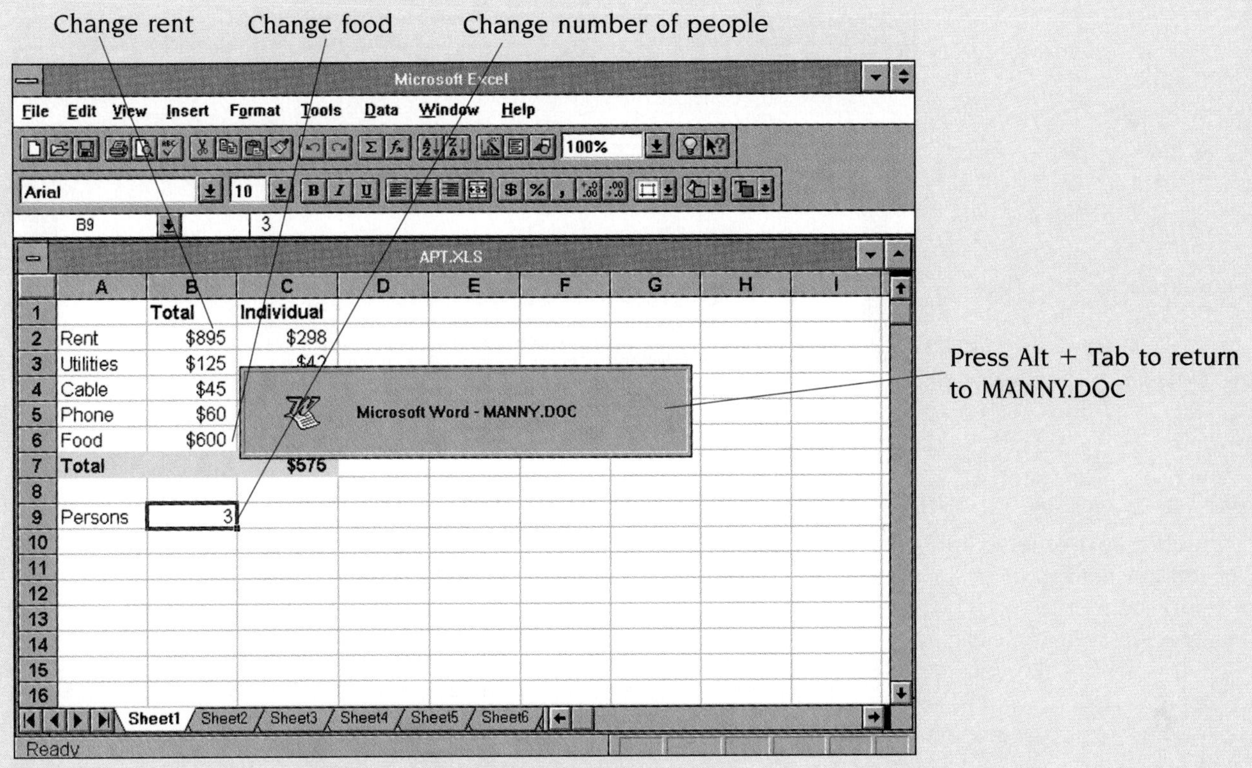

(f) Modify the Spreadsheet (step 7)

FIGURE A.4 Hands-on Exercise 2 (continued)

- Cells **A1 through C9** are still selected from step 4. Click outside the selected range to deselect the spreadsheet.
- Click in cell **B2.** Type **$895,** the rent for a three-bedroom apartment.
- Click in cell **B6.** Type **$600,** the increased amount for food.
- Click in cell **B9.** Type **3** to change the number of people sharing the apartment.
- Pull down the **File menu** and click **Save** (or click the **Save icon**) to save the modified spreadsheet.

Step 8: The modified documents

- Press and hold the **Alt key** while you press and release the **Tab key** repeatedly to cycle through the open applications. Release the Alt key when you see **Microsoft Word - MANNY.DOC** in a box in the middle of the screen as in Figure A.4f.
- The active application changes to Word and you should see the letter to Manny as shown in Figure A.4g; the document displays the modified spreadsheet because of the link established in step 5. Modify the text as shown to let Manny know about the new apartment. Save the document.
- Pull down the **Window menu.** Click **MOMDAD.DOC** to switch to the letter to your parents. The note to your parents also contains the updated spreadsheet (with three roommates) because of the link created in step 5.
- Exit Word.

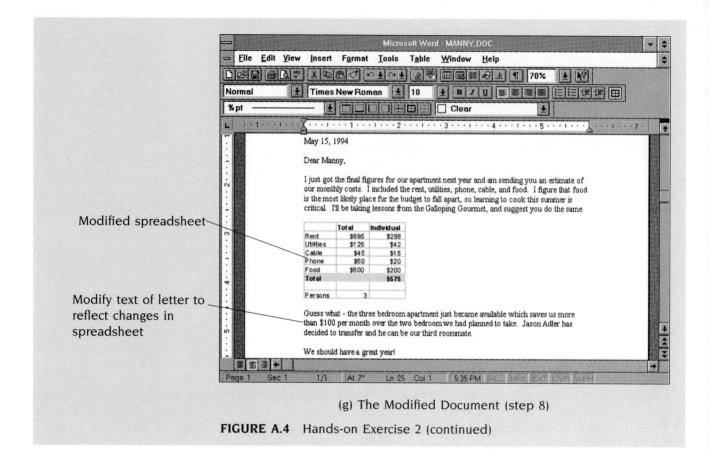

Modified spreadsheet

Modify text of letter to reflect changes in spreadsheet

May 15, 1994

Dear Manny,

I just got the final figures for our apartment next year and am sending you an estimate of our monthly costs. I included the rent, utilities, phone, cable, and food. I figure that food is the most likely place for the budget to fall apart, so learning to cook this summer is critical. I'll be taking lessons from the Galloping Gourmet, and suggest you do the same.

	Total	Individual
Rent	$895	$298
Utilities	$125	$42
Cable	$45	$15
Phone	$60	$20
Food	$600	$200
Total		**$575**
Persons	3	

Guess what - the three bedroom apartment just became available which saves us more than $100 per month over the two bedroom we had planned to take. Jason Adler has decided to transfer and he can be our third roommate.

We should have a great year!

(g) The Modified Document (step 8)

FIGURE A.4 Hands-on Exercise 2 (continued)

SUMMARY

Linking requires that the source document be saved as a separate file, and further that the link between the source and destination document be maintained. The link will be broken if you give a colleague a copy of the compound document without including the source document. Linking is useful when the same object is present in multiple destination documents. Any subsequent change to the object is made in only one place (the source document), and is automatically reflected in the multiple destination documents.

Embedding does not require a separate source document because the object is contained within the destination document. Embedding lets you give your colleague a copy of the compound document, without the source document, and indeed, there need not be a source document. You would not, however, want to embed the same object into multiple destination documents because any subsequent change to the object would have to be made in every destination document.

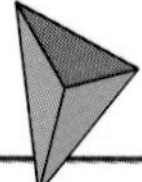

Key Words and Concepts

Client application
Clipboard
Common user interface
Compound document
Destination document
Dynamic connection
Embedded object
In-place editing
Insert Object command
Linking
Multitasking
Object
Object Linking and Embedding (OLE)
Server application
Source document
Static connection
Task list

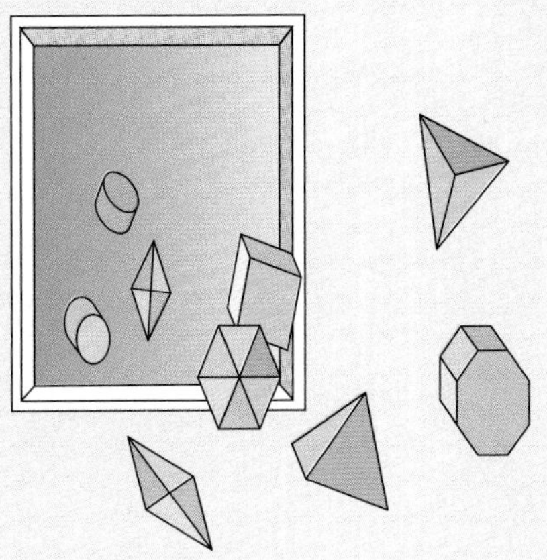

Appendix B: Toolbars

OVERVIEW

Word for Windows offers eight predefined toolbars to provide access to commonly used commands. The toolbars are displayed in Figure B.1 and are listed here for convenience. They are: the Borders, Database, Drawing, Formatting, Forms, Microsoft, Standard, and Word 2.0 toolbars. The Standard and Formatting Toolbars are displayed by default and appear immediately below the Menu Bar.

In addition to the predefined toolbars, which are displayed continually, six other toolbars appear only when the corresponding feature is in use. These toolbars appear (and disappear) automatically and are shown in Figure B.2. They are: the Equation Editor, Macro, Mail Merge, Master Document, Outlining, and WordArt toolbars.

The icons on the toolbars are intended to be indicative of their function. For example, clicking on the printer icon (fourth from the left on the Standard toolbar) executes the Print command. If you are unsure of the purpose of any icon, point to it and a Tool Tip will appear that displays its name.

You can display multiple toolbars at one time, move them to new locations on the screen, customize their appearance, or suppress their display.

- To display or hide a toolbar, pull down the View menu and click the Toolbars command. Select (deselect) the toolbar(s) that you want to display (hide). The selected toolbar(s) will be displayed in the same position as when last displayed. You may also point to any toolbar and click with the right mouse button to bring up a shortcut menu, after which you can select the toolbars to be displayed (hidden).
- To change the size of the tools, display them in monochrome rather than color, or suppress the display of the Tool Tips, pull down the View menu, click Toolbars, and then select/deselect the appropriate check box.
- Toolbars may be either docked (along the edge of the window) or left floating (in their own window). A toolbar moved to the edge of the window will dock along that edge. A toolbar moved anywhere else in the window will float in its own window. Docked toolbars are one tool wide (high), whereas floating

toolbars can be resized by clicking and dragging a border or corner as you would any window.

- To move a docked toolbar, click anywhere in the gray background area and drag the toolbar to its new location.
- To move a floating toolbar, drag its title bar to its new location.

➤ To customize one or more toolbars, display the toolbars on the screen. Then pull down the View menu, click Toolbars, click the Customize command button, and select the Toolbars tab. Alternatively, you can click on any toolbar with the right mouse button, select Customize from the shortcut menu, and then click the Toolbars tab.

- To move a tool, drag the tool to its new location on that toolbar or any other displayed toolbar.
- To copy a tool, press the Ctrl key as you drag the tool to its new location on that toolbar or any other displayed toolbar.
- To delete a tool, drag the tool off the toolbar and release the mouse button.
- To add a tool, select the category from the Categories list box and then drag the tool to the desired location on the toolbar. (To see a description of a tool's function prior to adding it to a toolbar, click the tool in the Customize dialog box and read the displayed description.)
- To restore a predefined toolbar to its default appearance, pull down the View menu, click Toolbars, select the desired toolbar, and click the Reset command button.

➤ Tools can also be moved, copied, or deleted without displaying the Customize dialog box.

- To move a tool, press the Alt key as you drag the tool to the new location.
- To copy a tool, press the Alt and Ctrl keys as you drag the tool to the new location.
- To delete a tool, press the Alt key as you drag the tool off the toolbar.

➤ To create your own toolbar, pull down the View menu, click Toolbars, and click the New command button. Alternatively, you can click on any toolbar with the right mouse button, select Toolbars from the shortcut menu, and click the New command button.

- Enter a name for the toolbar in the dialog box that follows. The name can be any length and can contain spaces.
- The new toolbar will appear at the top left of the screen. Initially, it will be big enough to hold only one tool. Add, move, and delete tools following the same procedures as outlined above. The toolbar will automatically size itself as new tools are added and deleted.
- To delete a custom toolbar, pull down the View menu, click Toolbars, and make sure that the custom toolbar to be deleted is the only one selected. Click the Delete command button. Click Yes to confirm the deletion.

Borders Toolbar

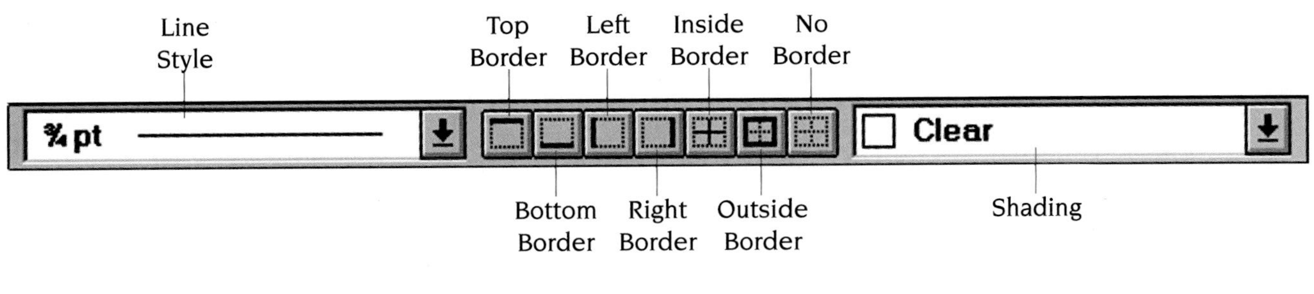

Database Toolbar

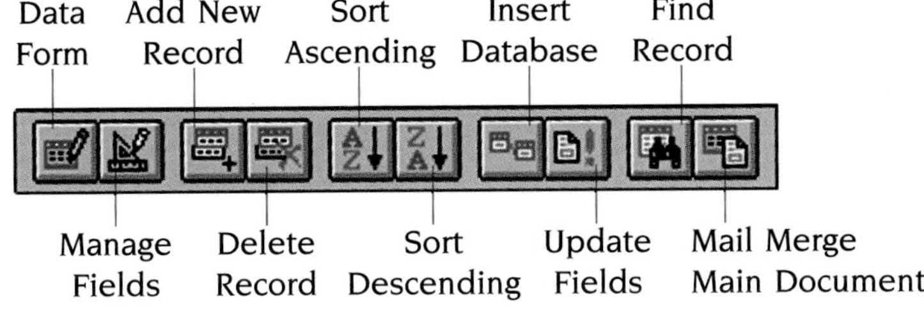

Drawing Toolbar

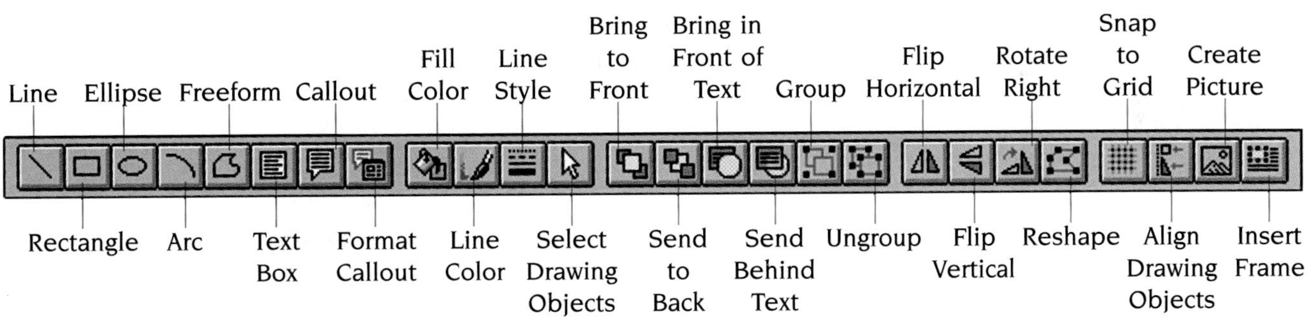

Formatting Toolbar

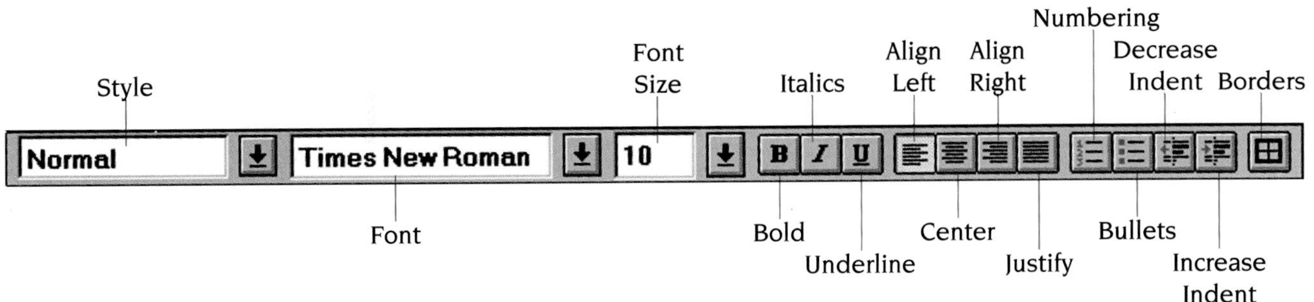

FIGURE B.1 Predefined toolbars

Forms Toolbar

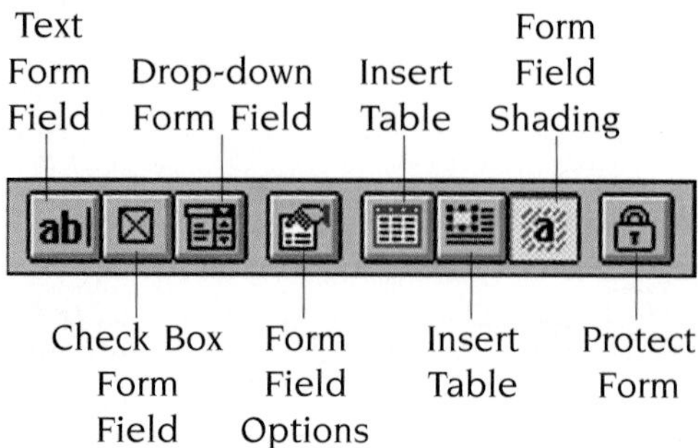

Microsoft Toolbar

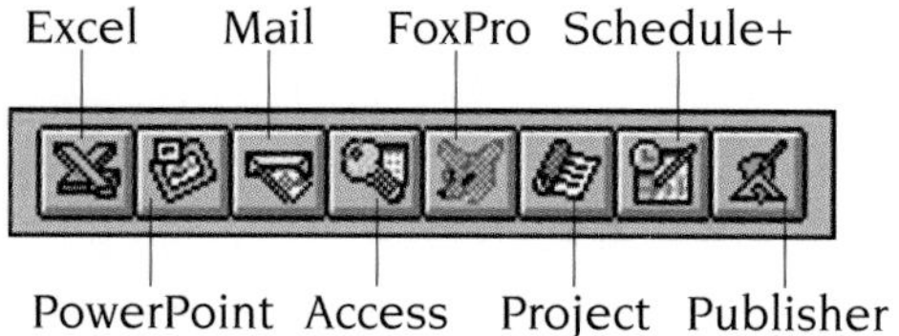

Standard Toolbar

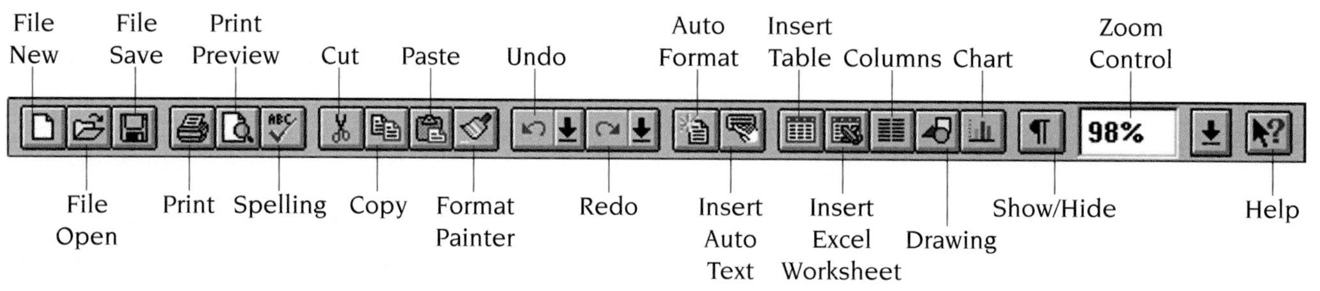

Word 2.0 Toolbar

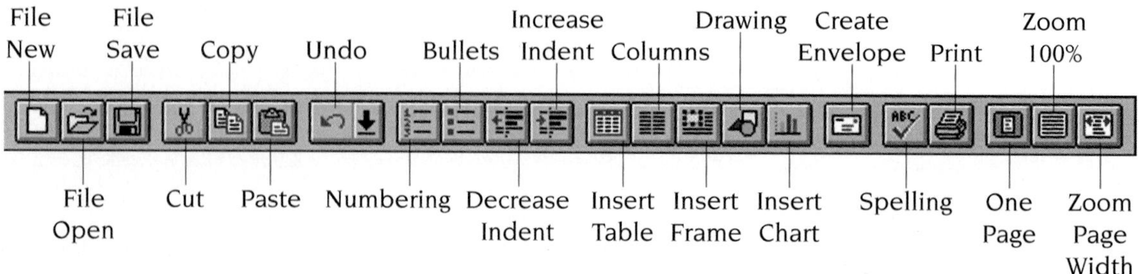

FIGURE B.1 Predefined toolbars (continued)

Equation Editor Toolbar

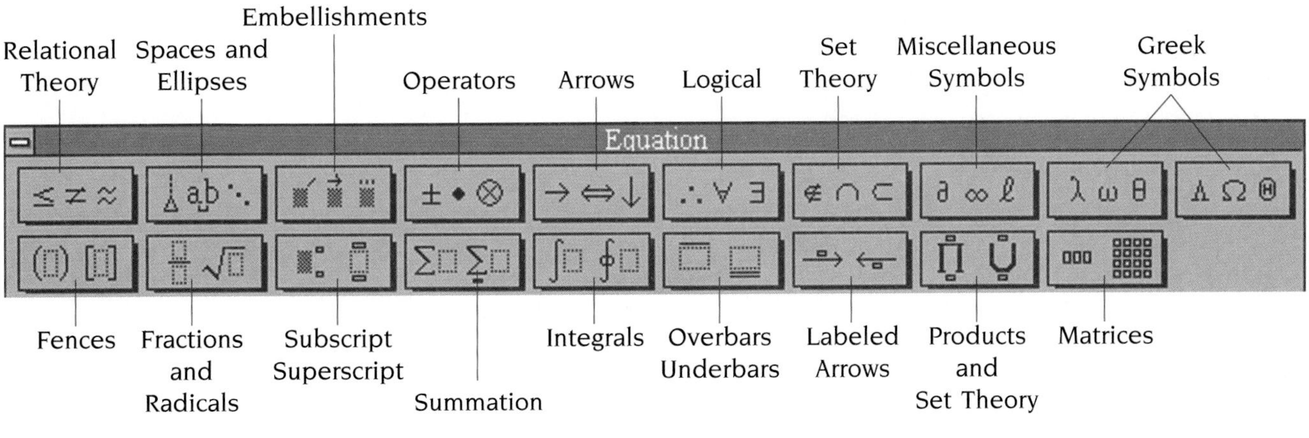

Macro Toolbar

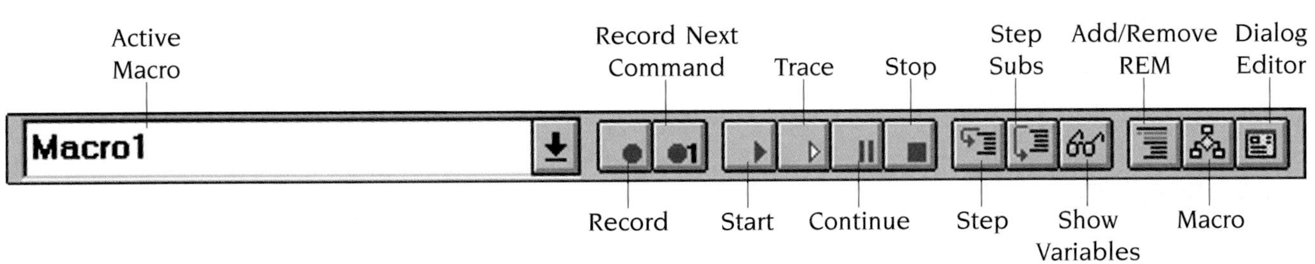

Mail Merge Toolbar

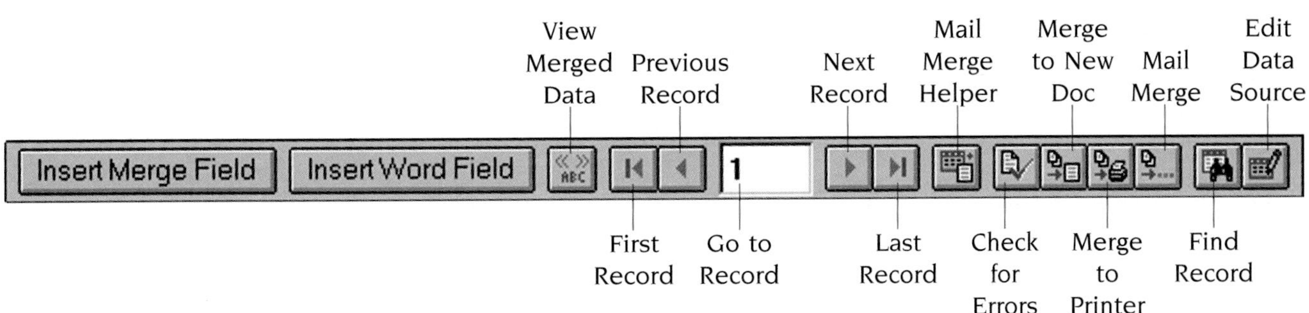

FIGURE B.2 Feature toolbars

Master Document Toolbar

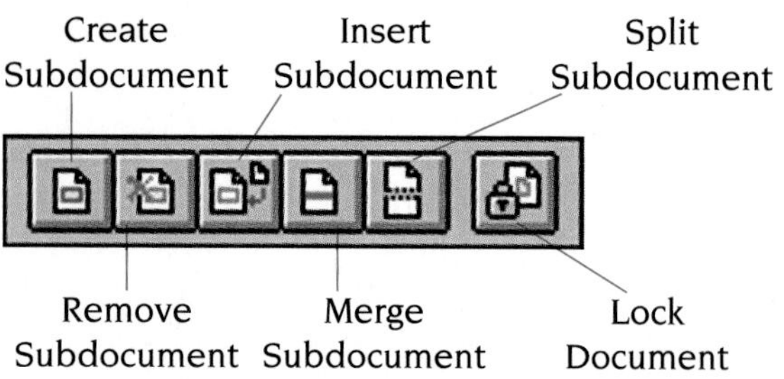

Outlining Toolbar

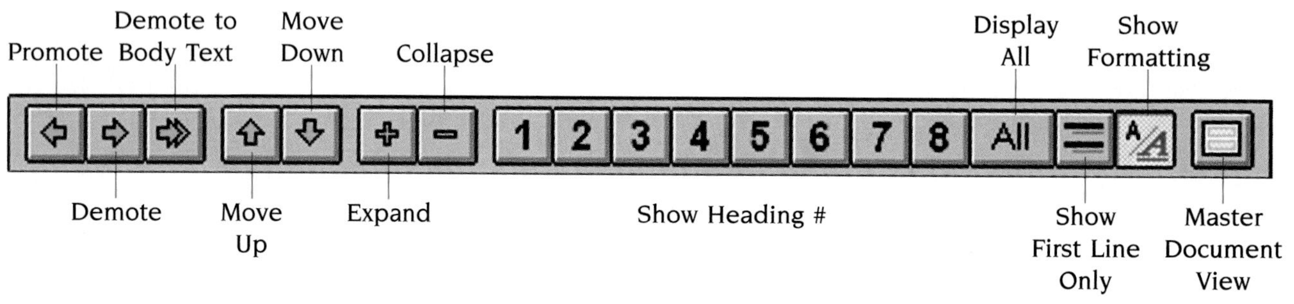

WordArt Toolbar

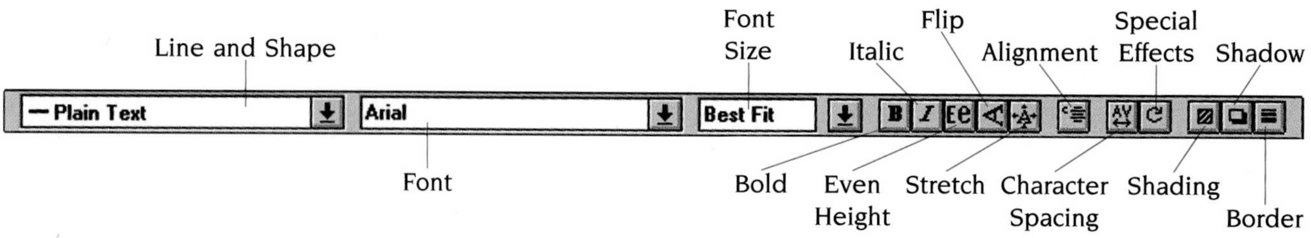

FIGURE B.2 Feature toolbars (continued)

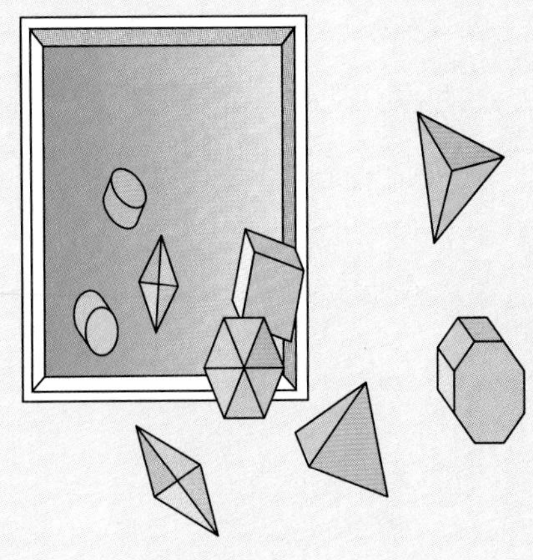

Index